a history of
Christian
Thought

Volume I

a history of
Christian
Thought

Volume I

From the Beginnings to the Council of Chalcedon

Justo L. González

abingdon - nashville

A HISTORY OF CHRISTIAN THOUGHT
VOL. I

ISBN 0-687-17174-1

Library of Congress Catalog Card Number: 74-109679

MANUFACTURED BY THE PARTHENON PRESS AT
NASHVILLE, TENNESSEE, UNITED STATES OF AMERICA

Therefore, since we are surrounded by so great a cloud of witnesses . . . let us run with perseverance the race that is set before us.

Hebrews 12:1 (RSV)

Contents

Foreword

When Jesus was asked which is the first of the commandments of necessity he replied by quoting a verse from the Old Testament, but in so doing he made a significant addition. The text that he cited is the very core of Judaism, "Hear, O Israel: The Lord our God is one Lord; and you shall love the Lord your God with all your heart, and with all your soul, and with all your might." So reads the verse in Deuteronomy 6:4-5 (RSV). But Jesus added, "You shall love the Lord your God with all your mind" (Mark 12:30 RSV). That addition provides the *raison d'être* for this book. There has been a continuous history of Christian thought because the Master called upon his disciples to love their God not only with heart and strength but also with the mind.

Yet, if the Master had never given this injunction, his disciples could scarcely have escaped using their minds, because they were driven to do so by the exigencies of their situation in the environment of the Greco-Roman world in which men of acute minds posed for the Christians questions calling for profound reflection and rigorous distinctions. The Christians refused to worship the emperor as a god. So also did the Jews. Their reason for refusal was obvious and self-consistent, based on that great command which Jesus quoted, "Hear, O Israel: the Lord our God is one Lord," and again, "You shall have no other gods before me." The Jews would not admit the worship of any other god than Yahweh, and in time they came to deny the existence of any other god. Above all they would not regard any man as a god. But the Christians refused to worship the emperor, a deified man, as incompatible with the sole worship of Christ. The pagans could then say, "Why do you refuse to worship a man as god? Was not your Christ a man?" If the Christian answered, "No, he was a god," the pagan would retort, "In that case you have two gods, and why then do you reproach us with polytheism?" The rejection of emperor worship thus demanded a Christology.

The Christians in their encounter with the pagan world despoiled the Egyptians. Just as the Israelites, when they escaped from Egypt, carried off some of the gods of their oppressors, so the Christians utilized the ideas and intellectual methods of their opponents in fashioning their replies. Broadly speaking, the intellectual concerns of the Christians, although theological rather than philosophical, placed them in the tradition of Greek philosophy, and even those Christians who, like Tertullian, decried the use of pagan learning, nevertheless in the acuteness of their reasoning were heirs of the classical heritage. But there was also a background in Judaism for intellectual pursuits. The synagogue was unique in the ancient world, a church without an altar, only a desk for the reading of the Law. And after the reading came the exposition, for the Law was to be interpreted. The desk in the synagogue was the lectern of a professor as well as the pulpit of a prophet. The rabbi was both. Significantly the first churches were modeled after the synagogue.

There was thus no absolute cleavage between the Hebraic and the Hellenic. They had enough in common to make possible a fusion, and this had been essayed prior to the advent of Christianity. Philo, the Jew, living in Greek-speaking Alexandria, was the first to effect the union so pregnant alike in richness and in tension for the thinking of the centuries to come. Philo harmonized Judaism and Hellenism largely by allegorizing the Old Testament in a Platonic sense. The Christians were really better Hebrews than Philo, for although open to Platonic influences, yet the Christians, by their insistence on the incarnation of God in the flesh of the man Jesus, persistently resisted the Platonic tendency to disparage the flesh as an enemy of the spirit.

The incarnation of God in the man Jesus involves another affinity of Christianity with Judaism and a divergence from the Hellenic approach to religion, because Judaism and Christianity see the primary self-disclosure of God to man in the events of history. The Eternal breaks into time. This is supremely the case with the incarnation, itself an event in time, when a decree went out from Augustus Caesar that all the world should be taxed. The Word became flesh at a point in time. Therefore, Christianity must always be historically oriented. This also means that God in Christ was disclosing himself to man. This is revelation. It comes down from above. But for the Greek, though the seer may experience visions and the devotee ecstasies, yet the knowledge of God is rather the result of inference from the observable in the world of nature and of man. This is essentially true of the Stoic and Aristotelian approaches and largely also in the case of the Platonic, where, from the shadows that he sees, man infers the realities that he does not see. In such a case, revelation, if such it can be called, proceeds from the ground up. It is not a deposit, but the object of a quest. It is not delivered in pronouncements, as Moses delivered the Law upon Sinai, but rather is adumbrated in the course of the dialogue in which the mind of man is matched with the mind of man. In the process previous insights may be entirely superseded. There need be no anchorage in the past, and there is nothing once and for all delivered.

Christianity, rooted in history, affirms a revelation once and for all given. But still, that revelation has to be explicated. And, after all, it was not given from Sinai in a set of commandments or drafted in the form of a set of propositions. It was given in a life, and even in the first generation the significance of that life was variously assessed, despite the surprising unanimity of the early Christian documents. The history of Christian thought is the record of man's wrestling with the implications of the self-disclosure of God in the man Christ Jesus. Moreover, Christians have in the main been ready to look upon the religious insights of the Greeks as a preparation for Christ and worthy to be taken into account in the understanding of Christ. Consequently, throughout the whole history of Christianity there has been a tension between the past and the present, between the given and the sought, between revelation as a deposit in some sense and revelation as the goal of an endeavor, between the faith to be conserved and the truth to be acquired. The tension has not been resolved by the centuries of Christian thought, but a solution cannot be attempted without taking them into account.

This first volume deals with the early period. The problems then raised are still ours. Dr. González has a splendid grasp of the cardinal ideas and a fine capacity for disengaging the significant from the trivial and ephemeral. His exposition is marked by singular clarity. He is in command of the linguistic tools for the reading of the ancient and the modern works. He shows a wide acquaintance with recent literature. His work can be heartily commended to readers in any tongue.

> Roland H. Bainton
> Titus Street Professor Emeritus
> of Ecclesiastical History
> Yale University

Preface to the English Edition

This book was born out of necessity. Teaching seminary students in Latin America, I became painfully aware of the need for a general introduction to the history of Christian thought, one that was simple enough to be read and understood by beginners, but that at the same time would give them a glimpse into the complexity and rich variety of the field they were entering for the first time. It was with these guidelines in mind that the book was written, and I therefore did not seek to be original in the sense of proposing a new interpretation of the historical course of Christian theology.

The English edition is in a sense a totally new book. I collected comments and suggestions from Protestant and Catholic colleagues throughout Latin America who knew and had used the book, and incorporated them into what I think are definite improvements. Also, while translating the book into English, I introduced corrections at several points in which further study had led me to correct my views, as well as at other points in which the actual use of the book had proved that I had not been sufficiently clear.

As to the contents of this volume—the first of three—I must point out that, for the sake of clarity, I have postponed for the second volume three subjects that chronologically would belong here: the theology of Augustine, the further development of penance after its early beginnings, and the problems of the form and authority of the ministry after its first stages. These three subjects the reader will find taken up and carried forward in the second volume of the *History*—the Spanish text of which is going to press at approximately the same time as this first English volume.

Following the almost unanimous suggestion of scholars who read this book in Spanish as well as in my original English text, I have decided not to include a chapter on the New Testament. It is hoped that this omission will be properly understood, not as a denial of the importance of the New Testament, but on the contrary, as an affirmation that the field of New Testament research is so vast and so crucial that it requires separate and special consideration.

Finally, a word of gratitude. So many people have contributed to this book that I can hardly call it my own. A general work such as this can only be written because from a much earlier date thousands of unknown monks and scholars have preserved and copied manuscripts, produced and published editions of ancient works, made exhaustive monographical studies of various subjects, and in general paved the way that I must follow. Others have taught me all I know of the methods of historical research, of languages ancient and modern, and of other such necessary tools for a work such as this. More concretely, Dr. Roland H. Bainton and Dr. David C. White have encouraged me in my work. Dr. Bainton has also honored me by writing the foreword to this book, while Dr. White has translated some sections of it. Mrs. Clara Sherman de Mercado has also translated two chapters. Mrs. Ramonita Cortés de Brugueras has very kindly typed and retyped my manuscript at several stages of production. With such debts of gratitude I offer this book to the reader, with the hope that it will somehow help him to understand the faith of which I consider myself an heir. If it fulfills that purpose, I shall feel more than amply rewarded. And I am certain that the many believers of all ages who have helped me write it would say the same.

J. L. G.

Carolina, Puerto Rico, July, 1969

NOTE ON THE 1975 REPRINT: The author regrets that the first two volumes of this *History* were written before there was widespread awareness of the degree to which gender-specific language excludes half of the human race. Technical problems have made the deletion of such language impossible at this time. Fortunately, the third volume reflects the new sensitivity of this situation.

List of Abbreviations

ACW	*Ancient Christian Writers*
AkathKrcht	*Archiv für katholisches Kirchenrecht*
ANF	*The Ante-Nicene Fathers*
Ang	*Angelicum*
AnglThR	*Anglican Theological Review*
AnnTh	*L'Année Théologique*
Ant	*Antonianum*
AntCh	*Antike und Christentum*
Aug	*Augustinus*
BAC	*Biblioteca de Autores Cristianos*
BLE	*Bulletin de Littérature Ecclésiastique*
BThAM	*Bulletin de Théologie Ancienne et Médiévale*
Byz	*Byzantion*
ByzZschr	*Byzantinische Zeitschrift*
BZNtW	*Beihefte zur Zeitschrift für die neutestamentliche Wissenschaft*
CAH	*Cambridge Ancient History*
CD	*La Ciudad de Dios*
CH	*Church History*
ChQR	*Church Quarterly Review*
CommVind	*Commentationes Vindobonenses*
CTM	*Concordia Theological Monthly*
DHGE	*Dictionnaire d'Histoire et de Géographie Ecclésiastiques*

DivThom	*Divus Thomas: Commentarium de Philosophia et Theologia*
DKvCh	*Das Konzil von Chalkedon: Geschichte und Gegenwart* (ed. Grillmeier und Bacht)
DomSt	*Dominican Studies*
DTC	*Dictionnaire de Théologie Catholique*
EphemTheolLovan	*Ephemerides Theologicae Lovanienses*
Est	*Estudios*
EstEcl	*Estudios Eclesiásticos*
ExpT	*The Expository Times*
GItFil	*Giornale Italiano di Filologia*
Greg	*Gregorianum*
HD	A. von Harnack, *History of Dogma* (New York: Russell & Russell, 1958)
HE	*Ecclesiastical History* (usually, that of Eusebius)
HJb	*Historisches Jahrbuch*
HTR	*Harvard Theological Review*
IDB	*The Interpreter's Dictionary of the Bible*
IER	*Irish Ecclesiastical Record*
IntkZtschr	*Internationale kirchliche Zeitschrift*
IrThQ	*The Irish Theological Quarterly*
JBL	*Journal of Biblical Literature*
JEH	*Journal of Ecclesiastical History*
JRel	*The Journal of Religion*
JRelSt	*The Journal of Religious Studies*
JRH	*The Journal of Religious History*
JTS	*Journal of Theological Studies*
Kairos	*Kairos: Zeitschrift für Religionswissenschaft und Theologie*
ΚΛΗ	Κληρονομία
KuD	*Kerygma und Dogma*
Lat	*Latomus: Revue d'Études Latines*
LCL	*Loeb Classical Library*
LumVie	*Lumière et Vie*

MScRel	Mélanges de Science Religieuse
MusHelv	Museum Helveticum
NAKgesch	Nederlands Archief voor Kerkgeschiedenis
NDid	Nuovo Didaskaleion
NedTheolTschr	Nederlands Theologisch Tijdschrift
NPNF	The Nicene and Post-Nicene Fathers
NRT	Nouvelle Revue Théologique
NTS	New Testament Studies
Numen	Numen: International Review for the History of Religions
OrCh	Orientalia Christiana Periodica
PG	Patrologiae cursus completus . . . series Graeca (ed. Migne)
PL	Patrologiae cursus completus . . . series Latina (ed. Migne)
PO	Patrologia orientalis
Prot	Protestantesimo
RAC	Reallexikon für Antike und Christentum
RET	Revista Española de Teología
RevBénéd	Revue Bénédictine
RevBib	Revue Biblique
RevEtGr	Revue des Études Grecques
RevScRel	Revue des Sciences Religieuses
RGG	Die Religion in Geschichte und Gegenwart. Dritte Auflage
RHE	Revue d'Histoire Ecclésiastique
RicRel	Ricerche Religiose
ROC	Revue de l'Orient Chrétien
RScF	Rassegna di Scienze Filosofiche
RScPhTh	Revue des Sciences Philosophiques et Théologiques
RScRel	Recherches de Science Religieuse
RStFil	Rivista Critica di Storia della Filosofia
RThAM	Recherches de Théologie Ancienne et Médiévale
RUOtt	Revue de L'Université d'Ottawa
SBAW	Sitzungsberichte der bayrischen Akademie der Wissenschaften in München
SC	Sources Chrétiennes
SCatt	La Scuola Cattolica
Sch	Scholastik: Vierteljahrschrift für Theologie und Philosophie

ScrVict	Scriptorium Victoriense
Sef	Sefarad: Revista de la Escuela de Estudios Hebraicos
SP	Studia Patristica
StCath	Studia Catholica
StTh	Studia Theologica
Th	Theology
ThBl	Theologische Blätter
ThGl	Theologie und Glaube
ThLit	Theologische Literaturzeitung
ThR	Theologische Revue
ThSK	Theologische Studien und Kritiken
ThSt	Theological Studies
ThViat	Theologia Viatorum
ThZschr	Theologische Zeitschrift
TIB	The Interpreter's Bible
TQ	Theologische Quartalschrift
TrthZschr	Trierer theologische Zeitschrift
VetTest	Vetus Testamentum
VieSpirit	La Vie Spirituelle
VigCh	Vigiliae Christianae
WuW	Wissenschaft und Weisheit
ZkT	Zeitschrift für katholische Theologie
ZntW	Zeitschrift für die neutestamentliche Wissenschaft und die Kunde der älteren Kirche
ZschrKgesch	Zeitschrift für Kirchengeschichte
ZTK	Zeitschrift für Theologie und Kirche

Introduction

Because of the nature of the material with which it deals, the history of Christian thought must of necessity be a theological undertaking. The task of the historian does not consist in mere repetition of what has happened—or, in this case, of what has been thought. On the contrary, the historian must begin by selecting the material he is to use, and the rules guiding him in this selection depend upon a decision that is to a considerable degree subjective. Whoever would write a history of Christian thought cannot include the entire contents of the 382 thick volumes of original sources edited by Migne—and even these do not go beyond the twelfth century—but is obliged to make a selection, not only as to which works he will include, but also as to the sources to be studied in preparation for his task. This selection depends in good part upon the author, which means that every history of Christian thought is of necessity also a reflection of the theological presuppositions of the writer, and the historian of Christian thought who suggests that his work is free of such theological presuppositions is deluding himself.

Harnack and Nygren, historians separated by decades in time as well as by diverse theological positions, are examples of the way theological presuppositions will influence the historian of Christian thought to write his history in a distinctive way.

Adolph von Harnack, possibly the most famous of the historians of dogma, published his monumental work, *Lehrbuch der Dogmengeschichte,* in the period running from 1886 to 1890. His theological position was derived from the thought of Ritschl,[1] whom he calls "the last of the Fathers of the Church." Ritschl constantly endeavored to limit the involvement of philosophy in the field of religion by showing the distortions that result when metaphysics is related to religious concerns. For him religion is preeminently practical and not speculative. This is not to say that religion should be dissolved into mere subjectivism. On the contrary, religion establishes those moral values which are the only means by which a man can free himself from the conditions of bondage that characterize the natural life. Neither dogmas nor mystical sentiment constitute the Christian faith, but rather those moral values which lift a man above his present misery.

Beginning with such theological presuppositions, Harnack's conclusions were inevitable. For him the history of Christian dogma was in large part the story of the progressive negation of the true principles of Christianity. Such principles were to be found in the moral teachings of Jesus. The starting point for Harnack was not so much the person as the teachings of Jesus.[2] Therefore, all the doctrinal development of the first centuries, which revolves around the person of Jesus rather than his teachings, could only be the progressive distortion of the original meaning of the gospel. The purpose, therefore, of Harnack's *History of Dogma* is to show that dogma—and especially christological dogma—which in today's world is antiquated, never was an authentic result of the gospel.[3]

---

[1] A brief and good introduction to Ritschl's theology may be found in Hugh R. Mackintosh, *Types of Modern Theology: Schleiermacher to Barth* (New York: Scribner's, 1937), pp. 138-80.

[2] Harnack sums up these teachings as follows: (1) the kingdom of God and its coming, (2) the Fatherhood of God and the infinite value of the human soul, (3) the superior justice and the commandment of love. *Das Wesen des Christentums* (Leipzig: T. C. Hinrichs, 1902), p. 33.

[3] See Joseph de Ghellinck, *Patristique et Moyen Age,* Vol. III: *Compléments a l'étude de la Patristique* (Gembloux: J. Duculot, 1948), pp. 1-102.

Nygren begins with very different presuppositions. Being one of the main exponents of the "Lundensian Theology," [4] he conceives the task of the historian of Christian thought as being an "investigation of motifs." This investigation has, itself, certain philosophical and theological foundations that determine its character. As an example of this we can mention the antithesis that Nygren establishes between what he considers the essential Christian motif, love of the *agape* type, and the Jewish motif, the Law or *nomos*. Because of this antithesis Nygren finds himself unable to relate adequately the Law with the gospel, which in turn produces not only theological difficulties, but also historical distortions—as when Nygren presents us with a picture of Luther in which the Law has lost the distinctive importance that it had for the Reformer. [5]

For their part, traditional Roman Catholic historians tend to interpret the history of Christian thought in such a way as to emphasize its continuity, for as Vincent of Lérins said (fifth century), only that is to be believed "which has been believed everywhere, always, and by all." [6] The presuppositions and value judgments of the historian determine his selection of the material, the bridging of gaps in the sources, and the very manner of presentation, which may appear so objective as to beguile the reader.

What are the presuppositions of the present author? The question must be asked and honestly answered, that the reader may the better exercise his right of dissent.

In dealing with the development of doctrine, this author is convinced that it is necessary to do so beginning with a theological concept, that is, a Christian concept of the truth, and that this

---

[4] See my Appendix to Hugh R. Mackintosh, *Corrientes teológicas contemporáneas* (Buenos Aires: Methopress, 1964), pp. 129-65.

[5] *Agape and Eros* (Philadelphia: Westminster Press, 1956), pp. 681-741. Cf. the critical comments of Gustaf Wingren, *Theology in Conflict: Nygren, Barth, Bultmann* (Philadelphia: Muhlenberg Press, 1958), pp. 85-107.

[6] *Commonitorium* 2. 3. This does not mean, however, that the question of the development of dogma is settled among Catholic theologians. On the contrary, Catholic scholars have produced many valuable studies of the issues involved, and there is almost as much variety of views among them as there is among Protestant scholars.

concept of truth—here we are not speaking of the truth itself, but only of its concept—is to be found in the doctrine of the Incarnation. According to this doctrine, Christian truth is such that it is not lost or distorted upon uniting itself with the concrete, the limited, and the transitory. On the contrary, the truth—or at least that truth which is given to men—is given precisely there where the eternal unites with the historical; where God becomes flesh; where a specific man, in a specific situation, is able to say: "I am the truth."

In order to clarify this concept of the truth let us compare it with two others with which it is incompatible and which, therefore, result in other interpretations of the person of Jesus Christ which deny the doctrine of the Incarnation.

First, we might affirm that truth exists only within the realm of the eternal, the permanent, and the universal, and therefore cannot be given in the historical, the transitory, and the individual. This concept of truth has exerted a strong attraction on the Greek mind, and through it, upon all of Western civilization. But such a concept, attractive though it might seem, has only led to the denial of the Incarnation, and to the affirming of that doctrine known as "Docetism" (see Chapter VI), which, while making of Jesus Christ an eternal, permanent, and even universal being, also sees him as quite distinct from that historic and individual man of which the Gospels speak to us.

Second, we could say that all truth is relative, that there is no such thing as absolute truth among men. This concept of truth has been in fashion for the last two or three centuries, a result of the enormous development in scientific and historical studies that have made us aware of the relativity of all human knowledge. But this viewpoint, attractive though it may be, is incompatible with the most fundamental doctrine of Christianity, namely the affirmation that in the historical event of Jesus Christ the very meaning of all life and history is encountered, and that this is as true today as in the first century of the Christian era. Such a concept of truth could be related to that christological doctrine called "Ebionism" (see Chapter V), which, while seeing in Jesus Christ a definite man, real and historical, also sees him as quite other than he whom the Gospels present to us as the Lord of all life and history—not that the Ebionites themselves were relativists, but that in modern times this understanding of truth often coincides with an Ebionite Christology.

Faced by these two positions Christianity affirms that the truth is given in the concrete, the historical, and the particular, contained and hidden within it, but in such a way as never to lose its veracity for all historical moments. In the historical humanity of Jesus Christ the Eternal Word of God comes to us who have not seen him "according to the flesh" nor experienced the urgency with which he confronted the first disciples. Only in his historical incarnation do we know this Word, yet we know it is the eternal Word, which has been and will be to us "a refuge in generation unto generation," and which comes to us at every moment in which we proclaim the incarnate Lord.

It is this understanding of the relation between truth and history which serves as one starting point in our interpretation and evaluation of doctrinal development. The truth of doctrine will never be such that we can say: here is the eternal and incommutable truth, free of any shadow or conjecture of historical relativism. The truth of doctrine is only present to that degree in which, through the various doctrines, the Word of God (which is the Truth) is able to confront the church with a demand for absolute obedience. When this happens that doctrine indeed becomes the standard of judgment of the church's life and proclamation. If this does not occur then doctrines are no more than documents that witness to the church's past. And whether this happens or not does not depend upon us, nor is it intrinsic in the character of the doctrine itself, but depends rather upon a decision from Above.

Are all doctrines then equally valid? Certainly not. Moreover, no doctrine is valid in the sense of being able to identify itself with the Word of God.[7] Doctrines are human words with which the church seeks to witness to the Word of God—and in this sense doctrines are a part of the church's proclamation. Just as in the sermon, doctrines become the Word of God only when God himself uses them as instruments of his Word, and nothing man can do will force God to speak through them.

But, because God in Jesus Christ gives himself to men and even makes himself an object of human action, and because the same thing occurs—although in a derived way—in the Scriptures and the sacraments, it is possible to pronounce judgment on the validity of one or another doctrine—always remembering that such judgment is ours and not God's. It is in the Scriptures—the "foundation of apostles and prophets"—that we have the measuring stick by which to judge doctrine.

On the other hand, doctrines do not come forth through spontaneous generation, nor are they directly sent from heaven, unrelated to particular human circumstances. Dogmas form a part of Christian thought, from which they come forth and to which they later serve as a starting point. Doctrines are forged through long years of theological reflection from established practices of worship, within the context of a spirituality that opposes those doctrines which might seem to attack the very center of the faith of an epoch, and even as the result of political intrigues. Moreover, there has never been unanimous agreement among Christians about how and when a doctrine becomes dogma. This is why my decision has been to write a "history of Christian thought" rather than a "history of dogma," which would tend to give more attention to the formal statement of doctrines than to the material process by which their content originates and eventually becomes widely accepted.

In the organization and presentation of subject matter I have

---

[7] Cf. Karl Barth, *Church Dogmatics* (Edinburgh: T. and T. Clark, 1936), 1: 306: "In dogmas there speaks the Church of the past—venerable, worthy of respect, authoritative, *non sine Deo*, as befits her—but the Church. . . .The Word of God is above dogma as the heavens are above the earth."

been guided by the necessities of a textbook for theological studies. Here for every historian there are two diverse possibilities: that of a chronological or a topical thematic order. In a book in which the primary purpose is to serve as an introduction to the history of Christian thought a discussion of themes does not appear advisable, for the reader who is not versed in the history of Christianity will be easily confused when presented with a unit of material which, while very much a part of Christian thought, comes from distinctive periods of history. The chronological presentation has the indisputable value of avoiding this type of confusion, but suffers the defect of insufficiently emphasizing the continuity of the diverse theological currents. It is for this reason that I follow an outline that, although essentially chronological, seeks to keep in mind the continuity of certain theological themes of primary importance.

II

The Cradle of Christianity

According to a tradition reflected in the Gospel of Luke, Christianity was born in a manger, a scene we often like to paint in quiet hues. Yet that manger scene was actually not an example of tranquil aloofness from the menacing world, but, quite the contrary, was the result of active involvement. Joseph and Mary were led to the city of David because of economic conditions at home and a decree from afar when Caesar Augustus ordered "that all the world should be enrolled" (Luke 2:1 RSV). The purpose of the census was taxation, and the world about the manger was rife with bitter complaint.

In short, from its very beginning Christianity has existed as the message of the God who "so loved the world" that he came to form part of it. Christianity is not an ethereal, eternal doctrine about God's nature, but rather it is the presence of God in the world in the person of Jesus Christ. Christianity is *incarnation*, and, therefore, it exists in the concrete and the historical.

Without the world, Christianity is inconceivable. Therefore, in a study such as this we should begin by describing, however briefly, the world where the Christian faith was born and took its first steps.

26

The Jewish World

It was in Palestine, among Jews, that Christianity arose. Among Jews and as a Jew, Jesus lived and died. His teachings were framed within the Jewish world view, and his disciples received them as Jews. Later, when Paul traveled about, preaching the gospel to the Gentiles, he usually began his task among the Jews of the synagogue. Thus, we must begin our history of Christian thought with a survey of the situation and thought of the Jews among whom Christianity was born.

The enviable geographical location of Palestine caused many misfortunes to the people who considered it their Promised Land. Palestine, through which crossed the trade routes from Egypt to Assyria and from Arabia to Asia Minor,[1] was always an object of the imperialistic greed of the great states that arose in the Near East. For centuries, Egypt and Assyria fought over that narrow strip of land. When Babylon supplanted Assyria, it also inherited Palestine, eventually destroying Jerusalem and taking into exile a part of the people. After the Persian conquest of Babylon, Cyrus permitted the exiles' return and made Palestine a part of his empire. By defeating the Persians at Issus, Alexander annexed their empire, including Palestine, which came under the rule of Macedonian governors. When Alexander died in 323, a period of unrest followed for more than twenty years. By the end of that time, Alexander's successors had consolidated their power, but for more than a century the two main houses springing from Alexander's generals, the Ptolemies and Seleucids, fought for the possession of Palestine and the surrounding region. In the end, the Seleucids gained the upper hand, but when Antiochus Epiphanes tried to force them to worship other gods alongside Yahweh, the Jews rebelled under the lead of the Maccabees or Hasmoneans, and as a result they gained religious liberty and, later,

---

[1] See Georges A. Barrois, "Trade and Commerce," *IDB*, 4: 677-83; Yohanan Aharoni, *The Land of the Bible: A Historical Geography* (Philadelphia: Westminster Press, 1967), pp. 39-57.

political independence. Such independence, however, was possible only because of the internal division of Syria, and it vanished as soon as the next great power appeared: Rome. In the year 63, Pompey took Jerusalem and defiled the Temple, penetrating even to the Holy of Holies. From then on, Palestine was subject to the Roman power, and in this condition we find it at the advent of our Lord.

Under the Romans, the Jews were notably intractable and difficult to govern. This was because of the exclusiveness of their religion, which admitted no "strange gods" before the Lord of Hosts. Pursuing its policy of respecting the national characteristics of each conquered people, Rome respected the Jewish religion. As a result, many parties in Palestine—notably the Pharisees—took a pacifistic stance and did not rebel against Rome. On a very few occasions, Roman governors interfered with Jewish religious practices, but the resulting disorder and violence obliged them to return at once to the former policy. Not one Roman governor succeeded in becoming popular among the Jews, although those who understood and accepted the religious character of their subjects did not encounter strong opposition. Thus, the more astute procurators took care not to mint small coins— the only ones used by the common people—with the Emperor's likeness, or to display the showy, idolatrous Roman insignia in the Holy City.[2]

All this was because the Jews were the people of the Law. The Law, or Torah, was the center of their religion and of their nationality, and that Law said, "Hear, oh Israel: The Lord our God is one Lord." The Law as we know it today was the result of a labor of compilation and organization undertaken by the religious leaders of Judaism in an attempt to unify the traditions of their people.[3]

---

[2] On the political circumstances of the period, see: Stewart Perowne, *The Later Herods: The Political Background of the New Testament* (Nashville: Abingdon Press, 1958); Robert H. Pfeiffer, *History of New Testament Times, with an Introduction to the Apocrypha* (New York: Harper, 1949); G. H. Stevenson, "The Imperial Administration," *CAH*, 10: 182-217. An old but still valuable work is that of Emil Shürer, *A History of the Jewish People in the Time of Jesus Christ*, 2nd ed. rev. (New York: Scribner's, n.d.; reprinted, New York, Schöcken Books, 1961).

[3] Arthur Weiser, *The Old Testament: Its Formation and Development* (New York: Asso-

Thus, with the passage of time, the priest came to supplant the prophet.

Instead of the vivid stories which embodied the interior meaning of prophetic faith, we have priestly teaching; instead of the intimate psychological portraiture of the Yahwist, we have individuals whose meaning for religion is their connection with institutions like the prohibition of blood (Gen. 9:1-7) and circumcision (Gen. 17:9-14); instead of a dramatic account of conflict and resolution, we have a fixed scheme into which are fitted in predestined fashion both history and human personality. History is subordinated to priestly faith and belief.[4]

Through the passage of years and of patriotic struggles, the Law became the symbol and bulwark of the Jewish national spirit. With the decline of the prophetic movement, and especially after the destruction of the Temple in A.D. 70, it came to occupy the center of the religious scene.

As a result, the Law, which had been codified by the priests to regulate temple worship and the people's daily life, became itself a source of the rise of a new religious caste, distinct from the priestly, and of a new spiritual interest centered not in the Temple, but in the Law. Although this Law paid more attention to the meaning of history than to the events themselves, this does not mean that it was doctrinal in character, but rather that it was ceremonial and practical. The compilers of the Law were less interested in God's attributes than in the cult and worship due him. This interest in religious practice led to the study and interpretation of the Law, for it was manifestly impossible that it could treat specifically of all cases that might arise. In the light of such a need, a new occupation originated, that of the scribe or teacher of the Law.

The scribes were responsible for the preservation of the Law as

ciation Press, 1961), pp. 70-142; Otto Eisfeldt, *The Old Testament: An Introduction* (New York: Harper, 1965), pp. 158-241. Other theories regarding the composition of the Law may be found in Martin Noth, *The Old Testament: An Introduction* (Harper, 1965) and Georg Fohrer, *Introduction to the Old Testament* (Nashville: Abingdon Press, 1968).

[4] James Muilenburg, "The History of the Religion of Israel," *TIB*, 1: 335.

well as for its interpretation. Although differences of school and temperament divided them, they produced a great body of jurisprudence concerning the application of the Law in diverse circumstances. Guignebert, in the following paragraph, gives an indication of the minutely detailed applications that were made:

The cauistry which grew up around the *Torah* . . . formed a dense and almost impenetrable jungle whose tortuous paths only the initiate might tread. He, and he alone, would have the inestimable advantage of knowing whether or not it was lawful to eat an egg laid on the Sabbath; whether he might, on that day of rest, set up a ladder against his dovecote to examine the cause of some disturbance there, or whether water poured from a clean vessel into an unclean one contaminated the source as well. The observance of the Sabbath raised especially thorny points and the scrupulous Jew had to make use of all his alertness and discernment to avoid the many pitfalls it presented.[5]

This happened because the Hebrew religion was becoming more and more personal, at a time when interest in Temple ritual was declining. In their long struggle, the Pharisees were beginning to overcome the Sadducees; the religion of personal conduct was superseding that of sacrifice and ritual. This was not, as is often said, a stifling of the vital religiosity of the Jewish people, for there was a great amount of activity in commenting on Scripture—*the midrashim*—both in its precepts—*midrash halakah*—and its narratives and inspirational sections—*midrash haggada*.[6]

We must pause to do justice to the Pharisees, so badly misunderstood in later times. The fact is that the New Testament attacks them, not because they were worse than other Jews, but because they were the best—the highest expression of human potentiality before

---

[5] Charles A. H. Guignebert, *The Jewish World in the Time of Jesus* (London: Kegan Paul, Trench, Trubner, 1939), p. 65.

[6] Furthermore, even the *midrash halakah* was more dynamic than is usually supposed. "The main characteristic of *Halakah* in all its forms and at all stages of its historical formation is its vitality, its ability to adapt and to evolve, which corresponds to its essential function of building a bridge between the fixed letter of the Torah of Moses and ever changing life." R. Bloch, "Ecriture et Tradition dans le judaïsme," *Cahiers Sioniens*, 8 (1954), 17.

God. Seeing them attacked in the New Testament,[7] we tend to consider them simply a group of the worst kind of hypocrites, but here we err in our interpretation, not only of Pharisaism, but also of the New Testament itself.[8]

Contrary to what we often imagine, the Pharisees emphasized the importance of a personal religion. For this reason the more conservative Jews accused them of being innovators who eased the yoke of the Law. At a time when the vitality of Temple worship was on the wane, the Pharisees strove to interpret the Law in such a way that it might serve as a daily guide for the religion of the people. Naturally, this led them into the legalism that has made them objects of so much criticism, and it was also the basic cause of their opposition to the Sadducees. But it is necessary to point out that the Pharisees were not "legalistic" in the sense that they demanded blind and unwilling obedience to the moral law and the ritual precepts—*halakah* —for a great deal of their literary remains are devotional, homiletical, and very human attempts to elicit voluntary obedience to the will of God—*haggada*.

The Sadducees were the Jewish conservatives of the first century. They accepted only the written Law as their religious authority, not the oral law that had developed out of Jewish tradition. Thus, they denied the resurrection, the future life, the complicated angelology and demonology of late Judaism, and the doctrine of predestination.[9] In this they opposed the Pharisees, who accepted all

---

[7] E. Haenchen, "Matthäus 23," *ZTK*, 48 (1951), 38 ff., argues that these accusations against the Pharisees became stronger because of the tension between the emerging church and the synagogue.

[8] George Foot Moore, *Judaism in the First Centuries of the Christian Era* (Cambridge: Harvard University Press, 1954), 1: 56-71; Robert T. Herford, *The Pharisees* (New York: Macmillan, 1924); J. Z. Lauterbach, "The Pharisees and Their Teaching," *Hebrew Union College Annual*, 6 (1929), 69-139; Louis Finkelstein, *The Pharisees: The Sociological Background of Their Faith* (Philadelphia: Jewish Publication Society of America, 1938); William D. Davies, *Introduction to Pharisaism* (Philadelphia: Fortress Press, 1967); Matthew Black, "Pharisees," *IDB*, 3: 774-81.

[9] One must take care, however, not to do an injustice to the Sadducees. "The Sadducees have not been permitted to speak for themselves before the bar of history: no document exists that is demonstrably, or even probably, sadducean. We know this sect only from reports in

these things, and for this reason the Talmud calls them—though quite inexactly—"Epicureans." [10] Their religion centered on the Temple and its rites rather than on the synagogue and its teachings.[11] Thus, it is not surprising that they disappeared soon after the destruction of the Temple, whereas the Pharisees were hardly affected by that event.

In contrast to the Sadducees, the Pharisees purposed to make religion a part of the intimate daily life. Like the Sadducees, their religion centered on the Law, yet theirs was not only the written Law, but also the oral. This oral legacy, handed down through centuries of tradition and interpretation, served to apply the written Law to the concrete situations of daily life, but it also served to introduce innovations into the religion of Israel. This is why the Sadducees, conservative by nature, rejected every possible use of the oral Law, while the Pharisees—making common cause with the scribes—hastened to defend it.

Thus, the Pharisees were not simply hypocrites. Rather, they were persons trying to give meaning to religion, although perhaps they were sometimes led to consider themselves better than others.

The Sadducees and the Pharisees did not comprise the whole of first-century Palestinian Judaism.[12] Rather, there was a multitude of sects and groups of which little or nothing is known. Among

NT and talmudic literature, which are hostile, and from Josephus, who is not sympathetic." Bernard J. Bamberger, "The Sadducees and the Belief in Angels," *JBL*, 82 (1963), 433. According to Bamberger, the Sadducees did not deny the existence of angels, but only the complicated angelogy that was found in relatively recent extra-biblical literature.

[10] Guignebert, *The Jewish World*, p. 162.

[11] The origins of the synagogue are still debated among scholars. The traditional view that it emerged during the Exile as a substitute for the Temple has been challenged by those who maintain that its background is not strictly religious, but is to be found in the ancient places set aside for local meetings, and by those who claim that it actually developed out of the Temple worship of the Diaspora, such as that which existed in Egypt in the fifth century B.C. See Isaiah Sonne, "Synagogue," *IDB*, 4: 476-91. In any case, the synagogue was an important factor in the shaping of Christian worship. On this latter point, see Clifford W. Dugmore, *The Influence of the Synagogue upon the Divine Office* (London: Faith Press, 1944).

[12] Erwin R. Goodenough has shown quite clearly that even in Palestine there were Hellenized Jews who had their own synagogues: *Jewish Symbols in the Greco-Roman Period*, (New York: Pantheon Books, 1965), 12: 185-86.

these we must not fail to mention the Essenes, to whom the majority of authors attribute the famous "Dead Sea Scrolls," and about whom, therefore, we know more than about the other groups.[13]

The Essenes—who seem to have numbered a few thousand—were a group with eschatological and purist leanings. They considered themselves to be the people of the New Covenant, which, while not essentially different from the Old, was its culmination and would finally acquire its true meaning on the "day of the Lord." The prophecies were being fulfilled in their time and in their community, and eschatological expectation was vivid among them.[14] This expectation consisted in the restoration of Israel around a New Jerusalem. Three important figures would contribute to the restoration of Israel: the Teacher of Righteousness, the Messiah of Israel, and the Messiah of Aaron. The Teacher of Righteousness had already come and had accomplished his task, which continued now among the chosen community of the Essenes until the day when the Messiah of Israel would wage war and destroy evil. Then the Messiah of Aaron would reign in the New Jerusalem.[15]

The community of the elect played a major role in the eschatological expectations of the Essenes, and for this reason they emphasized the laws of ceremonial purity and tended to withdraw from the great cities and the centers of political and economic life in Palestine, for in such places there were a great number of unclean persons, objects and customs, and every good Essene should avoid contact with such persons and things. This led them to establish communities like that of Qumran, where the Dead Sea Scrolls were discovered, and which seems to have been one of their principal centers. Although not all lived in this type of community, their interest in ceremonial purity

---

[13] Before the discovery of the Dead Sea Scrolls, we knew of the Essenes through Josephus (*War* 2:8. 2-13; *Ant.* 18. 1.5), Philo (*Apology*, quoted in Eusebius, *Praep. ev.* 8. 11; *Every Good Man* 12. 75-88), Pliny the Elder (*Nat. hist.* 5. 15), and Hippolytus (*Refutation* 9. 27).

[14] This is why the study of the prophets was a central feature of the Qumran community, for that study was the means by which the "signs of the times" could be discerned. See Frederick F. Bruce, *Biblical Exegesis in the Qumran Texts* (London: Tyndale Press, 1960).

[15] Otto Betz, "Dead Sea Scrolls," *IDB*, 1: 790-802.

and their intense eschatological expectation attracted them to such an environment, because only there could they avoid contact with the unclean. Matrimony raised a similar problem, for although not prohibited, it was frowned upon. Their discipline was very rigid; whoever violated it was judged by a tribunal of no less than a hundred persons, who could decree even the death penalty. Their rites included purifying baths, prayers chanted at sunrise, and communal worship—although not in the Temple of Jerusalem, which they believed had fallen into the hands of unworthy priests.

Although it is necessary to correct the sensationalistic reporting that took place when the Dead Sea Scrolls were discovered, it is still true that they have added a great deal to our knowledge of first-century Judaism. It is now possible to describe with some measure of accuracy an important trend in the Jewish spirituality of the time. It is also possible to gather more concrete information regarding the history of the Hebrew text of the Old Testament.[16] Finally, these discoveries have served to clarify the background of a number of New Testament passages that seem to originate from a similar type of religiosity—notably Matt. 18:15 ff.[17]

The Essenes were part of a wider circle of Jewish religion in which apocalypticism was predominant. Apocalypticism[18] is a religious and cosmic perspective that probably originated in Zoroastrianism, and entered the Jewish world during and after the Exile. From Judaism, it spread into certain circles, first Christian and later Muslim. The main tenet of apocalypticism is a cosmic dualism that sees in the present the beginning of the final struggle between the forces of good and those of evil. The present world—or age—is ruled by the

---

[16] Frank L. Cross, "History of the Biblical Text in the Light of the Discoveries in the Judean Desert," *HTR*, 57 (1964), 281-99.

[17] Helmer Ringgren, *The Faith of Qumran* (Philadelphia: Fortress Press, 1963), p. 249. The exact relationship between the Essenes and Christianity is still debated by scholars. See Krister Stendahl, *The Scrolls and the New Testament* (New York: Harper, 1957); Jean Daniélou, *The Dead Sea Scrolls and Primitive Christianity* (Baltimore: Helicon Press, 1958).

[18] Martin Rist: "The Revelation of Saint John the Divine: Introduction," *TIB*, 12: 347-51; Martin Rist, "Apocalypticism," *IDB*, 1: 157-61.

evil power; but the time approaches when, after a mighty battle accompanied by cataclysmic events, God will conquer evil and establish a new age in which he will be present and rule over the elect—usually a predetermined number. Meanwhile, the oppressed faithful find strength and consolation in the knowledge that the end of their suffering is at hand. Among the most important Jewish apocalypses are the book of Daniel, I Enoch, and the Apocalypse of Baruch. Their influence on certain segments of the early Christian community is attested by the apocalyptic nature of the Revelation of Saint John, as well as in the title of "Son of Man," popular in Jewish apocalyptic circles and very early applied to Jesus.

All this serves to give a bird's-eye view of the variety of sects and opinions that existed in Palestine at the time of Jesus. But this variety must not obscure the essential unity of the Jewish religion, which centered in the Temple, the Law, and eschatological hope. If the Pharisees differed from the Sadducees over the place of the Temple in the religious life of the people, or about the scope of the Law, this must not hide the fact that for the Jewish people both the Temple and the Law were fundamental aspects of Judaism. There was no direct contradiction between them, although the important practical difference was that the Temple worship could be celebrated only in Jerusalem, while obedience to the Law could be practiced everywhere. This is why the latter aspect of Jewish religious life gradually supplanted the former, even to the point where the destruction of the Temple in A.D. 70 did not shatter the heart of the Jewish religion.

On the other hand, this discussion of the various sects of first-century Palestinian Judaism should not give the impression that religious life had become stale. Quite the contrary. The diversity of sects and interpretations was due to the profound vitality of the Judaism of that time. Moreover, all these sects partook of the two principal tenets of Judaism: its ethical monotheism and its messianic and eschatological hope. Since earliest times, the God of Israel had been the God of justice and mercy, who because of his own justice demanded just and clean conduct of his children, not only in the

ceremonial sense, but also in their social relations. This ethical monotheism continued to be the center of Jewish religion, in spite of the
diversity of sects. Furthermore, through the rude blows that history
had dealt them, throwing them upon the divine mercy and justice,
the Jews had attained to a religion in which hope played a central
role. In one way or another, all expected God to save Israel from her
political and moral woes. This hope of salvation took on different
shades of meaning, sometimes centering in the Messiah and at other
times in a heavenly being that some called the "Son of Man." The
messianic hope was usually joined to the expectation that the kingdom
of David would be restored in this world, and the Messiah's task
consisted precisely in restoring the throne of David and sitting on
it.[19] On the other hand, the figure of the Son of Man, which appeared more frequently in apocalyptic circles, was a more universal
character than the Messiah, and would come to establish, not a
Davidic reign on this earth, but rather, a new era, a new heaven and
a new earth. Unlike the Messiah, the Son the Man was a celestial
being, and his functions included the resurrection of the dead and
the final judgment.[20] These two tendencies were drawn together
over the span of years, and by the first century there had appeared
intermediate positions, in which the reign of the Messiah would be
the last stage of the present era, and then would follow the new era
that the Son of Man was to establish. At any rate, the Jewish people
were still a people of hope, and it would be wrong to interpret their
religion simply in legalistic terms.

Another aspect of Jewish religion that would later develop into

---

[19] Ernst Jenni, "Messiah, Jewish," *IDB*, 3: 360-65; R. Meyer, "Eschatologie; III, Im Judentum," *RGG*, 2: 662-65; R. Meyer, "Messias; III, Im nachbiblishen Judentum," *RGG*,
4: 904-6.

[20] The phrase "Son of Man" has its roots in Dan. 7 and was later developed into a title
by the *midrashim* on that text. According to the synoptic tradition, Jesus claimed this title for
himself. Our exposition of this title and its meaning generally follows that of Sigmund Mo-
winckel, *He That Cometh* (Nashville: Abingdon Press, 1954), pp. 346-450. However, Norman Perrin, *Rediscovering the Teachings of Jesus* (New York: Harper, 1967), pp. 164-81,
argues that "Son of Man" was not a fixed title in first century Judaism, and that it was the
Christian community that turned it into a title and applied it to Jesus.

one of the pillars of trinitarian theology was the concept of Wisdom. Although it seems that Rabbinic Judaism had not gone as far as to fully hypostasize Wisdom, it did provide the basis for later Christian claims that Christ—or, if not, the Holy Spirit—is called Wisdom in the Old Testament.[21]

Judaism, however, was not confined to Palestine. On the contrary, the Jews formed important communities in Mesopotamia, Egypt, Syria, Asia Minor, and Rome. These Jews, together with the Gentile proselytes they had succeeded in attracting, constituted the Diaspora, or Dispersion, a very important phenomenon of first-century Judaism,[22] which contributed notably to the expansion and shaping of Christianity in its first years.[23]

The Jews of the Diaspora were not assimilated by the population of their new homelands, but rather, they formed a separate group that enjoyed a measure of autonomy within the civil government. In the great centers of the Diaspora—as in Egypt—the Jews lived in a certain zone in the city, not so much by obligation as because they themselves wanted to do so. There they elected their own local government and established a synagogue where they could study the Law. The Empire granted them certain legal recognition and provided laws to give them due respect, such as the law that prohibited forcing a Jew to work on his Sabbath day. In this way the Jewish community became a city within a city, with its own laws and administration. This is not surprising, but rather, a common practice in the Roman Empire. On the other hand, the Jews of the Diaspora, scattered throughout the world, felt themselves united by the Law and by the Temple. Although many of them died without ever having set foot in Palestine, every Jew over twenty years of age sent

---

[21] See H. Jaeger, "The Patristic Conception of Wisdom in the Light of Biblical and Rabbinical Research," *SP*, 4:90-106.

[22] A good summary of Diaspora Judaism may be found in William W. Tarn, *Hellenistic Civilisation* (Cleveland: World, 1961), pp. 210-38.

[23] Adolph von Harnack, *The Mission and Expansion of Christianity in the First Three Centuries* (New York: Harper, 1961), pp. 1-18; Kenneth Scott Latourette, *A History of the Expansion of Christianity* (New York: Harper, 1937-1944), 1:31-43.

an annual sum to the Temple. Moreover, at least in theory, the leaders of Palestine were also leaders of all the Jews of the Diaspora, though their power began declining in A.D. 70, when the Romans destroyed the Temple and scattered the Jewish population of Jerusalem.[24]

Almost from the beginning, differences began to spring up between Palestinian Judaism and that of the Diaspora. Of these the most important was language. Both in the Diaspora and in Palestine the use of Hebrew was declining, and it was more and more difficult to understand the Scriptures in their original language. As might be expected, the loss of Hebrew was much more rapid among the Jews of the Diaspora than among those who continued to live in Palestine. Whereas among the Palestinian Jews the Old Testament soon began to be translated into Aramaic—first orally and later in written form[25]—this process of translation was much more rapid and complete in the Diaspora, where the successive generations of Jews were losing the use of Hebrew and beginning to use the local tongues, especially Greek, the language of government and of commerce. It was at Alexandria that this linguistic Hellenization of Judaism reached its apex. This was a great center of Hellenistic culture, and, as we shall see later, the Alexandrian Jews wished to present their religion in such a way that it might be accessible to their educated neighbors. From this need arose the Greek translation of the Old Testament which was called the Septuagint.[26]

According to an ancient legend, which first appears in a work written about the end of the second century B.C.—the *Letter of Aristeas*[27]—this Greek version was produced in Egypt at the time

---

[24] Even at that time, however, Johanan ben Kakpai, who had fled Jerusalem in A.D. 69, managed to organize the Council of Jabneh, which held authority over Judaism for several centuries, and whose head was acknowledged by the Roman Empire as the leader of all Jews under Roman authority. Meanwhile, the Babylonian Jews developed their own hierarchy.

[25] These translations, of which a few fragments have survived, were called *Targumim*. See A. Jeffery, "Text and Ancient Versions of the Old Testament," *TIB*, 1: 46-62.

[26] The standard introduction to the Septuagint is still Henry Barclay Swete, *An Introduction to the Old Testament in Greek*, 2nd ed. (Cambridge: Cambridge University Press, 1914).

[27] Translated by H. T. Andrews in R. H. Charles, *The Apocrypha and Pseudoepigrapha of the Old Testament* (Oxford: Clarendon Press, 1913), 2: 83-122.

of Ptolemy II Philadelphus (285-247 B.C.), who brought seventy-two elders from Palestine—six of each tribe—to translate the Jewish Law. Later, in order to give more authority to this version, the legend was made more complex. It alleged that the elders worked independently, and when the time came to compare the results of their labors, they discovered that all their translations were identical. From this arose the name *Septuagint*, which is an abbreviation of the ancient title: *Interpretatio secundum septuaginta seniores*. The Roman numeral LXX is also used to refer to this version.

Separating history from legend, we may assert that the Greek version of the Old Testament, which we know as LXX, is not the product of a single effort. On the contrary, the LXX appears to have been in the making for more than a century, and there seems to have been no agreement among its various translators as to methods and purposes—while some are so literalistic that their results are almost unintelligible, others take excessive liberty with the Hebrew text.[28] Apparently the translation of the Pentateuch is the oldest, and could well have been done in the reign of Ptolemy II Philadelphus, as the legend asserts, although it is by no means the result of a homogeneous group of translators. Later, other translations were added to that of the Pentateuch, until the new version included the entire Hebrew canon of the Old Testament and some of the books that were later declared apocryphal.[29]

The LXX is of multiple importance. Scholars who devote themselves to the textual criticism of the Old Testament sometimes use it to rediscover the ancient Hebrew text. Those who study rabbinic

---

[28] In fact, whether or not there was a standard LXX translation is still an open question. P. Kahle has advanced the theory that the existing variants in the text of LXX are due to the fact that originally there was not a standard LXX, but rather several different and often fragmentary translations that were still in use at the beginning of the Christian era. Except in the case of the Torah, the Jews did not attempt to establish a standard text. This was done later by the Christian Church. See: Ernst Würthwein, *The Text of the Old Testament* (Oxford: Basil Blackwell, 1957), pp. 43-46.

[29] The LXX includes several books that are not included in the Hebrew canon of the O. T. The traditional interpretation of this fact is that Alexandrian Jews were more liberal than those in Palestine, and that this led them to accept the divine inspiration of books that did

exegesis are interested in the way it is reflected in the diverse methods employed by the translators of the LXX. In our case, it interests us because of its importance as part of the background of nascent Christianity.

The LXX played an important role in the formation of Hellenistic Jewish thought. In order to translate ancient Hebrew concepts, it was necessary to use Greek terms already bearing connotations completely foreign to biblical thought. Later, in order to understand the Greek text, interpreters studied the sense of its vocabulary in Hellenic and Hellenistic literature. On the other hand, educated Gentiles could now read the Old Testament and discuss its validity and significance with the Jews. To avoid being worsted in these discussions, the Jews were obliged to acquaint themselves better with the philosophical literature of the day, and to interpret the Bible in such a way that its superiority would be evident. Thus they even reached the point of affirming that the great Greek philosophers had copied the best of their wisdom from the Bible.

As for the history of Christianity, the LXX played an incalculably important part. The LXX was the Bible of the first known Christian authors, the Bible that almost all the writers of the New Testament used.[30] So much did the Christians claim ownership of it, that a Jew, Aquila, felt the need of producing a new version for the exclusive use of Jews.[31] Moreover, the LXX was the matrix in which

---

not have the same authority among Palestinian Jews. However, it is also possible that these books had great authority in Palestine as well as in the Diaspora, and that they were finally excluded from the canon because they lent themselves to heterodox interpretation. One must remember that the Hebrew canon was fixed about A. D. 90, and that by that time Christian use of Hebrew apocalyptic literature had made these writings suspicious among Jewish religious leaders. See Albert Carl Sundberg, "The Old Testament in the Early Church," HTR, 51 (1958), 205-25; Albert Carl Sundberg, The Old Testament of the Early Church (Cambridge: Harvard University Press, 1964).

[30] The book of Revelation seems to quote a version that is very similar to that usually known by the name of Theodotion. It seems, however, that the version quoted there is not that of Theodotion, but an earlier version that Theodotion later revised, and to which his name was given. This would explain the similarities as well as the differences between the text of Theodotion and that quoted in Revelation.

[31] Aquila was a Jewish proselyte from Pontus. Some ancient writers affirm that he was a Christian before his conversion to Judaism. In any case, he published his Greek translation of

the language of the New Testament was molded, and it is one of the best instruments we now possess to understand that language. "NT Koine is not simply the everyday Greek of an Eastern people in the first Christian century; its religious vocabulary derives ultimately, not from the Greek world, but from the Hebrew world of the OT through the medium of LXX Greek." [32]

The LXX was also a symptom of the state of mind of the Jews of the Diaspora, and above all those of Alexandria. The Hellenizing tendency had caught hold of them, and they felt obliged to show that Judaism was not so barbarous as one might think, but rather that it was closely linked to genuine Greek thought. An example of this state of mind is found in the work of Alexander Polyhistor—a Jewish author of the first century B.C.—and of the authors he quotes: Demetrius (third century B.C.) relates the history of the kings of Judah, making use of the methods of Alexandrian scholarship; Eupolemus (second century B.C.) makes Moses the inventor of the alphabet, which the Phoenicians took from the Jews and later introduced into Greece; Artaphanus (third century B.C.) even affirms that Abraham taught the principles of astrology to Pharaoh, and that Moses established the Egyptian cults of Apis and Isis. About the middle of the second century B.C., one Aristobolus wrote an *Exegesis of the Law of Moses*, whose purpose was to show that whatever there was of value in Greek philosophy had been taken from the Jewish Scriptures. We have already cited the work which—under the name of Aristeas—tried to give divine authority to the LXX. And all these are no more than a few examples that have come down to us of what must have been the state of mind of the Jews of the Diaspora during the Hellenistic period.[33]

The greatest expression of this intent on the part of the Jews to harmonize their tradition with the Hellenistic culture is found in

---

the Old Testament about A.D. 130, and it soon became popular among Jews. Perhaps as a reaction against Christian use of the LXX, Aquila's version is extremely literal.

[32] John W. Wevers, "Septuagint," *IDB*, 4: 277.

[33] Moses Hadas, *Hellenistic Culture* (New York: Columbia University Press, 1959), pp. 83-104; Tarn, *Hellenistic Civilization*, pp. 233-35.

Philo of Alexandria, a contemporary of Jesus, who strove to interpret the Jewish Scriptures in such a way that they might be compatible with the teachings of the Academy. According to Philo, the Scriptures teach the same things that Plato does, although they use allegories to do it. Thus, the wise interpreter's task is to show the eternal sense that may be found behind the scriptural allegories. Philo points out that Plato and the academicians are much later than Moses, and it is to be supposed that with all their learning they must have known the Scriptures, whence they derived the best of their teachings.[34] Certainly, Philo enjoyed the advantage of moving in circles where it was customary to interpret allegorically the more difficult passages of Scripture. The supposed epistle of Aristeas, which has been mentioned in connection with the origin of the LXX, already made use of this method of Scriptural interpretation, and later we shall see how Alexandrine Christianity was characterized by its allegorical interpretation of the Scriptures. Thus Philo could assert the infallible revelation of the Scriptures, and at the same time free himself from those aspects that were the most difficult to harmonize with Platonism.[35] As an example of this, one may cite the following passage, in which Philo discusses the curse of Adam:

"Thorns therefore and burrs shall it cause to spring up for thee" (Gen. iii: 18). Nay, what does grow and shoot up in the soul of a foolish man, but the passions which goad and wound it? To these, using figures, he has given the name of thorns. . . . He calls each of the passions "burrs" or "Three-spiked caltrops," because they are threefold, the passion itself, that which produces

---

[34] "Philo claimed in the name of Judaism everything which he took from the gentiles. The king theory, he assumed, was Jewish; the metaphysic of Plato, the numbers of the Pythagoreans, the cosmology of Greek science, the mysticism, ethics, and psychology of the hellenistic world, all this was, he says, nothing which he as a Jew took from the outside but something which the Greeks had taken from Moses." Erwin R. Goodenough, *An Introduction to Philo Judaeus,* 2nd ed. (New York: Barnes & Noble, 1963), p. 75.

[35] The Greeks also made use of allegorical interpretation in order to give new meaning to ancient myths that no longer seemed believable. Thus, for instance, Aphthonius interpreted the myth of Daphne and Apollo as an allegory having to do with the virtue of temperance. Robert M. Grant, *The Earliest Lives of Jesus* (London: S.P.C.K., 1961), pp. 45-46.

it, and the finished result of these. For instance, pleasure, the pleasant, feeling pleasure; desire, the desirable, desiring; sorrow, the sorrowful, feeling sorrow; fear, the fearful, fearing.[36]

As may be seen, this doctrine, although it might be very useful, is by no means an interpretation of the biblical text, but rather an effort to understand it in such a way that the Hellenistic mind will find it acceptable. We should point out, however, that Philo did not deny the historical and literal meaning of the Law—such denial would have been apostasy from Judaism—but rather, he insisted that, in addition to its literal sense, the Law also had an allegorical meaning.[37]

The God of Philo is a combination of Plato's idea of the beautiful and the God of the patriarchs and prophets. He is absolutely transcendent, so that no direct relationship exists between him and the world. Moreover, as Creator, God is beyond the ideas of the Good and the Beautiful.[38] God is essential being, and is not to be found in time or in space, but rather, these are found in him.[39]

Because God is absolutely transcendent and because—in his more Platonic moments—Philo conceives of him as an impassive being, the relationship between God and the world requires other intermediate beings.[40] The principal one of these is the *logos* or Word, which was created by God before the creation of the world. This *logos* is the image of God and is his instrument in creation. In it are the ideas of all things—in the Platonic sense of the word "idea"—so that it comes to occupy the place of Plato's demiurge. In addition, Philo incorporates into his doctrine of the *logos* certain Stoic elements,

---

[36] *Legum allegoria* 3. 248-50 (*LCL*, Philo 1: 469-71).

[37] *De migratione Abrahami* 89-91.

[38] Harry A. Wolfson, *Philo: Foundations of Religious Philosophy in Judaism, Christianity, and Islam* (Cambridge: Harvard University Press, 1948), 1: 200-204.

[39] *De somniis* 1. 117.

[40] This is the traditional interpretation of Philo's thought regarding the relationship between God and the world. Another interpretation may be found in Wolfson, *Philo,* 1: 282-89.

so that he also identifies the *logos* with the reason that constitutes the structure of all things. In order to explain these two functions of the *logos*, Philo introduces the distinction between the internal Word and the pronounced Word.[41] The difference is the same that exists between the word in thought and the spoken word. The internal Word corresponds to the world of ideas, while the external Word corresponds to the reason, which serves as form for the material world.[42]

As to the character of this *logos*, it should be pointed out that it is different from the *logos* of the Fourth Gospel. The *logos* of Philo is a being apart from and inferior to God, and it is found in a frame of reference that affirms the absolute transcendence of God and that therefore denies his direct relationship to the world. All this is far from the thought of the Fourth Gospel.

As for the end of man, Philo sustains—in typically Platonic fashion —that it is the vision of God. Man cannot understand God, since understanding implies a certain mode of possession, and man can never possess the infinite. But man can see God in a direct and intuitive way. This vision is such that man transcends himself and goes into ecstasy.[43]

Ecstasy is the goal and culmination of a long, ascending process, through which the soul is purified. In man, the body serves as ballast to the soul, and reason opposes the senses. Purification consists, then, in freeing oneself from the sensual passions that enslave the soul to the body. Here Philo introduces the Stoic doctrine according to which lack of passion, or apathy, is to be the goal of every human being. Yet in Philo apathy is not—as among the Stoics—the goal of morality, but rather the means that leads to ecstasy.

Much of this is foreign to biblical thought, although it is presented

---

[41] λόγος ἐνδιάθετος and λόγος προφορικός.

[42] *De vita Mosis* 2. 127.

[43] Wolfson, *Philo,* 2: 27-30.

simply as an interpretation of that thought.[44] This is the danger of an allegorical exegesis that tends to eclipse the unique character of the biblical message. As will be shown further on, this was also the weak point of the Christian theologians who flourished in Alexandria during the second and third centuries.

Finally, the picture of first-century Judaism must be completed with a word on the proto-gnostic trends that circulated in it, as may be seen in the *midrashim* of the time. These gnostic leanings probably evolved from apocalyptic dualism, whose followers found refuge in a trans-historical salvation when their apocalyptic expectations were not fulfilled. Their speculation centered on the throne of God, and developed into what has been called "throne-mysticism." [45] However, it is impossible to trace with any degree of certitude this gnostic trend in Judaism, and to determine how much of it is an autochthonous development of apocalypticism—and through it of Iranian patterns of thought—and how much is due to outside—and Christian—influences.[46] The best known of the early Judaizing gnostics, Elxai— or Elkesai, Elchasai—lived in the second century, and was clearly influenced by Christianity.[47] In any case, the existence of this type of speculative and mystical Judaism shows once more that that religion was not a petrified relic of a bygone age, but a vital movement with several very interesting ramifications.

---

[44] This has led Erwin R. Goodenough, *By Light, Light* (New Haven: Yale University Press, 1935), to claim that Philo's religion is really a mystery religion that is very far from Judaism as it was held and practiced in Palestine. Against this view, see: W. Völker, "Neue Wege der Philoforschung?" *ThBl*, 16 (1937), 297-301.

[45] Gershom G. Scholem, *Major Trends in Jewish Mysticism* (New York: Schoken Books, 1961), p. 44.

[46] Robert M. Grant, *Gnosticism and Early Christianity* (New York: Columbia University Press, 1959), pp. 39-69, has gathered an impressive amount of evidence to prove that the main features of gnosticism are already found in Jewish literature of the apocalyptic tradition, and that it was out of the failure of that tradition that gnosticism arose.

[47] Hans J. Schoeps, *Theologie und Geschichte des Judenchristentums* (Tübingen: J. C. B. Mohr, 1949), pp. 325-34; Jean Daniélou, *The Theology of Jewish Christianity* (Chicago: Regnery, 1964), pp. 64-67. The main sources on Elxai are: Hippolytus, *Philos.* 9. 8, 12; Eusebius, *HE*, 6. 38; Epiphanius, *Pan.* 19; Theodoret, *Haer. fab. comp.* 2. 7. See *infra*, p. 128.

The Greco-Roman World

Although for didactic reasons we have separated Judaism from the rest of the world in which the Christian church developed, the truth is that in the first century A.D. the Mediterranean basin enjoyed a political and cultural unity never since equaled. This unity was the result of the dissemination of Greek thought through Alexander's conquests and the ensuing Roman consolidation. From these had grown a universal culture that—while retaining important regional variations—united all the peoples of the Empire.

Alexander's conquests (334-323 B.C.) were at once cause and result of great changes in Greek thought. Before Alexander, and throughout the period from Homer to Aristotle, Greek thought had followed a path without which the great conquests of the fourth century would have been inconceivable. Ancient Greek thought had been typically aristocratic and racist. All the non-Hellenic peoples were "barbarians" by definition and were, therefore, inferior. With increasing commerce and intercommunication among various groups, Greek thought became less and less exclusive.[48] In Plato we find the affirmation that all are free, but we also find the old idea of an essential difference between Greeks and barbarians. Inspired by the desire to unite humankind in a single empire and culture, the conquests of Alexander put an end to Greek exclusivism. From that time on, Greek superiority to the barbarian was felt to be cultural rather than racial. Philosophy no longer concerned itself with the participation of the citizen in the life of the city, as in Plato's time, but rather with the individual in his new cosmopolitan environment. This, precisely, is one of the distinguishing marks of Hellenistic thought as opposed to Hellenic—its individualistic cosmopolitanism.

But Alexander's conquests did not take place in a cultural vacuum. Rather, they engulfed countries with very ancient cultures, such as Egypt, Syria, Persia, and Mesopotamia. In each of these countries, the influence of Greek culture had been felt even before the time of

---

[48] A process summarized by Hadas, *Hellenistic Culture*, pp. 11-19.

Alexander, but after the conquest the local culture was eclipsed for several centuries, only to reappear transformed and to expand far beyond its original frontiers.

This revival of the ancient Near-Eastern cultures took place simultaneously with the first century of the Christian era. For this reason, while studying the Hellenistic background of early Christianity one should keep in mind, on the one hand, the Hellenistic philosophy, and on the other, the many Eastern religions that were trying to invade the West. To these cultural and religious factors must be added the political and administrative—that is, the Roman Empire.

Greek philosophy had suffered a great change after the Alexandrian conquests. Aristotle, who had been Alexander's own teacher, fell into disuse. He was not completely forgotten, for the peripatetic school continued to exist through Theophrastus and Strato. But the metaphysical bent of the Aristotelian school became secondary to the study of botany, music, and other disciplines.[49]

The Platonic Academy continued its existence until Justinian closed it in A.D. 529, and through it Plato exercised considerable influence during the Hellenistic period. His sway extended far beyond the confines of the Academy, and it is interesting to note that, although the Museum of Alexandria was founded through the inspiration of the peripatetic, Demetrius of Phaleros, it was soon captured by the Platonic spirit and became one of its principal bulwarks.

Thus, although Hellenism was not ignorant of the contribution of Aristotle, it was to be Plato—and through him, Socrates—who would excercise the greater influence in molding the philosophy of the period.

There were certain aspects of Platonism, however, that did not conform to the spirit of the times any better than did Aristotelianism. Among these, the most important had to do with the contemporary political situation. Plato's thought, as well as Aristotle's, was forged within the framework of the ancient Greek city-state. Its objective

---

[49] Frederick C. Copleston, *A History of Philosophy*, Vol. I: *Greece and Rome*, rev. ed. (Paramus, N. J.: The Paulist/Newman Press, 1959), pp. 369-71.

was not so much the individual as the common good—although we must not forget that, above all in Plato, the goal of the common good is the individual's welfare. Man, in Plato and Aristotle, is a citizen, whose place in the world and in society is more or less assured, and whose religious and moral duties are regulated by long tradition. In such a situation, men could give themselves to speculation and could consider ethics as one aspect of philosophy. But when, at the time of Alexander, a cosmopolitan society arises, man finds himself lost in the immensity of the world, the gods enter into competition with other deities, and the rules of conduct with new customs. At this point a philosophy is needed which, in addition to speaking to man as an individual, will give him norms for daily living. Such a philosophy must not be limited by the ancient city-state as a frame of reference, nor by the distinction between Greeks and barbarians. Stoicism and Epicureanism fulfilled this need during a period of Greek philosophy. Later, as disbelief in the ancient gods became more rampant, philosophy would try to take their place— as it has attempted to do so often in human history—and thence would arise philosophical systems of a religious character, such as Neo-Platonism.

We cannot review here the whole of Greek and Hellenistic philosophy, but we should point out a few of the tenets that gave the different schools a share in the history of Christian thought.

Among all the ancient philosophers, it is Plato who had the greatest influence on the early development of Christian thought. Of his teachings, those that most concern us here are the doctrines of the two worlds, of immortality and the pre-existence of the soul, of knowledge as reminiscence, and of the Idea of the Good.[50]

The Platonic doctrine of the two worlds was used by several Christian scholars as a means of interpreting the Christian doctrine of the "world," and also that of heaven and earth. Using the Platonic teaching it could be demonstrated that the material things around us

---

[50] Adam Fox, *Plato and the Christians* (London: SCM Press, 1957) has attempted to collect those passages of Plato that have proved most interesting and influential to Christians.

are not the ultimate realities, but that there are others of a different order and of greater value. It is easy to understand the attractiveness of such a doctrine to a church enduring persecution. But some Christians were soon led into attitudes toward the material world that constituted a negation of the doctrine of creation. This was aggravated by the Platonic tendency to make an ethical distinction between the two worlds, in which the visible world is the homeland of evil, while the world of ideas is the goal of human life and morality.

From earliest times, the doctrine of the immortality of the soul attracted Christians who were searching in Greek philosophy for support for the Christian doctrine of the future life. If Plato had asserted that the soul is immortal, why should the pagans now scoff at the Christians, who also affirm life after death? Christians who argued in this manner did not usually recognize the difference between the Platonic immortality of the soul and the Christian hope of the resurrection. The Platonic system made the future life not a gift of God, but the natural result of the divine in the human. Platonic teaching affirmed the eternal life of the soul and the eternal death of the body, since only the spiritual can have permanence. It taught not only the immortality, but probably also the preexistence and the transmigration of souls. All this was very different from Christianity. But not a few Christian thinkers, eager to interpret their new faith in the light of Platonic philosophy, came to include part or all of this in their doctrinal system.[51]

The Platonic doctrine of knowledge is based on a distrust of the senses as the means of attaining true knowledge. This is no fault of the senses themselves, but is due to the fact that they can supply information only about objects of this world, not about ideas. Since true knowledge can only be knowledge of ideas, it is obvious that the senses are not an adequate means of reaching it. Plato utilized the theory of recall or reminiscence, which in turn requires the doc-

---

[51] See Oscar Cullmann, *Immortality of the Soul, or Resurrection of the Dead? The Witness of the New Testament* (New York: Macmillan, 1958).

trine of the pre-existence of souls.[52] Naturally, the mainstream of Christian thought, which never accepted the pre-existence of souls, could not interpret knowledge as reminiscence. But a distrust of sensory perception was readily accepted by Christians, and, through the epistemology of Augustine, dominated Christian thought for many centuries.

Finally, the Platonic Idea of the Good markedly influenced the formulation of Christian thought about God. In the *Timaeus*, Plato states that the origin of the world was the work of a divine artisan, or demiurge, that took formless matter and gave it form, imitating the beauty of the Idea of the Good. Whether or not Plato considered this a myth does not interest us at this point. Our concern is its powerful influence on early Christian thought. Because of their common theme, it was not difficult to draw parallels between the *Timaeus* and Genesis. The differentiation between the Idea of the Good and the demiurge or artisan of the universe established a dichotomy between the Supreme Being and the Creator, which is entirely foreign to biblical thought, but which soon became rooted in the minds of some scholars who wished to assert the impassiveness of God simultaneously with his activity in the world. From this source—and also from the monotheism that Plato's dialogue seemed to uphold— there arose the custom, deeply entrenched in some theological circles, of speaking of God in the same terms Plato used to refer to the Idea of the Good: God is impassive, infinite, incomprehensible, indescribable, and so on.

Next to Platonism, Stoicism was the philosophical system that most influenced the development of Christian thought. Its doctrine of the *logos*, its elevated moral tone, and its doctrine of natural law made a profound impression on Christian thinking.

According to Stoic teachings, the universe is subject to a universal reason, or *logos*. This *logos* is not simply an external force, but rather,

---

[52] See Francis M. Cornford, *Plato's Theory of Knowledge: The Thaetetus and the Sophist of Plato Translated with a Running Commentary* (London: Routledge & Kegan Paul, 1935).

it is the reason that is imprinted into the very structure of things. Our own reason is part of this universal *logos,* and thus we are able to know and to understand. All reason and all energy are to be found in this reason, which is called the *seminal logos.* This concept of the *logos,* originally independent of any speculative interest, would later be joined to Platonic thought—as had already taken place in Philo—to serve as the context within which the Christian doctrine of the *logos* would be elaborated.[53]

For the Stoics, the doctrine of the *logos* was only a part of their ethical concern, and it was this interest that caused their marked influence on some Christian thinkers. From the existence of the universal reason follows the existence of the natural order of things, and above all, of a natural order of human life. This order is what the Stoics call "natural law," and they find it imprinted in the very being of all men, so that we have only to obey it to be virtuous.[54] At the beginning, Stoicism tended to be a doctrine for minorities, and it established an absolute distinction, predetermined and unalterable, between the "wise" and the "foolish." [55] As time passed, however, Stoicism became more flexible, and when it was confronted with Christianity it had already become one of the most popular philosophical systems of the Empire. Christians saw in it an ally against those who scoffed at the austerity of their customs—in spite of the persecution under Marcus Aurelius, who was at the same time one of the greatest of the Stoics. Many soon reached the conclusion that the natural law of which the Stoics talked was also the foundation of Christian ethics. In this fashion a bridge was erected between

[53] Wilhelm Kelber, *Die Logoslehre von Heralkit bis Origenes* (Stuttgart: Urachhaus, 1958), pp. 48-88.

[54] J. Stelzenberger, *Die Beziehungen der frühchristlichen Sittenlehre zur Ethik der Stoa: Eine moralgeschichtliche Studie* (Munich: M. Hueber, 1933); Felix Flückiger, *Geschichte des Naturrechtes,* Bd. I: *Altertum und Frühmittelalter* (Zurich: Evangelischer Verlag, 1954), pp. 186-238; E. Galán y Gutiérrez, *Jus naturae* (Valladolid: Meseta, 1954); Henri und Marcel Simon, *Die Alte Stoa und ihr Naturbegriff* (Berlin: Aufbau Verlag, 1956), pp. 53-73 and 85-93; M. Spanneut, *Le stoïcisme des Pères de l'Eglise: De Clément de Rome à Clément d'Alexandrie* (Paris: Editions du Seuil, 1957).

[55] Eduard Zeller, *The Stoics, Epicureans and Sceptics* (New York: Russell & Russell, 1962), pp. 268-77.

the highest moral code of that age and Christian doctrine, but at a price—the casting of doubt upon the uniqueness and pristine newness of the Christian message.

Apart from Neoplatonism—which we shall not discuss yet, since its origin does not go back beyond the second century A.D.—the other philosophical movements of the Hellenistic period had little influence on Christianity. Epicureanism had lost its appeal even before the appearance of Christianity, and in any case, the disparity between the two doctrines was such that it would have been difficult for either to influence the other.[56] Skepticism, although it had not yet fallen into disuse, was the philosophy of a very small group, and its lack of positive teachings reduced its influence on other systems of thought. Aristotle continued to make himself felt through his logic and his doctrine of the "prime unmoved mover," but these had already been assimilated by contemporary Platonism—the so-called Middle Platonism[57]—so that Aristotle's influence reached the early church enveloped in systems that were essentially Platonic, like that of Philo.

In any case, we should bear in mind that an eclectic spirit characterized the first centuries of our era, an acceptance of that part of the truth that might be found in each of the philosophical schools. For this reason, some schools influenced others to such an extent that it is impossible to distinguish clearly among them. Even in the case of the two most clearly defined systems—Platonism and Stoicism—it is impossible to find in the first centuries after Christ a single adherent to one of them who has not appropriated some elements of the other. This spirit became manifest in the foundation of the "eclectic school" at Alexandria during Augustus' reign. But the eclectic spirit had long before taken possession of various philosophical schools—of Stoicism with Boethus of Sidon (second century B.C.), of Platonism with Philo of Larissa and Antiochus of Ascalon (first century B.C.), and of Aristotelianism with Galen (second century

---

[56] Cf., however, Richard P. Jungkuntz, "Christian Approval of Epicureanism," *CH*, 31 (1962), 279-93.

[57] Copleston, *History*, 1: 451-56; Nicolás Abbagnano, *Historia de la filosofía* (Barcelona: Montaner y Simón, S. A., 1955-1956), 1: 173-74.

A.D.)[58] The same tendency to combine doctrines from different sources can be seen in the religious syncretism of the time, which we are to discuss later. This syncretism combined different religions, as well as various philosophical doctrines that might be given a religious slant.

At the same time, strictly philosophical studies were the privilege of a very small minority. Of the educated population of the Empire, the majority did not go beyond grammar and rhetoric, and their acquaintance with the various schools of philosophy was derived only from the use of philosophical passages in their exercises in rhetoric, and perhaps the reading of some doxography in which the opinions of various philosophers were summarized.[59] In fact, some of the early Christian writers who are given the title of "philosophers" appear to be acquainted with classic philosophy only through some doxographic summary. As might be supposed, this lack of profound study of the thought of each philosopher contributed to the eclectic spirit of the period.

We have already said that in order to understand the framework in which Christianity developed, we must take into account not only the philosophical systems of the Hellenistic period, but also the religions that at that time were claiming men's allegiance. Olympic religion as found in the Homeric poems was not that faced by the first Christians. Since long before the conquests of Alexander, there existed in Greece, alongside the worship of the Olympic gods, other very different cults that were part of the group known as "mystery religions." These cults, of which the Eleusine mysteries are a classic example, were not a typically Greek phenomenon, but rather were a type of religiosity that tended to supplant the decadent national religions.[60]

---

[58] Abbagnano, *Historia*, 1: 164-71.

[59] Donald Lemen Clark, *Rhetoric in Graeco-Roman Education* (New York: Columbia University Press, 1957).

[60] The decadence of the ancient Olympic gods began even before the golden age of Greek culture. The mockery of Xenophanes is a witness to this, as is also the attempt of the Pythagoreans to Reform the Olympic religion. There is no doubt that Plato was greatly

A national religion, which is distinguished by its collective character and by the intimate connection between the gods and the nation, cannot subsist as such when the nation loses its individual identity, or when, in any society, the individual reaches a certain degree of autonomy in reference to the group. The ancient Egyptian religion could not persist intact when Egypt lost its national independence. In the same way, the ancient Greek religion could not remain unchanged before the advances of individualism. Hence the great popularity gained during the Hellenistic period by the mystery cults, which were so different from the national religions.

Apparently the mystery religions have their origin in the ancient fertility rites that were central in the religious practices of many primitive peoples. The miracle of fertility, both in human beings and in plants and animals, occupies an important place in the origin of most of the mysteries, and it is notable that even after their origin had been long forgotten, the feasts known as "rustic Dionysiacs" included symbols that suggested the origin of the cult to Dionysius as a god of fertility.[61] A miracle of death and resurrection that follow each other every year, with the change of seasons in the North and with the flooding of the Nile in Egypt, played an important role in the origin of these religions. In winter, the god died or withdrew, only to return in the spring with the priceless gift of fertility. From this followed, on the one hand, the myth that explained the annual death and resurrection in nature, and on the other, the participation of all nature in the life and death of the god, which in turn was the basis for the participation of the individual man in the death and renewed life of the divinity.

Besides these mythological aspects, which were central to the mysteries, one should point out that all these religions, in contrast to the national religions, were individualistic. Membership in them was not

---

influenced by Orphism; and, after all, Orpheus is Dionysius passing for an Olympic. See Francis M. Cornford, *From Religion to Philosophy: A Study in the Origins of Western Speculation* (New York: Harper, 1957).

[61] Angel Alvarez de Miranda, *Las religiones mistéricas* (Madrid: Revista de Occidente, 1961), pp. 79-80.

through mere physical birth, but rather it was necessary to be initiated. We do not know exactly what comprised these initiations, for the mysteries were noted for the secrecy of their rites. But we do know that initiation was a rite by means of which the neophyte became united to the god and thus shared in the divine power and immortality. The individualism and secrecy of these cults adapted them for diffusion across national boundaries, and thus we find that the cult of Isis and Osiris reached as far as Spain and that of Attis and Cybele, originally Phrygian, was widespread in Rome.[62] The initiates told others of the experiences afforded them by the mysteries, though without divulging the secrets, and in this way the cults were extended and intermingled.

Finally, one should note that these cults frequently included a ceremonial meal in which the faithful ingested the god and became participants in his divinity. In Thrace, the communicants of a certain divinity—which may well have been the rudimentary ancestor of the Greek Dionysius, who was probably of Thracian origin[63]—joined in a hunt that ended in an orgiastic feast, as the participants tore apart and devoured the still-throbbing carcass of the hunted animal.[64] In this way, they believed, the animal's life became theirs. Another example of this can be found in the ancient bacchanales, in which the purpose of imbibing wine was to be possessed by Bacchus and thus participate in his immortality.

The fact that these cults, whose intimate characteristics and secret rites are unknown, seem strange to us, should not conceal from us the great attraction that they held for men of the Hellenistic period. In fact, their popularity was so great that some—especially the cult

---

[62] On the cult of Isis and Osiris, see E. A. Wallis Budge, *Osiris: The Egyptian Religion of Resurrection* (New Hyde Park, N. Y.: University Books, 1961); on Attis and Cybele and their influence on Christianity, see P. Touilleux, *L'Apocalypse et les cultes de Domitien et de Cybèle* (Paris: Librairie Orientaliste Paul Geuthner, 1935).

[63] Such is the traditional view, based in ancient authorities. Henry Jeanmaire, *Dionysos: Historie du culte de Bacchus* (Paris: Gallimard, 1951), proposes a different theory, that Dionysius was originally Greek and was later merged in Thracia with some of the local gods.

[64] Alvarez de Miranda, *Las religiones*, p. 89.

of Mithra—were important rivals of Christianity in their missionary thrust.[65] In general, this popularity can be explained by the very character of the mysteries as religions of initiation. In an individualistic and cosmopolitan era, men could not be satisfied with merely collective and national religions. The mysteries, which appealed to the individual, and to individuals of all nationalities, responded effectively to the spirit of the times and thence their unusual growth. However, one should not forget that the essential character of the mysteries makes it impossible for non-initiates to understand them. Although it is difficult for us to feel the emotions that the mysteries aroused in their followers, we must at least understand that a great number of persons in the Hellenistic period found in them a spiritual home.[66]

Concerning the relationship between the mystery cults and Christianity, scholarly opinion has varied. During the first two or three decades of the twentieth century, it was thought that the mystery religions constituted a unity based on a common "mystery theology," and that Christianity was simply one of them, or at most, a distinct religion in which the influence of the mysteries was greatly felt. According to scholars of that time,[67] Christianity had taken from the mysteries its concept of the passion, death, and resurrection of the god; its rites of initiation—baptism; its sacramental meals—communion; its ascending stages of initiation—the orders; and a multitude of details needless to enumerate. But since then, a careful study has been made of the mysteries, and the conclusion reached by almost

---

[65] Mithra seems to be Persian in origin. He is often described as the god of light. Unlike other mysteries, that of Mithra does not include a feminine deity. It became very popular, especially among soldiers in frontier outposts, and for a time seems to have been a powerful rival of Christianity. Franz V. M. Cumont, *The Mysteries of Mithra*, 2nd ed., translated from the 2nd French ed. of 1902 (New York: Dover, 1956) is still a valuable introduction to Mithraism.

[66] The best insight into the allure of the mysteries may be had by reading the *Metamorphoses* of Lucius Apuleius, more commonly known as *The Golden Ass*.

[67] Wilhelm Bousset, *Kyrios Christos* (Göttingen: Vandehoeck & Ruprecht, 1965); Alfred F. Loisy, *Les Mystères païens et le mystère chrétien* (Paris, 1919); R. Reitzenstein, *Die hellenistischen Mysterienreligionen* (Leipzig, 1920); R. Reitzenstein, *Das iranishce Erlösungsmysterium* (Bonn, 1921).

all scholars is that there was no such thing as a common "mystery theology"—at least in the first century of our era. Quite the contrary, the mystery cults differed one from another so much that it is difficult even to explain the term "mystery religion." Moreover, the mysteries seem not to have reached their full development until the second and third centuries, which is the time when the majority of their characteristics in common with Christianity appear. It follows that such traits can be more easily explained as the influence of Christianity on the mysteries than the opposite, the more so when we learn that already in this period the pagan cults tried to imitate some of the characteristics of the dynamic new faith. But this should not lead us to the extreme of denying all influence of the mysteries on Christianity. For instance, the date, December twenty-fifth, so deeply cherished by Christians, was an important pagan feast connected with the cult of Mithra.[68] It was not until the end of the third century, or the beginning of the fourth, that it began to be observed as the birthday of Christ. The late date of such an innovation, however, seems to corroborate the fact that the mysteries reached their full growth after Christianity had become fixed in its central traits, and thus their influence was only peripheral.

There are two other aspects of Hellenistic religion that interest us: the cult of the Emperor and the syncretistic tendency of the times.

Emperor worship is not of Roman origin, but is rather one more instance of the invasion of the Roman world by the Eastern religions. Egypt worshiped its pharaohs; the Persians bowed before their sovereigns; the Greeks adored their heroes. These are the sources of Em-

---

[68] The winter solstice, being the day in which the sun begins to wax again after six months of waning, has often been connected with mystery and fertility cults. In pagan Rome, the feast was considered to be of great importance and was connected both with the cult of the Emperor and with Mithraism. In the fourth century, Christians appropriated the date on the basis that Christ is the sun of righteousness with healing in his wings. Bernard Botte, *Los orígenes de la Navidad y de la Epifanía* (Madrid: Taurus, 1964), pp. 90-96. However, Roland H. Bainton, "The Origins of Epiphany," in *Early and Medieval Christianity* (Boston: Beacon Press, 1962), pp. 22-38, claims that January 6, the date of the epiphany of Dionysus, was regarded as the date of the birth of Jesus even in the second century.

peror worship in the Roman Empire. At a time when the Mediterranean world had been fused into a more or less homogeneous culture, the customs of one region were reflected in others. When Alexander conquered the East, he adopted the practices that were followed there in respect to rulers, and had no difficulty in being accepted as a god.[69] Julius Caesar, and later Mark Anthony and Octavius, were revered as gods by the Egyptians. Rome, however, was wary of such extravagance. Even Octavius, who allowed himself to be worshiped in the Near East, did not pretend to be more than Emperor and Augustus while in Rome and dealing with Romans.[70] In Rome, the great were deified only after death—thus Vespasian said shortly before death: "Alas, I feel myself becoming a god!"[71] And even this practice was not accepted without criticism.[72] Generally it was the Roman aristocrats that were critical, for they opposed the influx of Eastern customs and religions. Moreover, Emperor worship foundered on the apathy of the masses, who felt that the cult did not satisfy their needs. For these reasons, it took years for Emperor worship to take root in the West, and there were some emperors who took it more seriously than their subjects.[73] In any case, this cult was not a vital force in the religious life of most of the Greco-Roman world, and if it became one of the principal points of conflict between the State and developing Christendom, this was only because of its use as a criterion of political loyalty.

On the other hand, the Hellenistic period is characterized by religious syncretism. The establishment of cultural, commercial, and political relationships among the different regions of the Mediterranean world inevitably had to lead to interrelationships and equivalency among the various regional deities. Isis was identified with Aphrodite and Demeter, and Zeus was fused with Serapis. Since polytheism was part of their fundamental structure, each mystery

[69] Roland H. Bainton, *Early Christianity* (New York: Van Nostrand, 1960), p. 22.
[70] What is "augustus" is sacred, but not divine. Cf. Ovid, *Fast.*, 1. 607-12.
[71] Suetonius, *De vita Caesarum* 8. 23 (LCL, *Suet.* 2: 318).
[72] Cf. Cicero, *Phil.* 1. 6. 31.
[73] Such was the case with Caligula. Suetonius, *De vita* 4. 22.

religion felt itself authorized to accept and adapt whatever it could find of value in other religions. If there is one characteristic of the religion of the Hellenistic period, it is syncretism. Every cult competed with the others, not to be the strictest, but to be the broadest, to include the most diverse doctrines. For our history, this spirit of the times—which is parallel to philosophical eclecticism and even becomes confused with it[74]—is of greatest importance. Only in such a context can we understand the importance and the difficulty of the decision the early Christians had to make when faced with the temptation to turn Christianity into a syncretistic cult like those that were then in vogue.

Finally, in discussing the cradle of Christianity, we must not overlook such an important factor as the Roman Empire. With its unity of structure and the facility of its means of communication, the Roman Empire, although it persecuted Christianity, provided necessary means for its expansion. The wise administrative organization of the Empire left its mark on the organization of the church, and the Roman legal code served not only canon law, but was also one of the quarries from which Latin theological vocabulary was drawn. But the great contribution of Rome to developing Christianity was its interest in the practical, the moral, and the human. This gave occidental Christianity its practical character and its deep ethical sense and laid the foundation for works of such profound psychological perception as Saint Augustine's *Confessions*.

All this goes to show what has already been said, that is, that Christianity was not born solitarily, in a vacuum, but that—incarnation that it is—it arose in the midst of a world in which it was to take form, and apart from which it is impossible to comprehend it, just as it is impossible to understand Jesus Christ apart from the physical body in which he lived.

---

[74] As is the case of Plotinus (see Chap. VIII), as well as of Porphyry and Iamblichus.

III

The Theology of the Apostolic Fathers

The earliest surviving Christian writings apart from those which now form part of the New Testament canon are those of the so-called Apostolic Fathers.[1] They have been given this title because at the time it was thought that they had known the apostles. In some cases this seems quite possible, but in others it was a mere product of imagination. The name "Apostolic Fathers" appeared in the seventeenth century, when it was applied to five writings or bodies of writings. But through the years three other members have been added to this group,[2] so that now the Apostolic Fathers are eight: Clement of Rome, the *Didache*, Ignatius of Antioch, Polycarp of Smyrna, Papias of Hierapolis, the *Epistle of Barnabas*, the *Shepherd* of Hermas, and the *Epistle to Diognetus*.

With the sole exception of the *Epistle to Diognetus*, all of these writings are addressed to other Christians.[3] Therefore, they are very useful to give us an idea of the life and thought of the young church. Reading the Apostolic Fathers, one can glimpse into the problems

---

[1] There is also a number of epitaphs and other inscriptions. Cf. G. Wilpert, *La fede della Chiesa nascente secondo i monumenti dell'arte funeraria antica* (Vatican City: Pontif. Instituto di Archeologia Cristiana, 1938).

[2] G. Jouassard, "Le groupement des Pères dits apostoliques," *MScRel*, 14 (1957), 129-34.

[3] The Epistle to Diognetus should be classified among the Apologists of the second century, and will be discussed not in this chapter but rather in that devoted to the Apologists.

posed by inner divisions, by persecution, and by the conflict with both Judaism and paganism.

The literary nature of these writings is not uniform. Among them there are several epistles, a sort of manual of discipline, an exegetical and theological treatise, a collection of visions and prophecies, and a defense of Christianity. This variety itself increases the value of the Apostolic Fathers, for it shows different aspects of the life of the early church.

Clement of Rome

The first of the writings of the Apostolic Fathers which can be dated with some degree of accuracy is the *First Epistle to the Co-rinthians*[4] of Clement of Rome. All that can be said with certainty[5]

---

[4] Preserved in the Greek original in two manuscripts, and in translations into Coptic, Syriac, and Latin. See Antonio Casamassa, *I Padri Apostolici* (Rome: Facultas Theologica Pontificii Athenaei Lateranensis, 1938), pp. 39-40.

[5] Clement belongs in part to history and in part to legend, for later Christians attributed to him many deeds that he never performed. Origen (*Comm. in Joh*, 6. 36), Eusebius (*HE*, 3. 4, 15), Epiphanius (*Haer*. 27. 6), and Jerome (*De viris illus* 15) affirm that Clement was with Paul while the latter founded the church in Philippi. The basis for this tradition is in Phil. 4:3. However, there is no reason to identify the "Clement" mentioned there with Clement of Rome. Others build around him a series of legends that are now called "Pseudoclementine" literature. This is the name given to a series of fictional writings in which Clement is the main character. They deal with Peter's travels, Clement's conversion to Christianity, and the struggles of Peter and Clement against Simon Magus. Among these writings there are *Twenty Homilies*, which claim to be Peter's, and ten books of *Recognitions*. The *Twenty Homilies* actually seem to have originated in Jewish Gnostic circles. The *Recognitions* tell the story of Clement's family, scattered by circumstances and later gathered together by Peter. Although they are more orthodox than the *Homilies*, it is quite possible that this is the result of corrections introduced by the translator Rufinus, for the *Recognitions* exist only in his Latin translation, and he avowedly corrected the errors he found in works that he translated. Both the *Homilies* and the *Recognitions* seem to have been written in the fourth century, although probably drawing from earlier sources.

There have also been attempts to identify Clement of Rome with Titus Flavius Clemens, a Roman consul who was condemned to death by his relative Emperor Domitian, in the year 95. As Flavius Clemens was accused of "atheism"—that is, of not worshiping the gods—and of having gone over to Jewish uses, it is quite probable that he was a Christian (the story of his death: Dio Cassius, *Hist. rom*. 67.14 and Suetonius, *De vita Caes*. 8. 15). But it seems quite unlikely that he was the bishop known to us as Clement of Rome.

about Clement is that he was bishop of Rome toward the end of the first century,[6] and that at that time—probably in A.D. 96—he wrote to the Corinthians an epistle that is his only genuine literary remain. Although there is no reason to doubt that Clement wrote it, his *Epistle*—usually called *I Clement*—is really a letter from the church in Rome to the church in Corinth.[7] It is a letter from church to church, and not from the bishop of Rome to another church.[8]

The reason for this letter is quite clear from the beginning, and it reminds us of the church of Corinth that is so well known through Paul's epistles. Once again Christians in that city are divided, and some of them[9] have assumed a rebellious attitude that worries Christians in Rome, for " 'the ignoble' rose up 'against the honorable,' those of no reputation against those of repute, the foolish against the wise,

---

[6] Ancient writers do not agree regarding the order of succession through which Clement became bishop of Rome. Irenaeus (*Adv. haer.* 3. 3.3) claims that Clement was the third bishop of Rome after Peter, and Eusebius (*HE* 3. 4, 15), and Jerome (*De viris illus.* 15) agree with him. Saint Augustine (Ep. 53.2), the *Apostolic Constitutions* (7.46), and several other sources (the *Liberian Catalog* and Optatus, *De schis. donat.* 2. 3) say that he was second after Peter. Finally, Tertullian (*De praes. haer.* 32) and the Pseudoclementine (in the so-called *Epistle of Clement to James*, which introduces the *Twenty Homilies: ANF*, 8: 218-22) claim that Clement was the immediate successor of Peter, and in this they are followed by other writers (Jerome, *Adv. Iovin.* 1. 12 and *In Isaiam* 52. 13). There have been several attempts to solve this conflict through various explanations—among them, that of Epiphanius, who claims that Clement was bishop of Rome twice (*Haer.*, 27. 6). Some modern scholars argue that during the first century Rome did not have a monarchical episcopacy, that is, that there was not one bishop, rather a college or group of bishops. According to this theory, it was later writers, used to thinking in terms of a monarchical episcopacy, who presented the list of bishops as a chronological succession, and this was the origin of the confusion regarding the exact place of Clement within that supposed succession (E. Kohlmeyer, "Zur Ideologie des ältesten Papsttums: Succession und Tradition," *ThSK*, 103 [1931], 230-42; Stanley Lawrence Greenslade, "Scripture and Other Doctrinal Norms in Early Theories of the Ministry," *JTS*, 44 [1943], 162-76).

[7] A letter into which two fragments of homilies by the same author have perhaps been inserted. L. Lemarchand "La composition de l'Épître de saint Clément aux Corinthiens," *RScRel*, 18 (1938), 448-57.

[8] The salutation opens: "The church of God which sojourns in Rome to the church of God which sojourns in Corinth" (Robert M. Grant *et al., The Apostolic Fathers*, 7 vols., Camden, N. J.: Thomas Nelson, 1964-1968, 2:15).

[9] Probably a group of "spiritualists" who opposed the authorities arguing for the freedom of the Spirit. P. Meinhold, "Geschehen und Deutung im ersten Clemensbrief," *ZschrKgesch*, 58 (1939), 82-129.

'the young against their elders.' " [10] Therefore, the epistle is mostly practical in nature, dealing with the vices that cause divisions and the virtues that strengthen unity, and treating other theological subjects only tangentially.

Clement seems to draw from two sources for his arguments against the rebellious: the Old Testament on the one hand, and the Stoic doctrine of the natural harmony of the universe on the other.

His use of the Old Testament for this purpose is quite simple: he refers to the main characters of Old Testament history and shows how they were obedient, hospitable, and humble. The section devoted to this type of argument—which includes chapters 9 to 19—opens with a summary very reminiscent of Hebrews 11:

> Let us take as an example Enoch, who because he was found righteous in his obedience was translated and never saw death. Noah, because he was found faithful in his service, proclaimed renewal to the world, for through him the Master saved the animals that entered peacefully into the ark.
>
> Abraham, who was called the friend, proved faithful in that he obeyed the words of God. For he went obediently from his land and kindred and from his father's house, with the result that by leaving a little country and a weak clan and a small household he became the heir of the promise of God.[11]

On the other hand, Clement's moral teaching also dwells on the Stoic theme of harmony or concord (ὁμόνοια). Harmony is manifest in all creation, for it derives from the character of God himself, who has established it in all things. God is the maker (δημιουργός) of the universe. But his activity, however, is not limited to the original creation, for he is also sovereign ruler (δεσπότης) over all things.[12] It is possible that in calling God "demiurge" Clement conceives his relation with the world in Platonic terms, as the artisan who takes a pre-

---

[10] 3. 3 (Grant, *The Apostolic Fathers*, 2:21).

[11] 9. 3-10. 2; 11. 1a; 12. 1 (Grant, *The Apostolic Fathers*, 2: 30-32). This is probably the reason why a tradition that goes at least as far back as Origen (quoted by Eusebius, *HE* 6. 25. 12-14) ascribes Hebrews to Clement (see also: *HE* 3. 38. 1-4 and Jerome, *De viris illus.* 15).

[12] 20.11. Here God is referred to as ὁ μέγας δημιουργὸς καὶ δεσπότης τῶν ἁπάντων.

existent matter and gives it a form in imitation of an idea that is above himself. But Clement does not say enough about creation to allow us to make a judgment regarding the connotations that the title of "demiurge" has for him. However, the title of "sovereign of all things," applied to God and united to the Stoic theme of harmony, shows without any doubt that the Stoic concept of providence has influenced Clement—which is not surprising at all if one takes into account the strength of Stoicism in Rome at the time. In any case, Clement's doctrine of God is clearly trinitarian, in the sense that several trinitarian formulas appear in the epistle.[13]

In Clement's Christology there is no doubt about the pre-existence of the Savior. This is the reason why he can quote the Psalms as Word of Christ through the Holy Spirit.[14] Jesus is a descendant of Jacob, but only according to the flesh.[15] Furthermore, it is possible that a certain text of doubtful reading refers to the sufferings of Christ as the "sufferings of God." [16]

In this epistle we find also the first claim for authority based on apostolic succession.[17] The apostles, inspired by Jesus, knew that there would come a time when the church would be in need of clearly established authorities. This led them to appoint certain holy men to succeed them, and these in turn have been succeeded by others as it has become necessary. These persons do not receive their authority from the congregation, and therefore it cannot depose them. Clement calls these persons who are charged with the direction of the church "bishops and deacons," [18] although sometimes he refers to the bishops as "presbyters." [19] Quite clearly, at this time there was not a clearly fixed distinction between bishops and presbyters.

---

[13] 46. 6; 58. 2. Cf. Jules Lebreton, *Histoire du dogme de la Trinité des origines au Concile de Nicée*, Vol. II, *De Saint Clément à Saint Irenée* (Paris: Beauchesne, 1928), pp. 249-81.

[14] 32. 1.

[15] 32. 2.

[16] 2. 1 (Alexandrine Codex).

[17] 44. 1-4.

[18] 42. 4-5.

[19] 44. 4-5.

Clement's popularity was the reason why, from a very early date, various works were attributed to him, with the purpose of circulating them under the cloak of his authority. The most ancient of these works, and the only one that will be discussed here, is the *Second Epistle of Clement to the Corinthians*.[20] This is really a homily, probably written before A.D. 150. Scholars do not agree as to its place of origin, although the majority argue for either Corinth or Rome. Its purpose is to exhort believers to repentance while they are still in this world, for there is no possibility of repenting hereafter.[21]

As will be seen later on, this call for believers to repent is to be found also in another Roman document of the same period, the *Shepherd* of Hermas, and is a witness to one of the central concerns of Christians in Rome toward the middle of the second century.[22]

Besides the doctrine of penance, whose proximity to that of Hermas is such that it does not need to be discussed separately, this homily is interesting because of his doctrine of the church and its Christology, both of which are developed in opposition to some who seemed to believe that the flesh had nothing to do with spiritual issues. Against these, the author says:

> Further, let none of you say that his flesh is not judged nor does it rise again. Consider: in what state were you saved, in what state did you regain your sight, if it was not in this flesh? Hence it is necessary to guard the flesh as the temple of God. For as in the flesh you were called, in the flesh you will come. If Christ the Lord who saved us was first spirit but became flesh and in that state called us, so we also shall receive our reward in this flesh.[23]

Within this context of emphasis on the spiritual significance of the flesh, the homily develops its ecclesiology, in which the salient feature is the pre-existence of the church.

---

[20] English translation: Grant, *The Apostolic Fathers*, 2: 112-32.

[21] 8. 1-3.

[22] "Between the *Shepherd* of Hermas and this homily one finds such an agreement in that which concerns the Christian life and penance, that one is inclined to see in *Secunda Clementis* a work, if not of the same author, at least of the same environment and time as the *Shepherd*." Pierre Batiffol, *La littérature grecque*, 3rd ed. (Paris: V. Lecoffre, 1901), p. 64.

[23] 9. 1-5 (Grant, *The Apostolic Fathers*, 2: 120-21).

So then, brethren, by doing the will of God our Father, we shall belong to the first Church, the spiritual one, which was created before the sun and the moon. . . . Moreover, the books and the apostles declare that the Church belongs not to the present, but existed from the beginning. For she was spiritual, . . . was made manifest in the flesh of Christ to show us that if any of us guard her in the flesh and it be not corrupted, he will receive her back in the Holy Spirit. For this flesh is the copy of the Spirit. No one who corrupts the copy will receive the original in its place. This, then, is what it means, brethren: guard the flesh, that you may share in the Spirit. If we say that the flesh is the Church and the Spirit is Christ, then he who does violence to the Church does violence to Christ. Such a man will not share in the Spirit, which is the Christ. This flesh is able to receive so great a life and immortality because the Holy Spirit is closely joined to it.[24]

From the texts quoted above, it seems that the Christology of this document is rather confused. On the one hand, there is no doubt that the author affirms Christ's divinity as well as his humanity. But on the other hand, he tends to confuse Christ and the Spirit. That is to say that, although there is in this work a clear doctrine of incarnation, its doctrine of the Trinity is still unclear.[25]

The Didache

The *Didache* or *Doctrine of the Twelve Apostles*—the Greek word *Didache* means "doctrine"—is without any doubt one of the most important literary discoveries of modern times. This work had been forgotten for centuries in ancient libraries until it was discovered in Istanbul in 1875. Besides this Greek text, there are fragments of translations into Latin, Arabic, Coptic, Georgian, and Syriac. Since its publication ten years after its discovery, this document has been studied by a great number of scholars, and its origin, author, and date

---

[24] 15. 1,5 (Grant, *The Apostolic Fathers*, 2: 125-27). Cf. G. Krüger, "ZU II. Klem. 14, 2," *ZntW*, 31 (1932), 204-5, and J. Beumer, "Die altchristliche Idee einer präexisterenden Kirche und ihre theologische Auswertung," *WuW* 9 (1942), 13-22, who discuss the relationship of the notion of the pre-existing church with Hermas and with Gnosticism.

[25] This may well be because of a survival of an archaic manner of referring to the persons of the Trinity. Cf. Jean Daniélou, "Trinité et angélologie dans la théologie judéo-chrétienne," *RScRel*, 45 (1957), 5-41.

have been and still are debated. There is no certainty as to its date of composition, for some scholars believe that it was written even before the destruction of Jerusalem in A.D. 70 [26] while others place it at a much later date.[27] It seems possible that it was written toward the end of the first century or the beginning of the second, although using earlier sources, and that its place of composition was some small community in Syria or Palestine, far from the main currents of Christian thought.[28] This would explain the greatest difficulty that scholars find in attempting to determine the origin and date of this document, which is the contrast between the proximity of this document to apostolic times in certain aspects, and its distance from the apostles in other matters.

The *Didache* has sixteen chapters, which can be divided in three main sections. The first of these sections (1.1-6.2) is usually called the "Document of the Two Ways." As will be seen later on, this document is found also in the so-called *Epistle of Barnabas*. It seems that it existed independently both of the *Didache* and of the *Epistle of Barnabas*, both of which used and modified it.[29] According to this document, there are two ways, one of life and one of death. The way of life is that followed by those who love God and their neighbors, and who also avoid evil in all its manifestations and fulfill their Christian duties. The way of death is accursed, and those who follow it are given to untruth, vice, hypocrisy, and avarice.

The second part (6.3-10.7) contains a series of liturgical instructions. Chapter 7 deals with baptism, which is normally to be administered by immersion in living water—that is, running water. But

---

[26] Jean-Paul Audet, *La Didachè: Instructions des Apôtres* (Paris: J. Gabalda, 1958), believes that the *Didache* had reached its present form by A.D. 70, and that already at that time it had received an addition by its own author, and several interpolations by another.

[27] Jean Colson, *L'évêque dans les communautés primitives* (Paris: Éditions du Cerf, 1951), argues that the *Didache's* archaicism is forged.

[28] Pella seems to be a good suggestion, although one that is impossible to prove. See Alfred Adam, "Erwägungen zur Herkunft der Didache," *ZschrKgesch*, 68 (1957), 1-47.

[29] It seems certain that the background of the "Document of the Two Ways" is to be found in Judaism, probably in its Essenian variety. See Jean-Paul Audet, "Les affinités littéraires et doctrinales du 'Manuel de discipline'," *RevBib*, 59 (1952), 219-38; 60 (1953), 41-82.

in cases of extreme scarcity of water, baptism may be administered by pouring water over the head three times in the name of the Father, the Son, and the Holy Ghost. This is the earliest text in which baptism other than by immersion is mentioned.

Now concerning baptism. Baptize as follows, when you have rehearsed the aforesaid teaching: Baptize in the name of the Father and of the Son and of the Holy Spirit, in running water. But if you do not have running water, use whatever is available. And if you cannot do it in cold water, use warm. But if you have neither, pour water on the head three times—in the name of the Father, Son, and Holy Spirit. And prior to baptism, both he who is baptizing and he who is being baptized should fast, along with any others who can. And be sure that the one who is to be baptized fasts for one or two days beforehand.[30]

Chapter 8 distinguishes Christians from "hypocrites"—that is, the Jews—on two scores: in their fast and in their prayers. The hypocrites fast the second and fifth day of the week, whereas Christians are to fast on two other days. In that which concerns prayers, Christians are distinguished from hypocrites in that they repeat the Lord's prayer three times a day.

Chapters nine and ten, together with chapter fourteen, have been subject to scholarly debate ever since the *Didache* was discovered. Chapters nine and ten deal with a meal of which only the bread and the wine are mentioned, and which is called "eucharist," but in which those present eat their fill. Chapter fourteen, on the other hand, refers to a meal that takes place on the Lord's day, preceded by an act of confession, and which is considered a "sacrifice." The question is whether the various chapters are to be understood as referring to a single type of celebration, or whether the first two refer to the *agape* or love feast, while the latter refers to the eucharist in the strict sense.[31] There is also a possibility that on certain occasions the eucharist was celebrated within the love feast.

---

[30] Grant, *The Apostolic Fathers*, 3: 163-64.

[31] F. E. Vokes, *The Riddle of the Didache* (London: S.P.C.K., 1938), p. 183, offers the following summary of the possible solutions to this question: "The following solutions are

The third part of the *Didache* (chapters 11-15) is a sort of manual of discipline. Chapters 11 to 13 deal with the problem of false prophets. How are they to be distinguished from the true prophets? The *Didache*'s answer is that the prophet is known by his behavior. If he asks for money, or orders that a table be set so that he may eat, or if he does not practice what he teaches, he is a false prophet and a "merchant of Christ." [32] On the other hand, true prophets deserve to be supported, and the community is to provide for them.

In the fourteenth chapter, there is another reference to the eucharist. This is called a "sacrifice"; but this seems to refer not to the sacrifice of Christ, but to communion as a sacrifice that Christians present before God. Chapter 15 deals with bishops and deacons, who are to be elected by the community, although the relationship between them and the prophet is not explained. The conclusion (Chapter 16) deals with the end of the world and how it is necessary to be prepared for it.

From the point of view of the history of Christian thought, the *Didache* is important above all as an expression of the moralism that very early took possession of some theological currents. At times, this seems to become a mere legalism. Thus, for example, the distinction between "hypocrites" and Christians is based principally on their different days of fast or on the fact that Christians repeat the Lord's prayer three times a day. In this sense, the *Didache*, rather than a monument to the faith of the early Christians, is an indication of how difficult it is to understand the true nature of the Christian faith.

But the *Didache* is also important from the point of view of the history of the liturgy, for it includes interesting instructions regarding baptism and eucharist. With reference to baptism, although it

---

possible: (i) that the *Didache* describes in chapters IX, X and XIV the eucharist, (ii) in IX and X the agape and eucharist and in XIV the eucharist, (iii) in IX and X the agape and in XIV the eucharist, (iv) in IX and X private house-eucharists and in XIV the public Sunday eucharist, (v) in IX, X and XIV the Christian ceremonial meals when agape and eucharist are still one undivided liturgy." Cf. Gregory Dix, *The Shape of the Liturgy* (London: Dacre Press, 1945), pp. 48-102.

[32] 11. 6, 8-10; 12.5.

takes for granted that this rite will normally be administered by immersion, it does allow baptism by pouring. As has already been said, this is the most ancient text in which this form of baptism is mentioned. With reference to the history of the eucharist, the *Didache* seems to witness to a time in which the agape and the eucharist were not clearly distinguished. Besides, the prayer of thanksgiving that appears in Chapter 9 seems to have been adapted from the ritual that Jews followed for the celebration of the Kedosh, and this shows how ancient Jewish celebration served as a source for Christian liturgy.

As a source for the history of ecclesiastical organization, the *Didache* reveals a period of transition between the primitive system of charismatic authority and the hierarchical organization that was slowly developing within the church. In the *Didache*, it is still the prophets that are most highly esteemed, but the problem of recognizing the authenticity of charismatic gifts has become acute, and bishops and deacons appear next to the prophets. Later on, prophets will disappear, and it will be the hierarchy that will lead the life of the church.

Ignatius of Antioch

Through the seven epistles of Ignatius of Antioch we are given a glimpse into the situation of the church at the beginning of the second century. Suddenly, in the midst of the shadows that cover Christianity at that time, these seven epistles appear as a light that illuminates one or two weeks of the life of the church in Syria and Asia Minor.

It was early in the second century, and Ignatius, bishop of Antioch,[33] had been condemned to die in the imperial capital, probably

---

[33] Apart from his seven letters, the most ancient sources for the life of Ignatius are: Polycarp, *Phil.* 9. 1 and 13. 2; Irenaeus, *Adv. haer.* 5. 28; Origen, *Prol. in Cant.* and *Hom. VI in Luc.*; Eusebius, *HE* 3. 36. In the tenth century the legend arose according to which Ignatius was the boy whom Jesus used as an example (Matt. 18:2). There is no basis for this legend, except that the title *Theophorus*—the bearer of God—which Ignatius gives himself in his epistles may have been interpreted in the passive sense—he who has been held by God. As to the order of succession that links Ignatius with the apostles, there is a confusion similar to

to be devoured by beasts. Toward that capital he was being led as prisoner by Roman soldiers when he wrote the seven epistles that have survived. There were several deep concerns in his mind. In Antioch there was the church that he had directed for several years. It was probably headless, threatened from outside by that persecution which had made Ignatius one of its victims, and from the inside by false teachers who twisted what he thought was the essential truth of Christianity. Ahead was Rome, the city of the final test, where he was to win his crown as a martyr or to succumb to fatigue and suffering. And around him, in that Asia Minor which he was now traversing, there was also a church in need of comfort and direction. He was concerned about what might happen in the church of Antioch, of which he had not had any news for a time. He was concerned about what might happen in Rome, where it was possible that his brethren in Christ would wrestle him from the claws of that martyrdom which he already suffered in his imagination, or even that he himself might weaken at the last moment. And he was concerned about Asia Minor, where he already saw the first signs of the same problems that he had had to face in Antioch. All this can be seen in the seven letters that have survived, four written from Smyrna and three from Troas.

From Smyrna, Ignatius wrote to the churches of Magnesia, Tralles, Ephesus, and Rome. The first three churches had sent some of their members to meet and comfort him, and Ignatius sent them a word of gratitude and of advice and affirmation in the faith. Bishop Damas, two presbyters, and a deacon had come to see him from Magnesia. As Tralles was somewhat further, only bishop Polybius had come. Ephesus, however, had sent a larger delegation headed by bishop Onesimus—the Onesimus of the New Testament? [34]—and one of

that which exists regarding Clement of Rome. Origen, *Hom. VI in Luc.;* Eusebius, *HE* 3. 22 and the *Apostolic Constitutions* 7. 46 do not agree. Thus, it is possible to argue that Antioch, like Rome, also had a collegiate episcopacy, which later developed into the rule of one bishop. In that case, this evolution must have been more rapid in Antioch than in Rome. Cf. Jean Colson, "Aux origines de l'épiscopat: Tradition paulinienne et tradition johannique," *Vie Spirit.,* Suppl. 3 (1949-50), 137-69.

[34] So John Knox, *Philemon among the Letters of Paul* (Chicago: Chicago University Press, 1935), pp. 50-56.

whose members was the deacon Burrhus, who served Ignatius as an amanuensis. The case of Rome was somewhat different. It seems that Ignatius had had news that some brethren in that church were planning to free him from martyrdom. He was opposed to such a project, for he was already anticipating the moment of his martyrdom. This is the reason why he wrote the Christians in Rome in order to ask them not to stand in the way that God had appointed for him,[35] but on the contrary, to allow him to be an imitator of the passion of his God.[36]

From Troas, Ignatius wrote to the church in Smyrna, to its bishop Polycarp, and to the church in Philadelphia. The tone of these three letters is more optimistic than that of the other four, for Ignatius had received news from his church in Antioch that it was meeting the difficulties that had caused him concern. In his letter to the Christians in Smyrna, Ignatius thanked them for their kindness and tried to strengthen them in their faith. He also wrote a letter to Polycarp, the bishop of Smyrna, giving him advice regarding his episcopal function, and asking him to send a messenger to Syria congratulating the church in Antioch for having overcome its difficulties. Finally, he congratulated the church in Philadelphia on the character of its bishop, and warned it against false teachers.

One should not expect that these seven epistles of Ignatius,[37] written within such a brief period and under such great pressures, would be a detailed, balanced, and systematic exposition of his theology. When he wrote these letters, certain problems were foremost in his

---

[35] *Rom.* 4. 1-2.

[36] *Ibid.*, 6.3.

[37] Because of the widespread fame of Ignatius, later writers attempted to ascribe to his name works that he never wrote. Thus, the Middle Ages produced four epistles that tried to show a relationship between Ignatius and the Virgin Mary. This corpus of four epistles includes two from Ignatius to Saint John, one from Ignatius to Mary, and one from Mary to Ignatius. There are also three different texts of the genuine epistles, usually called the *recensio longior,* the *recensio brevior,* and the *recensio brevissima.* Scholars generally agree that the *recensio brevior* is genuine. The *recensio longior* includes the seven genuine epistles, extensively interpolated, and six forgeries (from Mary of Cassobolon to Ignatius, and from Ignatius to Mary, to the Tarseans, to the Philippians, to the Antiochenes, and to Heron). The *recensio brevissima* is a summary of three genuine epistles.

mind. His epistles deal mainly with them. Quite possibly, Ignatius would have dealt with other subjects had the circumstances been different. In any case, in writing these seven letters the bishop of Antioch was concerned mostly about false doctrines and about the divisions that they caused in the church. Therefore, his main purpose was to attack those doctrines and to strengthen the authority of the bishop as the focal point for the unity of the church.

It seems that Ignatius was dealing with two different sorts of false doctrine.[38] On the one hand, there were some who denied the physical life of Jesus Christ[39] and refrained from partaking of communion.[40] These people seem to have thought of Jesus as a celestial being, with no real contact with the concrete situations of human life, and who was mostly the object of syncretistic speculation.[41] On the other hand, there were some Judaizing trends that turned Christ into a mere teacher within the framework of Judaism.[42] This was not, however, a Judaism of the pharisaic type, but rather an Essene Judaism similar to that of the Dead Sea Scrolls, although the Judaizers of Antioch made use of the name of Jesus Christ and did not practice circumcision.[43] In any case, Ignatius was certain that the teachings of these Judaizers, no less than those of the other false teachers, endangered the center itself of the Christian faith, for they denied the

---

[38] Some scholars have claimed that there was in Antioch a single heresy that combined in its teaching the various doctrines that Ignatius seems to refute in his letters. Such is the understanding of E. F. von der Goltz, *Ignatius von Antiochen als Christ und Theologe* (Leipzig: Hinrichs, 1894), p. 81, n. 1. More recently, this is also the view of Rudolf Bultmann, *Theology of the New Testament* (New York: Scribner's, 1951), 1: 171-72. Most scholars, however, do believe that there were two heretical groups in Antioch. Cf. Virginia Corwin, *St. Ignatius and Christianity in Antioch* (New Haven: Yale University Press, 1960), pp. 52-65; Cyril Charles Richardson, *The Christianity of Ignatius of Antioch* (New York: Columbia University Press, 1935), pp. 79-85.

[39] *Tral.* 10. 1; *Smyr.* 2. 5.

[40] *Smyr.* 7. 1.

[41] *Tral.* 6 (Grant, *The Apostolic Fathers*, 4:75-76): "I exhort you therefore—not I but the love of Jesus Christ—use only Christian food and abstain from every strange plant, which is heresy. For they mingle Jesus Christ with themselves, feigning faith, providing something like a deadly drug with honeyed wine, which the ignorant man gladly takes with pleasure; and therein is death."

[42] *Mag.* 9-10; *Philad.* 6. 1.

[43] Corwin, *St. Ignatius*, pp. 57-64.

incarnation of God in Jesus Christ. This was why he opposed both the Docetists and the Judaizers so violently.

It was at the point of Christology that Ignatius saw Christian doctrine most threatened. Therefore, he was categorically opposed to the doctrine of the Docetists. Jesus Christ was truly of the lineage of David; he was truly born; he truly ate and drank; he was truly baptized by John the Baptist; he was truly nailed to a cross; and he truly arose from the dead.[44] "For he suffered all this for us so that we might be saved; and he truly suffered just as he truly raised himself —not, as some unbelievers say, that he appeared to suffer—they are the apparent ones, and just as they think, so it will happen to them when they are incorporeal and demonic." [45]

Besides, even after the resurrection and ascension Jesus Christ still exists in the flesh and still reveals himself, even more clearly than before.[46]

This affirmation of the reality of Christ's humanity did not lead Ignatius to leave aside his divinity. In the contrary, Ignatius clearly stated that Jesus Christ is "our God." [47] Jesus Christ is God made man.

> There is one Physician:
> both flesh and spirit,
> begotten and unbegotten,
> in man, God,
> in death, true life,
> both from Mary and from God,
> first possible and then impassible,
> Jesus Christ our Lord.[48]

---

[44] *Smyr.* 1.

[45] *Smyr.* 2 (Grant, *The Apostolic Fathers*, 4:115).

[46] *Ibid.*, 3.1.

[47] *Eph.*, *salut.*; 15.3; 18.2; *Rom.* 3. 3; *Pol.* 8. 3. In *Rom. 6.* 3, Ignatius calls Christ "my God." The title "god," without the definite article, is applied to Christ in *Eph.* 1. 1; 7. 2; 19. 3; *Tral. 7.* 1; *Smyr.* 10. 1. Von der Goltz, *Ignatius*, pp. 21-28, does not think that this title is to be understood in its absolute sense. Against this view, see M. Rackl, *Die Christologie des heiligen Ignatius von Antiochen* (Freiburg im Breisgau: Freiburger Theologische Studien, 1914), pp. 150-231.

[48] *Eph. 7.* 2 (Grant, *The Apostolic Fathers*, 4: 38).

Jesus Christ "is above every moment of time—eternal, invisible, for our sake visible, intangible, impassible, for our sake passible." [49]

Ignatius never posed the question of how this union of humanity and divinity in Jesus Christ is possible.[50] The same can be said about how the divinity of Jesus Christ is related with that of the Father.[51] After all, his interest was not in the speculative problems posed by the Christian faith, but rather in affirming that God is present in the historical existence of the man Jesus of Nazareth.

Ignatius is closer to John than to Paul in the interpretation of the work of Christ. For him, the core of Christianity is revelation. God cannot be known apart from his revelation in Christ. God is silence, and Jesus Christ is the Word that comes from silence, although the unity between silence and the Word is such that the latter expresses the essence of silence.[52] Thus, the work of Christ is, above all, one of revelation.[53] Jesus has come to make God known to us rather than to save us from the bonds of sin. In this Ignatius differs from Paul, for whom the great enemy of man is sin, which enslaves him, and who sees salvation, above all, as a liberation. In fact, in the epistles of Ignatius the word "sin" appears only once.[54]

However, one should not exaggerate this contrast between Ignatius and Saint Paul. After all, the revelation of which Ignatius speaks is not a mere intellectual knowledge of God, but consists rather in the divine action through which man is united to God and is thus freed from his great enemies, which, according to Ignatius, are death and

---

[49] *Pol.* 3. 2 (Grant, *The Apostolic Fathers*, 4: 132).

[50] Rackl, *Christologie*, p. 284.

[51] The clear affirmations of Ignatius regarding the divinity of Jesus Christ have led some interpreters to accuse him of patripassianism—that is, the doctrine according to which the Father and Son are one in such a manner that the Father suffered in Jesus Christ. Such is the interpretation of E. Kroymann in his introduction to Tertullian's *Adversus Praxeam* (Tübingen: Mohr, 1907). Against this, see Rackl, *Christologie*, pp. 229-31. Perhaps all that one can say is that Ignatius is not explicit on this point.

[52] *Mag.* 8.1. Cf. *Eph.* 19. 1.

[53] This, according to the interpretation of Corwin, *St. Ignatius*, pp. 116-53. Hans Werner Bartsch, *Gnostisches Gut und Gemeindetradition bei Ignatius von Antiochen* (Gütersloh: Werner, 1940), plays down the importance of revelation for Ignatius.

[54] *Smyr.* 7. 1. The verb "to sin" appears in *Eph.* 14.2

division. The problem of man is not a mere ignorance that can be overcome by an intellectual illumination. On the contrary, the Devil plays an important role in Ignatius' theology, and the work of Christ consists, in part at least, in conquering the Devil and making the believer a partaker of that victory.

Thus all magic was dissolved and every bond of wickedness vanished; ignorance was abolished and the old kingdom was destroyed, since God was becoming manifest in human form for the newness of eternal life; what had been prepared by God had its beginning. Hence everything was shaken together, for the abolition of death was being planned.[55]

In Christ and in his victory over the Evil One, God offers us victory over death and division, which are the instruments of the evil powers over men. This is why Ignatius constantly underlined the importance of immortality and unity as a result of the work of Christ. This work of Christ comes to us through the church and the sacraments.

Ignatius saw the church as one, and he was the first to speak of the "catholic church."[56] This unity of the church is due not to the harmony or the good feelings of Christians among themselves, but to the presence of Jesus Christ himself in the church. This does not mean, however, that unity is a purely spiritual matter. On the contrary, it is based on a hierarchy that represents God the Father, Christ, and the Apostles. "Similarly all are to respect the deacons as Jesus Christ and the bishop as a copy of the Father and the presbyters as the council of God and the band of the apostles. For apart from these no group can be called a church."[57]

---

[55] *Eph.* 4.3 (Grant, *The Apostolic Fathers,* 4:51).

[56] *Smyr.* 8. 2. A. A. Garciadiego, *Katholike Ekklesia: El significado del epíteto "Católica" aplicado a "Iglesia" desde San Ignacio de Antioquía hasta Orígenes* (Mexico: Editorial Jus, 1953), argues that "catholic" for Ignatius is not used in the sense of world wide, but rather as that which is whole, in opposition to the partiality of the sects. One should also note that Ignatius is, as far as is known, the first to call the new faith "Christianity"—Χριστιανισμός. *Mag.* 10. 1,3; *Rom.* 3. 3; *Philad* 6. 1. It is significant that the first person to speak of "Christianity" was precisely a bishop of that city in which the followers of Jesus were first called "Christians" (Acts 11:26).

[57] *Tral.* 3. 1 (Grant, *The Apostolic Fathers* 4:73). Cf. *Mag.* 6.1; *Tral.* 13; *Smyr.* 8.1.

Ignatius underlined the importance of the bishop in the local church, and he was actually the first witness to the existence of a monarchical episcopacy.[58] Nothing is to be done in the church without the bishop,[59] and he who is not subject to him is not subject to God.[60] Without his consent, it is not lawful to celebrate baptism or the eucharist,[61] and Ignatius also advised that marital union take place with the bishop's consent.[62]

In the unity of this church which is subject to God the Father, to Christ, and to the apostles through the bishops, presbyters, and deacons, one is united with Christ. This takes place especially through the sacraments.

The church is more than a human institution. The church of the Ephesians, for example, was predestined before the beginning of the centuries, and is also worthy of every blessing.[63] Yet, this does not mean that Ignatius tried to hide or ignore the weaknesses of Christians. He knew too well the divisions and baseness of which believers are capable. But in spite of all this, it is still true that in the church, even in the midst of human meanness, Christ is present.[64] In the unity of the church, and especially through the eucharist, believers are united to Christ.

Ignatius did not offer a systematic exposition of the sacraments, but

---

[58] The only epistle in which Ignatius does not refer to the bishop and to the tripartite hierarchy is *Romans*. Is this because of the particular nature of this letter, whose purpose is not to exhort or to teach, but rather to plead that he be allowed to suffer martyrdom? Or is it rather because of the lack of a monarchical episcopacy in Rome, of which Ignatius would have been aware had such been the case? Given the scant materials available, it is impossible to answer these questions with any degree of certainty.

[59] *Mag.* 7.1; *Tral.* 2.2; *Pol.* 4.1.

[60] *Eph.* 5.3; *Tral.* 2.2; *Pol.* 4.1.

[61] *Smyr.* 8.1.

[62] *Pol.* 5.2.

[63] *Eph., salut.*

[64] "This proclaims his confidence that it is not in some abstract ideal church that true holiness and glory lie, but in these local congregations, with all their persistent difficulties which as bishop he had known so well. The Church is *in* the churches, transforming the ugly and the ephemeral into the noble and the eternal. The churches, thus, are more than human institutions, for they are carrying out the divine intent, and are touched with the divine glory." Corwin, *St. Ignatius*, p. 191.

there is no doubt that for him the eucharist was of great importance. He called it "the flesh of Jesus Christ," [65] and also "the medicine of immortality, the antidote which results not in dying but in living forever in Jesus Christ." [66] However, this is not necessarily to be understood as a clear affirmation that the bread becomes physically the flesh of Christ, for in other contexts Ignatius spoke of the gospel and faith as the flesh of Christ, and of love as his blood.[67] When Ignatius said that the gospel or the eucharist are the flesh of Christ, he was simply underlining the unity that exists between Christ and the gospel, or between him and the eucharist. On the other hand, this does not imply that Ignatius saw the eucharist as a mere symbol of Christian unity. On the contrary, communion is necessary for the Christian life, and only heretics withdraw from it.[68] In it the believer is united with Christ, and especially with his passion.[69] Furthermore, in the eucharist "the powers of Satan are destroyed and his destructive force is annihilated by the concord of your faith." [70]

It would be an anachronism to ask whether Ignatius saw the eucharist in symbolic or realistic terms. The truth seems to be that Ignatius—perhaps influenced by mystery religion—saw in the eucharist an act through which, in representing the passion of Christ, the believer is united to that passion.

This would agree with what Ignatius said about baptism, in which, when Christians repeat the rite to which Christ submitted, they also participate in his purifying power. This is the reason why Christ was baptized, for in doing so he purified the waters with which we ourselves are purified.[71]

What are the sources of Ignatius' theology? This is a question that scholars have debated and on which they do not agree, for the answer

---

[65] Smyr. 7.1.
[66] Eph. 20. 2 (Grant, The Apostolic Fathers, 4:53).
[67] Tral. 8.1; Rom. 7.3; Philad. 5.1.
[68] Smyr. 7.1.
[69] Philad. 4.
[70] Eph. 13. 1 (Grant, The Apostolic Fathers, 4:44).
[71] Eph. 18.2. It was also for a similar reason that Christ was anointed: Eph. 17.1.

that one gives to it depends on the manner in which one answers a whole series of questions regarding primitive Christianity. It seems certain that Ignatius had read the Gospel of Matthew and Paul's First Epistle to the Corinthians, although it is more difficult to determine whether he knew the other Synoptic Gospels, as well as which other Pauline epistles he had read.[72]

In any case it is quite clear that Ignatius is closer in his theology to the Fourth Gospel than to the Apostle Paul.[73] However, the problem of the relationship between Ignatius and the authors of the Johannine writings is very complex. Although Jerome affirms that Ignatius, together with Polycarp and Papias, was a disciple of John at Ephesus,[74] this assertion is not trustworthy, for other ancient writers do not mention it,[75] and Ignatius himself, in his Epistle to Polycarp, implies that he had not met the bishop of Smyrna before a very recent date.[76] In any case, there is no doubt that there is a close relationship between Ignatius and Johannine theology. But scholars do not agree as to the exact nature of that relationship. It is possible that Ignatius knew the Fourth Gospel and the Epistles of John; but it is also possible that their proximity is due, not to the influence of one upon the other, but to both writers belonging to the same theological school.[77]

Finally, there is the question of how Ignatius is related to Gnosticism on the one hand and to mystery religions on the other. It would be fair to say that the relationship between Ignatius and Gnosticism is mostly negative, except perhaps in some details of vocabulary—as, for example, the "silence" of God.[78] The problem of

---

[72] Corwin, *St. Ignatius*, pp. 66-68.

[73] *Ibid.*, pp. 66-69; von der Goltz, *Ignatius von Antiochen*, pp. 178-96; Richardson, *The Christianity of Ignatius of Antioch*, pp. 60-67; Walter von Loewenich, *Das Johannes-Verständnis im zweiten Jahrhundert* (Giessen: A. Töpelmann, 1932).

[74] *Chron. ad. an. Abr.* 2122 (quoted by Casamassa, *I Padri*, p. 105).

[75] See *supra*, n. 32.

[76] *Pol.* 1.1.

[77] See Richardson, *The Christianity of Ignatius of Antioch*, pp. 68-75.

[78] Many scholars believe that Gnosticism has greatly influenced the theology of Ignatius. Their basic arguments are well summarized in Corwin, *St. Ignatius*, pp. 11-13. However, one of Corwin's theses is that the influence of Gnosticism on Ignatius is rather peripheral and negative.

the relationship between the mysteries and Ignatius' theology is more difficult to solve, for many of the documents through which the mysteries can be studied are later than Ignatius, and it is therefore very difficult to distinguish between those common elements which have passed from the mysteries to Ignatius' theology, and those which, on the contrary, reflect the influence of Christianity on the mystery cults.[79] In any case, there is an undeniable point of contact between Ignatius and the mysteries in the way in which the bishop of Antioch underlines the reality of the believers' participation in the unity and victory of Christ through the common meal of the eucharist.

By way of conclusion, one can say that Ignatius is a theologian who is not inclined to systematic or speculative construction, but who has a profound sense of the importance of some of the fundamental doctrines of Christianity, as well as a far-reaching vision of the consequences of those doctrines. This, coupled with his ecclesiastical and pastoral interest, and with his attitude of total devotedness at the threshold of martyrdom, make his epistles one of the richest treasures bequeathed to us by Christian antiquity.

Polycarp of Smyrna

Among the Apostolic Fathers, there is also an *Epistle of Saint Polycarp to the Philippians,* written in connection with the martyrdom of Ignatius.[80] It is probable that the actual *Epistle* was not

---

[79] The bibliography relevant to this may be found in Corwin, *St. Ignatius,* p. 211, n. 20.

[80] Polycarp is known not only by his epistle, and by the one that Ignatius wrote to him and that has already been mentioned, but also through his disciple Irenaeus, who later became bishop of Lyon in Gaul (*Adv. haer.* 3.3.4). Eusebius has also preserved a letter that Irenaeus wrote to Victor, bishop of Rome, in which he tells of an interview that Polycarp had with Bishop Anicetus in about A.D. 155 in order to discuss the controversy that was taking place regarding the date of the celebration of Easter (*HE* 5. 24). There is also an account of Polycarp's martyrdom which claims to have been recorded by the church of Smyrna shortly after the event (Grant, *The Apostolic Fathers,* 5:51-82). Other sources are Tertullian (*De praes. haer.* 32) and Jerome (*De vir. illus.* 17), who draws on Tertullian and Eusebius.

Some biographical data may be gathered from these sources. Polycarp seems to have been a

originally one letter, but two. According to this hypothesis, Chapter 13 and probably 14 are part of a first letter, in which Polycarp responded to the request of the Philippians that he send them those letters of Ignatius which he had, and also asked them for news regarding Ignatius and his companions. The other twelve chapters would then be a later letter of Polycarp, also addressed to the church in Philippi.[81]

No matter whether we have here one or two epistles, the important fact is that this document shows a theological outlook similar to that of Ignatius and of the Fourth Gospel, although with a more practical intent. Polycarp does not reach the depths of the Fourth Gospel or of Ignatius, but he does follow them in underscoring the reality of the humanity of Christ,[82] whom he places in the center of his doctrine of salvation.[83]

In any case, the importance of this epistle is not so much in its doctrine, which is neither original nor profound,[84] as in its witness to the authenticity of Ignatius' epistles.

This is probably the best place to mention the *Martyrdom of Polycarp*, which is the most ancient document of its nature that has been preserved.[85] It is a letter written by the church of Smyrna to the church of Philomelium and to the entire church, shortly after the

---

disciple of John—whoever that may have been—together with Papias and, according to some dubious authorities, Ignatius (see *supra*, n. 32). Early in the second century, when Ignatius passed through Smyrna on his way to martyrdom, Polycarp was bishop of the church in that city. In A.D. 155, he went to Rome and there met with Bishop Anicetus. Shortly after his return to Smyrna, possibly in February, A.D. 156, Polycarp suffered martyrdom in the same city where he had led the Christian flock for many years.

[81] Such is the thesis of P. N. Harrison, *Polycarp's Two Epistles to the Philippians* (Cambridge: Cambridge University Press, 1936). A summary of it may be found in pp. 15-19. It has been generally well received by scholars, for it solves the contradiction between chapter thirteen, where Polycarp asks the Philippians for news regarding Ignatius, and the rest of the document, in which the martyrdom of the bishop of Antioch is taken for a fact.

[82] *Philip.* 7.1.

[83] *Ibid.*, 8.1.

[84] Cf. D. Ruiz Bueno in *Padres apostólicos* (BAC, 65), p. 648.

[85] And even this in a Latin translation, for only a few fragments of the Greek original have survived.

events it narrates.[86] The sheer dramatism of its narrative and the sincerity of its style suffice to make this document extremely interesting. But from our point of view it is important especially because it contains the most ancient allusion to the custom of preserving the relics of martyrs, [87] as well as because it throws light on the nature of the conflict between Christians and pagans, which we shall study in the next chapter.

Papias of Heriapolis

Papias was also among the disciples of John, and later became bishop of Heriapolis.[88] He took upon himself the task of collecting every saying or teaching of the Lord which he heard. Thus, he compiled and composed his *Exposition of the Sayings of the Lord*, of whose five books only a few fragments have survived—and even these are of limited significance for the history of Christian thought.

In ancient times, Papias was often discussed because of his chiliasm. It is usually in order to criticize him on this score that Eusebius quotes him, whereas Irenaeus uses him to support that doctrine. In some cases the chiliasm of Papias oversteps the boundary between the poetical and the ridiculous, as when he says that

> The days will come
> when vineyards shall grow
> each with ten thousand vines,
> and on one vine ten thousand branches,
> and on one branch ten thousand shoots,
> and on every shoot ten thousand clusters,
> and in every cluster ten thousand grapes,

---

[86] Although probably with some later interpolations. See Grant, *The Apostolic Fathers*, 5:48-49.

[87] *Mart. Pol.* 28. 2, 3.

[88] The most ancient references to Papias are to be found in Irenaeus (*Adv. Haer.* 5. 33.4) and Eusebius (*HE* 3. 39). Although scholars place him at different dates, he probably wrote early in the second century. See E. Gutwenger, "Papias: Eine chronologische Studie," *ZkT*, 69 (1947), 385-416.

and every grape when pressed will give twenty-five measures of wine;
and when one of the saints grasps a cluster,
another cluster will cry out:
"I am better,
take me,
bless the Lord on my account." [89]

More recently, scholars have discussed the fragments of Papias inasmuch as they refer to the authorship of the first two Gospels[90] and to the existence of two Johns, the apostle and the elder.[91]

The Epistle of Barnabas

Such is the title that was given to an ancient document that was sometimes included among the canonical writings of the New Testament, and that was probably written in Alexandria about A.D. 135. [92] Although some ancient Christian writers claim that its author is Barnabas, the companion of Paul, he most certainly did not produce this work.[93]

This so-called *Epistle of Barnabas* is composed of two clearly distinguishable parts. The first (chapters 1-17) is doctrinal in character, whereas the second (chapters 18-21) is more practical.

The doctrinal part is devoted mostly to an allegorical interpretation of Old Testament texts. The question of the proper understanding of the Old Testament had been a serious one for some time among Hellenistic Jews. Thus, we have already seen how Philo offered an allegorical interpretation of the Old Testament which made the an-

---

[89] Fragment found in Irenaeus (*Adv. haer.* 5. 33.3). Translated in Grant, *The Apostolic Fathers*, 5: 95.

[90] Fragment found in Eusebius (*HE* 3. 39.15-16).

[91] Fragment found in Eusebius (*HE* 3. 39.4).

[92] It is impossible to ascertain the date of this document, for the inner evidence seems to be contradictory. Chapter four would lead one to date it toward the end of the first century, whereas chapter sixteen would seem to indicate a date around A.D. 135. See Ruiz Bueno, *Padres*, pp. 753-56; Grant, *The Apostolic Fathers*, 3: 42-43.

[93] The first to ascribe this work to Barnabas is Clement of Alexandria, who is sympathetic toward its allegorical exegesis, and therefore quotes it repeatedly: *Paid*, 2.10; *Strom*. 2. 6, 7; 2. 15; 2. 18; 2. 20; 5.8; 5. 10. Origen quotes it as Scripture: *Comm. in Rom*. 1. 18.

cient scriptures compatible with his own Neoplatonic philosophy. Similarly, Christians were now facing the seeming incompatibility between some of the texts of the Old Testament and the teachings of the New. Furthermore, the emergence of the Christian church had produced a controversy between Christians and Jews, and that controversy had to do mostly with the correct interpretation of the Old Testament.[94] Christians thus found themselves forced to seek means of interpretation that would link the two Testaments. One of these methods was allegorical interpretation, a procedure by which it was possible to rid the precepts of the Old Testament from that rather primitive nature that Christians and even some Jews found difficult to accept. It was in Alexandria that this allegorical interpretation flourished, first among Jews such as Philo, and then among Christians such as Pseudo-Barnabas, Clement, and Origen. This is one of the reasons why both Clement and Origen held the so-called *Epistle of Barnabas* in high esteem, and even included it among the canonical writings of the New Testament. And it is also one of the reasons why modern scholars believe that Alexandria was the place of composition of this document.

As an example of the allegorical interpretation to be found in this *Epistle,* one may take the manner in which it understands the Old Testament prohibition to eat pork. According to the author of this document, this precept really tells us that we are not to join men who are like pigs, that sometimes remember their master and at other times forget him, according to their convenience.[95] In another passage, he affirms that the commandment regarding circumcision had only an allegorical meaning, and that it was an evil angel that led Jews to understand literally what really referred to the circumcision of the ears and of the heart.[96] This is, in general, the way in which Pseudo-

---

[94] An echo of this controversy may be heard in the following passage of Pseudo-Barnabas: "Do not be like certain people, compounding your sins by claiming that your covenant is irrevocably yours. But they lost it completely . . ." (4. 6, Grant, *The Apostolic Fathers*, 3: 89-90).

[95] 10. 3.

[96] 9. 4-5.

Barnabas interprets the commandments of the Old Testament.[97]

This does not mean, however, that the so-called *Epistle of Barnabas* denies the historical character of the Old Testament. On the contrary, most of the narratives of the Old Testament are historically true, and Pseudo-Barnabas does not doubt them, although he does affirm that they point to Jesus. The sacrifice of Isaac,[98] the goat that was led into the desert,[99] Moses with his arms extended in the shape of the cross,[100] and the serpent that was raised in the desert[101] are figures or "types"[102] of Jesus Christ and his work of salvation. All these things really happened, but their deeper significance was in the fact that they announced Christ.[103]

The second part of the *Epistle of Barnabas* repeats the teaching of the two ways that we have already found at the beginning of the *Didache*. It seems that Pseudo-Barnabas draws this material from the "Document of the Two Ways," which was also one of the sources of the *Didache*.[104]

Although the doctrinal interest of Pseudo-Barnabas lay mostly in the relationship between the Old Testament and Christianity, one can also discover in his work some other aspects of his theology. Thus, for instance, he affirmed the pre-existence of Christ as well as his par-

---

[97] Cf. 5. 3; 6. 8-17; 10. 4-8; 15. 3-9.

[98] 7. 3.

[99] 7. 6-11.

[100] 12. 2-3.

[101] 12. 5-7.

[102] The term "type" appears at least once in each of the passages cited in notes 98-101.

[103] Pseudo-Barnabas seems to waver on his interpretation of circumcision, for first he tells us that God did not intend it to be taken literally (see *supra*, n. 96) and later goes on to say that Abraham circumcised the 318 men of his house "while looking forward in the spirit to Jesus" (9. 7, Grant, *The Apostolic Fathers*, 3:108), for the letters by which 318 is written in Greek can be understood as a sign of the cross (T) and the first two letters of the name of Jesus (IH). Thus, one finds here elements of a purely allegorical interpretation, which would tend to say that the literal understanding of the commandment was due to an evil influence, and another interpretation, which would rather say that the commandment and the event were true, but that their real significance is to be found in their being a "type" of Christ.

[104] See *supra*, n. 29.

ticipation in creation.[105] The son of God "came in flesh for this reason, that he might bring to summation the total of sins of those who persecuted his prophets to death," [106] that is, in order to condemn the Jews; but he also came in order to make himself known to mankind, who could not behold him in his pre-existent glory, just as it is impossible to gaze directly upon the Sun.[107] Besides, Christ died in order to "fulfill the promise given to the fathers," to "destroy death," and to "show forth the resurrection," that is, in order to show that "he will judge after he accomplishes resurrection." [108] This judgment will take place in the near future,[109] for Pseudo-Barnabas believes that God will fulfill all when the world is six thousand years old, in view of the fact that God made the world in six days, and a thousand years are like a day before his eyes.[110]

The Shepherd of Hermas

The most extensive work in the body of literature gathered under the title of "Apostolic Fathers" is the Shepherd of Hermas,[111] who probably lived toward the end of the first century and the first half of the second,[112] and whose work consists of a collection of materials

---

[105] 5. 5.

[106] 5. 11.

[107] 5. 10.

[108] 5. 6-7.

[109] 4. 3; 21. 3.

[110] 15. Does this imply a chiliastic eschatology on the part of Pseudo-Barnabas? 15. 5, 7 would seem to imply so, although his rejection of all that seems grossly material would make his view of the millennium very different from that of Papias. See Jean Daniélou, "La typologie millénariste de la semaine dans le christianisme primitif," VigCh 2 (1948), 1-16.

[111] Herbert A. Musurillo, "The Need of a New Edition of Hermas," ThSt 12 (1951), 382-87, gives a list of the different manuscripts and versions of the Shepherd, and discusses their main characteristics.

[112] According to the Muratorian canon, Hermas was a brother of Bishop Pius, who was bishop of Rome in the fifth decade of the second century. Some scholars have questioned this statement and suggested an earlier date for the Shepherd. Stanistas Giet, Hermas et les Pasteurs: Les trois auteurs du Pasteur d'Hermas (Paris: Presses Universitaires de France, 1963), proposes a theory according to which Hermas may have been the one who wrote the visions; later a second writer added what is now the ninth parable; finally, a third hand added the other nine parables and the mandates. Although this theory has not been generally accepted, the various settings in which different parts of the book are placed require either a

produced at different stages during his career as a prophet in the Roman church.[113] His main concern seems to have been the lack of zeal and dedication of some brethren, and especially the problem posed by post-baptismal sins, that is, by sins committed after conversion and baptism. There were many who had fallen into apostasy because of fear of persecution, and who later had sincerely repented of their weakness. Hermas himself felt guilty because he had coveteously looked upon a woman to whom he owed the greatest respect. What hope did then remain for such persons? Should they be given up as entirely and irremissibly lost? If, on the other hand, they were forgiven, what guarantee was there that they would not fall again? The *Shepherd* of Hermas faces these questions in a collection of five visions, twelve mandates, and ten parables.

The five visions are an exhortation to penance and to steadfastness in the face of persecution. Hermas begins in the first vision by confessing his own guilt for having coveted Rhoda, the Christian lady whose slave he had been.[114] But the center of this section is the third vision, or "vision of the tower," which is closely related to the ninth parable. In this third vision, the church comes to Hermas in the shape of a lady, and shows him a great tower that is being built. Six young men build the tower with stones that a multitude brings, some from the bottom of the sea and others from different parts of the earth. Those that come from the bottom of the sea are ready to be placed in the tower. But only some of those that come from the earth can be used for the construction, while others are thrown aside. Then the lady explains to Hermas that she herself—that is, the church—is the tower, and the stones are the persons with whom the church is built. The good stones are those who live in sanctity, and the stones brought

---

theory of multiple authorship, or one of several additions by the original author, with perhaps some interpolations by a later hand.

[113] A. V. Ström, *Der Hirt des Hermas. Allegorie oder Wirklichkeit?* (Uppsala: Wretmans Boktryckeri, 1936), studies the personality and inspiration of Hermas from a psychological point of view, and concludes that the biographical data that appear in the *Shepherd* are authentic, and that Hermas really thought that he was an inspired prophet.

[114] *Vis.* 1. 1. 1-2. 1.

from the bottom of the sea are the martyrs who have suffered for the Lord. The stones that have been set aside are those who have sinned but are willing to repent, and for this reason they are not thrown too far away from the tower, for at a later time they will find a place in its construction. But there are other stones that break to pieces when they are cast away, and these are the hypocrites, those who do not abandon evil, and who therefore have no hope of salvation or of belonging to the church.

The twelve commandments are a summary of the duties of a Christian, and Hermas affirms that in obeying them there is eternal life.[115] It is in the fourth commandment that one finds the clearest expression of the doctrine of Hermas according to which it is possible to repent once more after baptism, and he who sins again after this second repentance will find it very difficult to be forgiven. "After that great and holy calling, if anyone sins who has been tempted by the devil, he has one repentance. But if he continually sins and repents, it is of no advantage to such a man, for he will hardly live." [116] This doctrine of penance for post-baptismal sins has been interpreted in various ways, for it is possible to see in Hermas a rigorist who is making a concession to human weakness, a reformer calling the church to its lost purity, or a man of such vivid eschatological expectation that he believes there will be no possibility of further repentance.[117] In any case, one should note that according to this document there is no sin that is unforgivable if the sinner has recourse to the second opportunity to repent.[118]

The ten parables bring together the teachings of the visions with those of the mandates, and they deal especially with practical and

---

[115] At the end of most of them, the promise is made that he who keeps them "will live to God."

[116] *Mand.* 4. 3. 6 (Grant, *The Apostolic Fathers, 6:* 72).

[117] See B. Poschmann, *Poenitentia secunda: Die kirchliche Busse im ältesten Christentum bis Cyprian und Origenes* (Bonn: P. Hanstein, 1940); J. Hoh, "Die Busse im Pastor Hermae," *TQ*, 111 (1930), 253-88; J. Hoh, *Die kirchliche Busse im II. Jahrhundert* (Breslau: Müller und Seiffert, 1932); Serafino Prete, "Cristianesimo antico e riforma ortodossa: Note intorno al 'Pastore' di Erma (II sec.)," *Convivium* (1950), 114-28.

[118] *Vis.* 2. 2. 4.

moral matters. In the ninth parable the vision of the tower appears again, although we are now told that the construction has been temporarily stopped in order to allow for the repentance of sinners.[119]

It seems that for Hermas Christianity is, above all, a series of precepts that must be followed. One does not find here the profound mystical sense of Ignatius, nor the theological investigation of Pseudo-Barnabas. This practical interest in sins and their remission leads Hermas to offer for the first time in the history of Christian thought the theory that it is possible to do more than the commandment of God requires, and thus to attain a greater glory.[120] Although there is no mention here of a treasury of merits, or of their transference, one can see in this doctrine some of the first roots of what would later become the elaborate penitential system of the Roman Church.[121]

Hermas refers to the Savior as "Son of God," and identifies him with the Holy Spirit.[122] The pre-existent Holy Spirit dwelt in the Savior, and the latter in such a way obeyed the divine will that he was made a partner with the Holy Spirit.

The pre-existent holy Spirit, which created all creation, God caused to dwell in that flesh which he wished. So this flesh, in which the Holy Spirit dwelled, served the Spirit well, living in reverence and purity, and did not defile the Spirit in any way. So because it conducted itself appropriately and purely and worked with the Spirit and collaborated in every deed, acting with strength and courage, he chose it as partner with the holy Spirit, for the conduct of this flesh pleased God because it was not defiled while it possessed the holy Spirit on earth. So he took the Son as a counselor, and the glorious angels,

---

[119] It is possible that this parable was written some time after the parallel vision, and that the fact that in the parable the construction has been halted reflects the progressive loss of eschatological expectation during the second century.

[120] "If you do something good beyond the commandment of God, you will gain greater glory for yourself and you will be more honored before God than you would have been." *Parab.* 5. 3.3 (Grant, *The Apostolic Fathers*, 6: 103).

[121] However, how much of this is a continuation of the Roman practical spirit that we have already seen in Clement, and how much is drawn from Jewish apocalypticism, is still an open question. See Erik Peterson, "*Die Begegnung* mit den Ungeheuer. Hermas, Visio IV," *VigCh*, 8 (1954), 52-71; Erik Peterson, "Kritische Analyse der V. Vision des Hermas," *HJb* 77 (1958), 362-69.

[122] *Parab.* 9. 1. 1.

that this flesh also, after it served the Spirit blamelessly, should have some place to dwell and not seem to have lost the reward of its servitude.[123]

It is difficult to coordinate in a systematic whole the doctrine of the church to be found in the *Shepherd*. There is no doubt that its author believes that the church is of great importance, for it is she that leads him and interprets his visions. She is pre-existent,[124] and the world was created for her.[125] But Hermas does not attempt to clarify the relationship between the pre-existent church and this local church of Rome, full of difficulties, which he addresses. On the matter of the hierarchy, Hermas is not clear, for he refers to the "apostles, bishops, teachers, and deacons," [126] while in another passage he speaks of "the elders who preside over the church." [127] In any case, it is interesting to note that it is almost the middle of the second century, and we still have no word regarding the monarchical episcopate in Rome.

Other Christian Literature of the Same Period

Besides the works that are usually included among the Apostolic Fathers, there are Christian writings of the same period which should be discussed here. Many of these writings claim to be ancient Jewish texts in which the work of Christ was foreseen, and it is for this reason that they are usually included among the pseudepigrapha of the Old Testament. Some of these Christian pseudepigraphical books are Jewish documents that have been interpolated by Christians, and that must be studied in order to establish the exact nature of the Christian interpolations before one can use them as a source for the study of early Christian theology. Finally, there are some works that claim to be apostolic in origin and are thus included among the apocryphal books of the New Testament.

---

[123] *Ibid.*, 5. 6. 5-6 (Grant, *The Apostolic Fathers*, 6: 107-8).
[124] *Vis.* 2. 4. 1.
[125] *Ibid.*, 1. 1. 6.
[126] *Ibid.*, 3. 5. 1.
[127] *Ibid.*, 2. 4. 3.

The most important Christian books in the Old Testament pseudepigrapha are the *Ascension of Isaiah,* the *Testaments of the Twelve Patriarchs,* and the *Second Book of Enoch.*

The *Ascension of Isaiah* is a composite document that seems to have taken shape in Antioch toward the end of the first century or the beginning of the second.[128] Its most interesting section is that in which the prophet is taken up in a progressive ascension to the seventh heaven. There he sees God, the Lord "Christ who shall be called Jesus," [129] and "the angel of the Spirit." [130] Thus, the trinitarian theology of this document is undeniable, but it is still shaped within the framework of Jewish angelology.[131] From the seventh heaven, the Lord descends to earth passing unknown through each heaven, for in every case he takes the form of the angels of that heaven, in accordance with the words of God to him:

Let no one of the angels of this world know that you are with me the Lord of the seven heavens and of their angels. Let them not know that you are with me until I have called the heavens, their angels and their lights to the sixth heaven, so that you may destroy the princes and the angels and the gods of this world and the world in which they rule.[132]

After a birth that takes place with remarkable Docetic undertones,[133] Jesus is crucified, resurrected, and ascends in human form through each heaven, where there is a great sadness because the Lord had previously come by and was not recognized or worshiped. Finally,

---

[128] The book is composed of a Jewish *Martyrdom of Isaiah,* the Christian *Vision of Isaiah,* and a brief Christian apocalypse. Probably the *Vision* is the latest part, for it dates from the first half of the second century. See Eugène Tisserant, *Ascension d'Isaïe* (Paris: Letouzey et Ané, 1909), pp. 59-60.

[129] 10. 7.

[130] 10. 4.

[131] Cf. J. Barbel, *Christos Angelos: Die Anschauung von Christus als Bote und Engel in der gelehrten und volkstümlichen Literatur des christlichen Altertums* (Bonn: P. Hanstein, 1941).

[132] 10. 11-12. Cf. Ignatius, *Eph.* 19.

[133] 11. 7-14.

in the seventh heaven he sits at the right hand of the "Great Glory" while the "angel of the Holy Spirit" sits at the left.[134]

The *Testaments of the Twelve Patriarchs* seem to be the result of a work of compilation, correction, and interpolation which some Christian of Essenian background undertook, probably also in Antioch late in the first century. The work as it now stands is Christian in origin, but it seems certain that the author used some "testaments" of patriarchs which were already circulating among the Essenes.[135] The *Second Book of Enoch* is similar to the foregoing, and it also seems to have been written in about the same place and time.[136]

Among the interpolated Jewish writings, the most important is the *Sibylline Oracles*, whose fifth book contains Christian interpolations of the period that we are now studying, whereas the sixth and seventh books are a Christian work probably written in Egypt in the middle of the second century.[137]

Finally, the apocryphal literature of the New Testament is very abundant, and it is impossible to discuss it here. But among the documents that most probably belong to the period of the Apostolic Fathers, one should mention the *Gospel of Peter*,[138] the *Revelation of Peter*,[139] the *Gospel according to the Hebrews*,[140] and the *Epistle of the Twelve Apostles*.[141] The first two of these come from Syria

---

[134] 11. 32-33.

[135] Jean Daniélou, *The Theology of Jewish Christianity* (London: Darton, Longman & Todd, 1964), pp. 14-16. English translations: *ANF* 8: 9-38; Robert Henry Charles, *The Apocrypha and Pseudoepigrapha of the Old Testament in English* (Oxford: Clarendon Press, 1913), 2: 296-367.

[136] Daniélou, *Theology*, p. 16. English translation: Charles, *Apocrypha*, 2: 431-69.

[137] Daniélou, *Theology*, pp. 17-19. See Johannes Geffcken, *Komposition und Entstehungszeit der Oracula Sibyllina* (Leipzig: J. C. Hinrichs, 1902). English trans.: Milton S. Terry, *The Sibylline Oracles* (New York: Hunt & Eaton, 1890).

[138] English trans. in Montague Rhodes James, *The Apocryphal New Testament* (Oxford: Clarendon Press, 1953), pp. 90-94. Brief introduction, Greek text, and Spanish trans.: Aurelio de Santos Otero, *Los evangelios apócrifos BAC*, 148 (1956), 398-417.

[139] Ethiopic text, Greek fragments, and French trans.: Sylvian Grébaut, "L'Apocalypse de Pierre," *ROC*, 5 (1910), 208 ff. and 307 ff.

[140] Reconstruction of the Greek and Latin text, and Spanish trans.: de Santos Otero, *Los evangelios*, pp. 37-50.

[141] Ethiopic text and French trans.: L. Guerrier, "L'Epître des Douze Apôtres," PO, 9: 143-326.

toward the end of the first century or the beginning of the second. The *Gospel according to the Hebrews* was probably written early in the second century, although it is difficult to determine where. Finally, the *Epistle of the Twelve Apostles* seems to have been written in Asia Minor, probably also early in the second century.[142]

Although it is difficult to determine their exact date, and although their cryptic language often makes it difficult to interpret their thought, these works also shed light upon the period that we are studying, and therefore upon the theology of several of the Apostolic Fathers. In fact, these works do not belong to a distinct theological school, but rather reflect, according to the place and date of their composition, the type of theology that was dominant there and that can be seen also in the Apostolic Fathers who wrote in the same time and place.

General View

When one studies the Apostolic Fathers, one discovers the beginning of certain schools or theological tendencies whose later development will become clearer as this history progresses. But one also finds a basic unity behind this diversity.

Among the various tendencies, one can speak in the first place of one comprising Asia Minor and Syria. Further on, the thought of Asia Minor would be different from that of Syria. But at this time these two regions are united in contrast with Rome on the one hand and Alexandria on the other. This Christianity of Asia Minor is known to us by the Johannine literature, the works of Ignatius, Polycarp, and Papias, and several pseudepigraphic works. In these writings Christianity is not principally a moral teaching but a union with the Savior by which immortality is attained. Thus, what is fundamental is not simply following a certain code of ethics, but rather being closely united with the Lord Jesus Christ. Hence the importance of the eucharist for Ignatius. Hence also his appeal for the unity of the

---

[142] Questions of date and place of composition of these and other similar documents are summarized in Daniélou, *Theology*, pp. 19-28.

church, for it is in the union of Christians among themselves that they find their union with Christ.

The main outside forces influencing this Christianity of Syria and Asia Minor were the mystery cults, Gnosticism, and Essenian Judaism. The influence of the mysteries is probably found above all in the understanding of the eucharist as an act of union with Christ. Gnosticism has also influenced the Christianity of this region, above all, with its doctrine of revelation. But its influence upon Christology and cosmology can also be traced in documents such as the *Ascension of Isaiah,* and negatively in Ignatius' insistence on the historical reality of the incarnation. The influence of Judaism upon this type of Christianity comes from the Essenian movement rather than from Pharisaism, and it is quite possible that this is the source of several of the elements of this type of Christianity which some scholars have interpreted in terms of purely mysteric influences.

In Rome, we see the beginning of a different type of Christianity. There, as can be seen in the *First Epistle to the Corinthians* of Clement and in the *Shepherd* of Hermas, Christianity takes a practical and ethical direction that can even lead to moralism and legalism. Clement and Hermas are not interested in speculative thought nor in mystic union, but in practical obedience. Whatever his intention may have been, Hermas already shows the interest in penance for post-baptismal sins which Western Christianity would later develop into a complex penitential system,[143] and he is also the first to speak of works beyond those needed for salvation. This salvation is, then, not so much a gift of God through union with Jesus Christ as a reward that a God who has shown his mercy in Christ gives to those who obey his commandments. And Jesus, rather than the beginning of a new era, is the teacher of a new law.

This theological school develops under the sign of Stoicism and of the practical spirit of the Roman people. The influence of Stoicism can

---

[143] Paul Galtier, *Aux origines du sacrement de pénitence* (Rome: Universitas Gregoriana, 1951), pp. 107-87.

be seen in the manner in which Clement stresses harmony as a fundamental element of the Christian life, while the influence of the Roman practical spirit can be seen throughout all the work of Clement and Hermas.

In the so-called *Epistle of Barnabas*, we have the first document of the young Alexandrine school of theology. This school, which is characterized by the influence of Middle and Neoplatonism upon it and by its allegorical interpretation of the Old Testament, has its background in the Jewish Alexandrine philosopher Philo, as well as in the canonical Epistle to the Hebrews, which also makes extensive use of the Philonic tradition.[144] It combines the ethical interest that we have already found in Rome with a speculative approach, and is less interested in the historical events of the Old Testament than the two other types of Christianity that we have discussed. Thus, the historical reality of the Old Testament often disappears behind allegorical interpretations that turn the ancient Jewish Scriptures into a moral teaching or an announcement of Jesus Christ. On the other hand, and perhaps in part on account of its lack of interest in historical events, this type of Christianity has little to say regarding the fleshly life of Jesus.

The most marked influence upon this Alexandrine school is that of Jewish hellenism of the type found in Philo. One should point out, however, that books six and seven of the *Sibylline Oracles*, which seem to be Alexandrine in origin and which show several points of contact with the *Epistle of Barnabas*, have an apocalyptic nature that can hardly be ascribed to the influence of Philo.

Regarding the organization and government of the churches, there is a great variety of forms. In some of the Apostolic Fathers the monarchical episcopate and the tripartite hierarchy are stressed, whereas others do not seem to know such an episcopate, nor to distinguish between bishops and presbyters.

---

[144] See *TIB*, 11: 585.

But this diversity of outlook should not lead us to think that there was not in the church of the time a certain unity of doctrine and thought. On the contrary, in certain aspects one finds a surprising uniformity.

Thus, regarding the person of Christ, the Apostolic Fathers agree in affirming his pre-existence, as well as his divinity and his humanity. And in that which refers to the relationship between Christ, the Father, and the Holy Spirit, apart from the lack of clarity to be found in Hermas, all the Apostolic Fathers agree in making use of diverse trinitarian formulas, no matter how primitive.[145]

All the Apostolic Fathers see in baptism a true power of purification, but they seem to have forgotten the symbolism of death and resurrection that is found in the Apostle Paul.[146] Regarding the eucharist, there is no doubt that it is the center of Christian worship, although we do not yet find systematic or clear discussions of the presence of Christ in it, nor is there any power attributed to the words of institution themselves.

Not only in their understanding of baptism, but also in their total theological outlook, one senses a distance between the Christianity of the New Testament—especially that of Paul—and that of the Apostolic Fathers. References to Paul and the other apostles are frequent; but in spite of this the new faith becomes more and more a new law, and the doctrine of God's gracious justification becomes a doctrine of grace that helps man to act justly.[147]

The influence of the Apostolic Fathers in the further development of Christian thought was not uniform. Some of them were practically

---

[145] Hermas' understanding of trinitarian matters is similar to that of the *Testaments of the Twelve Patriarchs*, and is not due to a personal interpretation, but is rather a survival of an early effort to understand trinitarian issues by means of Jewish angelology. See supra, notes 25 and 131.

[146] André Benoit, *Le baptême chrétien au second siècle: La théologie des Pères* (Paris: Presses Universitaires de France, 1953).

[147] Cf. E. Aleith, *Paulusverständnis in der alten Kirche* (Berlin: A. Töpelmann, 1937); W. Roslan, *Die Grundbegriffe der Gnade nach der Lehre der Apostolischen Väter* (Rettenburg: A. Bader, 1938); Thomas Forsyth Torrance, *The Doctrine of Grace in the Apostolic Fathers* (Grand Rapids: Eerdmans, 1959).

unknown to later Christians. Others, such as Hermas and Pseudo-Barnabas, were sometimes included in the canon of the New Testament. But most influential of all were Clement and Ignatius, probably because their theology was less tied to Jewish Christian patterns and issues.[148]

---

[148] Robert M. Grant, "The Apostolic Fathers' First Thousand Years," *CH*, 31 (1962), 421-29.

IV

The Greek Apologists

Toward the middle of the second century, a number of Christian writers took upon themselves the task of defending their faith in the face of the false accusations that were at the heart of persecutions. Although most of these works are addressed to the Emperors, their authors actually hoped that they would be read by a wide circle of educated persons. This was extremely important, for the lot of Christian communities in each place greatly depended on local public opinion. During most of the second century the policy of the Empire toward Christianity was that which Trajan had set in his letter to Pliny the Younger, that Christians were not to be sought out by the authorities, but that it was necessary to punish them if somebody took the trouble to accuse them.[1] This is why the Christians of Asia Minor could visit Ignatius, who already had been condemned as a Christian, without thus endangering their lives. In the *Martyrdom of Polycarp*, it is the mob that actually accuses, condemns, and sentences the bishop of Smyrna.[2] And in the epistle in which the churches of Lyon and Vienne tell of the death in A.D. 177 of some of their members on account of their faith, it is once again the mob that takes the leading role in their trial.[3]

---

[1] Pliny, *Ep.* 10. 97.
[2] *Mart. Pol.* 3. 2; 12. 2-13. 1.
[3] Eusebius, *HE* 5. 1. 7-8.

In their attempt to defend Christianity, these Apologists found it necessary to attack paganism on the one hand, and to refute the accusations made against Christians on the other. Although the Apologists themselves did not establish such a distinction, one can say that these accusations were of two sorts: some of them were mere popular gossip, while others were more sophisticated attacks on Christian faith and practice.

The popular accusations were based on rumors regarding the customs and beliefs of Christians. Thus, some claimed that Christians committed incest, that they ate children, that they worshipped the sexual organs of their priests, that their god was a crucified ass, and many similar things. Most of these rumors seem to have arisen out of a gross misunderstanding of some Christian practices. Thus, for example, the *agape* or love feast seems to have been the basis for the legend according to which Christian meetings were orgies in which, after much eating and drinking, the lights went out and the most disorderly sexual unions took place. Similarly, the assertion that Christ was present in the eucharistic banquet, probably coupled with some nativity stories, was the origin of the rumor according to which Christians covered a child with flour and then, presenting it to a neophyte and telling him that it was a loaf of bread, they ordered him to cut it. When the child's blood started flowing, the Christians ate it. The neophyte, an unwilling participant in that crime, was thus involved in it in such a way that he was forced to keep silent.[4]

The more sophisticated accusations—known to us mostly from the *Octavius* of Minucius Felix and Origen's *Contra Celsum*[5]—consisted mostly in showing the ignorance and incompetence of Christian teachers. Much was made of the fact that the so-called teachers of the Christians were really ignorant people belonging to the lowest strata

---

[4] Although these rumors were already circulating in the second century and may be discovered behind the works of the Apologists, this particular list has been taken from the *Octavius* of Minucius Felix, a Christian apology written in Latin early in the third century, in which a pagan lists these accusations (*Octav. 9*). Cf. Tertullian, *Apol. 7*.

[5] Pierre de Labriolle, *La réaction païenne* (Paris: L'artisan du livre, 1950), studies these accusations in detail.

of society. This is why Christians approach only those who are ignorant—that is, women, children, and slaves—for they know that their "science" would not resist a solid refutation.[6] These Christians, although perhaps not atheists in the strict sense, at least adore an unworthy god, who is constantly getting involved in insignificant human matters.[7] Their gospels themselves are full of contradictions, and the little good that can be found in their doctrines they have taken from Plato and other Greek philosophers, although even that they have corrupted.[8] Such is the case with the absurd doctrine of resurrection, which is no more than a gross misunderstanding of the Platonic doctrines of immortality and the transmigration of souls.[9] Besides, Christians are subversive people, opposed to the state, for they do not accept the divinity of Caesar nor do they respond to their civil and military responsibilities.[10]

It is these accusations that the Greek Apologists of the second century faced. In the case of the popular rumors, quite clearly the product of fantasy, the Apologists found it sufficient simply to deny them.[11] But the more sophisticated attacks could not be set aside with such ease, but had to be seriously refuted. It was the need to respond to these accusations that impelled the Apologists to write the works that we must now study, and that for the first time posed and attempted to answer several questions that would be of great importance for the further development of Christian theology.

Aristides

As the apology of Quadratus to which Eusebius refers seems to have been lost,[12] the most ancient apology that has survived is that of

---

[6] Minucius Felix, *Oct.* 5; Origen, *Contra Cel.* 3. 50; 3. 55.

[7] Minucius Felix, *Oct.* 10.

[8] Origen, *Contra Cel.* 6. 1.

[9] *Ibid.*, 7. 28.

[10] *Ibid.*, 8. 68-69.

[11] Their most detailed denial of these charges is to be found in Athenagoras, *A Plea for the Christians* 31-36.

[12] See further on in this chapter the section devoted to the *Letter to Diognetus*.

Aristides, who addressed his defense of Christianity to emperor Hadrian,[13] and who therefore must have written it before the year A.D. 138.[14]

Aristides begins with a brief discourse regarding the nature of God and the world.[15] God is the first mover of the world, and he made all things because of man. This means that every man who fears God must also respect his fellowmen. God has no name, and Aristides defines him in negative terms: without beginning, without end, without composition, etc.

After this brief introduction, Aristides classifies mankind in four categories: the barbarians, the Greeks, the Jews, and the Christians.[16] Taking each of these groups in turn, the Apologist shows that the barbarians as well as the Greeks and the Jews have followed a religion that is contrary to reason. The barbarians have made gods that have to be guarded so as not to be robbed; and that being the case, how do they expect these gods to have the power to guard them? [17] The Greeks have made gods that are like men, and even worse, for they commit adultery and all sorts of evil.[18] Finally, the Jews, although

---

[13] Eusebius, *HE* 4. 3. 3; Eusebius, *Chronica Ol.* 226. *Christus* 125. *Adr.* 8. The Syriac and the Armenian texts include the name of Hadrian in the dedication. The Greek text does not; but this is clearly because of its adaptation in order to make it fit into the setting of the *Legend of Barlaam and Joasaph*. See n. 14.

[14] This apology was lost for several centuries, and was rediscovered late in the nineteenth century in a Syriac version, in the monastery of Saint Catherine in Sinai. Its discoverer, J. Rendel Harris, published it in 1893 in the Cambridge series *Texts and Studies* (I,1). Some years earlier (1878) an Armenian fragment had been published in Venice (of which a Latin translation may be found in *BAC*, 116: 117-32). Through these discoveries, J. Armitage Robinson was able to recognize the Greek text of the lost apology in two chapters of a well-known Greek work—the *Legend of Barlaam and Joasaph*. His edition of the Greek text may be found in the same volume of *Texts and Studies*. However, the Syriac version seems to be more trustworthy than the Greek adaptation that appears in the *Legend*. Not only are there reasons in the Greek text itself which would seem to deny its fidelity to the original, but the Armenian text, and even some Greek fragments discovered later, seem to agree with the Syriac rather than the Greek of the *Legend of Barlaam and Joasaph*. Therefore, we shall follow the Syriac version.

[15] *Apol.* 1.

[16] *Ibid.*, 2. 1. Thus, according to the Syriac and Armenian versions. The Greek text says that there are three groups: the pagans, the Jews, and the Christians.

[17] *Apol.* 3. 2.

[18] *Ibid.*, 8. 1-13. 8. In the middle of this passage dealing with the Greeks, there is a

better than Greeks and barbarians in affirming that God is only one, have also fallen into idolatry, for they actually adore the angels and their own laws, and not God.[19]

Over against these peoples stand the Christians, who are the only ones that have found the truth. Christians are a new nation that has a divine admixture,[20] and this new race is known for its superior customs and for the love that binds its members among themselves.[21]

Because of this manner of presenting Christianity, Aristides says little about the beliefs of this new nation.[22] Besides what has already been said about the character of God and how Christians constitute a new nation, it is important to note that a sharp eschatological expectation is found in this Apologist. The world will be subject to a "terrible judgment which will come upon all mankind through Jesus," [23] and meanwhile it only subsists on account of the prayers of Christians.[24] Finally, there is a text in which Aristides affirms that children are sinless.[25]

Justin Martyr

Not only for the number and extension of his works, but also for the depth and originality of this thought, Justin Martyr is without any doubt the most important of the Greek Apologists of the second century. His city of origin was the biblical Shechem, which was then called Flavia Neapolis.[26] A philosopher at heart, he came to Chris-

---

refutation of Egyptian religion which does not seem to follow the orderly argument of the author (*Apol.* 12).

[19] *Apol.* 3. 2.

[20] *Ibid.*, 16. 4.

[21] *Ibid.*, 15. 2-10.

[22] The Greek text attempts to correct this by adding some lines on Jesus, his life and his disciples, and on the Trinity (15. 1-3).

[23] *Apol.* 17. 7.

[24] *Ibid.*, 16. 6.

[25] *Ibid.*, 15. 9: "When one of them has a child, they praise God; and if it also happens to die in its infancy they greatly praise God, as for one who has gone through the world without sin."

[26] *I Apol.* 1.

tianity after an intellectual pilgrimage of which he himself tells in his *Dialogue with Trypho*[27] But even after his conversion he did not set aside the cloak of the philosopher, but rather claimed that in Christianity he had found the true philosophy. This is the thesis of his two Apologies—which are probably two parts of a single one.[28]

As is to be expected in works of this nature, the Apologies of Justin are not systematic treatises on the Christian faith. In the *First Apology*, after a very brief introduction, Justin says that it is reasonable to abandon those traditions which are not good and to love only truth. This is precisely what those to whom this work is addressed must do, for they are known as wise men and philosophers, and justice requires that Christians be not condemned only for their name, but that one take into consideration what that name implies before condemning them. Hence the need for an exposition of what the name "Christian" really means, and what is the relationship of Christians with the Empire, with good customs, and with paganism. This is in short the argument of the *First Apology*, which is repeated several times with some variations. Besides, there are in this document some interesting data for the history of liturgy and of early Christian heresies.[29] In the so-called *Second Apology* Justin centers his attention mostly on the relationship between Christianity and pagan philosophy.

The *Dialogue with Trypho* is somewhat later than the Apologies, and it claims to be the record of a conversation regarding the correct interpretation of the Old Testament which Justin held with a Jew called Trypho.[30] At the beginning of this dialogue, Justin offers a

---

[27] *Dial.* 2. 3-8. 2. See J. Champonnier, "Naissance de l'humanisme chrétien," *Bulletin de la Association G. Budé*, nouv. sér., 3 (1947), 58-68.

[28] The *II Apol.* has no heading of its own, but seems to be rather an appendix to the *I Apol.* There is no way of telling how much time passed between the writing of these two documents. See P. Keresztes, "The So-Called Second Apology of Justin," *Lat*, 20 (1965), 858-69.

[29] P. Keresztes, "The Literary Genre of Justin's First Apology," *VigCh*, 19 (1965), 99-110; Wolfgang Schmid, "Die Textüberlieferung der Apologie des Justins," *ZntW*, 40 (1941), 87-138.

[30] Perhaps the same as Tarpho in the Talmud. Eusebius (*HE* 4. 18. 6) says that he was the

brief summary of the path that led him to Christianity. The rest is an apology against Judaism on the interpretation of the Old Testament, the divinity of Jesus, and the New Israel.[31]

In his task of defending Christianity, Justin faces two basic problems: on the one hand, that of the relationship between Christian faith and classical culture, and on the other, that of the relationship between that faith and the Old Testament.

Justin bases his solution to the first of these problems on his doctrine of the *logos* or Word. This is certainly not a creation of Justin, for the doctrine of the logos has a long history in Greek and Hellenistic philosophy. In the Judeo-Christian tradition, Philo of Alexandria had already introduced the Hellenistic concept of the logos, and the Fourth Gospel had used the same term for understanding the divine and pre-existent nature of the Savior. In fact, Justin's doctrine of the logos follows very closely that of Philo, which seems to be his main source.[32]

Making use of a very widespread idea among Greek philosophers, Justin affirms that all knowledge that men have is the product of the logos. For him, this logos is not only the rational principle of the universe, but is also the pre-existent Christ of the prologue of the Fourth Gospel. Therefore, combining these two traditions regarding the logos, Justin concludes that every knowledge is a gift of Christ, and that

those who lived reasonably are Christians, even though they have been thought atheists; as, among the Greeks, Socrates and Heraclitus, and men like them; and among the barbarians, Abraham, and Ananias, and Azarias, and Misael, and Elias, and many others whose actions and names we now decline to recount, because we know it would be tedious.[33]

---

most famous Jew of his time. See Marie Joseph Lagrange, *Saint Justin* (Paris: J. Gabalda, 1914), p. 28.

[31] F. M. M. Sagnard, "Y-a-t-il un plan du 'Dialogue avec Tryphon'?" *Mélanges Joseph de Ghellinck*, I (Gembloux: J. Duculot, 1951), 171-82.

[32] Apart from the incarnation, the main difference between Justin and Philo in their doctrine of the logos is that Justin affirms the personal nature of the Word.

[33] *I Apol.* 46. 3-4 (*ANF*, 1: 178).

These men of old only knew the Word "partially."[34] They only knew those truths which the Word revealed to them,[35] but they could not behold the Word himself. This Word, however, has been made flesh, and thus Christians know the Word "entirely."[36] Christians behold as a whole what the ancients only saw in part. In other words, Justin distinguishes between the *seminal logos* and the *seeds of the logos*.[37] This vocabulary he borrows from the Stoics, but he uses it in a different manner than they did.[38] For the Stoics, the seeds of the logos were universal data that all men know regarding morality and religion. The *seminal logos* is the universal reason, in which individual reason participates and which acts upon the seeds of the logos in order to develop them. For Justin, on the contrary, the seeds of the logos are neither universal nor natural, but result rather from the direct and individual action of the seminal logos. Furthermore, these are not basic data that the human mind must perfect, but are rather illuminations that only the logos himself can lead to perfection. This is why Justin uses the rather unphilosophical term of "part of the logos": for the part can only be completed by the whole. The part of the logos that Plato had could never have been completed by Plato's mind, but only by the logos himself.[39] Philosophy contains only part of the truth, but by itself it cannot even distinguish that part of truth from the

---

[34] *II Apol.* 10. 2.

[35] According to Justin, the Greeks made use of another source of knowledge, apart from the direct inspiration of the Word: the Hebrew Scriptures. It was from them that Plato drew some of his knowledge, although he did not understand them correctly (*I Apol.*, 44. 8-10; 60).

[36] *II Apol.* 10. 3.

[37] *Ibid.*, 7. 3.

[38] In general, Justin's "Platonism" is really the Middle Platonism of his times, which already included several Stoic elements. Carl Andresen, "Justin und der mittlere Platonismus," *ZntW*, 44 (1952-53), 157-95.

[39] On the *seminal logos* and its *seeds*, see: Jean Daniélou, *Message evangélique et culture hellénistique aux II* *at III* *siècles* (Paris: Desclée & Co., 1961), pp. 45-46; Ragnar Holte, "Logos Spermatikos: Christianity and Ancient Philosophy According to St. Justin's Apologies," *StTh*, 12 (1958), 109-68; Jan Hendrik Waszink, "Bemerkungen zu Justins Lehre vom Logos Spermatikos," *Mullus: Festschrift Theodore Klauser* (Münster: Aschendorff, 1964), pp. 380-90.

great deal of falsehood in which it is enveloped.[40] Only the Word, which is the truth and the measure of all truth, can be the basis of that distinction. The Word, who was known in part by the philosophers, is now known as a whole by Christians. This is why Christians can say that this or that assertion of the philosophers is true, and that this or that other assertion is false: because they know truth incarnate.

In summary, as a true Middle Platonist and a Christian as well, Justin takes elements of Stoicism and adds them to his basically Platonic philosophy, although affirming always that total truth can only be known in the Word incarnate. This is the reason for the rather strange character of Justin's thought, so clearly Platonic, but at the same time so deeply Christocentric.

Justin discusses the problem of the relationship between the Old Testament and the Christian faith in his *Dialogue with Trypho*.[41] For him, the Old Testament refers to the New in two manners: by means of events that point to other events in the New Testament, and by means of prophecies that speak of that which becomes a reality in the New Testament.[42] The first of these are "types" or "figures," [43] and the latter are "sayings." [44]

The "sayings" in which Justin finds a witness to the Christian message need not detain us here, for, with some exceptions, they are

---

[40] The errors of the pagans are due, not only to the partial nature of their knowledge of the Word, but also to the work of demons, who are constantly striving to lead men into evil and error, and one of whose favorite wiles is to plant among men myths and rites that are in fact parodies of Christian doctrines and practice. *I Apol.* 54; 56; 58; 62. 1-2; 64. 4; *II Apol.* 4. 3-4.

[41] L. W. Barnard, "The Old Testament and Judaism in the Writings of Justin Martyr," *VetTest*, 14 (1964), 395-406, shows that Justin's education was purely Hellenistic, and that he came to the Old Testament by way of Christianity, and not vice versa. However, his information regarding Jewish exegesis and traditions is correct.

[42] *Dial.* 116. 1 (*ANF*, 1:256): "For the Holy Spirit sometimes brought about that something, which was the type of the future, should be done clearly; sometimes He uttered words about what was to take place, as if it was then taking place, or had taken place."

[43] τύποι.

[44] λόγοι.

the prophetic texts that seem to have circulated in books of *Testimonia*.[45]

The "types" are much more interesting, for here we see the development of an exegetical tradition that will become very important in patristic theology. According to this typological interpretation, there are in the Old Testament certain events that prefigure other events to come. Thus, Justin affirms that the paschal lamb with whose blood the houses of the Israelites were anointed was a "type" of Christ, for by the blood of the Savior those who believe in him are saved. Similarly, the lamb that was to be sacrificed and roasted pointed to the passion of Christ, for the lamb is roasted in the shape of the cross. And the proof that this and other similar commandments in the Old Testament were only temporary has been given by God himself with the destruction of Jerusalem, for it is now impossible for the Jews to fulfill such commandments.[46]

This typological interpretation must not be confused with allegory. In the latter, the importance of the historical realities of the Old Testament events threatens to disappear behind a new mystical meaning—and Pseudo-Barnabas goes to the extreme of claiming that the literal interpretation of the Old Testament was due to an evil angel[47]—whereas in Justin's typology the significance is to be found in the historical fact itself, although it transcends it.[48]

---

[45] See Daniélou, *Message,* pp. 196-97. On Justin's use of prophecy, see: J. Gervais, "L'argument apologétique des prophéties messianiques selon saint Justin," *RUOtt,* 13 (1943), section spéciale, 129-46, 193-208.

[46] *Dial.* 40. 1-3.

[47] Although, as has already been said, Pseudo-Barnabas also makes use of typological exegesis.

[48] One should note also that Justin's typology includes, not only the Old Testament, but also the total structure of the universe, for he sees "types" of the cross everywhere. "For consider all the things in the world, whether without this form [of the cross] they could be administered or have any community. For the sea is not traversed except that trophy which is called a sail abide safe in the ship; and the earth is not ploughed without it: diggers and mechanics do not their work, except with tools which have this shape. And the human form differs from that of the irrational animals in nothing else than in its being erect and having the hands extended, and having on the face extending from the forehead what is called the nose, through which there is respiration for the living creature; and this shows no other form than that of the cross." (*I Apol.* 55. 1-2; *ANF,* 1: 181.)

Justin conceives the logos that spoke in the philosophers and prophets in the fashion of Middle Platonism. According to him, God is wholly transcendent, without any name except that of Father.[49] In order to communicate with this world, God has begotten the logos, whose function is to act as an intermediary between the Father and his creation. The multiple manifestations of God in the Old Testament are theophanies not of the Father, but of the logos, which is his mediator and revealer,[50] for even "he who has but the smallest intelligence will not venture to assert that the Maker and Father of all things, having left all supercelestial matters, was visible on a little portion of the earth." [51] Hence a certain tendency to establish a distinction between the Father and the Word in terms of the transcendence and immutability of the one and the immanence and mutability of the other, and also the tendency to speak of the Father and the Word as if they were two gods, the one absolute and the other secondary. Justin even calls the Word "another God." [52] However, this is not to be understood in such a way that it denies Christian monotheism, for according to Justin the unity between God and the Word is similar to that which exists between the sun and its light, "just as they say that the light of the sun on earth is indivisible and inseparable from the sun in the heavens." [53] It is rather that Justin attempts to interpret the relationship between the Father and the Son by combining elements taken from Jewish angelology with others taken from Middle Platonism. The first source leads him to stress the unity of God, and to see in the Word an attribute or "power" of that one God. The second source leads him to stress the divine transcendence, and the Word then becomes a subordinate God that serves as a bridge between the world

---

[49] On the divine transcendence in Justin, see Goodenough, *Theology*, pp. 123-38. According to Goodenough, Hebrew thought conceives of transcendence in terms of spatial distance, whereas Greek thought conceives of it in terms of immutability. Justin combines both trends.

[50] See B. Kominiak, *The Theophanies of the Old Testament in the Writings of St. Justin* (Washington: Catholic University of America Press, 1948).

[51] *Dial.* 60.2 (*ANF*, 1:227).

[52] *Ibid.,* 56.11.

[53] *Ibid.,* 128.3 (*ANF*, 1:264).

and that supreme God who exists only in absolute transcendence. This tension between these two sources is not characteristic of Justin alone, but appears rather generally in the theology of the first centuries. As we shall see later on, it was only through long and bitter controversies that it was possible to clarify Christian doctrine in this regard.[54]

The importance of Justin for the historian is to be found not only in what he has to say regarding the relationship of the Christian faith with pagan philosophy and with the Old Testament, but also in the information that he has preserved regarding early Christian worship, and especially baptism[55] and the eucharist.[56] With reference to the eucharist, Justin affirms that the food that is taken in it is the flesh and blood of Jesus; but he also asserts that it is still food in the sense that it nourishes the bodies of those who partake in it.

For not as common bread and common drink do we receive these; but in like manner as Jesus Christ our Saviour, having been made flesh by the Word of God, had both flesh and blood for our salvation, so likewise have we been taught that the food which is blessed by the prayer of His word, and from which our blood and flesh by transmutation are nourished, is the flesh and blood of that Jesus who was made flesh.[57]

Although Justin's apologies attempt to use Hellenistic philosophy in order to present the Christian faith, this does not mean that their author disregards the distance that separates Christianity from

---

[54] Although Justin does not expound his thought regarding the Holy Spirit, there is no doubt that he believes in the existence of "a third" next to the Father and the Son. See *I Apol.* 60.6.

[55] *I Apol.* 61; *Dial.* 87-88. Does Justin distinguish between baptism and confirmation? Cf. E. C. Ratcliff, "Justin Martyr and Confirmation," *Th*, 51 (1948), 133-39; P. Carrington, "Confirmation and St. Justin," *Th*, 52 (1949), 448-52.

[56] *I Apol.* 65, 67. See H. B. Porter, "The Eucharistic Piety of Justin Martyr," *AnglThR*, 39 (1957), 24-33.

[57] *I Apol.* 66.2 (*ANF*, 1:185). J. Beran, "Quo sensu intelligenda sint verba Iustini Martyris 'ὅση δύναμις αὐτῷ' in I Apologia, N. 67," *DivThom*, 39 (1936), 46-55, argues on the basis of *I Apol.* 57.5 that Justin knows of a special priestly power that is employed in the consecration of the eucharist. This is rather doubtful, for the text can be interpreted otherwise.

philosophy. His sense of the proper character of Christianity is clearly seen in the manner in which Justin stresses the doctrines of incarnation and of the resurrection of the dead. Later on, we shall see other so-called defenders of the Christian faith attempting to free it from this entanglement with the historical, the particular, and the material. Justin does not attempt to deny, or even to leave aside, the doctrine of incarnation, but rather places it at the center of his Apologies. On the other hand, the doctrine of a life after death was also an object of mockery among the pagans, and in the face of such mockery some Christians sought support in the Platonic doctrine of immortality. This gave Christianity a certain intellectual veneer, but led to a confusion between the Greek doctrine of the immortality of the soul and the Christian doctrine of the resurrection of the dead. This confusion could easily be followed by a long series of doctrines and values of a Platonic rather than a Christian nature. Here again, Justin does not allow himself to be seduced by the seeming similarity between Platonic and Christian doctrines, but rather affirms that the soul is by nature mortal and that Christians lay their hope, not in a universal immortality, but in the resurrection of the dead.[58]

Justin's eschatology[59] includes not only the doctrine of the resurrection of the dead, but also that of the return of Christ in royal glory,[60] and the establishment of a reign of a thousand years in the New Jerusalem.[61]

In summary, one can say that Justin's theology, as it is known through his works that have survived, is an attempt to achieve a Christian interpretation of Hellenism and Judaism. Both have a place within the divine plan.[62] This does not lead Justin to deny the unique

---

[58] *Dial.* 5. 1, 3; 80.

[59] L. W. Barnard, "Justin Martyr's Eschatology," *VigCh,* 19 (1965), 86-98.

[60] Jean Leclercq, "L'idée de la royauté du Christ dans l'oeuvre de saint Justin," *AnnTh,* 7 (1946), 83-95.

[61] *Dial.* 80. 5. See Oronzo Giordano, "S. Giustino e il millenarismo," *Asprenas,* 10 (1962), 155-71.

[62] The plan, dispensation, or οἰκονομία of God, a term that Justin takes from Paul, is basic in his thought, as it will also be in that of his disciple Tatian, and later in Irenaeus and Tertullian.

character of Christianity in order to make it more palatable to the world around him. On the contrary, Christianity is the only vantage point from which Judaism as well as Hellenism may be judged correctly. This implies a doctrine of history of which certain glimpses may be seen already in the work of Justin,[63] but which would later develop in other theologians who would build upon his foundations, notably Irenaeus. Perhaps if posterity had spared some of Justin's works that have been lost,[64] we would find dimensions in his thought which his existing works can only suggest.

Tatian

Tatian is one of those personalities in Christian antiquity who are surrounded by a wall of darkness which no effort seems capable of penetrating. Born in the Orient—if not in Assyria at least in Syria[65]—Tatian seems to have been converted to Christianity in Rome through the efforts of Justin, who was then teaching at the imperial city. After Justin's martyrdom, around A.D. 165, Tatian founded his own teaching center. Some years later he left Rome for Syria, where we are told that he founded a heretical school. Ancient Christian writers agree in claiming that he founded the sect of the Encratites, but very little is known about his heresy.[66] After this,

[63] B. Seeberg, "Die Geschichtstheologie des Justins des Märtyrers," *ZschrKgesch,* 58 (1938), 1-81; Antonio Quacquarelli, "La storia nella concezione di S. Giustino," *RScF,* 6 (1953), 323-39.

[64] Eusebius (*HE* 4.18) mentions *Against the Greeks, Refutation, On the Divine Monarchy, Psalter, On the Soul,* and *Against Marcion.* Justin himself mentions a work *Against all Heresies* (*I Apol.* 26), and the notes of his *Debate with Crescens,* which circulated in Rome (*II Apol.* 8.5). The various works with some of these titles which have been attributed to Justin are not genuine. Pierre Prigent, *Justin et l'Ancien Testament: L'argumentation scripturaire du traité de Justin contre toutes les hérésies comme source principale du Dialogue avec Tryphon et de la première Apologie* (Paris: Lecoffre J. Gabalda, 1964), believes that portions of *Against All Heresies* are behind the *I Apol.* and *Dial.,* as well as in some fragments preserved by John of Damascus. But these latter are probably to be attributed to Melito, as shown by Walter Delius, "Ps.-Justin: 'Über die Auferstehung,' " *ThViat,* 14 (1952), 181-204.

[65] Tatian himself affirms that he was born in Assyria (*Address to the Greeks* 43). But at that time it was customary to include Eastern Syria in Assyria.

[66] The main sources for the life of Tatian and the sect of the Encratites are: Irenaeus,

possibly around the year 180, Tatian simply disappears from history.[67]

In his *Address to the Greeks* Tatian attempts to show the superiority of what he calls "barbarian religion" over the culture and religion of the Greeks. He begins by reminding the Greeks of the barbarian origin of the inventions of which they now boast. Furthermore, the Greek philosophers themselves were unworthy people, as may clearly be seen in the many anecdotes that are told about them. Finally, Greek religion has no right to consider itself better than that of the "barbarians," for the Greeks worship in their gods the loose women who served as models to the sculptors, and in any case the stories that circulate regarding the gods themselves are not very worthy of imitation. And if all this does not suffice, let the Greeks remember that Moses was earlier than Homer, and that any good which may be found in Hellenic religion has simply been taken from the Old Testament.[68]

It is within this attack on Greek civilization that Tatian expounds what he calls the "barbarian religion" of Christians. Naturally, one cannot expect a systematic exposition of Tatian's theology within such a context. But it is clear that the center of his Christian theology is God and his Word or logos. This logos springs from God in a manner similar to that in which from one light others may be lit, with no loss for the first. This logos made the world, not out of a pre-existent matter, for nothing is without beginning except God.

Adv. haer. 1:28; Tertullian, *On Fasting* 15; Hippolytus, *Philos.* 2. 8.10 and 10.18; Clement of Alexandria, *Strom.* 3.12-13; Origen, *De orat.* 24; Eusebius, *HE* 4.18,19. It was forbidden for the Encratites to marry. Probably they also abstained from wine. Some of these sources claim that the Encratites held a Christology and a doctrine of the Godhead similar to those of Valentinus and Marcion (on these two, see the following chapter).

[67] Apart from his *Address to the Greeks*, Tatian composed the *Diatessaron*, which was the first attempt to harmonize the Four Gospels, and treatises *On animals*, *On demons*, *On Perfection according to the Savior*, and *On problems*. Except for translations of the *Diatessaron*, all these works have been lost.

[68] The chronological priority of Moses over Homer is one of the main theses of Tatian, who tries to prove it through various chronologies. In short, he claims that "Moses was older than the ancient heroes, wars, and demons. And we ought rather to believe him, who stands before them in point of age, than the Greeks, who, without being aware of it, drew his doctrines [as] from a fountain." (*Address* 40; *ANF*, 2:81.)

God was in the beginning; but the beginning, we have been taught, is the power of the Logos. For the Lord of the universe, who is Himself the necessary ground (ὑπόστασις) of all being, inasmuch as no creature was yet in existence, was alone; but inasmuch as He was all power, Himself the necessary ground of things visible and invisible, with Him were all things; with Him, by Logos-power (διὰ λογικῆς δυνάμεως), the Logos Himself also, who was in Him, subsists. And by His simple will the Logos springs forth; and the Logos, not coming forth in vain, becomes the first-begotten work of the Father. Him (the Logos) we know to be the beginning of the world. But He came into being by participation, not by abscission; for what is cut off is separated from the original substance, but that which comes by participation, making its choice of function, does not render him deficient from whom it is taken. For just as from one torch many fires are lighted, but the light of the first torch is not lessened by the kindling of many torches, so the Logos, coming forth from the Logos-power of the Father, has not divested of the Logos-power Him who begat Him. I myself, for instance, talk, and you hear; yet, certainly, I who converse do not become destitute of speech (λόγος) by the transmission of speech, but by the utterance of my voice I endeavour to reduce to order the unarranged matter in your minds. And as the Logos, begotten in the beginning, begat in turn our world, having first created for Himself the necessary matter, so also I, in imitation of the Logos, being begotten again, and having become possessed of the truth, am trying to reduce to order the confused matter which is kindred with myself. For matter is not, like God, without beginning, nor, as having no beginning, is of equal power with God; it is begotten, and not produced by other being, but brought into existence by the Framer of all things alone.[69]

Within this creation, men as well as angels were made free, and it is we who through the wrong use of our freedom have created evil.

Our free-will has destroyed us; we who were free have become slaves; we have been sold through sin. Nothing evil has been created by God; we

---

[69] *Address* 5 (*ANF*, 2:67). Robert M. Grant, "Studies in the Apologists," *HTR*, 51 (1958), 123-34, points out that this manner of understanding the *logos* springs from grammar and rhetoric rather than from philosophy.

ourselves have manifested wickedness; but we, who have manifested it, are able again to reject it.[70]

Man's soul is not immortal, but rather dies with the body and later is resurrected with it in order to suffer an eternal death. But the soul who knows the truth continues living even after the destruction of the body.[71]

Athenagoras

Athenagoras "the philosopher" was a contemporary of Tatian, although his spirit and style are very far from those of Justin's disciple. Very little is known about Athenagoras, but through his writings one can discover a refined and ardent spirit. His style, although not classical, is the finest, most clear and correct of all Christian writers of the second century. Two of his works have been reserved for posterity: *A Plea for the Christians* and *On the Resurrection of the Dead*.

In the *Plea for the Christians*, after a brief dedication and an introduction that has led scholars to date the work around A.D. 177, Athenagoras goes on to refute the three main charges against Christians: atheism, Thyestean banquets, and incest. He answers to the charge of atheism by quoting a long list of poets and philosophers who have said about God things similar to those which Christians now say, and who in spite of this were not atheists.

His doctrine of the relationship between God and the Word is clearly summarized in the following quotation:

The Son of God is the Logos of the Father, in idea and in operation; for after the pattern of Him and by Him were all things made, the Father and the Son being one. And, the Son, being in the Father and the Father in the Son, in oneness and power of spirit, the understanding and reason (νοῦς καὶ λόγος) of the Father is the Son of God. But if, in your surpassing intelligence, it

---

[70] *Address* 11 (*ANF*, 2:70).
[71] *Ibid.*, 13.

occurs to you to inquire what is meant by the Son, I will state briefly that He is the first product of the Father, not as having been brought into existence (for from the beginning, God, who is the eternal mind [νοῦς], had the Logos in Himself, being from eternity instinct with Logos [λογικός]); but inasmuch as He came forth to be the idea and energizing power of all material things. . . . The Holy Spirit Himself also, which operates in the prophets, we assert to be an effluence of God, flowing from Him, and returning back again like a beam of the sun. Who, then, would not be astonished to hear men who speak of God the Father, and of God the Son, and of the Holy Spirit, and who declare both their power in union and their distinction in order, called atheists.[72]

As may be seen from this text, the doctrine of the Word which Athenagoras holds is similar to that of Justin, although Athenagoras lays more emphasis on the unity of the Word with the Father.[73]

As to the charges of immorality leveled against Christians, Athenagoras simply rejects them categorically. How could anyone believe that Christians are capable of such actions, which all men find repulsive, when their moral doctrine is so palpably higher than that of other men? Christians certainly cannot eat children, for homicide and even abortion are forbidden for them. Nor can they commit incest, for they condemn the most fleeting thought against chastity and praise virginity above every other way of life.

In his treatise *On the Resurrection of the Dead,* Athenagoras tries to show that the resurrection of the body is possible, proving on the one hand that it agrees with the nature of God, and on the other hand that human nature itself requires it. He sees no contradiction between the resurrection of the dead and the immortality of the soul, but on the contrary affirms that the latter doctrine requires the former, for a man is only such when the soul is united to the body.[74]

---

[72] *Plea* 10 (*ANF*, 2:133).
[73] Cf. *ibid.,* 24 (*ANF* 2:141): "We acknowledge a God, and a Son his Logos, and a Holy Spirit, united in essence,—the Father, the Son, the Spirit, because the Son is the Intelligence, Reason, Wisdom of the Father, and the Spirit an effluence, as light from fire."
[74] *On the res.* 15.

The attitude of Athenagoras regarding the relationship between philosophy and theology is similar to that of Justin. Justin sees a positive value in the truths that are to be found in pagan philosophy; and in the *Plea* we are told that Plato knew the essential points of the Christian doctrine of God.[75] But Athenagoras affirms that the great difference between the philosophers and the Christians is in the fact that the former followed the impulses of their own souls, whereas the latter follow the revelation of God himself.[76] This is why the philosophers contradict each other—although Athenagoras does not stress such contradictions, as would be done by some later apologists.

Theophilus of Antioch

Theophilus, bishop of Antioch, wrote his *Three Books to Autolycus* around the year 180 or slightly thereafter.[77] His purpose in these books was to persuade his friend Autolycus that Christianity is true. But his work is neither as profound as that of Justin, nor as elegant as that of Athenagoras. His knowledge of classical culture seems to have been rather superficial, and such is the case also with his defense of Christianity.[78]

The first of the *Three Books to Autolycus* deals with God; the second, with the interpretation of the Old Testament and the errors of the poets; and the third, with the moral superiority of Christianity. It is not necessary to summarize here the content of each of these three

---

[75] *Plea* 23.

[76] *Plea* 7.

[77] Eusebius, *HE* 4.24. Through this report, and through that of Jerome (*De viris illus.* 25) it is known that Theophilus also wrote *Against the Heresy of Hermogenes, Against Marcion,* several catechetical works, and biblical commentaries. All these works have been lost. Friedrich Loofs, *Theophilus von Antiochen Adversus Marcionem und die anderen theologischen Quellen bei Irenaeus* (Leipzig: Hinrichs, 1930), believes that one of the sources of Irenaeus, which he calls IGT, is Theophilus' *Against Marcion*. His thesis has been refuted by F. R. M. Hitchcock, "Loof's Asiatic Source (I.Q.A.) and the Pseudo-Justin *De Resurrectione,*" *ZntW*, 36 (1937), 35-60; "Loof's Theory of Theophilus of Antioch as a source of Irenaeus," *JTS*, 38 (1937), 254-66.

[78] Daniel Ruiz Bueno, usually moderate in his criticism, says that he is "a deeply antipathical character, who despises that which he has not been able to understand." (*Padres Apologistas, BAC,* 116:578.)

books, but only to discuss what Theophilus has to say regarding the knowledge and nature of God.

According to Theophilus, only the soul can know God. To Autolycus, who has asked him to show him his God, Theophilus answers that he must first see his man—that is, that his friend must first show the purity that is necessary in order to see God. The soul of man is like a mirror, which must be clear in order to be able to reflect an image.[79]

This God who can only be known by those whose souls are pure is triune. Actually, Theophilus is the first Christian author to use the term "trinity."[80] Theophilus, as well as Justin, Tatian, and Athenagoras, calls the second person of the Trinity the logos, and he introduces in the Christian doctrine of the Word the distinction that Philo had already made between the immanent Word, which has always existed in the mind or heart of God, and the expressed Word, who was begotten before all things, so that it is in this latter sense that he is said to be "the first-born of all creation."[81] The introduction of this distinction in the field of Christian theology is of great importance, for it was soon accepted and used by some of the most influential theologians, and it played an important role in the controversies of later centuries.

Hermias

The *Mockery of the Pagan Philosophers,* written by Hermias, is usually included among the Greek apologists of the second century. However, its date of composition is very doubtful, and some critics place it in the second century, whereas others place it as late as the sixth.[82] Although Hermias has sometimes received the title of

---

[79] I *Ad Autol.* 2.

[80] τριάς (*Ad Autol.* 15).

[81] II *Ad Autol.* 22.

[82] See the discussion of this issue in O. Bardenhewer, *Geschichte der altkirchlichen Literatur;* Erster Band: *Vom Ausgang des apostolischen Zeitalters bis zum Ende des zweiten Jahrhunderts* (Darmstadt: Wissenschaftliche Buchgesellschaft, 1962), pp. 326-28.

philosopher, his work requires no more knowledge of philosophy than that which could be found in any manual of the time. It is totally lacking in literary elegance, as well as in theological interest. Its author says very little about his own Christian theology, but rather concentrates on the manner in which the various wise men of antiquity contradicted one another, thus hoping to show that none of them is worthy of respect. If there is some positive value in this brief document, it is as a witness to the sense of humor of an early Christian.

The Epistle to Diognetus

The situation is very different when we come to another apologist that it is also difficult to date.[83] This is the unknown author of the *Epistle to Diognetus*, whose style compares favorably with other Christian writers of the same period.

In twelve brief chapters—that is, if the last two are genuine[84]—this unknown Christian presents one of the most beautiful and noble defenses of the new faith. Without going to the extremes of Tatian or Hermias, the *Epistle to Diognetus* points out the senselessness of the pagan religion as well as of Jewish customs, and it expounds in a positive and simple way the nature of the Christian faith, which does not come from men but from the God who has created the universe, as may be seen in the lives of its followers.

For the Christians are distinguished from other men neither by country, nor language, nor the customs which they observe. For they neither inhabit cities of their own, nor employ a peculiar form of speech, nor lead a life which is

---

[83] Some critics have dated it in the thirteenth century, and even in the Renaissance; but such late dates are most unlikely, and there is reason to believe that we have here a document that is roughly contemporary with the others that we have studied in this chapter. Daniel Ruiz Bueno, *Padres Apostólicos, BAC,* 65:818-20, summarizes scholarly discussion on this point. He himself sees some value on the theory of D. P. Andriesen according to which this document is the lost apology of Quadratus (pp. 820-30). F. Ogara, "Aristidis et epistolae ad Diognetum cum Theophilo Antiocheno cognatio," *Greg* 25 (1944), 74-102, argues for Theophilus as its author, but not with great success.

[84] Arguments of style, vocabulary, and content have led some critics to suggest that they are a later addition. See *SC,* 33:219-40.

marked out by any singularity. The course of conduct which they follow has not been devised by any speculation or deliberation of inquisitive men; nor do they, like some, proclaim themselves the advocates of any merely human doctrines. But, inhabiting Greek as well as barbarian cities, according as the lot of each of them has determined, and following the customs of the natives in respect to clothing, food, and the rest of their ordinary conduct, they display to us their wonderful and confessedly striking method of life. They dwell in their own countries, but simply as sojourners. As citizens, they share in all things with others, and yet endure all things as if foreigners. Every foreign land is to them as their native country, and every land of their birth as a land of strangers. They marry, as do all [others]; they beget children; but they do not destroy their offspring. They have a common table, but not a common bed. They are in the flesh, but they do not live after the flesh. They pass their days on earth, but they are citizens of heaven. They obey the prescribed laws, and at the same time surpass the laws by their lives. They love all men, and are persecuted by all. They are unknown and condemned; they are put to death, and restored to life. They are poor, yet make many rich; they are in lack of all things, and yet abound in all; they are dishonoured, and yet in their very dishonour are glorified. They are evil spoken of, and yet are justified; they are reviled, and bless; they are insulted, and repay the insult with honour; they do good, yet are punished as evil-doers. When punished, they rejoice as if quickened into life; they are assailed by the Jews as foreigners, and are persecuted by the Greeks; yet those who hate them are unable to assign any reason for their hatred.[85]

Melito of Sardis

Several apologies that are mentioned by ancient Christian writers have been lost,[86] and there is no way to know what may have been their theological content. In the case of Melito of Sardis, however, although his apology has been lost,[87] there is a homily that has sur-

---

[85] *Ad Diog.* 5 (*ANF*, 1:26-27).

[86] According to Eusebius (*HE* 4. 3), the first apology was that of Quadratus. Aristo of Pella wrote the first work against the Jews (*HE* 4. 6; Origen, *Contra Cel.* 4. 52). Miltiades (*HE* 5. 17) and Apollinaris of Hierapolis (*HE* 4. 27) wrote, among other works, apologies in favor of Christianity.

[87] Melito was a prolific writer, but all his production has perished, except for his *Paschal Homily*. See Eusebius, *HE* 4. 26.

vived.[88] In it, he summarizes the history of Israel, laying special emphasis on the Exodus and the paschal institution, and interpreting the totality of that history typologically, so that it refers to Jesus Christ.

This is he who rescued us from slavery to freedom, from darkness to light, from death to life, from oppression to an eternal kingdom, and made us a new priesthood and a chosen people for ever. He is the Passover of our salvation, he it is who in many men suffered many things. This is he who in Abel was slain, in Isaac was bound, who in Jacob dwelt in a strange land, who in Joseph was sold, who in Moses was cast out, in the lamb was sacrificed, and in David was hunted, in the prophets was dishonored.[89]

This homily differs from the apologies that we have studied in that philosophical concepts do not play a role in it. But its theology agrees with that of the other apologies. Christ is pre-existent and divine, and this is stressed to such a point that the distinction between the Father and the Son is almost erased.[90] As in the case of Justin, Melito does believe in the Holy Spirit, but has not developed a doctrine of his relationship with the Father and the Son. Finally, Melito clearly affirms that Christ is at once God and man, and in this homily we are told that the Savior is "by *nature* God and man." [91]

General View

In passing from the Apostolic Fathers to the Greek Apologies of the second century, one meets a totally different atmosphere. We are now

---

[88] A very illuminating suggestion regarding the nature of this homily is put forth by Παναγιώτης Κ. Χρήστου, "Τὸ ἔργον τοῦ Μελίτωνος περὶ Πάσχα καὶ ἡ ἀκολουθία τοῦ Πάθους," ΚΛΗ, 1 (1969), 65-77.

[89] *Paschal Hom.* 68-69 (trans. Campbell Bonner, *The Homily on the Passion by Bishop Melito of Sardis*, London: Christophers, 1940, p. 176).

[90] "Melito's theology, as far as this homily reveals it, is dominated by the conception of the divinity and the pre-existence of Christ. . . . But this emphasis upon his divinity and pre-existence made it natural and almost inevitable that in naive, unguarded speech the personal distinction between God the Father and God the Son should be obscured." Bonner, *The Homily*, pp. 27-28.

[91] *Paschal Hom.* 8. He also speaks of the "two substances (οὐσίαι)" of Christ, and for him "substance" and "nature" seem interchangeable. Bonner, *The Homily*, pp. 28-29.

witnessing the early encounters of Christianity with classical culture, and the various efforts of Christian thinkers to interpret the relationship between them. Thus, some are willing to grant validity to the spark of truth that they believe can be found in pagan philosophy, whereas others see no other possible relationship between Christianity and Hellenism than a war to the bitter end.[92] On the other hand, in their effort to present the faith in such a manner that it may be understood by pagans, Christians find themselves forced to systematize their thought, and it can thus be said that the Apologists are the first systematic theologians of Christianity.[93] The importance of these writers for the history of Christian thought is precisely in this task of systematizing Christian theology, as well as in their doctrine of the logos, which opens the way to dialogue between Christian faith and classical culture.

There are, however, some dangers involved in this work, for as it defines the faith of the church it also gives rise to new problems that earlier Christians had not suspected. Thus, the development of the doctrine of the logos, with all its philosophical implications, will some years later be the cause of grave theological controversies. Already in the Apologists, one sees the diversity between Justin, who affirms that the Word is "another God," and Melito, who tends to identify the Son with the Father. And somewhere between them is Theophilus, who distinguishes between an inner Word, which exists eternally in the mind of the Father, and a spoken or expressed Word, which is the creative agent that will later become incarnate in Jesus Christ.

In general, the Apologists seem to look upon Christianity as a doctrine, be it moral or philosophical. Christ is above all the teacher of a new morality or of the true philosophy. But one must not forget that in the homily of Melito Christ appears as the conqueror of death and of the powers of evil, and Christianity is presented as participation in

---

[92] However, all of them make use of classical culture, even if some do it unwillingly. See G. L. Ellspermann, *The Attitude of the Early Christian Writers Toward Pagan Literature and Learning* (Washington: Catholic University of American Press, 1949).

[93] "By their intellectualism and exclusive theories the Apologists founded philosophic and dogmatic Christianity." Harnack, *HD*, 2: 228.

that victory. That is to say, it is possible that the apologists, who in addressing pagans speak of Christ almost exclusively as a teacher and illuminator, had a wider and more profound understanding of his saving work than that which can be seen in their writings that have survived.

In any case, the Apologists contributed to the progressive Hellenization of Christianity. Their position before philosophy is not uniform, as may be seen in the contrast between Justin, Athenagoras, and Theophilus on the one hand, and Hermias and Tatian on the other. Even among those who make most use of philosophical instruments, such as Justin and Athenagoras, the doctrines of incarnation and the resurrection of the dead, which are not palatable to the Hellenic spirit, do not lose their centrality. But in spite of this, one must say that the concept of God which the apologists took from Hellenistic philosophy, and which emphasized the divine immutability, would long be a burden on Christian theology and would be a factor making more difficult the trinitarian and christological controversies of later centuries.

Meanwhile, the problems that threatened the inner life of the church were others, and it would be erroneous to interpret them exclusively in terms of the opposition between the Hebrew spirit and the Greek mind. These problems were the first heresies, to which we must now turn.

V

The Early Heresies: Challenge and Response

From a very early date, the Christian church had to struggle with various interpretations of its faith which seemed to many to endanger a crucial aspect of that faith. Converts were coming to Christianity from several different religious and cultural backgrounds. As was to be expected, these various origins influenced their interpretation of Christianity. At the same time other religious movements were taking important elements of the Christian faith and incorporating them into their systems. Was this sufficient to call them Christian? Where was the line to be drawn between true Christianity and what was in fact a different religion with Christian elements? Quite clearly, that line could not be drawn *a priori,* for those who were eventually considered heretics did not work outside the Christian community, but rather counted themselves as faithful Christians attempting to explain the gospel in terms that their contemporaries might understand. Also, those who were eventually declared orthodox did not agree on all matters, and therefore a contemporary observer would have had great difficulty in distinguishing them from the others. Thus arose a variety of doctrines, all claiming to be the correct understanding of Christianity, but many of which seemed to contradict, or at least to leave aside, some of the fundamental tenets of the Christian faith in its traditional form.

The existence of this diversity of doctrines may be seen already in the New Testament, whose authors are constantly attempting to put an end to them. Galatians, Colossians, the so-called Johannine literature, and I Peter show the struggle of the early Christians against such doctrines. We have already seen how Ignatius of Antioch opposed those who denied the real incarnation of Jesus Christ. A few years later, Justin once again attacked the teachers of what he took to be a false Christianity. Furthermore, almost all the Apologists wrote works against the heretics, although these have not been preserved. During the second century, and especially in its later years, these doctrines became so widespread that they provoked in the church at large a reaction that was to be of enormous significance for the history of Christian thought. Therefore, before the discussion of those theologians whom the church later considered to be the great defenders of orthodoxy, we must give a brief summary of the doctrines that they opposed.

Judaizing Christianity

The first doctrinal problem that confronted the primitive church was that of its relationship with Judaism. The progressive solution of this problem may be seen in Acts as well as in the Epistles of Paul. There were, however, some persons who never accepted Paul's solution, which eventually became that of the vast majority of Christians.

It is difficult to determine the exact nature of the doctrines held by each of the diverse Judaizing movements, as well as to distinguish among them. This difficulty, which is due in part to the scarcity of the sources for their study, was already faced by the ancient Christian writers who discuss the Judaizers, for they, too, seem confused regarding the various groups and their doctrines. The reason for this is probably that these Christians were not at first organized in clearly defined groups, such as churches, but simply formed movements that frequently coalesced.

However, for the sake of clarity, it seems possible to distinguish several levels at which the issue of the relationship between Christianity and Judaism was posed.

At first this had to do only with whether a Christian should follow the Law of the Old Testament or not. At this level, there were some moderate Judaizers, who themselves obeyed the Law but did not attempt to compel others to do likewise, and those of a more extreme position, who not only followed the Law but felt that all true Christians should do so.[1]

At another level, however, there were some Judaizing Christians who affirmed, not only that it was necessary to obey the Law of the Old Testament, but also that Paul was an apostate from the true faith, and that Christ had not been Son of God from the beginning, but had been adopted because of his moral excellence in fulfilling the Law. This was the position of the "Ebionites," a sect that seems to have continued to exist for several centuries.[2]

The sources of our knowledge of Ebionism are, apart from the witness of the ancient antiheretical writers,[3] the translations of the Old Testament by the Ebionite Symmachus, as well as certain portions of the Pseudo-Clementine literature. Among the sources that came together to form this body of literature, scholars believe that it is possible to distinguish that which they call the "Preaching of Peter," whose theology agrees with what we are told of Ebionism by other Christian writers. Therefore, it is believed that the "Preaching of Peter" is Ebionite in its origin, and that therefore we have in it a direct witness to the doctrine of this sect.[4]

From these sources, it is possible to reconstruct Ebionite theology, at

---

[1] Justin, *Dial.* 47.

[2] The term "Ebionite" first appears in Irenaeus, *Adv. haer.* 1. 26. 2. Its etymological origin is usually found in the Hebrew for "poor."

[3] Justin, *Dial.* 47; Irenaeus, *Adv. haer.* 1. 26; Origen, *Contra Cel.* 2. 1, 3; 5. 61, 65; Epiphanius, *Pan.* 29-30; Eusebius, *HE* 3. 27; Hippolytus, *Philos.* 7. 34.

[4] J. N. Reagan, *The Preaching of Peter: The Beginning of Christian Apologetic* (Chicago: The University of Chicago Press, 1923).

least in its main traits. It seems that in its origin Ebionism is related to Essenian Judaism, for some of its principles seem to have been taken from that type of Judaism—the rejection of animal sacrifices, the doctrine of the existence of a principle of good and a principle of evil, although both come from God, and several minor details.[5]

According to the Ebionites, there is a principle of good and a principle of evil. The latter is lord of this age, but the former will rule in the age to come. Meanwhile, the principle of good is revealed in this world through its prophet, who has come in several incarnations. Adam, Abel, Isaac, and Jesus are incarnations of the prophet of good. But, ever since the time of Adam, each incarnation of the prophet of good is accompanied by its counterpart, which serves the purposes of the principle of evil. Cain, Ishmael, and John the Baptist are manifestations of the principle of evil, which is also called the feminine principle.[6]

Within this system of thought, Jesus is above all a prophet of the masculine principle, or principle of good. Apart from this, Jesus is merely a man whom God had chosen to proclaim his will. Jesus was not born of a virgin, and it was at his baptism that he received from on high the power that enabled him to fulfill his mission. This mission did not consist in saving humanity—a work that is beyond the capabilities of any man—but in calling mankind to obedience to the Law, which has been given by the masculine principle. In fact, the Law was the core of Ebionite spirituality and, although they did not offer bloody sacrifices, they did emphasize circumcision and the observance of the Sabbath.[7] The Laws in the Old Testament which refer to sacrifices were not given by God, but rather have been added to the sacred text through the influence of the feminine principle.[8] This is

---

[5] Jean Daniélou, *The Theology of Jewish Christianity* (London: Darton, Longman & Todd, 1964), pp. 56-58, offers a valuable comparison between Ebionism and the Dead Sea Scrolls.

[6] *Hom.* 2. 15-17.

[7] The foregoing has been summarized from Daniélou, *Theology*, pp. 63-64.

[8] *Hom.* 2. 38.

why, in spite of their strict observance of the Law, Epiphanius tells us that the Ebionites did not accept the Pentateuch in its entirety.[9]

As to the relationship of Jesus to the Law, the Ebionites insisted that he had not come to abolish the Law, but to fulfill it. This fulfillment of the Law by Jesus does not mean in any way that the Law has now been accomplished, and that it is therefore no longer binding, but rather that Jesus set an example for all to follow. It was Paul who introduced the idea that in fulfilling the Law Jesus had done so for every other man. This teaching on the part of Paul was to be expected, for he too was a servant of the feminine principle.[10]

Thus, this type of Judaizing Christianity was a variant of Essenian Judaism, from which it was distinguished mainly by the role that Jesus played in its theology.[11]

Ebionism was never a very widespread doctrine, and it seems to have disappeared as the church became more and more gentile and less Jewish. This does not mean, however, that it did not present a challenge to the church of the early centuries. On the contrary, what was at stake here was the uniqueness of Jesus Christ, over against the possibility of adapting him in such a way that he could simply be juxtaposed to the ancient Jewish religion. When this was done, Jesus was no longer unique and central. He was no longer the only begotten Son of God, but a mere prophet within the sequence of prophets. He was no longer the Savior, but simply an element—sometimes secondary—of the action of God within this age.

Finally, at another level there were discussions of the relationship between Christianity and Judaism which attempted to reinterpret not only Christianity itself, but Judaism as well. This was the case of a

---

[9] *Pan.* 30. 18.

[10] Paul is not directly attacked in Pseudo-Clementine literature. But there are frequent references to an "enemy" or a "hostile man" who is probably Paul.

[11] Such is the view of Daniélou, *Theology,* pp. 55-64. In this he follows Oscar Cullmann, "Die neuentdeckten Qumrantexte und das Judenchristentum der Pseudo-Klementinen," in *Neutestamentliche Studien für R. Bultmann, BZNtW,* 21 (1954), 35-51. Cf. Joseph A. Fitzmeyer, "The Qumran Scrolls, the Ebionites, and Their Literature," in Krister Stendahl, ed., *The Scrolls and the New Testament,* pp. 208-31.

certain type of Judaizing Christianity which, while having probably a close connection with Ebionism, was also influenced by Gnosticism.

The main exponent of this type of Judaizing Christianity seems to have been Elxai (also called Elkesai, Elcesai, or Elchasai). He lived in the first half of the second century, but hardly anything is known of his life.[12] His doctrine is clearly Ebionite, although with a strong Gnostic influence. It is based on a revelation that Elxai claimed that he had received from an angel who was ninety-six miles tall. This angel was the Son of God. Next to him there was another angel of similar proportions, although feminine, and this was the Holy Ghost.

The content of this revelation of Elxai is known only through the quotations and other references to be found in the Christian writers who attack it. From their witness, one may conclude that Elxaism was only a form of Ebionism—it was necessary to keep the Law and be circumcised, and Jesus was only a prophet—with certain Gnostic influences—astrological speculations, numerology, and dualistic tendencies.[13] Its main strength seems to have been in the East, especially beyond the Euphrates, where Elxai himself was probably born. In any case, this sect, although small, is important, for it may have influenced Mohammed, the founder of Islam.

Gnosticism

Under the general title of "Gnosticism" are included several religious doctrines that flourished in the second century, and whose main characteristic was their syncretism.[14] The Gnostics would take

---

[12] Hippolytus, *Philos.* 9. 8-12; Eusebius, *HE* 6. 38; Epiphanius, *Pan.* 19; Theodoret, *Haer. fab. comp.* 2. 7.

[13] This is held by Hans Joachim Schoeps, *Theologie und Geschichte des Judenchristentums* (Tübingen: J. C. B. Mohr, 1949), pp. 325-34. Cf. Daniélou, *Theology*, pp. 64-67. While the latter believes that Elxaism is an Ebionism that has been influenced by orthodox Christianity, the former affirms that Gnostic influences are to be credited with the difference between Ebionism and Elxaism. This last theory is more in agreement with the Fathers; but one must concede that the existing data are insufficient to pronounce a definitive verdict. See also, on the relationship between Elxaism and Gnosticism, Ethel Stefana Drower, "Adam and the Elkasaites," *SP* 4 (1961), 406-10.

[14] Alexander Böhlig, "Synkretismus, Gnosis, Manichäismus," in *Koptische Kunst: Chris-*

any doctrine that they found valuable, without any regard for its origin or for the context from which it was taken. When they came to know early Christianity and saw its great appeal, they attempted to take those aspects of Christianity which seemed most valuable to them and adapt them to their systems. This procedure posed an urgent challenge for those Christians who did not accept it, for it became necessary to show that Gnosticism misrepresented Christian doctrine, and to show reasons why one should not turn Jesus Christ into a mere element within a Gnostic system.[15]

There has been a great deal of scholarly debate regarding the origins of Gnosticism, but this debate probably can never be settled because of the syncretistic nature of Gnosticism itself, which makes use of Persian dualism as well as oriental mysteries, Babylonian astrology, Hellenistic philosophy, and practically every doctrine that circulated in the second century. Therefore, Harnack's dictum that Gnosticism is "an acute hellenization of Christianity" is not quite accurate. Although it is true that there are strong Greek influences in Gnosticism, it is also true that this is only one of the many sources from which the Gnostic teachers drank.[16]

Although there are very important speculative elements in

---

tentum am Nil (Essen: Villa Hügel, 1963), pp. 42-47; M. Mazza, "Gnosticismo e sincretismo: Osservazioni in margine alla letteratura recente sulle origine gnostiche," *Helikon*, 5 (1965), 570-87.

[15] The best introductions to Gnosticism in English are still: Robert M. Grant, *Gnosticism and Early Christianity* (New York: Oxford University Press, 1960), and Hans Jonas, *The Gnostic Religion: The Message of the Alien God and the Beginning of Christianity* (Boston: Beacon Press, 1958).

[16] Beginning in the eighteenth century, there has been a great deal of scholarly debate regarding the origins of Gnosticism. The only conclusion that can be drawn from this debate is that Gnosticism cannot be understood as flowing from a single source, but rather as a mingling of various currents of religious thought. On this issue, see the bibliographical summary in Eugène de Faye, *Gnostiques et Gnosticisme: Etude critique des documents du Gnosticisme chrétien aux IIe et IIIe siècles* (Paris: Librairie Orientaliste Paul Geuthner, 1925), pp. 499-540. After that date, there has been an upsurge of interest in the Jewish elements in Gnosticism. See: Grant, *Gnosticism;* Gershom Gerhard Scholem, *Jewish Gnosticism, Merkabah Mysticism and Talmudic Tradition* (New York: Jewish Theological Seminary, 1960); Willen Cornelis van Unnik, "Die jüdische Komponente in der Entstehung der Gnosis," *BigCh*, 15 (1961), 65-82; Hans-Martin Schenke, "Das Problem der Beziehung zwischen Judentum und Gnosis: Ist die Gnosis aus dem Judentum ableitbar?" *Kairos*, 7 (1965), 124-33.

Gnosticism, its usual presentation as consisting primarily of various systems of numerological speculations has made it impossible to understand how it could have been a strong rival of the church. The fact that Gnosticism became an appealing alternative to orthodox Christianity was due above all to its soteriological interest. In order to understand that appeal one must interpret Gnosticism above all as a way of salvation. The cosmopolitanism that followed Alexander's conquests had its counterpart in the individualism of men who found that the ancient national religions were no longer able to satisfy their needs. For this reason, the centuries in which Christianity was beginning to make its way in the world were characterized by a search for individual salvation, and by the consequent growth of those religions which claimed to offer it—besides Christianity, the mysteries and Gnosticism.

Gnosticism is, then, above all a doctrine of salvation. But, what is the nature of that salvation?[17] According to Gnosticism, it consists in the liberation of the spirit, which is enslaved because of its union with material things. The body and the animal soul of man belong to the material world, for the soul is only that which gives the body its life, desires, and passion.[18] The spirit does not really belong to this world, but is part of the divine substance. For some reason that is usually explained mythologically, it has fallen into this world and become a prisoner of matter. It is then necessary to free the spirit from that prison; and this is achieved through knowledge or *gnosis*—whence the name of Gnosticism.

This knowledge does not consist in mere information, but is rather a mystical illumination that results from the revelation of the eternal. Knowledge is, then, an understanding of the human situation, of what we once were and what we should become; and through it we can be freed of the bonds that tie us to the material world. On the other hand, as we are enslaved by our union with matter in such a way that

---

[17] J. Zandee, "Gnostic Ideas on the Fall and Salvation," *Numen*, 11 (1964), 13-74.

[18] Although one should point out that the status of the soul is neither uniform nor clear in many Gnostic systems.

we are unable to know eternal truth by our own means, it is necessary that a messenger be sent from the transcendent spiritual world to bring us its liberating revelation. This messenger is characteristic of all Gnostic systems, and in Christian Gnosticism it will be Christ who will accomplish this mission.[19]

However, the doctrine of salvation must be grounded in an understanding of man and the universe, and this is the place of the complicated speculative constructions within the various Gnostic systems. If man's spirit is imprisoned in matter, there must be a reason for that condition; and that reason the Gnostics attempt to offer in their speculations.[20] There are two main characteristics in this speculation: its derivative dualism and its numerology. The dualism of Gnosticism, which many scholars have emphasized as one of its main characteristics, is not a primary or initial dualism, but results rather from an initial monism.[21] Gnostic speculation sets out from a single eternal principle, from which other principles or aeons are produced in a declining process, until—usually through an error of one of the lower aeons—the material world is produced. Thus appears the derivative dualism between matter and spirit, or between the heavenly and the earthly. Within the process of the production of the various levels of aeons, numerology—a rather common feature in Hellenistic speculation—plays an important role, for the aeons are usually produced following certain numerical patterns. Gnostic cosmology springs from this combination of derivative dualism and numerological speculation, and it is characterized by complex series of aeons that stand between the absolute and the material world. These

---

[19] References regarding this messenger collected from various Gnostic sources may be seen in Jonas, *Gnostic Religion,* pp. 75-80.

[20] However, the importance of the long series of aeons of Gnostic speculations is not merely as an explanation of our present situation, but also as a religious description of it. "The religious significance of this cosmic architecture lies in the idea that everything which intervenes between here and the beyond serves to separate man from God, not merely by spatial distance but through active demonic force." Jonas, *Gnostic Religion,* p. 43.

[21] A point clearly proved by Antonio Orbe, *Estudios valentinianos,* Vol. I, Pt. I, *Hacia la primera teología de la procesión del Verbo* (Rome: Apud Aedes Universitatis Gregorianae, 1958), pp. 203-85.

beings are often seen as spheres that the spirit must traverse in its return to eternity. Finally, the ethics of the Gnostics are based on their anthropology and cosmology. If whatever good there is in man is to be found in his spirit, and the body is by nature evil, two opposed conclusions may be drawn: either one is to subject the body to strict discipline and live an ascetic life, or whatever the body does makes no difference, for it cannot mar the purity of the spirit, and one may therefore allow the body to do as it pleases. It is for this reason that some Gnostic sects were extremely ascetical while others were libertine.[22]

When the general Gnostic view was conjoined with Christian teaching, there were three basic points at which most Christians felt that their faith was threatened: the doctrine of creation and of the divine rule over the world, the doctrine of salvation, and Christology.

Gnosticism was opposed to the traditional Christian doctrine of creation because it saw in the material world, not the work of the eternal God, but the result of an error committed by an inferior and evil or ignorant being. According to the Gnostics, the things of this world are not merely worthless, but even evil. In this they were opposed to the mainstream of the Judeo-Christian tradition, which affirmed that all things were made by God, who still acts in the history of the world.

From this first disagreement between Gnosticism and traditional Christianity, there followed a similar disagreement regarding the doctrine of salvation. According to Gnosticism, salvation consists in the liberation of the divine and immortal spirit that is imprisoned within the human body. The latter's role in the plan of salvation is merely negative. Over against this view, most Christians affirmed that salvation included the human body, and that the final fulfillment of God's plan for the salvation of men will not take place without the resurrection of the body.

Finally, Gnostic dualism had devastating consequences when applied to Christology. If matter, and above all this matter which forms our body, is not the product of the divine will, but rather of

---

[22] On Gnostic libertinism see de Faye, *Gnostiques*, pp. 413-28.

some other principle that is opposed to that will, it follows that matter and the human body cannot serve as a vehicle for the revelation of the supreme God. Therefore Christ, who came to make that God known to man, cannot have come in flesh. His body cannot have been a truly physical body, but only a bodily appearance. His sufferings and his death cannot have been real, for it is inconceivable that the supreme God would thus give himself up to the evil and destructive power of matter. Thus the Gnostics are led to the christological doctrine that is known as Docetism—from the Greek δοκέω, to seem or suppose— which we have already found in discussing the opponents of Ignatius of Antioch. Over against this theory, most Christians affirmed that in Jesus of Nazareth—in his body, in his life, his sufferings, his death and resurrection—is to be found the saving revelation of God. This is why such Christians saw Gnosticism, not as a different version of their own faith, but as an attempt to deprive that faith of the very heart of its message.

Although Gnostic schools were many, and the relationship among them is not clear, one may attempt to describe some of their systems as a means to illustrate their general traits.

Our knowledge of Gnosticism derives from their writings and from the works in which some ancient Christian writers attack them. Until a few decades ago, only a very limited number of Gnostic writings seemed to have survived, and scholars were forced to follow only the testimony of writings directed against them. Naturally, the question that was always left unanswered was how far should these anti-Gnostic writings be trusted. Recently vast amounts of Gnostic materials have been discovered, and thereby our knowledge of Gnosticism has been greatly amplified and clarified.[23]

---

[23] See: Jean Doresse, *The Secret Books of the Egyptian Gnostics: An Introduction to the Gnostic Coptic Manuscripts Discovered at Chenoboskion* (New York: Viking Press, 1960); Kendrick Grobel, ed. and trans., *The Gospel of Truth: A Valentinian Meditation on the Gospel* (Nashville: Abingdon Press, 1960); Johannes Leipoldt and Hans-Martin Schenke, *Koptisch-gnostiche Schriften aus den Papyruscodices von Nag Hamadi* (Hamburg: H. Reich, 1960); J. D. McCaughey, "The Nag Hammadi or Chenoboskion Library and the Study of Gnosticism," *JRH*, 1 (1960), 61-71; Bertil Gärtner, *The Theology of the Gospel According*

According to a very ancient tradition, whose first exponent is Justin,[24] Simon Magus was the founder of Gnosticism.[25] The historical truth seems to be, not that Simon founded this type of religion, but that in Chapter 8 of Acts we have a record of one of the earliest encounters between Christianity and Gnosticism. In Samaria, where Simon lived, there were people from various parts of the ancient world, and thus an atmosphere was developed that was very adequate for a syncretistic doctrine such as Gnosticism. According to Justin and other ancient Christian writers, Simon Magus had an ample following. He claimed that he was God himself, or that he had the power of God, and that his companion Helena was the Holy Spirit. The book of Acts affirms that he was baptized as a Christian. Although there is no evidence that he appropriated other Christian doctrines, this episode exemplifies the syncretistic spirit of Gnosticism.

Menander, a disciple of Simon Magus, is an obscure person who seems to have been a Jewish gnostic rather than a Christian. According to the ancient heresiologists,[26] Menander specialized in magic, as his teacher had done before him. He claimed that he himself was the Savior, sent by the heavenly beings as their messenger, in order to teach the magic procedures by which one could overcome the angels that created this world and that still hold mankind in slavery.

Probably the first Gnostic who attempted to reinterpret the Christian gospel was Cerinthus.[27] He lived at Ephesus towards the end of

---

to Thomas (New York: Harper, 1961); Hans Jonas, "The Secret Books of the Egyptian Gnostics," JRel, 42 (1962), 267-73.

[24] Justin, I Apol. 26. Also Pseudo-Clementine, pass.; Irenaeus, Adv. haer. 1. 23; Tertullian, De anima 34, 57; Ps.-Tertullian, Adv. omn. haer. 1; Hippolytus, Philos. 6. 2-15; Epiphanius, Pan. 21. 2, 4. Justin saw in Rome a statue erected to the Sabine god Semo Sancus, and on that basis affirmed that the Romans had built a statue to Simon Magus. His error was discovered when the Roman inscription was unearthed in 1574.

[25] See Eizo Kikuchi, "A Type of Primitive Gnosticism Represented by Simon Magus," JRelSt, Vol. 36 (1962), no. 172.

[26] Only Justin, I Apol. 26, 56, seems to have firsthand knowledge of him. However, de Faye goes too far in casting doubts upon his existence (Gnostiques, p. 432).

[27] Irenaeus, Adv. haer. 1. 26. 1 and 3. 3. 4; Eusebius, HE 3. 28 and 7. 25. According to this last text, some opponents of the New Testament book of Revelation claimed that it had been written by Cerinthus.

the first century, and in his system one finds the derivative dualism that is characteristic of Gnosticism in general. He also distinguished between Jesus and Christ: Jesus was the man, son of Mary and Joseph, whereas Christ was the divine being that descended upon Jesus at his baptism. Therefore, Cerinthus was not a Docetist in the strict sense, although he solved the problem of the union of humanity and divinity in Christ by establishing a radical distinction between them. When Christ had accomplished his mission as a messenger to humanity, he abandoned Jesus, and it was the latter who suffered, died, and rose from the dead, for Christ himself is impassible. According to tradition, the great opponent of Cerinthus at Ephesus was Saint John—whoever that may have been.[28] One should know that the First Epistle of John in our New Testament seems to be directed against him.[29]

Satornilus—or Saturninus—was a disciple of Menander.[30] According to him, the world was made by seven angels, one of which was the God of the Jews. These angels attempted to make man in the image of the supreme God, but failed. Then the supreme God, moved by his mercy, gave the man who had been created by the angels a portion of his eternal substance, and he later sent Christ to give man the means to be freed from the slavery of matter. The most important of these means seem to have been sexual continence and special dietary observances.

The sect of the Carpocratians seems to have been born in Alexandria, where it is said that their teacher Carpocrates lived around the year A.D. 130.[31] The philosophical school that dominated Alexandrine

---

[28] See Eduard Schwartz, "Johnannes und Kerinthos," in his *Gesammelte Schriften*, 5 (Berlin: W. de Gruyter und Co., 1963), 170-82.

[29] See I John 2: 22; 4: 1-3; 5: 1, 5, 20.

[30] Justin, *Dial.* 35; Irenaeus, *Adv. haer.* 1. 24. 1-2; Hippolytus, *Philos.* 7.16.

[31] The stories regarding Carpocrates and his son Epiphanius are so legendary that one is inclined to doubt the very existence of these two men. Furthermore, Origen (*Contra Cel.* 5. 62) mentions a sect of "Harpocratians." This has led scholars to suggest that the name of the Carpocratians is not derived from their founder, but from the Egyptian god Horus-Carpocrates, worshiped under the name of Harpocrates. See H. Leisegang, *La Gnose* (Paris: Payot, 1951), pp. 176-84. The main sources are: Irenaeus, *Adv. haer.* 1. 25; Clement Alex., *Strom.* 3. 2-18; Tertullian, *De anima* 35; Hippolytus, *Philos.* 7. 20; Eusebius, *He* 4.7.

thought in the first centuries of the Christian era was Neoplatonism, and we have already seen how Alexandrine Judaism and Christianity received a strong influence from that philosophical school. The same is true of the Carpocratians, who included in their Gnostic syncretism, not only certain Christian elements, but others that were Neoplatonic in origin. According to them, the world was created by spirits who were inferior to the Father. The souls of men existed before their birth, and salvation is achieved by recalling that pre-existence. Those who do not gain such recollection are condemned to a series of reincarnations. Jesus was a man, the Son of Joseph and Mary, but a perfect man, who remembered his previous existence with total clarity and proclaimed the eternal realities that had been forgotten.

Alexandria was also the place of activity of Basilides,[32] who flourished between the years A.D. 120 and 140, and claimed to have been a disciple of the apostle Matthias. According to him, the origin of all heavenly realities is the Father, from whom several orders of beings emanate up to the number of 365 heavens. The angels who created this world, one of which is the God of the Old Testament, dwell in the last of these heavens. The God of the Old Testament chose a people and attempted to establish its rule over the entire world; but the other angels prevented him from doing so. As all the angels were ignorant of the nature of the Father, from whom they were separated by 364 heavens, their creation was extremely imperfect. But even in the imperfection of that creation there is still a portion of the divine spirit, imprisoned in the bodies of men. In order to liberate that divine element the Father sent his Only-begotten Son. This Son was not made man, but rather seemed to be so. His mission was to awaken in the spirits that had fallen asleep the recollection of heavenly realities. In order to do this, it was not necessary to suffer. Therefore Jesus was not crucified, but it was rather Simon of Cyrene who suffered the passion and death.

---

[32] *Frag. Murat.;* Irenaeus, *Adv. haer.* 1. 24; 2. 35; Clement Alex., *Strom.* 2. 8; 3. 1; 4. 12, 24, 26; 5. 1; Ps.-Tertullian, *Adv. omn. haer.* 1; Hippolytus, *Philos.* 7. 1-15; 10. 10; Eusebius, *HE* 4. 7. See Werner Foerster, "Das System des Basilides," *NTS,* 9 (1962-1963), 233-55.

Finally, we must devote a few paragraphs to Valentinus, who also lived part of his early life in Alexandria. It is not known where or how he developed his theological positions, for all that is known of him is that he was at Rome toward the middle of the second century and that he was expelled from the church in that city around the year A.D. 155. Valentinus is important for the history of Christian thought, not only for his doctrines, but also because in his case it is possible to compare the witness of orthodox Christian heresiologists with the writings of the heretic himself—or at least of his school. Also, in him the expansion of Gnosticism from Syria and the Orient reached Rome, and it was after that time that the Western wing of the Christian church began to show a deeper consciousness of the threat posed by Gnostic teaching.

From the works of the heresiologists,[33] the following outline of the doctrine of Valentinus may be drawn: The eternal principle of all beings is the Abyss (Bythos). This is incomprehensible and unfathomable, and in him Silence (Sigē) is to be found. In Silence, the Abyss begat two other beings: Mind (Nous) and Truth (Alētheia). Thus, the first "tetrad" was completed: Abyss, Silence, Mind, and Truth. But Mind (masculine), being united to Truth (feminine), gave origin to Word (Logos) and Life (Zoē). From these in turn Man (Anthrōpos) and Church (Ekklēsia) are begotten, and the "ogdoad" is thus completed. However, this is still not the end of the divine emanations, for each of the last two couples or aeons wished to honor the Abyss by multiplying, and thereby twenty-two more beings were originated, ten from Word and Life and twelve from Man and Church. Thus the Pleroma or Plenitude was completed, being formed by thirty aeons arranged in fifteen couples. The last of these aeons is Wisdom (Sophia), and it is from her that the material world had its origin. This took place when Wisdom went beyond the limits of her possibilities in attempting to know Abyss—of which only Mind is

---

[33] Irenaeus, *Adv. haer.* 1. 1-93, ll; 2.14; Clement Alex., *Strom.* 2. 8; 4. 13; 5. 1; Tertullian, *Adv. Valent.* pass.; *Adv. Prax.* 8; Hippolytus, *Philos.* 6. 12, 24-32; 10. 9; Eusebius, *HE* 4. 11.

capable. This led Wisdom to such a violent passion that she produced a new being, although without the participation of her mate. Due to its origin, this new being is an "abortion," and therefore creates a disorder within the Pleroma. Finally, Abyss decides to produce two new aeons, Christ and the Holy Spirit, in order to re-establish order within the Pleroma. This is accomplished, but there is always the product of Wisdom's passion, which is called Achamoth. Achamoth is expelled from the Pleroma and kept outside by the Cross or limit. The aeons, wishing to help this abortion of Wisdom, produce a new aeon, Jesus, in whom their plenitude is to be found. Jesus frees Achamoth from her passions, which become matter; then he leads her to repentance, and from that repentance the soul originates; finally, he grants Achamoth the *gnosis* from on high, and that illumination is the origin of the spirit. These three elements—matter, soul, and spirit—are still to be found in this world, although its creator does not know of the existence of the third. The creator of this world is a Demiurge formed by Wisdom in order to give form to matter and the soul. Then Wisdom herself placed within the men that had been created by the Demiurge the seeds of the spirit. These seeds developed until, once ready, Christ came to rescue them by presenting himself in the man Jesus—who is not to be confused with the aeon of the same name. Christ descended upon Jesus in his baptism, and then left him before his passion. Christ's mission was to bring *gnosis,* so that through it the spirits of men, which truly belong in the Pleroma, may return there.

The foregoing is a summary of what the heresiologists tell us regarding the system of Valentinus.[34] But the teachings of that Gnostic—or at least of his disciples—are to be found also in a recently discovered document that is known as the *Gospel of Truth.*[35] Ac-

---

[34] One should point out, however, that the heresiologists do not agree on several details. The foregoing follows the reconstruction of Jonas, *Gnostic Religion,* pp. 174-97.

[35] Edited by Michel Malinine, Henri-Charles Puech, and Gilles Quispel, *Evangelium Veritatis* (Zürich: Rascher, 1956). An attempt to reconstruct the Greek text: Jacques E. Ménard, *L'Evangile de Vérité* (Paris: Letouzey et Ané, 1962). English translation by K. Grobel cited above, n. 23.

cording to Irenaeus, the Valentinian sect had a *Gospel of Truth*,[36] and it seems safe to assume that the recently discovered document is the one to which the ancient writer referred.[37] However, there are several points of contrast between this *Gospel of Truth* and what we learn from Irenaeus himself as well as from other heresiologists regarding the theology of Valentinus. Given this contrast, three basic theories have developed in order to explain them: first, that the heresiologists are not to be trusted; secondly, that the *Gospel of Truth* was written by Valentinus before his definitive break with the church, and therefore before his system had reached its full maturity; third—and most probable—that both the *Gospel of Truth* and the witness of the heresiologists are basically trustworthy,[38] and that their divergencies may be explained by their different purposes. According to this theory, the heresiologists tried to underline the least plausible aspects of Gnostic speculations, precisely in order to undermine it, whereas the *Gospel of Truth* is much more interested in the question of salvation, which was the main interest of Gnosticism and the reason for its appeal. Furthermore, there are in the *Gospel of Truth* certain cosmogonic allusions that would not be understandable apart from the witness of the heresiologists.

This seems to confirm what has been previously said: the great attraction of Gnosticism during the early centuries of the Christian era cannot be understood on the basis of its cosmogonic speculations, but rather on the basis of its doctrine and promise of salvation. Therefore the Christian heresiologists, while serving the orthodox church by showing the least favorable aspects of Gnosticism, acted in detriment of historical accuracy by obscuring the great spiritual attraction of Gnosticism as a religion of salvation.

On the other hand, Gnosticism was admirably well adjusted to the

---

[36] *Adv. haer.* 3. 11. 9.

[37] Hans Jonas, "*Evangelium Veritatis* and the Valentinian Speculation," SP, 6 (1962), 96-111, defends this identification, as well as the view that both the *Gospel of Truth* and the heresiologists are trustworthy as witnesses to Valentinus' fully developed doctrine.

[38] With due allowance for the details in which the heresiologists disagree among themselves.

syncretistic spirit of its time. Each teacher took from the others whatever seemed convenient, and the sects and schools were so interwoven that modern historians must simply confess that they are unable to establish precise distinctions between the various Gnostic tendencies. Thus Gnosticism, which poses an academic problem for the historian, posed an urgent problem for Christians in the second and third centuries, who saw their faith threatened not only by violent external attacks, but also and even more by doctrines that attempted to take into account what they took to be the most valuable aspects of Christianity and to render them more readily acceptable to contemporary men.

Marcion

Among the many varying interpretations of its message which the early Christian church had to face, none was so dangerous as that proposed by Marcion, a native of Sinope, in Pontus, where his father was bishop.[39] After leaving that city, he traveled to Asia Minor and later to Rome, where he was expelled from the church, probably in A.D. 144.[40] He then founded a Marcionite church, and it was this step which made him one of the most dangerous rivals of orthodox Christianity. The various Gnostic teachers were only that: teachers who never founded more than schools. Marcion founded a church to rival that which already existed, and that church soon had so many members that at one time the final result of the conflict was seriously in doubt. Although after the third century Marcionism began its decline and soon disappeared from the Western part of the Empire, before that time it had posed a very real challenge.

Marcion has traditionally been counted among the Gnostics. Har-

---

[39] The main source is Tertullian, *Adv. Marc.* pass. Also: Justin, *I Apol.* 58; Irenaeus, *Adv. haer.* 1. 27; Clement Alex., *Strom.* 3. 3; Origen, *Contra Cel.* 5. 54; 6. 53, 74; *Comm. im Job.* 5. 4; 10. 4; Hippolytus, *Philos.* 7. 17-19; 10. 15; Eusebius, *HE* 4. 9; 5. 13. The classical study is that of Adolph von Harnack, *Marcion! Das Evangelium vom fremden Gott* reprint (Darmstadt: Wissenschaftliche Buchgesellschaft, 1960).

[40] On this date, see Edwin Cyril Blackman, *Marcion and His Influence* (London: S.P.C.K., 1948), pp. 20-21.

nack, the great historian of doctrines, protested against this, for he saw in Marcion an original thinker who at some points had a clearer grasp of essential Christian teachings than did the Gnostics. One's final decision on this matter greatly depends on what he understands by "Gnostic," for there is no doubt that there are some elements in Marcion's theology that bring him very close to Gnosticism, while others would lead the historian to discuss him separately, as I have decided to do here.

Marcion's theology is dualistic in the same derivative sense in which Gnosticism is dualistic.[41] In this material world, law and justice reign. Over against this, grace is the center of the Christian gospel, the gospel of the God whose love is such that he forgives even the worst sinners. Therefore, the gospel is the word of a god who can best be described as the "other," or the "foreign god," and who is radically different from the god who rules this world.

The god who rules this world is he whom the Jews worshiped. It is he who made all things "and saw that it was good." It is he who requires bloody sacrifices, who leads his people in battle, who orders entire populations to be slaughtered, who is best described as "a jealous god, visiting the iniquities of the fathers upon the children to the third and the fourth generation" (Exodus 20. 5).

Far above this vindictive god, there is another, the "unknown god," who is love. He is not related to this world, but is rather "the foreign god." While the Creator is just, fierce and bellicose, this supreme god is loving, peaceful, and infinitely good.[42] It is probable that Marcion began by affirming that the Creator was an evil god, and that it was later—perhaps through the influence of the gnostic Cerdo—that he came to describe him as a just god.[43] Thus, the contrast became not so

---

[41] There is, however, no text that clarifies the relationship between the Creator and the Supreme God, so that the statement that Marcion's dualism is not initial, but derivative, can only be based on inferences that may well be mistaken. See Orbe, *Hacia la primera teología*, pp. 259-65.

[42] Tertullian, *Adv. Marc.* 1. 6.

[43] As is held by Blackman, *Marcion,* pp. 66-71.

much that which exists between good and evil, but that between love and justice.

Marcion's dualism brings him very near to Gnosticism. The problem of evil seems to have been a primary concern for Marcion as well as for the principal Gnostic teachers. Like most of them, Marcion had a negative view of matter, and therefore of the body, and especially of sex. Like many of them, he was willing to grant some truth to the Old Testament, but only as the revelation of an inferior god or principle. Furthermore, the idea of an "unknown god" who is above the creator is not original with Marcion, but seems to have been drawn from the doctrine of Cerdo, Cerinthus, and Basilides.

The consequences of these points of contact with Gnosticism is that Marcion's theology also excludes this world from the sphere in which the Supreme God rules. This is why Tertullian, with his characteristic perspicacity to discover the weak points of an opponent's doctrine, made mockery of Marcion's Supreme God, who had taken so long to make himself known[44] and who meanwhile had not been able to produce even a sad little vegetable.[45]

But there are also other aspects of Marcion's theology which are different from Gnosticism. First, Marcion does not claim to have a secret knowledge through which salvation may be achieved. According to him, his doctrine follows from a careful study of the Christian message as it was preached by Paul. This message is to be found in the Epistles of Paul and in the Gospel of Luke, although it is necessary to revise those writings in order to eliminate the many Judaizing interpolations that have been introduced in them. Paul was the herald of a radically new message, of the message of the revelation of a god theretofore unknown. The Old Testament cannot be taken as the word of the god who reveals himself in Jesus Christ. In consequence, the references to the Old Testament to be found in the Pauline Epistles are later additions. And the same may be said regarding the Gospel of Luke, Paul's companion. Thus, Marcion formulated the first canon

---

[44] *Adv. Marc.* 1. 15.
[45] *Ibid.*, 1. 11.

of the New Testament.[46] His doctrine is then based on the study of these Scriptures, for he does not claim to be a prophet or to have any secret source of knowledge, but only to be a true exponent of Christian Scriptures.

Second, Marcion does not show the speculative interest that is characteristic of Gnostic systems. Numerology and astrology have no importance in his thought. His understanding of the human condition does not lead him to construct the endless series of aeons that were so important in Gnosticism.

Finally, Marcion went beyond the Gnostics through his interest in organization. All the Gnostic teachers founded schools. Marcion founded a church. This probably followed from his conviction that his doctrine was not an individual revelation that he had received, but the correct interpretation of the message that the church at large had adulterated. On the basis of that conviction, it was necessary to found a new church that would restore the proclamation of the original message. In founding such a church, Marcion posed a greater challenge to the church at large.

But what made Marcion's teachings absolutely unacceptable to most Christian leaders was the same thing that made Gnosticism unacceptable: Docetism. Like the Gnostics, Marcion denied that Christ was truly man. The great stumbling block that he found in the common story of the life of Christ was his birth. If the Savior was born as a child, he would have been placed under the rule of the Creator, which would in turn deny the radical newness of the gospel.[47] This is why Marcion affirms that Christ appeared as a fully grown man in the fifteenth year of the reign of Tiberius. However, the data that have survived do not suffice to determine whether Marcion thought that

---

[46] The importance of Marcion for the history of the New Testament canon is great, but must not be exaggerated. The idea of a scriptural canon was common among Christians, who continually made use of the Old Testament. Nor was the notion new that certain apostolic writings were divinely inspired. Marcion's contribution was in joining both of these ideas—which he was compelled to do once he rejected the Old Testament without claiming a private revelation or tradition to take its place.

[47] Blackman, *Marcion*, p. 100.

Christ's body was a mere appearance, or rather that it was made of an ethereal substance.

In summary, one may say that Marcion's doctrine is an exaggerated Paulinism. He himself, in composing the New Testament canon only of the Pauline epistles and the gospel written by Paul's companion, showed that he believed that Christianity is to be understood only in the light of the message of the Apostle to the Gentiles. The contrast between law and gospel, the doctrine of divine grace, and his radical Christocentrism, showed that in some respects Marcion had a clearer grasp of Paul's message than most of his contemporaries. As has been said earlier, already at the time of the Apostolic Fathers there was a tendency to turn Christianity into a new moral doctrine and thus to forget the Pauline emphasis on the free gift of God. A word of warning was necessary, and Marcion attempted to give it. But in his extreme emphasis on the contrast between Paul's message and the proclamation of the church he was led to some positions that were clearly opposed to the Pauline message, such as his theory of two Gods, his negative view of the Old Testament, and his Docetism. His call for a new discovery of the unmerited grace of God was necessary and relevant in the midst of the legalism that threatened to sweep the church. But his denial of God's action in the history of Israel and his dualistic interpretation of the history of salvation made the church attack him with such vigor that the positive values of his doctrines did not receive the attention that they merited.

Montanism

Montanus was a pagan priest who had been converted to Christianity and baptized around A.D. 155.[48] Some time after his baptism, he declared himself possessed by the Holy Spirit, and began prophesying on the basis of that possession.[49] He was soon joined by two wom-

---

[48] The main sources for Montanism are Tertullian's Montanist writings. Also Epiphanius, *Pan.* 48-49 and Eusebius, *HE* 5. 14-19.

[49] His words in which he seemed to claim that he was the Paraclete are not to be taken literally, but rather as oracles given in the name of God. In any case, later Montanists

en, Priscilla and Maximilla, who also prophesied. This was not unique, for the custom of allowing those who were inspired to prophesy was still continued in many regions. What was new was the content of the prophecies of Montanus and his companions, who claimed that a new dispensation had begun with the new revelation given by the Spirit to them. This new revelation did not contradict what had been given in the New Testament, but surpassed it in the rigor of its ethics and in certain eschatological details.

The Montanist code of ethics was very rigorous, and was in fact a protest against the ease with which the rest of the church forgave sinners, as well as against the progressive adaptation of the church to the requirements of secular society. Regarding martyrdom, they opposed the traditional view that it was not to be sought, but rather avoided if it was possible to do so without denying the faith. Marriage was not totally evil, but it was not seen as a great good, and widows and widowers were not allowed to remarry.[50]

This code was based in an imminent eschatological expectation. According to Montanus and his two prophetesses the period of revelation had come to an end with them, and immediately thereafter the end of the world would come. The New Jerusalem would be established in the town of Pepuza in Phrygia—and many Montanists gathered there in order to witness the great events of the final days.

Montanus and his followers were good organizers who saw no contradiction between the new revelation of the Spirit and good ecclesiastical organization. Therefore, they soon adopted a hierarchical structure, and the church that was thus founded rapidly spread

identified Montanus with the Holy Spirit. See Jaroslav Pelikan, "Montanism and Its Trinitarian Significance," *CH*, 25 (1956), 100-104. The general thesis of the whole article (pp. 99-109), that Montanism was of less significance in the development of trinitarian doctrine than is usually supposed, is correct. The contribution of Montanism was mostly in drawing attention to the Holy Spirit.

[50] Hans Lietzmann, *The Founding of the Church Universal* (New York: Scribner's, 1950) pp. 260-61 claims that the early Montanists rejected marriage. If such is the case, Tertullian's opposition to remarriage must reflect a later stage in the development of Montanism.

throughout Asia Minor, and later to Rome and Northern Africa, where it was able to gain the adherence of Tertullian, who was without any doubt the most remarkable Latin Christian theologian of his time. Therefore, one should not interpret Montanism as a protest against the excessive organization of the church, and in favor of a purely charismatical structure. Furthermore, in its origin Montanism does not seem to have advocated a return to the practice of prophecies, but claimed rather that Montanus and his two prophetesses had received a special and final revelation, so that one was not to expect that the prophetic spirit would be extended to the rest of Christians. It was only at a later time that Montanists in general, attempting to imitate their founders, claimed the gift of prophecy.

The reasons why other Christians opposed Montanism were twofold: practically, Montanism weakened the emerging structure of the church, which to many seemed necessary to oppose the various heresies; theologically, the Montanist claim of having received a new revelation endangered the finality of that given in Christ.

Monarchianism

While many were turning to Gnosticism in order to find what they thought was a clear understanding of Christianity, others were attempting to clarify the relations between the Father, the Son, and the Holy Spirit. The earliest mentions of the so-called Monarchians show that originally this term was used in defense of the "monarchy" or unity of God over against the multiplicity of aeons and the duality of gods proposed by the Gnostics and by Marcion. Some of the earliest Monarchians—who were called "alogoi" by reason of their opposition of the doctrine of the logos—rejected the Fourth Gospel, which they claimed had been written by Cerinthus, and whose doctrine of the logos seemed to serve as a basis for the various Gnostic speculations regarding multiplicity within the divinity. According to the alogoi, the divinity of Christ cannot be distinguished in any way from that

146

of the Father, for such distinction would destroy the divine monarchy.[51]

After the first and rather obscure alogoi, two unrelated doctrines developed that attempted to safeguard the unity of God. These doctrines are usually called Dynamic and Modalistic Monarchianism.

In spite of its inadequacy, the term "Dynamic Monarchianism" is traditionally used to refer to the attempt to preserve the divine unity by claiming that the divinity that was in Christ was an impersonal power proceeding from God but was not God himself. It is called "dynamic" by reason of the Greek term *dynamis,* which means "power" or "force" and which was employed to refer to the impersonal power that dwelt in Christ. The earliest known person to have held this doctrine was Theodotus, who refused to give Jesus the title of God, and from whom the Dynamic Monarchians are often called "Theodotians." [52] This sect or school—condemned by the church in Rome since A.D. 195—was continued by Artemon, who attempted to support it on the basis of Scriptures and of an older tradition that he said had been abandoned by his contemporaries.[53] But its greater exponent was Paul of Samosata, whose doctrines will be studied further on.[54] Although Dynamic Monarchianism did have some followers during the third and fourth centuries, it was not widespread enough to pose a real threat to the church. Its Christology was too close to that of the Ebionites, turning Christ into little more than a mere man, and this diminished its allurement among Christians.

There was, however, another doctrine that also emphasized the unity of God and that at the same time did not in any way limit the divinity of Jesus Christ. This doctrine is usually called "Modalist Monarchianism"—although one must make clear that the common

---

[51] Irenaeus, *Adv. haer.* 3. 11; Epiphanius, *Pan.* 51.

[52] There seem to have been two men of the same name who held this doctrine. The first seems to have come from Byzantium to Rome late in the second century. The other was a Roman, and probably a follower of the first Theodotus.

[53] Eusebius, *HE* 5. 28; Augustine, *Conf.* 7. 19. See James Franklin Bethune-Baker, *An Introduction to the Early History of Christian Doctrine to the Time of the Council of Chalcedon* (London: Methuen & Co., 1903), pp. 99-100.

[54] Chap. X.

name of monarchianism does not mean that there was any direct rela-tionship between this doctrine and that of "Dynamic Monarchian-ism," to which in fact it was radically opposed.

Modalist Monarchianism did not deny the full divinity of Christ, but simply identified it with the Father. Because of that identification, which implied that the Father had suffered in Christ, this doctrine is sometimes called "Patripassianism." Its most ancient teachers seem to have been Noetus of Smyrna[55] and Praxeas,[56] an obscure person whom some have identified with Pope Callistus. Although Christian writers attempted to refute Modalism from a very early date, they were not able to destroy it. Early in the third century, it found its greatest teacher in Sabellius, from whom it also took the name of Sabellianism. It is impossible to know precisely what Sabellius himself taught;[57] but he probably denied all distinctions within the Godhead, which he called "Son-Father" (*hyiopatōr*), and affirmed that the Son and the Spirit were simply modes in which God appeared—much as the sun appears in its rays—for the purposes of redemption and inspiration.[58]

As was to be expected, these diverse doctrines and attempts to un-derstand the Christian faith in various ways served as a challenge and a point of departure for the great theological development of the sec-ond and third centuries, and were among the main factors that gave impulse to the great theologians who flourished at that time. But

---

[55] Hippolytus, *Contra Noetum*, passim.

[56] Tertullian, *Adversus Praxeam*, passim. See Raniero Cantalamessa, "Prassea e l'eresia monarchiana," *SCatt*, 90 (1962), 28-50.

[57] "Unfortunately, we are very badly informed on his authentic doctrine: we know sufficiently well what his disciples said, and the authorities of the fourth century present under the name of Sabellianism a rather complex doctrine, which in several points approaches that of Marcellus of Ancyra." E. Amann, "Monarchianisme," *DTC*, 10: 2201-2202. The main sources are Hippolytus, *Philos.* 9. 11-12; Epiphanius, *Pan.* 62, 69.7 (where Arius is quoted on the subject); Athanasius, *Orat. contra Ar.* 3. 4. 36; Ps.-Athanasius, *Orat. contra Ar.* 4, in several scattered references.

[58] Sabellius probably did not use the term *prosōpon* in the sense of "mask" to refer to the Father, Son, and Holy Spirit, but rather spoke of all three as one *prosōpon*. It was later, when it became clear that the *prosōpon* could be understood as outward appearance, that orthodox theologians accused of Sabellianism those who spoke of three prosopa.

before we turn to those theologians we must attempt to outline some of the means by which the church at large attempted to refute and to counteract the various systems that it saw as a threat to its faith.

The Response

Although the organization of the church during the second century was not such as to allow it to make quick and final decisions, the church at large reacted to the heresies in a surprisingly uniform way. There were indeed differences of schools—and in the next three chapters we shall study representatives of three different theological tendencies—but, in spite of these differences, orthodox Christians throughout the Mediterranean world appealed to similar instruments in order to combat heresy. In truth, these various instruments were simply practical and particular variations of the fundamental argument that could be adduced against the various heresies: apostolic authority. That authority is the final argument that lies behind such antiheretical instruments as the New Testament canon, the rule of faith, the creeds, and the emphasis on apostolic succession. The canon of the New Testament was supposed to be no more than the collection of the apostolic books, or at least of those whose doctrine could claim to be apostolic because they were written by the companions or disciples of the apostles. The rule of faith is an attempt to outline and summarize the faith of the apostles. The creeds are the expression of that faith which the believer accepts in his baptism—and it is important to note that the legend soon developed according to which one of the most common of those creeds had been composed by the apostles. The importance of apostolic succession is precisely in the claim that the churches that possess such a succession can judge what is and what is not apostolic doctrine. Finally, those theologians whom we shall study in the next three chapters, and a large part of whose work was devoted to the refutation of heresy, believed that their task consisted in clarifying and affirming the faith of the apostles, and that their various arguments and methods were subsidiary to that task.

Because of the challenge of heresies, as well as the normal development of human movements, the church during the second century moved toward a fixed and more uniform organization, and this gave rise to what is usually called the "Old Catholic Church." What marks the beginning of this Old Catholic Church—whose difference from the apostolic and sub-apostolic church is not to be exaggerated—is precisely the appearance of the various antiheretical instruments that we have already mentioned and whose direct consequence is a general tendency toward uniformity. Therefore, we must pause to consider at least the first stages in the development of these instruments, and their relationship with the struggle to preserve the purity of the faith.

The first of these antiheretical instruments which we shall discuss here is the emphasis on apostolic succession. As was to be expected, the apostles, and later their disciples, had a great authority over the early generations of Christians. Already late in the first century, Clement of Rome appealed to apostolic succession, although not against heresies but against schismatics.[59] A few years later, Ignatius of Antioch, now against heretics, emphasized the authority of the bishops and the elders as representatives of Christ and his apostles. Thus, Clement appealed to succession without even mentioning monarchical episcopacy, while Ignatius appealed to the authority of the bishops without mentioning the matter of succession. Soon the impact of heresies led Christians to join the ideas of apostolic succession and of monarchical episcopacy, and thus began the emphasis on the uninterrupted chain of bishops who unite the present church with apostolic times. According to this argument—which soon became generally accepted doctrine—the apostles were the depositaries of the true faith, which they communicated to their best disciples, whom they also made their successors in the episcopacy of the churches that they founded. These disciples of the apostles did the same with their own disciples, and so on successively, so that even in the second century it is possible

---

[59] Other contemporary indications of the growing authority of the apostles may be found in the New Testament. Eph. 2:20; Rev. 21:9-14.

to point to churches that can prove that their bishops are direct successors of the apostles. Although these churches are only a few, for the apostles did not found many churches, they are the true depositaries of the faith. But other churches are also apostolic, for their faith agrees with that of those founded by the apostles.

What we have just summarized is that which may be found in early antiheretical writers such as Irenaeus and Tertullian. But one must point out that at this time the understanding of apostolic succession was still not such that succession is required to confer validity to the episcopal office. On the contrary, some bishops had that succession and others did not have it; but all their churches were apostolic because their faith agreed with the faith of the apostles as it had been preserved in churches whose bishops were in their succession. Later, and through a development that would take several centuries, this doctrine of apostolic succession would be developed to a point that would never be recognized by those who first advocated it.

The canon of the New Testament was another instrument that the church used in its struggle against heresy. This instrument has the peculiarity of having been taken from the heretics themselves, for the first New Testament canon seems to have been that proposed by Marcion. However, while the church may have taken from Marcion the idea of a canon or a fixed list of inspired Christian books, it did not take from him the notion of the existence of such books. On the contrary, from its very beginning the Christian church adopted the Old Testament as its Scriptures, and at an early date there were Christian writings that were used as Scripture together with the Old Testament. As was to be expected, the Gospels, which contained the very words of Jesus, were soon placed side by side with the Old Testament. Justin Martyr is a witness to this when he says that in Christian worship portions are read from the writings of the prophets or from the "memoirs of the apostles"—as he calls the Gospels.[60] Therefore, what the church took over from Marcion was not the concept of canonical

---

[60] *I Apol.* 57. 3.

literature, but rather the impulse that led it to determine which of the many Christian books should be considered as part of Scripture. Furthermore, even that process is not to be attributed exclusively to Marcion, for other heretics, with their constant production of books that claimed to be inspired, made it necessary to determine which books were to be counted as Scripture and which were not to be so counted. It took centuries for the New Testament canon to reach its final form; but its basic outline was fixed during the second half of the second century. After that time the general structure of the New Testament was accepted as composed of "gospels" and "apostles," following perhaps the example set by Marcion. Although after the middle of the second century the inclusion of the Fourth Gospel in the canon was still debated, as is shown by its warm defense by Irenaeus,[61] after that time the fourfold witness to the gospel was accepted.[62] Quite possibly the various gospels were included in order to show that the faith of the church was not based on the witness of single apostles, as was claimed by Marcion and some Gnostics.

As to the "apostles," the book of Acts and the Pauline epistles enjoyed great authority from the time of their publication. Marcion's canon did not include Acts; but it did include the Pauline epistles. After that time, all the lists of sacred books that have survived include Acts as well as the Pauline epistles. The Pastoral Epistles, probably composed early in the second century in order to combat heresy, were soon added to the genuine epistles of Paul. Hebrews was first included in Alexandria, where its doctrine and general point of view found more sympathetic hearing than in other circles. As to the universal epistles of James, Peter, John, and Jude, their acceptance was neither unanimous nor uniform. The first to have been universally accepted seems to have been the First Epistle of John. The others appear in some lists but are absent in others. The same may be said regarding Revelation, which took some time to be accepted universally

---

[61] *Adv. haer.* 3. 11. 8.

[62] It is noteworthy that Tatian's *Diatessaron*, which attempted to provide a unified Gospel, used the four canonical Gospels and no others.

because of the suspicion with which some sectors within the church regarded apocalyptic thought.

There were also other writings which, although eventually excluded from the canon of the New Testament, were taken for inspired at certain times and places. Such are Clement's *First Epistle to the Corinthians, Second Clement,* the *Epistle of Barnabas,* the *Didache,* the *Shepherd* of Hermas, the *Acts of Paul,* and other writings of the same period.

In any case, what interests us here is not the history of the canon itself,[63] but how that history reflects the response of Christians to the challenge of heresy. The canon took centuries to reach its definitive form, and there is no list of books written before A.D. 367 which exactly agrees with the actual canon. But the idea itself of a canon appears and is firmly established in the second century as a response to the need of finding norms to distinguish the "apostolic doctrine" from the many heresies that claimed to be founded on the authority of an apostle.

However, emphasis on apostolic succession and the formation of a New Testament canon were not enough to determine whether a doctrine was apostolic or not. Apostolic succession could guarantee a certain measure of continuity, and it was a very valuable norm, but it did not include an exposition of the correct doctrine. The New Testament, on the other hand, did expound that doctrine, but it did so in such an extensive and unsystematic way that it by itself was not enough for a quick and definitive recognition of unorthodox doctrine. It was therefore necessary to develop a systematic summary of the faith of the church—a summary of such a nature that it could serve to distinguish clearly between that faith and the various doctrines that modified or supplanted it. It was that need which gave rise to the idea of a *rule of faith,* and which at the same time increased the importance of the creeds as a proof of orthodoxy.

---

[63] See Frank W. Beare, "Canon of the NT," *IDB,* 1: 520-32; Edgar J. Goodspeed, "The Canon of the New Testament," *TIB,* 1:63-71; L. Vischer, "Kanon: II, Kirchengeschichtlich," *RGG,* 3: 1119-22.

While the New Testament was being formed, the Roman church was developing a formula that would later become the nucleus of our present Apostles' Creed, and that is usually known as the "Ancient Roman Symbol"—abbreviated by "R." It seems that R first appeared, not as an affirmative formula, but as a series of questions that were asked of the catechumen at his baptism.[64] These questions were three, following the very ancient tripartite formula of baptism, and at first were limited to asking the candidate for baptism whether he believed in the Father, in the Son, and in the Holy Spirit.

Soon the Roman church saw the increasing need to use these questions as a manner of assuring the orthodoxy of the newly baptized. As the point at issue had to do mostly with Christology, several clauses were added to the second question. Thus developed a baptismal formula that must have been very similar to that which is quoted by Hippolytus in his *Apostolic Tradition* (early in the third century):

> Dost thou believe in God the Father almighty?
> Dost thou believe in Christ Jesus, the Son of God,
> Who was born by the Holy Spirit from the Virgin Mary,
> Who was crucified under Pontius Pilate, and died,
> and rose again on the third day living from the dead,
> and ascended into the heavens,
> and sat down on the right hand of the Father,
> and will come to judge the living and the dead?
> Dost thou believe in the Holy Spirit, in the
> holy Church, and in the resurrection of the flesh? [65]

This baptismal formula was later adapted in order to serve as an affirmation of faith and as the basis and culmination of the catechism. Thus was established the practice of the *traditio et redditio symboli,* in

---

[64] Here we follow John Norman Davidson Kelly, *Early Christian Creeds* (London: Longmans, Green & Co., 1950), pp. 100-130, regarding the original interrogative form of R. But we depart from him in his effort to deny the importance of antiheretical concerns in the formation of R.

[65] Kelly, *Creeds,* p. 114.

which the bishop taught the symbol or creed to the catechumen, who then repeated it as an affirmation of faith.[66]

Although already in Tertullian we find a text that seems to reflect a certain knowledge of a similar formula to that quoted by Hippolytus,[67] it is in the fourth century, with Marcellus of Ancyra[68] and Rufinus of Aquileia,[69] that we find the first uses of R as a clearly affirmative formula. On the basis of the witness of Marcellus and Rufinus, the following text of R as it existed in the fourth century has been reconstructed:

I believe in God the Father Almighty (*pantokratora*); and in Christ Jesus his only-begotten son, our Lord, who was born of the Holy Spirit and the virgin Mary, who under Pontius Pilate was crucified and buried, in the third day rose from the dead, ascended unto the heavens, and sat at the right of the Father, from whence he shall come to judge the living and the dead; and in the Holy Spirit, the holy church, the remission of sins, and the resurrection of the flesh.[70]

It will readily be seen that the transformation of R since the time of Hippolytus to that of Rufinus and Marcellus is practically nil as far as its content is concerned—the main addition being the clause that refers to the forgiveness of sins—while, in its form, the interrogatory formula has become affirmative. The absence of great changes in its content show that already early in the third century the nucleus of R was taken as a fixed formula. Furthermore, given the conservative character of Hippolytus, it is not too daring to say that the text that he quotes is probably much more ancient, and that by A.D. 170 or 180 the basic traits of R had been fixed.

---

[66] On the origin of the term "symbol" as a name for the Creed, see Kelly, *Creeds*, pp. 52-61.

[67] *De virg. vel.* 1. Note, however, that in this text the clause on the Holy Spirit is missing.

[68] Quoted by Epiphanius, *Pan.* 72. 3.

[69] *Comm. in symbolum, passim.*

[70] Translated from the Greek and Latin texts as reconstructed by Arthur Cushman McGiffert, *The Apostles' Creed: Its Origin, Its Purpose, and Its Historical Interpretation* (New York: Scribner's, 1925), pp. 42-43.

As to its structure, R is simply a development of the ancient tripartite series of baptismal questions.[71] This development was greater with reference to the christological question, for what was at issue in the second century was above all the Christology of the church.

The antiheretical—and especially anti-Marcionite—purpose of R is evident from the manner in which it repeatedly denies Gnostic and Marcionite views. The fact that the terms that it uses are earlier than the heresies that it combats should not be a reason to deny its antiheretical purpose. What actually seems to have happened is that the church, being convinced that it was defending traditional apostolic doctrines, used traditional terms in order to refute the innovations of the heretics.

In the first clause, the union of the term "Father" and "Almighty" is significant. The Greek term[72] that is here used—and there is no doubt that Greek was the original language of R—in order to describe the nature of God does not mean simply "almighty" in the sense that he has power to do anything that happens to be his will, but means rather "all-governing." This means that the God who rules this physical world in which we live is also God the Father, and that therefore it is not possible to distinguish between a spiritual world in which God reigns and a material world that exists apart from the divine will—in contrast to what was being affirmed in Rome at that time by Marcion and Valentinus.

There is no doubt that the second clause has a marked antiheretical interest. In the first place, the possessive adjective, "his," [73] establishes even more clearly the identity between the Father of Jesus Christ and the God who rules this world—an identity that Marcion would deny. Then, the reference to Mary, "the virgin," which excluded the Ebionites, also served to point out that Jesus was born of a woman and of a particular woman—a doctrine that most Docetists did not accept.

---

[71] A development in which it is possible that a previously independent christological formula was appended to the second clause of the trinitarian formula.

[72] παντοκράτωρ.

[73] τὸν υἱὸν αὐτοῦ.

The reference to Pontius Pilate serves to establish a date and to underline the historical nature of the crucifixion and burial of Christ. Finally, the clause on the judgment contradicts Marcion's doctrine of the contrast between the just God of the Old Testament and the loving and forgiving God of the New.

The mention of the Holy Spirit in the third clause is earlier than the formation of R; but the mention of the resurrection of the flesh probably has an antiheretical purpose. The Gnostics as well as Marcion rejected the doctrine of the resurrection and preferred to speak of the immortality of the human spirit.

Beginning late in the second century, and much more frequently during the third, the "rule of faith" is mentioned repeatedly by Christian writers. The first to use this term is Irenaeus.[74] But the fact that very soon thereafter it appears also in Clement of Alexandria, writing practically at the other end of the Mediterranean world,[75] shows that the idea of a rule of faith had been circulating for some time. In modern times, some scholars have identified this rule of faith with some primitive form of the Creed—or of various creeds. This identification does not seem to be justified, for the variations to be found in this rule of faith from one writer to another, and even within the works of a single author, are too great to allow one to believe that there was a fixed formula behind them. One can illustrate this situation with the case of Tertullian, in whose work three different expositions of the rule of faith may be found.[76] One of them, it is true, is very similar to R; but the fact that the other two do not even follow the same order shows that, although Tertullian saw in R—or in some other creed of the same family—an adequate summary of the rule of faith, that rule was not exactly the same as that creed. Therefore, it seems possible to say that the rule of faith was not a fixed text, which it was necessary to repeat word by word, but that it was rather a sum-

---

[74] *Epideixis* 3.
[75] The references may be found in Richard Patrick C. Hanson, *Tradition in the Early Church* (London: SCM Press, 1962), p. 77.
[76] *Adv. Prax.* 2; *De praes.* 13; *De virg. vel.* 1.

mary of the fundamental contents of the Christian message, probably underlining those aspects of that message which the heretics denied.

This way of understanding the rule of faith as a fluctuating summary of the basic events of the history of salvation would explain why in various regions of the Empire the rule of faith was essentially the same, but at the same time reflected the influence and tendencies of each school, and even of each theologian. Thus, Irenaeus includes his doctrine of recapitulation in the "rule of faith"; Tertullian, his doctrine of the new law; and Origen, the distinction between the various meanings of Scripture.[77]

Thus, the challenge posed by heresy provoked a series of reactions that would have great consequences for the future life of the church. The creed, the New Testament canon, and the doctrine of apostolic succession are three of those reactions.[78] It is quite possible that all these would have eventually developed even without the challenge of heresy. But there is no doubt that during the second century the various attempts by Christians to understand their faith in ways that seemed to most other Christians to deny the truth of the gospel was the catalytic agent that led to the development of these new phenomena.

On the other hand, the challenge posed by heresies drew another response whose consequences were also great: theological activity. The thoughts and the pens of many Christians were stimulated by the challenge of those who attempted to show that other versions of Christianity were more reasonable than the traditional one, and thus

---

[77] Hanson, *Tradition,* pp. 91-92.

[78] One should point out, however, that the various antiheretical instruments that have been discussed here were not applied independently from each other, but rather corrected and complemented one another. Thus, for instance, the rule of faith was sometimes used to determine the spuriousness of a book that claimed to be written by an apostle—if the doctrine of the book did not agree with the rule of faith, its author could not have been an apostle—and the authority that bishops had as successors of the apostles was also used in order to refute the scriptural interpretations of heretics. Therefore, these various instruments, which we have separated here for their brief study, had an organic unity in the minds of those who used them.

many theological works were produced whose influence went far beyond the direct denial of heresy.

These antiheretical writers who flourished late in the second century and early in the third were exponents of various theological traditions. In Gaul lived Irenaeus, a native of Asia Minor, who represented that type of theology which we have already seen in the earlier writers from Asia Minor. Tertullian in Carthage, while drawing from Irenaeus, was also an exponent of the practical and moral interests that we have earlier seen in the Western church. Finally, Clement and Origen, whose theological activity was centered in Alexandria, reflected the intellectual atmosphere of that city.

VI

Irenaeus

During the second century many Christians undertook to refute the various doctrines in which they saw a threat to their faith. As has already been said, Justin wrote *Against All Heresies* and *Against Marcion,* and Theophilus of Antioch wrote *Against Marcion* and *Against Hermogenes.* All these works, as well as many others that the historian Eusebius mentions, have been lost. Therefore the earliest antiheretical author whose works have survived is Irenaeus of Lyon.

Very little is known of the life of Irenaeus. He seems to have been born in Asia Minor—probably Smyrna—in approximately A.D. 135. There he knew Polycarp of Smyrna, although he must have been a young man when the aged bishop ended his life in martyrdom. Later—probably around A.D. 170—he went to Gaul and settled in Lyon, where there was a Christian community some of whose members were also immigrants from Asia Minor. In A.D. 177, when he was a presbyter in that community, he was entrusted with a letter to the bishop of Rome. Upon returning from his mission, he found that the bishop of Lyon, Pothinus, had suffered martyrdom, and that he was to be his successor in the episcopate. As bishop of Lyon, Irenaeus led the church in that city, evangelized the Celts who lived in the region, defended his flock against heresy, and sought peace and unity in the church.[1] This last concern led him to intervene in the Paschal controversy when Victor, the bishop of Rome, was about to break communion with the churches of Asia Minor over a disagreement regarding the date for celebrating Easter.[2] However, what gave Irenaeus his great importance for the history of Christian thought was his struggle against heresy and his concern to strengthen the faith of Christians, for these were the reasons that led him to write his two surviving works. As to his death, it is said that he died as a martyr, although no more details are given. He probably died in A.D. 202, when many Christians were killed in Lyon.

The two surviving works of Irenaeus are his *Denunciation and Refutation of the So-called Gnosis* and his *Demonstration of Apostolic Preaching*. His other works, which were several, have been lost.[3]

The *Denunciation and Refutation of the So-called Gnosis*, usually known as *Adversus haereses*, consists of five books of which the Greek original has been almost entirely lost; but there is an entire Latin translation[4] and an Armenian version of the last two books.[5]

In the first book of *Adversus haereses*, Irenaeus simply expounds the doctrines of the Gnostics, and "especially of the disciples of Ptolemaeus"—who was a disciple of Valentinus. His presupposition here is that Gnosticism is senseless and that its attraction is so based on its supposed secrets that the mere exposition of Gnostic teaching is in itself a victory over it.[6] In this exposition, Irenaeus pays more atten-

---

[1] But see: Bertrand Hemmerdinger, "Saint Iréné évêque en Gaul ou en Galatie?" *RevEtGr*, 77 (1964) 291-92; Jean Colin, "Saint Irénée était-il évêque de Lyon?" *Lat*, 23 (1964), 81-85; Sante Rossi, "Ireneo fu vescovo di Lione," *GItFil*, 17 (1964), 239-54.

[2] See Marcel Richard, "La lettre de saint Irénée au Pape Victor," *ZntW*, 56 (1965), 260-81.

[3] A list of his works may be seen in Albert Houssiau, *La christologie de saint Irénée* (Louvain: Publications Universitaires, 1955), pp. 3-5.

[4] This Latin translation is literal to the point of violating Latin grammar, and has therefore been subject to attempted corrections by copyists. See Sven Lundström, *Studien zur lateinischen Irenäusübersetzung* (Lund: C. W. K. Gleerup, 1943).

[5] The use of this Armenian translation is the most valuable characteristic of the new edition published by *SC*.

[6] See the *praefatio* and the last two paragraphs of Book 1.

161

tion to Valentinus and his disciples than to the other Gnostics, although he does make a list of the principal Gnostic teachers and attempts to establish the relationships between them.[7] The reason for his concentration on the system of Valentinus was that he had first felt impelled to write his work when he learned that a friend of his had been lured by Ptolomaeus' Gnosticism; but in any case he feels that by refuting one Gnostic system he has refuted all, for, as he says, "it is not necessary to drink up the ocean in order to learn that its water is salty." [8]

In his second book, Irenaeus tries to refute Gnosticism on the basis of common sense. Here he attacks the doctrines of the Pleroma and aeons with an implacable logic, although without attempting to develop a speculative alternative. Humor is not altogether lacking. As in the first book, most of the space is dedicated to Valentinus and his disciples, and it is only toward the end of the book that Irenaeus attempts to make his refutation extend to other Gnostic systems.[9]

Finally, the last three books are devoted to a refutation of Gnosticism on the basis of Scriptures. At first Irenaeus had hoped to include this in his second book; but he later found it necessary to devote three separate books to the subject. In general, his use of the Old Testament in these three books is reminiscent of Justin's doctrine regarding "prophecies" and "types." The doctrines that Irenaeus was attacking tended either to a rejection of the Old Testament or to its adulteration by means of allegorical interpretation. They claimed that redemption was radically discontinuous with creation, and that there was therefore a definite opposition between the God of the Old Testament and the Supreme God. Over against this, Irenaeus tries to show the continuity between the events of the Old Testament and those of the New—a concern that often leads him to what modern scholars would call typological exegesis.[10]

---

[7] *Adv. haer.* 1. 23-31.

[8] *Ibid.*, 2. 19. 8.

[9] On his polemical methods, see Bruno Reynders, "La polémique de saint Irénée: Méthode et principes," *RThAM*, 7 (1935), 5-27.

[10] See, for instance, *Adv. haer.* 4. 20. 7-25. 3; *Epid.* 43-51.

The originality of Irenaeus in the *Adversus haereses* has been disputed. There have been attempts to distinguish the various sources that Irenaeus is supposed to have used, and thus to discover his own contribution.[11] Because of the almost total lack of points of reference outside the works of Irenaeus himself, these attempts are not wholly convincing.[12] In any case, there is no doubt that Irenaeus does not claim to be an original theologian, but rather sees himself as an exponent of the church's doctrine and as one of its defenders against the heresy of the Gnostics. In some instances, it is clear that Irenaeus is using arguments that he has taken from a different context.[13] But in spite of this there is a unity in his theology, given, not by a systematic principle, but by certain concerns and themes that appear repeatedly in his works.

The *Demonstration of Apostolic Preaching,* usually called *Epideixis,* is a catechetical work, although with some apologetic undertones.[14] Its purpose is not the training of catechumens, but the strengthening in the faith of those who are already believers. As anti-Gnostic polemics are not foremost here, this work is more systematical than *Adversus haereses,* although even here one would seek in vain an original and daring theology. Irenaeus is an exponent of the doctrine that he has received from the church, and has no desire to be considered an original or speculative theologian.

The *Epideixis* starts out by a confession of faith that Irenaeus then expounds, first systematically (chapters 3-7), and then historically (chapters 8-42a). The rest of the work (chapters 42b-97) attempts to prove on the basis of Scripture the faith that has been expounded

---

[11] The most important of these attempts is that of Friedrich Loofs, *Theophilus von Antiochien Adversus Marcionem und die anderen theologischen Quellen bei Irenaeus* (Leipzig: J. C. Hinrichs, 1930).

[12] F. R. M. Hitchcock, "Loofs' Theory of Theophilus of Antioch as a source of Irenaeus," *JTS,* 38 (1937), 254-66 has shown some of the weaknesses of Loofs' study.

[13] A clear instance is *Adv. haer.* 3. 22. 1, as is shown by Houssiau, *Christologie,* p. 13. Here Irenaeus makes use of an anti-Ebionite argument that proves that Christ was born of a virgin in order to argue against the Gnostics that Christ had a human origin.

[14] Only an Armenian version has been preserved. There is an English translation by Joseph P. Smith (*ACW,* 16).

earlier. Finally, the conclusion (chapters 98-100) repeats the purpose of the work, which Irenaeus hopes will be also the purpose of his readers: to flee from unbelievers and defend the correct doctrine against heresy, in order to achieve salvation.

In attempting to expound Irenaeus' theology, one should keep in mind that we are not dealing with a systematic theologian who derives all his conclusions from a few speculative principles. Therefore, rather than attempting to discover the ruling principle of that theology, it is best to follow the same order that Irenaeus suggests in his *Epideixis*: to start with the Creator and then to pursue the history of salvation up to its final consummation.

The god of Irenaeus has existed from the beginning, and created all things out of nothing.[15] Irenaeus is interested in creation because it has great implications for the world and for man. Valentinian Gnosticism as well as many other doctrines then current attempted to absolve God from the responsibility of having made this world with its matter and its imperfections. In order to do this, Gnosticism developed long series of aeons that stood between the supreme deity and the error from which the world originated. This was also the reason why Marcion distinguished between the God and Father of Jesus Christ and the Creator of the world. Over against this, Irenaeus flatly affirms and repeats that the God of our salvation is the same as the God of our creation.[16]

All things have been created by God, and none can exist against his will. Even the Devil has been created by God, and his present power is only temporal and limited. Even here and now, it is not Satan but God who rules the world. The Devil may rebel and upset the order of divine creation, but even then God rules over all things.[17]

God has created and rules this world by means of his two "hands": the Son and the Holy Spirit. Most of the texts in which Irenaeus refers to the doctrine of the Trinity are too brief to allow historians to draw

---

[15] *Adv. baer.* 2. 10.
[16] *Ibid.*, 4. 6. 2; 4. 20. 2.
[17] *Ibid.*, 5. 24.

conclusions regarding that doctrine. Irenaeus bypasses the more subtle aspects of trinitarian doctrine and simply affirms, as he must have heard from his fathers in the faith, that God is Father, Son, and Spirit, without discussing the relationships between the three.[18] Here he makes use of the doctrine of the Word as well as of his own metaphor of the two hands of God. However, when he speaks of the Son as "Word of God," he does not use that term as referring to an intermediate being between God and the world, as Justin had done, but rather emphasizes the unity between God and his Word. The same may be said regarding the hands of God—the Son and the Holy Spirit—which are not intermediary beings between God and the world, but are God himself as he relates to the world.[19]

This triune God created man according to his image.[20] But man himself is not the image of God; that image is the Son, in whom and by whom man has been created. "As the image of God hath He made man; and the 'image' is the Son of God, in whose image man was made." [21] Therefore, the image of God is not something to be found in man, but is rather the direction in which we are to grow until we attain "to mature manhood, to the measure of the stature of the fullness of Christ" (Eph 4:13 RSV). This idea of growth is important for an understanding of Irenaeus.[22] According to him, Adam was not created as a perfect man in the sense that he was all that God called him to be, but was rather created so that he could develop and grow in that image of God which is the Son. Irenaeus has no place for an original state of man in which Adam, gifted with powers far above

---

[18] Antonio Orbe, *Hacia la primera theología de la procesión del Verbo* (Rome: Gregorian University Press, 1958), pp. 114-43, is right in claiming that Irenaeus never affirms the eternal generation of the Word. His trinitarian doctrine is "economic" in the sense that it is developed in terms of God's dealing with the world rather than in immanent terms.

[19] See Jean Mambrino, "Les *Deux Mains de Dieu* dans l'oeuvre de saint Irénée," *NRT*, 79 (1957), 355-70.

[20] Erik Peterson, "L'homme, image de Dieu chez saint Irénée," *VieSpirit*, 100 (1959), 584-94.

[21] *Epid*. 22 (*ACW*, 16:61).

[22] Charlotte Hörgal, "Die göttliche Erziehung des Menschen nach Irenäus," *NDid*, 13 (1963), 1-28.

our own, wandered in Paradise. For him, Adam was only the beginning of God's purpose in creation. Adam was "like a child," whose purpose was to grow unto a closer relationship with God. Furthermore, that growth was not something to be achieved by Adam on his own power, but was rather part of the continuing creation of God.[23]

As a creature of God with the purpose of growth, man is free. This freedom is not understood in idealistic terms, but is simply the possibility of fulfilling God's purpose. Adam's freedom was in no way incompatible with the divine omnipotence, but was rather its result and expression.[24]

However, creation was followed by the fall of Satan and of man.[25] Like man, angels were created by God, although they were not made with the purpose of growth, but were created in their full maturity. This provoked Satan's envy, and he therefore tempted man, not to oppose the purpose of creation, but rather to accelerate the purpose that God had ordained and thus to disrupt the order established by God. When Satan said to man, "You will be like God," he was simply affirming God's purpose in creation. But when man succumbed to temptation he broke the divine plan and thus became a slave of sin and death.

Although the relationship between God's power and that of the Devil has been mentioned, it is necessary to insist on this subject, for it is fundamental for an understanding of the theology of Irenaeus. The opposition between God and the Devil is not fictitious. The Devil is really opposed to God's plans, and he even manages to upset them. Furthermore, he is able to achieve undeniable, although partial and temporary, victories. But there is no doubt that God will triumph in the end. And even now, it is God who rules the world, although in it the Devil makes every effort to detain God's plans. In his struggle

---

[23] *Epid.* 12. Cf. Gustaf Wingren, *Man and the Incarnation* (Philadelphia: Muhlenberg Press, 1959), pp. 26-38.
[24] *Epid.* 11.
[25] *Ibid.*, 16.

against the Devil, God is Lord even of the very instruments that the Devil employs. Finally, in the consummation, all things will be subjected to God and the Devil will be destroyed. Meanwhile, the struggle continues, and the promised victory does not make the present battle less real.

As to man, by his fall he was made a servant of the Devil. The opposition between God and Satan is such that man has to be subject to one of the two, and in the garden Adam gave himself up to Satan. Therefore, man is a slave of the Devil, which means, first, that his growth has been interrupted and, second, that he is now held by the two powers of Satan: sin and death.

One should note here that this understanding of the Fall as an interruption in man's development is very different from what later became common in Western theology. According to Irenaeus, the Fall is not so much the loss of certain perfections that man had as the interruption of what ought to have been his growth.[26]

Although sin and death are the Devil's instruments to which man has succumbed in becoming a servant of Satan, God's power is such that even these diabolic instruments can be used to achieve his ends. Thus, death serves as a limit to man's sinful possibilities, and his enslavement to sin is an occasion for man to acknowledge God's goodness and to praise him for his grace.[27]

In spite of the Fall, God does not abandon man, but rather loves him continually. In so doing, God is simply carrying forward his plan, which he had conceived from the beginning.[28] This plan or dispensation (οἰκονομία) is a single one, but is made manifest in a series of particular covenants that culminate in Christ.[29] These covenants are

---

[26] See Wingren, *Man and the Incarnation*, pp. 50-63.

[27] *Adv. haer.* 3. 23. 6.

[28] A. Verriele, "Le plan du salut d'apres saint Irénée," *RevScRel*, 14 (1934), 493-524; K. Prümm, "Göttliche Plannung und menschliche Entwicklung nach Irenäus Adversus Haereses," *Sch*, 13 (1938), 206-24.

[29] See André Benoit, *Saint Irénée: Introduction a l'étude de sa théologie* (Paris: Presses Universitaires de France, 1960), pp. 219-27, especially his emphasis on the unity of the divine *oikonomia* in opposition to Gnosticism.

four, and they succeed one another in chronological order. The first is
that of Adam, and it lasted until the flood; the second is that of Noah,
and extended until the Exodus; the third is that of Moses, which
ended with the advent of Christ. The fourth covenant is that of
Christ, which will continue until the end of time.[30] Of these covenants, Irenaeus only develops his thought regarding the last two: that
of the Law and that of Christ.

The Law was given by God as part of his loving plan, in order to
restrain the sinfulness of man. Obedience to the Law is not the final
end of man. The Law creates a form of servitude, different from and
opposed to that of sin, it is true, but which is still far below the freedom that man requires in order to fulfill the purpose of his creation.
This is why the Law itself promises the establishment of a new covenant that will surpass it. The Law is not only a rule, but also a
promise; and therefore it itself implies that the time of its validity will
come to an end. However, as the Law has been given by God as a
means to lead men toward the fulfillment of his will, and as that will
never changes, the law cannot be completely abolished. Its heart—the
moral law, and especially the Decalogue—still demands our obedience,
although that obedience is now different from what it was when the
Law itself was in vigor. On the other hand, the ancient rites of ceremonial Law have been abolished by the advent of Christ, for their
purpose was to announce the coming of the Savior. Thus Irenaeus
emphasizes the unity—of continuity as well as of fulfillment—between the Old Testament and the New, and thereby rejects
the teachings of those who attempt to establish a radical opposition
between both Testaments.[31]

Christ is the center of Irenaeus' theology. He is the basis for the
continuity between creation and redemption—a continuity that most
heretics denied. Man was made by the same God who now in Christ

---

[30] *Adv. haer.* 3. 11. 8. Compare the Latin version (which we follow here) with the extant
Greek fragment.

[31] See Jean Daniélou, "Saint Irénée et les origines de la théologie de l'histoire," *RScRel,*
34 (1947), 227-31.

offers him salvation. In Christ, that image according to which and for which man was made has come to dwell among men. This is the work of Christ, which Irenaeus calls "recapitulation." [32]

Recapitulation is one of Irenaeus' fundamental doctrines, and it is necessary to understand it in order to understand his theology.[33] The term "recapitulation" has various meanings in ancient writers,[34] and Irenaeus himself uses it in more than one sense.[35] But the principal and characteristic meaning of the term "recapitulation" in Irenaeus is that which sees in it the best way to express the work of Christ as head of a new humanity.

Although God's plan for the redemption of mankind was operating from the very beginning, that plan finds its greatest and final expression in the recapitulation of all things by Christ which began in the incarnation. Before that time, while it is necessary to affirm that the Son was present in God's actions, one cannot speak of a recapitulation in the strict sense. Recapitulation is a summary and culmination of what has happened before, and it can only be understood within the context of those previous events.

To a certain extent, Christ's recapitulation is a new starting point; but it is also closely related with what went before it. Although the incarnation is a new beginning in the history of the world, it is not opposed to creation, but is rather its continuation and fulfillment. Christ is the new Adam, and in him the history of the old Adam is repeated, although in an opposite direction. In Adam, man had been created to be like the Son, and in Christ the Son takes humanity unto himself. As a man, Christ is all that Adam should have been had he not suc-

---

[32] recapitulatio, ἀνακεφαλαίωσις.

[33] Emmeran Scharl, *Recapitulatio mundi: Der Rekapitulationsbegriff des heiligen Irenäeus und seine Anwendung auf die Körperwelt* (Freiburg im Breisgau: Herder, 1941); R. Potter, "St. Irenaeus and Recapitulation," *DomSt*, 3 (1951), 192-200.

[34] The earliest use of the term in Christian literature is in Eph. 1. 10. Irenaeus quotes a text of Justin in which the term may appear; but it is impossible to determine where the quotation ends, and therefore whether the phrase where the term appears is part of Justin's quotation or of Irenaeus' comments. See J. Armitage Robinson, "On a quotation from Justin Martyr in Irenaeus," *JTS*, 31 (1930), 374-78.

[35] See Houssiau, *Christologie*, pp. 216-24.

cumbed to temptation. Christ is the new point of departure in which man, who in Adam had given himself over to the Devil, is once again free to grow in the image that is the Son. It is for this reason that Irenaeus emphasizes the parallelism between Adam and Christ. Adam was formed from the virgin soil, and Christ came to the world through Mary, the virgin; the Fall of man took place through the disobedience of a woman, and the obedience of another woman was the occasion for his restoration; Adam was tempted in Paradise, and Jesus in the desert; through a tree did death enter into the world, and through the tree of the cross has life been given unto us.[36]

Another fundamental aspect of Christ's recapitulation is his victory over Satan. Irenaeus sees the whole history of salvation as the struggle between God and the Devil, which will end in God's final victory. In Adam, man had made himself a subject of the Devil, and therefore Christ's recapitulation involves a victory over Satan, and our consequent liberation. In Adam, Satan managed to alienate man from that image of God for which he had been created. In Christ, that very image is united to man, and thus the Devil's purposes are overthrown. Therefore, the initial victory of Christ is not his resurrection but his incarnation. When God is united to man Satan suffers the first of the great defeats that will lead to his final destruction.

Irenaeus does not discuss the union of divinity and humanity in Christ as if these were two opposed natures.[37] On the contrary, man was created to enjoy union with God, and in Christ that union achieves its highest goal. Furthermore, God and man in Christ are not understood as two "substances" or "natures." It is rather that in Christ divinity is united to humanity because he is the Word that God addresses to man, and is also the man who responds to that Word. In thus making use of dynamic rather than substantialist concepts, and in not defining the divine nature in opposition to the human, Irenaeus avoids the difficulties that would later give rise to bitter christological controversies.

---

[36] A list of references would be endless. The best is probably *Epid.* 31-34.
[37] See Wingren, *Man and the Incarnation,* pp. 100-112.

God's incarnation in Christ is only the beginning of his victory over evil. The whole life of Christ is part of the work of recapitulation, which now continues until the final consummation. After being united to man, the Son of God must live a human life and die a human death. His temptation in the desert is another decisive victory over Satan, who is unable to achieve the Fall of this new Adam.[38] Throughout his life and ministry, living the totality of a human life,[39] Christ saves that life from its ancient servitude to the power of Satan. In his death and resurrection, he makes use of the most formidable weapon of evil, death itself, in order to conquer the empire of Satan. The final fulfillment that we now await—when all things will be subjected to him—will be Christ's last victory over the Devil. Meanwhile, we who live between the resurrection and the consummation are not living in a period of truce in this struggle of centuries, but are living precisely at the time in which Christ is making effective his victory on the cross, in order to lead us to the final day.

The church has an important role in this work of recapitulation. Just as in Adam all sinned because Adam was the head of humanity, in Christ the whole church overcomes Satan because Christ is the head of the church. Although Christ has overcome the Devil, and thus has returned to man the possibility of growing until he achieves the plenitude of God's image, that possibility is given only in the body whose head is Christ. The church is Christ's body, and in her he advances his work of recapitulation through baptism and the eucharist by which man is united to Christ himself.

Although Irenaeus does not devote to baptism as much attention as he does to the eucharist, there is no doubt that he sees in baptism in the name of the Father, the Son, and the Holy Ghost the starting point of Christian life. Baptism is "the seal of eternal life," and it is also "rebirth unto God, that we be no more children of mortal men,

---

[38] *Adv. haer.* 5. 21. 2.

[39] This seems to be the reason why Irenaeus prefers the tradition according to which Jesus lived fifty years on earth. *Adv. haer.* 2. 22.

but of the eternal and everlasting God." [40] Through baptism, man becomes a part of that new humanity which is the body of Christ, and thus comes to share in the resurrection of the head of that body, Christ the Lord.

As the *adversus haereses* does not claim to be a systematic exposition of Christian doctrine, Irenaeus discusses the eucharist only in order to refute heresies, and especially in order to contradict their contempt for flesh and for matter. Therefore, we have no detailed and orderly exposition of his eucharistic theology.[41] However, one can draw some conclusions regarding this matter from the polemical texts of the *Adversus haereses*.[42] According to Irenaeus, in the eucharist the members of the body of Christ are nourished by him, being united to their Lord and sharing in his life and his blood. In drinking of the cup and eating of the bread, the believer is nourished by the body and the blood of Christ in such a real way that he can trust in his final resurrection, because the body and the blood that he has taken are immortal.[43] In the eucharist, furthermore, Christ tells us that creation is not to be despised, for he himself uses bread and wine, which are part of creation, as nourishment for those who believe in him.

On the other hand, the church can only fulfill this work of uniting men to Christ if it is really his body, and for this reason it must keep and teach the correct doctrine, and it must preserve the unity of the body. Hence Irenaeus' zeal in attacking those whom he considered heretics: they are a threat, not simply to this institution which is called "church," but also to the effectiveness of the work of Christ, for they teach false doctrines and divide the body of believers. Therefore, Christians must be firm in the doctrine that they have

---

[40] *Epid.* 3 (*ACW*, 16:49).

[41] Oddly enough, in spite of the importance that the eucharist seems to have had for Irenaeus, he does not discuss it in the *Epideixis*.

[42] *Adv. haer.* 4. 18. 4-5; 5. 2. 2-3. It is in the first of these texts that the very debated phrase appears: "eucharistia ex duabus rebus constans, terrena et coeleste." See: H. D. Simonin, "A propos d'un texte eucharistique de saint Irénée," *RScPhTh*, 23 (1934), 281-92; Damien van den Eynde, "Eucharistia ex duabus rebus constans," *Ant*, 15 (1940), 13-28.

[43] *Adv. haer.* 5. 2. 3.

received. It is at this point that Irenaeus introduces the doctrine of apostolic succession,[44] which was a very useful instrument in the early centuries of Christianity and which later would be the subject of many controversies. The norm by which error is to be distinguished from truth is the doctrine that has been received from the apostles. Supposing that the apostles had some secret knowledge, as the Gnostics claim, they would not have communicated that knowledge to other men than those whom they trusted enough to appoint them leaders of the churches which they founded, that is, the bishops. These in turn would have done likewise, entrusting the true doctrine to those who would succeed them. Therefore, the Gnostics lie when they claim to have a secret doctrine that their teachers received from one or another of the apostles.[45]

The significance of Irenaeus as a theologian is much greater than would seem to follow from the brevity of the foregoing. His theology, grounded in the Bible and the doctrine of the church rather than on his personal opinion, has repeatedly been a source of theological renewal.[46] Because of the wide cosmic views that follow from his doctrine of the divine plan and of recapitulation in Christ, he may be said to have been among the first Christian writers to seek the theological meaning of history.[47] His chronological position between the imme-

---

[44] Henri Holstein, "La tradition des Apôtres chez saint Irénée," *RScRel*, 36 (1949), 229-70; Einar Molland, "Irenaeus of Lugdunum and the Apostolic Succession," *JEH*, 1 (1950), 12-28.

[45] *Adv. haer.* 3. 3. The second paragraph of this chapter, where Rome is mentioned, has been and is debated by scholars. It seems safe to say that the text is hopelessly ambiguous, and that no definitive conclusions may be reached regarding its significance for the issue of Roman primacy. Among the many studies on the subject, see: H. Katsenmeyer, "Petrus, der Primat, die Kirche in den auf uns gekommenen Schriften des Bischofs Irenäus von Lyon, der 'Widerlegung und Abwehr der falschen Gnosis' und der 'Darlegung der apostolischen Verkundigung,'" *IntkZtschr*, 56 (1948), 12-28, 82-88; Jean Colson, "L'union des évêques et l'évêque de Rome aux deux premiers siècles de l'Église," *VieSpirit*, Suppl. 4 (1950), pp. 181-205; Dominique J. Unger, "St. Irenaeus and the Roman Primacy," *ThSt*, 13 (1952), 359-418. Unger's article includes ample bibliographical references to other studies.

[46] See L. S. Thornton, "St. Irenaeus and Contemporary Theology," *SP*, 2 (1957), 317-27.

[47] My friend and former student, Luis N. Rivera, in a doctoral dissertation presented at Yale (1970), has shown how the divisive tendency of Gnostic theology regarding God, man,

diate successors of the apostles and the catholic church of the third and fourth centuries places him at an important crossroads in the history of Christian thought. But it is, above all, his insistence in the unique and cosmic nature of Christianity that has placed him among the greatest theologians of all times.

Jesus Christ, and the Church led Irenaeus to a profound understanding of that unity—of God, man, Jesus Christ, and the Church—which, in a dialectic relationship to truth, is at the base of Irenaeus' theology.

VII

Tertullian

It is interesting to note that the origins of Latin Christian literature are to be found not in Rome but in North Africa. Although the First Epistle of Clement to the Corinthians, which comes from Rome, is one of the most ancient Christian writings, this document was written in Greek. During several centuries Africa, rather than Rome, was the center of Latin Christian thought. It was there that the theological vocabulary of the Western church received its basic shape. And there flourished the most significant Latin Christian writers of the early centuries—men such as Tertullian, Cyprian, Augustine, and others.[1]

Some have identified Tertullian with a lawyer of that name who appears in the *Corpus Iuris Civilis*, although it is not possible to make a final decision regarding that identification. In any case, Tertullian lived in Rome for several years, and after his conversion, which took place when he was about forty years old, he returned to Carthage, where he had been born in about A.D. 150. There he undertook an extensive literary production in favor of his new faith, which he defended against those who persecuted it as well as against those who

---

[1] Although North African Christianity is usually believed to have come from Rome, there are reasons to believe otherwise. It is possible that, founded originally by Christians from the East, the Church in North Africa later developed closer bonds with Rome. W. Telfer, "The Origins of Christianity in Africa," *SP*, 4: 512-17. Cf. E. Buoniauti, *Il cristianesimo nell' Africa romana* (Bari: Laterza, 1928).

seemed to pervert it. However, early in the third century—probably in A.D. 207—he left the communion of the African church in order to become a Montanist. The reasons why he took this step are not clear, but it seems that Montanism embodied for him the spirit of protest against the growing power of the hierarchy and against its supposed laxity in dealing with repentant sinners. It was this aspect of Montanism which appealed to Tertullian, who had always shown an excessive moral rigor.[2]

After his conversion to Christianity, Tertullian wrote several works addressed to the pagans in order to defend his new faith.[3] The most important of these is his *Apology—Apologeticus adversus gentes pro christianis*—written in A.D. 197. Here Tertullian attempts to defend Christianity in a manner that is very reminiscent of a lawyer. Thus, for instance, referring to the famous letter in which Trajan ordered Pliny to condemn those Christians who were accused before him, but not to search those who were not accused, Tertullian writes:

O miserable deliverance,—under the necessities of the case, a self-contradiction! It forbids them to be sought after as innocent, and it commands them to be punished as guilty. It is at once merciful and cruel; it passes by, and it punishes. Why dost thou play a game of evasion upon thyself, O Judgment? If thou condemnest, why dost thou not also inquire. If thou does not inquire, why dost thou not also absolve?[4]

Besides this Apology, Tertullian wrote other works that shed light on the persecutions and the attitudes of Christians before them. Among these one should mention *To the Gentiles, The Testimony of the Soul,* and *To the Martyrs,* which is one of the most exalted ex-

---

[2] H. von Campenhausen. "Urchristentum und Tradition bei Tertullian," *ThBl*, 8 (1929), 193-200; M. S. Enslin, "Puritan of Carthage," *JRel*, 27 (1947), 197-212; Heinrich Karpp, *Schrift und Geist bei Tertullian* (Gütersloh: C. Bertelsmann, 1955); W. Bender, *Die Lehre über den Heiligen Geist bei Tertullian* (Munich: M. Hueber, 1961); cf. Jerome, *De viris illus.* 53.

[3] J. Lortz, *Tertullian als Apologet.* 2 vols. (Münster: Aschendorff, 1927-1928).

[4] *Apol.* 2 (*ANF*, 3: 19).

pressions of the heroic spirit of early Christians. All these were written before Tertullian became a Montanist.

On the other hand, and thus showing his inclination to controversy, Tertullian wrote a long series of polemical works against all sorts of heretics. His *Prescription Against Heretics*—*Liber de Praescriptionibus adversus haereticos*—will be discussed as we attempt to expound Tertullian's theology. The same may be said of his work *Against Praxeas*—*Adversus Praxeam*. His five books *Against Marcion* are the main source from which historians draw their knowledge of the doctrines of that heretic. Besides, Tertullian wrote against Hermogenes, against the Valentinians, and against the Gnostics and Docetism in general. All these works are of fundamental importance for the history of Christian thought, not only as a source for Tertullian's theology, but also as a source for the controversies that took place toward the end of the second century and the beginning of the third.

Finally, Tertullian wrote several works of a moral and practical nature. Some of these were written before he became a Montanist, such as *On penance, On patience,* and *To His Wife.* Others are written from a Montanist point of view, such as *On Monogamy, On Fasting, On Modesty,* and the *Exhortation to Chastity.* All these writings reflect Tertullian's rigorism, although, as was to be expected, this is more clearly manifested in his Montanist works. In any case, these documents are of great importance for the information that they provide regarding the moral life and the worship practices of Christians in Tertullian's time. When historians attempt to reconstruct the development of Christian liturgy or the history of Christian customs, Tertullian proves to be an invaluable source of information. However, that which is of interest to us here is his theology, especially inasmuch as he inherits certain aspects of that theology from earlier thinkers, and at the same time announces that which was to come.

The sources for Tertullian's theology are to be found in Christian tradition, in the legal training that he probably had, and in his philosophical background. There is no doubt that a great deal of Tertullian's theology has been drawn directly from Christian tradition such as it is found in the Greek apologists, in Irenaeus, and in Hermas. As far as his legal background is concerned, Tertullian never left it behind: his arguments do not seek to convince as much as to overwhelm; when he seems to be cornered by his opponents, he weaves his way out by rhetoric; for him, the gospel is a new law; his argument in defense of Christianity is a legal argument; the same may be said regarding his basic argument against the heretics; and some scholars have claimed that his trinitarian doctrine is expressed in legal terms. Finally, although Tertullian explicitly and repeatedly rejects every intrusion of philosophy in matters of faith,[5] it is a fact that—probably without even knowing it—he himself is often influenced by Stoicism,[6] and he even speaks so highly of Seneca that he almost contradicts his general rejection of pagan philosophy.[7]

Tertullian is above all a practical and concrete thinker. None of his works was written for the mere pleasure of writing or speculating, but with a definite and practical purpose. Among these works, probably the best introduction to his thought is his *Liber de praescriptionibus adversus haereticos,* which we shall henceforth call the *Praescriptio.*

In Roman legal practice, a *praescriptio* was an argument that a party in a trial presented, not usually referring to a particular aspect of the trial, but to the proceedings themselves. Thus, the *praescriptio* is often an objection that affirms that the opposite party is out of order, and that the proceedings should not continue.[8] Therefore, when Tertullian wrote a *Prescription against heretics* he was not trying to discuss the doctrines themselves of the heretics, but was rather at-

---

[5] A. Labhart, "Tertullien et la philosophie ou la recherche d'une 'position pure'," *MusHelv,* 7 (1950), 159-80.

[6] C. de L. Shortt, *The Influence of Philosophy on the Mind of Tertullian* (London: Elliot Stock, 1933); F. Seyr, "Die Seelen-und Erkenntnislehre Tertullians und die Stoa," *CommVind,* 3 (1937), 51-74.

[7] *De anima,* 20.

[8] See the various interpretations of J. L. Allie, "Nature de la prescription ou des prescriptions dans le De praescriptione." *RUOtt,* section spéciale, 6 (1937), 211*-25*, 7 (1938), 16*-28*; L. De Witte, "L'argument de prescription et Tertullien," *Collect. mechlin.,* 25 (1936), 239-50; and J. K. Stirnimann, *Die Praescriptio Tertullians im Lichte der römischen Rechts und der Theologie* (Fribourg, Switzerland: Paulus Verlag, 1949).

tempting to deny them the very right to argue against the orthodox.

The first seven chapters of the *Praescriptio* deal with heresies in general, and claim that one is not to marvel at their existence, for the New Testament fortells their coming, and they serve to strengthen the faith of believers, who see the words of Scripture being fulfilled. In any case, heresies spring not from faith, but rather from philosophy. They are simply the ancient errors of the philosophers transposed to the level of faith, for the philosophers as well as the heretics ask the same questions regarding the origin of evil and of man. The confusion of philosophy with revelation results in an unfaithfulness to the latter, for "what indeed has Athens to do with Jerusalem? What concord is there between the Academy and the Church? What between heretics and Christians?" [9]

This text, as well as the following one from his treatise *On the Flesh of Christ,* have been the main reasons why Tertullian has been accused of being anti-intellectual:

The Son of God was crucified; I am not ashamed . . . *of it.* And the Son of God died; it is by all means to be believed, because it is absurd. And He was buried, and rose again; the fact is certain, because it is impossible.[10]

But the truth is that Tertullian is not a blind irrationalist. He does believe that there are things that are simply too wonderful to be understood, such as the crucifixion or the power of baptism. But this is not a general claim that belief has to be based on rational impossibility.[11] He rather believes that unrestrained speculation can lead far afield, and that the actual revelation of God is what is really im-

---

[9] *De praes. haer.* 7 (*ANF*, 3: 246).

[10] *De carne Christi,* 5 (*ANF*, 3: 525). See also *De bapt.* 2, and the comments of B. Leening, "Note on the Reading in Tertullian's *de Baptismo,* 'Credo quia non credunt'," *Greg,* 14 (1933), 423-31.

[11] Etienne Gilson, *La philosophie au moyen âge* (Paris: Payot, 1944), pp. 97-98; F. Refoulé "Tertullien et la philosophie," *RevScRel,* 30 (1956), 42-45; Vianney Décarie, "Le paradoxe de Tertullien," *VigCh,* 15 (1961), 23-31.

portant to the Christian. This may be seen in the following text, in which he is refuting the argument of Praxeas that the Father, being omnipotent, could become the Son:

We must not, however, because He is able to do all things suppose that He has actually done what He has not done. But we must inquire *whether he has really done it*. God could, if He had liked, have furnished man with wings to fly with, just as He gave wings to kites. We must not, however, run to the conclusion that He did this because He was able to do it. He might also have extinguished Praxeas and all other heretics at once; it does not follow, however, that He did, simply because He was able. For it was necessary that there should be both kites and heretics; it was necessary also that the Father should be crucified.[12]

The seven chapters that the *Praescriptio* devotes to error are followed by seven others that deal with the nature of truth. Christian truth is such that, once it has been found, there is no reason to seek further. This truth has been given to the church once and for all in Jesus Christ, and the believer's task is simply to accept it, without a vain curiosity that can only lead to error.

The core of the argument of the *Praescriptio* appears in Chapter 15, where Tertullian affirms that every discussion with heretics on the basis of Scripture is out of order, for heretics have no claim on the sacred texts. From this point on, the real argument of the book unfolds, affirming that the Scriptures belong to the church and that only she may use them. Scriptures, as well as the true doctrine—summarized in the rule of faith—were given by the apostles to their successors, and by them to their own successors and so on until the present. The heretics are unable to prove that they are the legitimate successors of the apostles, whereas the church can prove her claim to that inheritance. In Corinth, in Philippi, in Thessalonica, in Ephesus, in Smyrna, and in Rome there are churches that were founded by the apostles and that can show the succession that links the apostles with the present

---

[12] *Adv. Prax.* 10 (*ANF*, 3: 605).

bishops. All these churches teach the same doctrine, and even those which were not founded by the apostles are apostolic, for their doctrine is the same.[13] The orthodox church can show this succession and this unity of doctrine, and on this ground it can claim the Scriptures as her undivided inheritance. The heretics cannot do the same, for they are upstarts and they teach new doctrines. Therefore, they have no right to appeal to Scripture. Here Tertullian makes use of the *praescriptio longi temporis*, according to which the use of a property for a prolonged period eventually gave the user a legal right. Thus, according to this type of *praescriptio*, the church that has always made use of the Scriptures is the only one that now has the right to use and interpret them.

Tertullian's argument is overwhelmingly final. If the heretics have no right to use the Scriptures, it becomes impossible for them to discuss with the orthodox in order to draw them from the true faith. The *praescriptio* is total: the heretics are excluded from every discussion, and only the orthodox and apostolic church has the right to determine that which is Christian doctrine and that which is not.[14]

However, a short time after writing this defense of the authority of apostolic churches and of their exclusive right to interpret the Scriptures, Tertullian himself broke with those churches and became a Montanist. Although this was in no way a break with orthodoxy, Tertullian now found that he needed to undertake precisely that type of argument against the heretics which the *praescriptio* would seem to have excluded. Once one denies the final authority of the apostolic churches, the argument of the *praescriptio* loses all its power, and it is necessary to refute the heretics in another way.[15] This was one of the

---

[13] *De praes. haer.* 32.

[14] The exact place of Rome within the framework of Tertullian's theology is subject to various interpretations. Cf. H. Koch, "Zu Tertullian *De pudicitia* 21, 9 ff.," *ZntW*, 31 (1932), 68-72; W. Köhler, "Omnis ecclesia Petri propinqua," *ZntW*, 31 (1932), 60-67) H. Stoeckius, "Ecclesia Petri propinqua: Eine kirchengeschichtliche Untersuchung der Primatsfrage bei Tertullian," *AkathKrcht*, 117 (1937), 24-126; Berthold Altaner, "Omnis ecclesia Petri propinqua," *ThR*, 38 (1939), 129-38. The text that is at the heart of this discussion is *De pudicitia* 21. 9.

[15] In *De praes. haer.* 44, Tertullian had already promised a further refutation of various

reasons why Tertullian wrote some of his most significant works, among them his *Against Praxeas*.

Nothing is known about Praxeas. It seems that he came from Asia Minor, where he had come to know Monarchianism as well as Montanism, and had accepted the former and rejected the latter. In coming to Rome, he was made welcome, and he then took a hand in combating Montanism and in spreading Monarchianism in that city. This is why Tertullian says that Praxeas "did a twofold service for the devil at Rome: he drove away prophecy, and he brought in heresy; he put to flight the Paraclete, and he crucified the Father." [16]

Tertullian's treatise *Against Praxeas* is significant because some of its phrases and terminology seem to foreshadow what would be generally accepted formulas centuries later. This is so in that which refers to trinitarian doctrine as well as in that which refers to Christology.

In order to respond to the claims of Praxeas, Tertullian develops his trinitarian doctrine, making use of the juridical terminology of his time.[17] According to him, Praxeas affirms that the distinction between the Father and the Son destroys the "monarchy" of God, but does not realize that the unity of the monarchy does not require that it be held by only one person.[18] The "monarchy," that term which

---

heresies. But, if one takes his *praescriptio* seriously, these refutations would not be as extensive and detailed as they became after he joined the Montanists.

[16] *Adv. Prax.* 1 (*ANF*, 3: 597). There is some doubt as to whether Praxeas existed at all. This name may well be Tertullian's veiled way to refer to Noetus of Smyrna or Callistus of Rome.

[17] Not all scholars agree on the importance of legal terminology for a correct interpretation of Tertullian. Hans Rheinfelder, *Das Wort "Persona": Geschichte seiner Bedeutungen mit besonderer Berück sichtigung des französischen und italienischen Mittelalters* (Halle: H. Niemeyer, 1928) follows this interpretation, which stems from Harnack. Against this view, see H. C. Dowdall, "The Word 'Person,'" *ChQR*, 106 (1928), 229-64, and Ernest Evans, "Tertullian's Theological Terminology," *ChQR*, 139 (1944-45), 56-77. See also Th. L. Verhoeven, *Studiën over Tertullianus' Adversus Praxeam, voornamelijk betrekking hebbend op monarchia, oikonomia, probola in verband met de Triniteit. Proefschrift* (Amsterdam: Noord-Hollandsche Uitgevers Maatschappij, 1948).

[18] See Antonio Quacquarelli, "L'antimonarchianesimo di Tertulliano nell 'Adversus Praxeam,'" *RScF*, 3 (1950), 31-63; Th. Verhoeven, "*Monarchia* dans Tertullien, *Adversus Praxeam*," *VigCh*, 5 (1951), 43-48.

is so cherished by Praxeas and his followers, means simply that a government is one, and does not prevent the monarch from having a son or from managing his monarchy as he pleases. Furthermore, if the Father thus wishes, the Son may share in the monarchy without thereby destroying it. Therefore, the divine monarchy is no reason to deny the distinction between Father and Son, as is claimed by "the simple, indeed, I will not call them unwise and unlearned," who deny this distinction.[19]

But this does not suffice to refute Praxeas, for it is necessary to explain how it is possible that the Father, the Son, and the Holy Spirit be one God and that they, however, be different. Here Tertullian appeals once again to his legal background and introduces two terms that the church would continue using for many centuries: "substance" and "person." "Substance" is to be understood here, not in its metaphysical, but rather in its legal sense.[20] Within this context, the "substance" is the property and the right that a person has to make use of it. In the case of the monarchy, the substance of the Emperor is the Empire, and this is what makes it possible for the Emperor to share his substance with his son—as was in fact common in the Roman Empire. The "person," on the other hand, is to be understood as "legal person" rather than in its usual sense. The "person" is one who has a certain "substance." It is possible for several persons to share one substance, or for one person to have more than one substance—and this is the core of Tertullian's doctrine regarding not only the Trinity, but also the person of Christ.

On the basis of this concept of substance and person, Tertullian affirms the unity of the Father, the Son and the Holy Spirit without denying their distinction: the three share in a single and undivided substance, but this does not prevent them from being three different persons,

---

[19] *Adv. Prax.* 3 (*ANF*, 3: 598)
[20] However, as has been stated in n. 17, scholars do not agree on this point.

three, however, not in condition, but in degree; not in substance, but in form; not in power, but in aspect; yet of one substance, and of one condition, and of one power, inasmuch as He is one God, from whom these degrees and forms and aspects are reckoned, under the name of the Father, and of the Son, and of the Holy Ghost.[21]

However, when one seeks to discover the exact meaning of the terms with which Tertullian points to the unity of God (*status, substantia, potestas*), as well as those which point to his diversity (*gradus, forma, species*), one finds that the formula, which seems to be so explicit, is rather ambiguous. *Substantia* may have different meanings, in a scale that goes from being itself or its reality to a man's food, including the legal sense that has been pointed above. The meaning of *status* also varies, and may refer to a mere position such as the social condition of a person, which in legal practice may be the same as his being or substance. Finally, *potestas* refers usually to the external capability of doing something, but may also be applied to the inner nature of a thing. Therefore, the divine unity, which Tertullian seems to have defined with such precision, is still ambiguous. And the same may be said of those terms which Tertullian uses to distinguish between the persons of the Trinity. This is why it is possible to interpret this passage in such a way that the Trinity seems to be an essential unity with secondary distinctions, or to interpret it in such a way that there are three beings whose unity consists in the fact that all three are divine.

When one reads further in Tertullian, it becomes clear that he tends to emphasize the distinction between the persons of the Trinity, even at the expense of their essential unity. In Chapter 9 of this very treatise *Against Praxeas* one finds that "the Father is the entire substance, but the Son is a derivation and portion of the whole," [22] and that the distinction between the Father and the Son means that one is invisible and the other visible.[23] In *Against Hermogenes* we are

---

[21] *Adv. Prax.* 2 (*ANF*, 3: 598).

[22] *Adv. Prax.* 9 (*PL*, 2: 164; *ANF*, 3: 603-4): *"Pater enim tota substantia est Filius vero derivatio totius et portio."*

[23] *Ibid.*, 14.

told further that there was a time when the Son did not exist.[24] These assertions establish between the Father and the Son a distinction that later will be considered heterodox. On the basis of these and other texts Tertullian has been accused of subordinationism.[25] And it is true that there is such a tendency in his thought. But one must remember that the purpose itself of *Against Praxeas* would naturally lead Tertullian to emphasize the distinction between the Father and the Son rather than their unity. Furthermore, it would be unjust to expect in Tertullian a precision that would not appear in the history of Christian thought before long and bitter controversies. For these reasons, his undeniable subordinationist tendencies must not obscure Tertullian's genius in foreshadowing the basic formula that the Western church would adopt for many centuries in order to express the triune nature of God.[26]

Another significant aspect of Tertullian's trinitarian doctrine is his insistence on the divine "economy"—*oeconomia,* a word that he transliterates into Latin rather than translating it from the Greek. According to him, God is one, "but under this dispensation, which we call oeconomia:" [27] that the one God also has a Son. This divine economy is necessary for a proper understanding of the monarchy, for it is under it that God is one. On this basis, Tertullian's doctrine has been characterized as "organic monotheism," [28] that is, a monotheism that is understood in terms of an organic relationship. Perhaps, prop-

---

[24] *Adv. Herm.* 3 (PL, 2: 200): *"Fuit autem tempus cum et delictum et filius non fuit."* This is to be understood in the light of *Adv. Prax.* 5, where Tertullian takes up the ancient distinction between the inner Word (which he calls *ratio*) and the spoken Word (which he calls *sermo*). The first is eternally present in God; the latter—which is also called "Son" and "Wisdom"—was spoken before creation so that all things could be made by him (*Adv. Prax.* 6).

[25] See B. Piault, "Tertullien a-t-il été subordinatien?" *RScPhTh,* 47 (1963), 181-204.

[26] Although the importance of Tertullian's formula has often been denied, it seems to have been clearly shown by J. Moingt, *Théologie trinitaire de Tertullien,* 3 vols. (Paris: Aubier, 1966).

[27] *Adv. Prax.* 2 (PL, 2: 156).

[28] George L. Prestige, *God in Patristic Thought* (London: W. Heinemann, 1936), pp. 97-106. Cf. the critical review of Charles E. Raven, *JTS,* 39 (1938), 89-92.

erly investigated, this aspect of Tertullian's trinitarian theology will be found to be more significant than his use of the terms substance and person.[29]

Tertullian's Christology, whose most fortunate expression is also found in *Against Praxeas*, is above all an anti-Docetic Christology. In all his works there is a clear interest in affirming the reality of Christ's body. For him, the truth of that body is not a mere doctrine, but is the basic point on which all Christian soteriology depends.[30] On the other hand, his opposition to Modalist Monarchianism forces Tertullian to pay attention, not only to the need to affirm the reality of Christ's humanity, but also to the way in which that humanity is related to the Savior's divinity. This is the task that he takes up in chapter twenty-seven of *Against Praxeas*. For this task, he employs the same tools that he had found so useful in discussing the relationship between the Father, the Son, and the Holy Spirit. These tools are the terms "substance" and "person."

It seems that Praxeas and his followers affirmed that it was possible to establish a distinction between the Father and the Son, but that that distinction could only be made with reference to Jesus Christ: the Father is the spirit, and is called Christ; the Son is the flesh, and is called Jesus. Tertullian responds to this by affirming the unity of Jesus Christ, and denying the possibility of distinguishing between Jesus and Christ—an error whose origin he attributes to the school of Valentinus.[31]

But it is not enough to deny the position of Praxeas. One must also try to express the correct doctrine. "This must be the point of our inquiry: How the Word became flesh,—whether it was by having been transfigured, as it were, in the flesh, or by having really clothed

---

[29] Prestige, *God*, p. 111: "It must therefore be concluded that Tertullian and Hippolytus put forward a statement of the eternal relationships of the divine triad which is, apparently, unique in patristic theology." Cf. K. Wölfl, *Das Heilswirken Gottes durch den Sohn nach Tertullian* (Rome: Gregorian University Press, 1960).

[30] *De carne Chr.* 1, claims that heretics deny the reality of Christ's flesh in order to be able to reject the doctrine of resurrection.

[31] *Adv. Prax.* 27.

Himself in flesh." [32] In his answer, Tertullian adopts the second alternative, for it preserves the divine immutability. If one were to say that in Christ the Word has been transformed in order to unite with the flesh, the result would be an intermediate being between the divine and the human—a being that would be neither truly divine nor truly human, but would be, as Tertullian says, a *tertium quid*. Therefore, just as there are in God three persons and only one substance, in Jesus Christ there are two substances[33]—divinity and humanity—both of which belong to a single person.[34] This union is such that the properties of both substances or natures—Tertullian uses both terms—are completely preserved and shown in the actions of Christ. Thus, in such actions one can see the power of God—or, as Tertullian would say, of the spirit[35]—as well as the qualities of the man—or, as he would say, of the flesh.

The property of each nature is so wholly preserved, that the Spirit on the one hand did all things in Jesus suitable to Itself, such as miracles, and mighty deeds, and wonders; and the Flesh, on the other hand, exhibited the affections which belong to it.[36]

This Jesus Christ was born of Mary, who conceived him as a virgin, but whose womb was truly opened in his birth.[37]

---

[32] *Ibid.* (*ANF*. 3: 623).

[33] A doctrine that may well derive from Melito, as is suggested by Raniero Cantalamessa, "Tertullien et la formule christologique de Chalcédoine," *SP*, 9 (1966), 141-42.

[34] Cantalamessa, "Tertullien," pp. 145-48, argues that Tertullian did not use the term "person" in its christological sense, but was simply refuting the doctrine of Praxeas that the one divine person was Christ, united to the flesh in Jesus. The conclusion of this interpretation is that Tertullian did not contribute to the eventual use of the term "person" in christological discussions. It may well be so, for his work in this direction has no trace in other Latin theologians, and Augustine and the West may have come to this use of the term quite independently of Tertullian.

[35] Tertullian sometimes uses the term "spirit" to refer to the Holy Spirit, and at other times uses it to refer to the divinity of Christ.

[36] *Adv. Prax.* 27 (*ANF*, 3: 624). Cf. *De carne Chr.* 5.

[37] *De carne Chr.* 23. Cf. J. A. De Aldama, "La virginidad *in partu* en la exégesis patrística," *Salmaticensis* 9 (1962), 113-53. He also affirms that Christ had brothers. *De carne Chr.* 7.

Another important aspect of Tertullian's theology is his doctrine of the transmission of the soul and of original sin, in which one can see the consequences of his Stoic outlook and its ulterior influence in the formation of Western theology. Tertullian's Stoicism led him to conceive of the soul as well as of God as corporeal beings,[38] and this in turn led him to affirm that the soul was derived from the souls of its parents, just as the body is derived from the bodies of its parents.[39] This doctrine, known as "traducianism," is the basis on which Tertullian affirms that, just as the soul is transmitted from parents to children, so is sin.[40] Thus, original sin becomes an inheritance that children derive from their parents, just as they derive their body. This is certainly not the only way in which original sin may be understood; but, due to a great extent to the influence of Tertullian through Saint Augustine, it has become so common in the West that this is what is usually understood by "original sin." During the Middle Ages, when traducianism was abandoned by most theologians on account of its materialistic implications, the doctrine of original sin as an inheritance was preserved.

What Tertullian has to say with reference to baptism is important for the history of Christian worship, because in his treatise *On Baptism* he offers detailed descriptions of how that sacrament was administered in North Africa in his time. His own view of the efficacy of baptism is rather realistic, and he opens his treatise on the subject by exclaiming: "Happy is our sacrament of water, in that, by washing away the sins of our early blindness, we are set free and admitted into eternal life!" [41]

On the eucharist, he is neither as clear nor as detailed, and there is

---

[38] Tertullian's main source for his treatise *On the Soul* is the physician Soranus of Ephesus. Heinrich Karpp "Sorans vier Bücher und Tertullians Schrift *De anima*," *ZntW*, 33 (1934), 31-47; André Jean Festugière, "La composition et l'esprit du *De anima* de Tertullien," *RScPhTh*, 33 (1949), 129-61.

[39] *De anima* 27.

[40] *De test. animae* 3; *De anima* 40.

[41] *De baptismo* 1 (*ANF*, 3: 669). See also Robert E. Roberts, *The Theology of Tertullian* (London: Epworth Press, 1924), pp. 191-98.

some question as to whether he interpreted it in realistic or in symbolic terms,[42] although probably the posing of the question itself is an anachronism.

The work of Tertullian is of great importance for the history of Christian thought.[43] Although there was already in existence some Christian Latin literature when Tertullian began writing,[44] this literature had not yet developed a terminology capable of expressing the more refined theological issues. It was Tertullian, at least as far as we know, who produced that terminology.[45] In so doing, he did not simply translate terms taken from Greek writers, nor did he only use

---

[42] F. R. M. Hitchcock, "Tertullian's Views on the Sacrament of the Lord's Supper," *ChQR*, 134 (1942), 21-36, sets forth the various possible interpretations, although he himself is inclined to understand Tertullian in symbolic terms.

[43] There are three aspects of Tertullian's theology which have not been discussed in this chapter, but which should at least be mentioned as points of importance for a total understanding of his thought: his theory of penance, his rigoristic ethics, and his eschatology. On penance, see: J. Hoh, "Die Busse bei Tertullian," *ThGl*, 23 (1931), 625-38; C. Chartier, "L'excommunication ecclésiastique d'après les écrits de Tertullien," *Ant*, 10 (1935), 301-44, 499-536; C. B. Daly, "The Sacrament of Penance in Tertullian," *IER*, series V, 69 (1947), 693-707, 815-21; 70 (1948), 731-46, 832-48; 73 (1950), 156-69. On Tertullian's ethics, see: Th. Brandt, *Tertullians Ethik: Zur Erfassung des systematischen Grundanschauung* (Gutersloh: Bertelsmann, 1928). On his eschatology, see: Roberts, *The Theology*, pp. 203-18; H. Finé, *Die Terminologie der Jenseitsvorstellungen bei Tertullian* (Bonn: P. Hanstein, 1958).

[44] Minucius Felix, whom we shall not study here, may have been earlier than Tertullian, as is held by the following: H. J. Baylis, *Minucius Felix and His Place among the Early Fathers of the Church* (London: S.P.C.K., 1928); F. Lavallée, "L'apologétique de L'Octavius," *Mélanges J. Saunier* (Lyon: Facultés catholiques, 1944); E. Paratore, "La questione Tertulliano-Minucio," *RicRel*, 18 (1947), 132-59; Gilles Quispel, "Anima naturaliter christiana," *Latomus*, 10 (1951), 163-69; S. Rossi, "L'*Octavius* fu scritto prima del 161," *GItFil*, 12 (1959), 289-304; S. Rossi, "*Feriae vindemiales e feriae judiciariae* a Roma (a proposito dell' *Octavius* di Minucio Felice)," *GItFil*, 15 (1962), 193-224. On the other hand, see: J. J. De Jong, *Apologetiek en Christendom in den Octavius van Minucius Felix* (Maastricht: Booston en Stols, 1935); H. Diller, "In Sachen Tertullian-Minucius Felix," *Philologus*, 90 (1935), 98-114, 216-39; B. Axelson, *Das Prioritätsproblem Tertullian-Minucius Felix* (Lund: C. W. K. Gleerup, 1941).

[45] His work in this direction did not consist in creating new terms—although a list of such creations may be seen in R. Braun, "*Deus Christianorum*": *Recherches sur le vocabulaire doctrinal de Tertullien* (Paris: Presses Universitaires de France, 1962), pp. 547-48—but rather in fixing the theological use of those already in existence. Cf. Franz Joseph Dölger, "Der Heiland," *AntCh*, 6 (1950), 241-72; J. Moingt, "Une étude du vocabulaire doctrinal de Tertullien," *RScRel*, 52 (1964), 248-60.

the language of the Latin Bible[46] or of the legal profession,[47] but he also imprinted his own personality on that terminology, and through it, on the whole of Latin theology.[48] His legalism, which was already a product of the atmosphere around him, both Christian and pagan, became a further factor strengthening the legalistic inclinations that have been characteristic of Latin Christianity.[49] Some of his sayings—"the blood of Christians is seed," "what has Athens to do with Jerusalem?" "the soul is naturally Christian," etc.—have become part of the common inheritance of cultured Western man. His doctrines regarding apostolic succession, the origin of the soul, and original sin have left a profound imprint on the development of Christian thought. His trinitarian formula greatly anticipated the ulterior development of that doctrine, and to an extent the same is true of his Christology. And all this he was able to achieve in spite of the fact that a great deal of his theological production bears the stamp of his Montanist beliefs.

---

[46] Christine Mohrmann, "Observations sur la langue et le style de Tertullien," *NDid*, 4 (1950-51), 41-54.

[47] A. Beck, *Römisches Recht bei Tertullian und Cyprian: Eine Studie zur frühen Kirchenrechtsgeschichte* (Halle: H. Niemeyer, 1930).

[48] On the direct use of his works by later Christian writers, see Gustave Bardy, "Tertullien," *DTC*, 15: 168-69.

[49] See, however, the objections of E. Langstadt, "Some Observations on Tertullian's Legalism," *SP*, 6: 122-26, who points out that Tertullian's conception of "Law" is not as rigid as ours, and that therefore his "legalistic religion" is not as it has usually been described.

VIII

The School of Alexandria: Clement and Origen

In the last two chapters we have studied two theological positions
that differ in some aspects, but that do have several points of contact.
We turn now to another theological current that was flowing at
the same time as those two, but that was very different from them:
the theology of Alexandria.

At the end of the second century and the beginning of the third,
Alexandria was one of the principal cities of the Empire. Only Rome
and Antioch could rival it in political and economic importance. But
its cultural activity was superior even to that of the capital. Only
twenty-five years after the city was founded—by Alexander the
Great in 332 or 331 B.C.—Ptolemy Soter adorned it with the Library
and the Museum which would make it famous. The Library, whose
directors were among the most remarkable scholars of the world, grew
to the point where it had 700,000 volumes, which made it an arsenal
of knowledge astounding for its time. The Museum, as its own name
proclaims, was dedicated to the Muses, and was a sort of university in
which the most distinguished writers, scientists, and philosophers
gathered and worked. Largely because of these institutions, Alexandria soon became famous as a rich center of knowledge and
wisdom.[1]

---

[1] *CAH*, 7: 142-54; 12: 619-28. See also P. J. G. Gussen, *Het leven in Alexandrië volgens*

On the other hand, the geographical position of Alexandria gave a special flavor to the thought that was developed in that city. This is all the more important because the intellectual work produced in Alexandria was precisely of that type for which the world was athirst. Egypt had been admired by the ancient Greeks, who saw in it a mysterious land, pregnant with hidden wisdom. Besides, all different sorts of doctrines proceeding from the East converged in Alexandria and there formed an eclectic mass. In an earlier chapter it has already been said that long before the beginning of the Christian era there were many Jews in that city, and that they translated their Scriptures and interpreted their religion in a fashion that clearly showed the influence of the local atmosphere. The Jews with their Scriptures were not the only ones who came to Alexandria, but also the Babylonians with their astrology, the Persians with their dualism, and many others with their different and often confused mystery religions.

All these currents, meeting and flourishing in a city that was itself new enough not to have a stern tradition, contributed to make Alexandria the center of a type of thought that seemed to meet the needs of men at that time. It has already been pointed out that the Hellenistic period was characterized by its individualism and its cosmopolitanism—in contrast with the thought and religion of ancient Greece, which focused on the city. The individualism of the times made men listen more attentively to those doctrines which promised them a way to rule their lives and to achieve salvation— whatever that might mean. Cosmopolitanism, on the other hand, gave momentum to the syncretistic tendencies of the times, and prepared certain circles for the reception of eclectic doctrines. Precisely because of the many influences that converged upon it, Alexandria was especially well prepared to produce this type of doctrine. This is why that city, toward the end of the second century, was like a pot boiling with diverse teachings, all of them eclectic in nature: the Gnosticism held by Basilides, the Neoplatonism of Ammonius Saccas

de cultuur-historische gegevens in de Paedagogus (boek II en III) van Clemens van Alexandrië (Assen: Van Gorkum & Co., 1956).

and Plotinus, the Hellenistic Judaism that followed in the tradition of Philo, and—what is most interesting to us—the esoteric and Platonist Christianity of Clement and Origen.

Since we have already studied Hellenistic Judaism, as well as the gnosticism of Basilides and others, we must now offer a brief description of Plotinian Neoplatonism, in order to have a general picture of the intellectual background of the Christian school of Alexandria.[2] Like all philosophers of his time, Plotinus was an eclectic who drew on Plato and Aristotle as well as on Stoicism. His system begins with the ineffable One, which is beyond all essence and every name that could be given to it. From this absolutely transcendent One all that exists comes, although not by an act of creation, but rather by what can best be understood by means of the metaphor of emanation.

Quite clearly, once divinity is conceived in this fashion, creation cannot be conceived of as an act of the will, which would imply a change in the divine essence. Creation takes place in such a way that God remains motionless in the midst of it, without willing it nor consenting to it. It is a process of *emanation*, similar to the manner in which light spreads around a luminous body or heat around a hot one; or, even better, like the perfume which spreads from a body.[3]

This emanation goes forth from the perfect One toward imperfection and multiplicity. First, there is the Intellect (νοῦς), which combines features of Plato's Demiurge and of Philo's Logos. Next, there is the Soul of the World, of which every human soul is a part. Thus an entire hierarchy of being unfolds, and its last level is matter in the sense of the extreme of multiplicity.

Within this framework, man is conceived of as a soul imprisoned

---

[2] Quite clearly, this book can include only the briefest summary of the Neoplatonism of Plotinus. For further reading, the best short introduction is still that of Emile Bréhier, *The Philosophy of Plotinus* (Chicago: University of Chicago Press, 1958).

[3] Nicolás Abbagnano, *Historia de la filosofía* (Barcelona: Montaner y Simón, 1955), 1: 178.

within a body. Thus, our task is to overcome the bonds of our bodies and ascend to that mystical union with the One which is called ecstasy.

Clement and Origen, to whose thought this chapter is devoted, and who were very much indebted to Neoplatonism, serve to illustrate a way of opposing heresies which is very different from that of Irenaeus or Tertullian.[4] That is the reason why their theology is also much wider in scope than an apology or a refutation of heresies. Therefore, this chapter—which might seem exceedingly extended at first sight—is the turning point between two fundamental periods in our history. On the one hand, Clement and Origen were still living in the period of persecutions and Gnosticism—which gives their work a point of contact with the thinkers that have been discussed up to now. On the other hand, their theology is not limited to an apology or to a refutation of heresies, but rather is free to rise in high speculative flights—and this is what makes their work the beginning of a new type of theological activity, with its values and its dangers.

It is difficult to reconstruct the historical development of the School of Alexandria. The traditional interpretation has been that there existed a formal institution that scholars called the "Catechetical School of Alexandria," and which offered, not only the basic teaching that served as a preparation for baptism, but also a higher level of philosophical and theological training. It seems more accurate to say that Pantaenus—of whom very little is known—founded in Alexandria a private school such as those which philosophers commonly had, or the one that Justin had led in Rome. Upon the death of Pantaenus, he was succeeded as head of that school by Clement. When Clement had to abandon Alexandria because of the persecution of Septimus Severus, his school was probably closed. Later, when Origen was eighteen years old, he received the responsibility of preparing candidates for baptism. It was probably at a later time, as his fame grew and many showed an interest in the higher level of knowledge that he could offer them, that Origen founded a new school of higher studies,

---

[4] Harold Arthur Blair, "Two Reactions to Gnosticism," *ChQR*, 152 (1951), 141-58.

similar to that which had been led by Pantaenus and Clement.[5] He then left the catechetical task in the hands of Heraclas. Thus, the term "School of Alexandria" as it is used here does not refer to a particular institution, such as a catechetical school or a center of higher studies. It is used rather in the sense of a theological school or tendency, although one must not forget that this theological school did a great deal of its work through the institutions of catechesis and higher learning which were directed by Pantaenus, Clement, and Origen.

Clement of Alexandria

As all the literary work of Pantaenus—if he did indeed write anything—has been lost, Clement is the first theologian whom we must study in this chapter.

Very little is known about the life of Clement. One may suppose that his parents were pagan, for such was the religion of his youth. He seems to have been born in Athens, where he was educated and where he lived until his conversion. He then set out in a search for wisdom which took him to Italy, Syria, and Palestine, until he met Pantaenus in Alexandria and found in him the guiding light that his spirit needed. He studied and then worked with Pantaenus, whom he succeeded, probably in the year 200. But soon the persecution of Septimius Severus (A.D. 202) forced him to leave Alexandria, and after that his life is even more difficult to follow. One can only say that he visited Cappadocia and Antioch, and that he died some time between A.D. 211 and 216.

Apart from some fragments quoted by later writers, the works of Clement that have been saved for posterity are five: *Exhortation to the Heathen, The Instructor, The Stromata, Who Is the Rich Man That Shall Be Saved?* and *Excerpts from Theodotus.* This last work is really just a series of notes that Clement seems to have gathered for some future project, and is not very helpful for the study of his theol-

---

[5] Jean Daniélou, *Origen* (New York: Sheed & Ward, 1955), pp. 9-20; Manfred Hornschuh, "Das Leben der Origenes und die Entstehung der alexandrinischen Schule," *ZschrKgesch,* 71 (1960), 1-25, 193-214.

ogy, because, among other reasons, it is difficult and at times even impossible to distinguish between that which Clement has taken from Theodotus and his own comments. *Who Is the Rich Man That Shall Be Saved?* is a homily of only secondary value for our purposes, although it does have a measure of interest. The other three works merit a more detailed discussion.

The *Exhortation to the Heathen*—usually called *Protreptikos*—is the first of a series of three works that Clement planned to write, relating each of them with one of the three functions of the Word, who exhorts, leads, and teaches. This is the reason why the first work was to be called *Protreptikos*, that is, the exhorter; the second was to be the *Paidagogos*, the instructor; and the third was to be the *Didaskalos*, the teacher.[6] As an exhorter, the Word invites men to abandon paganism and follow the way of salvation. This is precisely the theme of the *Exhortation to the Heathen*, whose twelve chapters are devoted to attacking the errors of the pagans and inviting the reader to accept the Christian faith. Yet, even in this work of an apologetic character, Clement shows appreciation for the values of Hellenistic culture, and affirms that truth is to be found also in the ancient philosophers and poets.

The Instructor is the second work of this triology, and its purpose is to lead the believer in his Christian life, teaching him certain rules of conduct and freeing him from his passions.

Finally, the *Stromata* does not fulfill the promise that its author had made of completing his trilogy with a work on the function of the Word as teacher. It is impossible to know the reason for this. The two most common explanations are that Clement decided that he was unable to write the systematic work that he had promised, and that the *Stromata* is only a series of notes that Clement was preparing in order to write his third work, which he was unable to do before death claimed him.[7] In any case, it is quite clear that this work is not a

---

[6] *Paid.* 1. 1.

[7] On the various solutions to this problem, see: J. Munck, *Untersuchungen über Klemens von Alexandrien* (Stuttgart: W. Kohlhammer, 1933), pp. 1-126.

systematic study of any kind, but is rather a series of miscellaneous notes, or perhaps something like a tapestry, where the threads of thought come to the surface only to be lost later on without giving the reader any clue as to what has happened to them. It is in this fashion, and with an almost total lack of order and system, that Clement expounds the highest aspects of his doctrine.

The best point of departure for a summary of Clement's theology is the way in which he conceives the relationship between Christian truth and the truth to be found in Greek philosophy. On this point Clement places himself squarely within the tradition of Justin and Athenagoras, and against the attitude of Tatian and Tertullian.

Clement does not doubt that truth can be found in the philosophy of the Greeks, and he offers two different and partially contradictory explanations for the presence of truth in it. He sometimes affirms that the philosophers took their best ideas from the Hebrews.[8] But he also asserts that they knew truth by a direct action of God, in a fashion similar to that by which the Jews received the Law.

> As many men drawing down the ship, cannot be called many causes, but one cause consisting of many;—for each individual by himself is not the cause of the ship being drawn, but along with the rest;—so also philosophy, being the search for truth, contributes to the comprehension of truth; not as being the cause of comprehension, but a cause along with other things, and cooperator; perhaps also a joint cause. And as the several virtues are causes of the happiness of one individual; and as both the sun, and the fire, and the bath, and clothing are of one getting warm: so while truth is one, many things contribute to its investigation. But its discovery is by the Son.[9]

Therefore "the same God that furnished both Covenants [that of the Law and that of Philosophy] was the giver of Greek philosophy to the Greeks, by which the Almighty is glorified among the Greeks." [10]

---

[8] *Strom.* 1. 25; 5. 14. See Thomas Finan, "Hellenism and Judeo-Christian History in Clement of Alexandria," *IrThQ*, 28 (1961), 83-114.

[9] *Strom.* 1. 20 (*ANF*, 2: 323).

[10] *Ibid.*, 6. 5. (*ANF*, 2: 489).

It is the second of these explanations which seems to be the true position of Clement when it comes to the relationship between the truth found in philosophy and that found in Scripture. The other explanation he probably saw as a traditional argument, useful in polemics and perhaps partially true, but which fails to do justice to the greatness of Greek philosophy. As truth is only one, it must be acknowledged as such wherever it is found, and its origin must also be confessed to be one: God.

On this point Clement goes one step beyond Justin. The latter had granted a certain degree of truth to pagan philosophy; he had tried to show that the higher doctrines of the philosophers agreed with the Scriptures; and he had even affirmed the divine origin of that truth which the philosophers had. But Clement claims that philosophy was given to the Greeks with the same purpose with which the Law was given to the Jews: to serve as a handmaiden to lead them to Christ.[11] Furthermore, philosophy is the covenant that God has established with the Greeks,[12] and—just as the Jews have their prophets—there have been under this covenant inspired men such as Homer, Pythagoras, and Plato.[13] Truth is one and comes from God, so that Christians can and must see in philosophy the reflection of the same truth that has been revealed to them. If some fear that this may lead them into error, they lack faith in the power of truth, which can overcome its enemies.[14]

This does not mean, however, that faith is not necessary in order to know truth. It is true that philosophy works mostly on the basis of ra-

---

[11] *Ibid.*, 1. 20.

[12] *Ibid.*, 6. 8.

[13] *Ibid.* 5. 5, 14.

[14] Actually, the difference between Justin and Clement regarding the relationship between philosophy and the Scriptures results from their different circumstances and purposes. Justin writes for unbelievers, and his purpose is to show them that Christianity is rational. Clement writes for believers, and his purpose is to show them the value of philosophy for the Christian life.

tional demonstrations. But even the philosophers agree that it is impossible to prove the first principles upon which every other demonstration is founded. These first principles can be accepted only by an act of the will, that is, by faith. On the other hand, it is not enough to say that faith is the point of departure of knowledge; one must add that knowledge is also necessary for faith. Faith is not a mere guessing or an arbitrary decision as to what principles are true. That decision is made on the basis of knowledge. "Knowledge, accordingly, is characterized by faith; and faith, by a kind of divine mutual and reciprocal correspondence, becomes characterized by knowledge." [15]

The fact that "knowledge is to be believed" is the core of Clement's answer to those who try to develop an autonomous philosophy. The parallel fact that "faith is to be known" is the core of his opposition to the heretics. These latter are like men who cannot distinguish between a true and a false coin, for they do not have the knowledge necessary to make a judgment.[16] If faith is not an arbitrary decision, but makes use of the help that knowledge gives it, the heretics do not have true faith, for their "faith" is based on their own likings and not on the knowledge of Scripture.

Clement never doubts that the Scriptures are inspired by God. His assurance on this point is such that he never develops a theory of inspiration.[17] God speaks in the Scriptures, and the manner in which this fact is related to the men who actually wrote the sacred text is not a problem of primary importance.

What is indeed important is to determine the manner in which God does speak in Scripture, for if one believes that he can find there the literal expression of the Word of God his interpretation will be very

---

[15] *Strom.* 2. 4 (*ANF*, 2: 350). E. F. Osborn, *The Philosophy of Clement of Alexandria* (Cambridge: Cambridge University Press, 1957), pp. 113-74.

[16] *Strom.* 2. 4. Cf. *Strom.* 7. 17, where the heretics are said to have a counterfeit key that does not permit them to enter into truth.

[17] Claude Mondésert, *Clément d'Alexandrie: Introduction à l'étude de sa pensée religieuse à partir de l'Ecriture* (Paris: Aubier, 1944), p. 83.

different from what it would be if he thought that in the sacred text God speaks through allegories or symbols.

As a faithful member of the exegetical tradition that we have already met in the Alexandrian Judaism of Philo and in the Epistle of Barnabas, Clement believes that the allegorical interpretation of Scripture is one of the main instruments of hermeneutics.

For many reasons, then, the Scriptures hide the sense. First, that we may become inquisitive, and be ever on the watch for the discovery of the words of salvation. Then it was not suitable for all to understand, so that they might not receive harm in consequence of taking in another sense the things declared for salvation by the Holy Spirit. Wherefore the holy mysteries of the prophecies are veiled in the parables—preserved for chosen men, selected to knowledge in consequence of their faith; for the style of the Scriptures is parabolic.[18]

However, one must be careful not to exaggerate Clement's proneness to allegorism, for he tries not to abandon the historical sense of Scripture, as has often been done by many an allegorical interpreter. For example, whereas the author of the so-called Epistle of Barnabas thought that a bad angel had led the Jews to interpret the Law literally, Clement says once and again that the Scriptures do have a literal historical sense.[19] This is why, referring to Clement, Claude Mondésert can say that "the Bible is for him . . . the narration of a revelation which has been experienced in history; it is the story, in concrete facts and in personal actions, of the acts of God towards men, and of repeated divine interventions in world history." [20]

In order to keep at once this historical sense of Scripture and the freedom and depth that are born out of allegorical interpretation, Clement proposes the doctrine of the various senses of Scriptures. This doctrine is based on a total cosmological conception that is

---

[18] *Strom.* 6. 15 (*ANF*, 2: 509).
[19] *Ibid.*, 1. 21; 2. 19; 3. 6; 6. 3, 8; 7. 3.
[20] Mondésert, *Clément*, p. 87.

typically Platonic, and according to which the realities of this world are symbols of eternal truths.[21] Just as things in this world are true, but have their greatest value as signs that point to the world of ultimate reality, the historical and literal meaning of the sacred text is true, but that text has its greatest value when it is interpreted as signs or allegories that show the more profound truths of the universe. Every text has at least two meanings: a literal and a spiritual one. This is the basic rule of Clement's exegesis, although sometimes he finds several levels within the spiritual sense.[22]

The literal sense is that which is found directly in the text itself, without attempting to discover any hidden meaning. This does not mean that the literal sense is always that which follows from a literalistic or naïve interpretation of the text, and for this reason it may be more accurate to call this the "first meaning," in contrast with the "further meanings" that may be discovered through allegorical interpretation. There are cases in which this first meaning coincides with the literal sense of the words found in the text. Such is the case in the historical texts of the Old Testament. But there are also instances in which the first meaning is not strictly the literal or naïve one, for such an interpretation would be completely false. This is the case of the many parables, metaphors, and allegories that can be found in Scripture, and whose first meaning is not their literalistic interpretation, but their figurative sense.

This primary meaning of a biblical text is certainly not the highest, and the Christian who hopes to achieve a profound understanding of his faith must not be content with it; but this does not imply that the "first meaning" is unimportant, or that it can be left aside without forsaking biblical truth. On the contrary, the "first meaning" is the point of departure of every other meaning of the text. Especially in the case of historical and prophetic texts, to deny this first and literal sense of Scripture would imply a denial of God's action and promises. There is only one reason that can be adduced in order to deny the

---

[21] *Ibid.*, pp. 131-35.
[22] Cf. *Strom.* 1. 26; 6. 15; 7. 16.

literal meaning of a particular text: that it says something that is un-worthy of God. Thus, for example, the texts that refer to God in anthropomorphic terms must be interpreted in such a way that it is clearly seen that their anthropomorphism is an allegory that points to more profound truths.[23]

In every text there is always one or more "further meanings," beyond and above its primary or immediate sense. These are to be un-covered through allegorical interpretation. The bountifulness of God is such that it would be folly to believe that there can only be one teaching in a particular text. God is so loving and merciful that in the same text he reveals himself to the most ignorant as well as to the wisest of men, speaking to them at different levels that are adequate to the level of perception of each group of believers. Therefore, a Chris-tian who wishes to reach a higher echelon in this philosophy which is Christianity must constantly seek, behind the first or literal meaning of a biblical text, a further sense, of an allegorical or spiritual nature, which can even unfold into several different and valuable interpreta-tions. This doctrine of the various senses of a biblical text is the start-ing point of Clement's allegorical interpretation, which in turn is one of the main characteristics of his theological work. One must bear in mind, however, that his is not a boundless allegorism, nor one that leaves historical truth aside. Clement's allegorical interpretation is usually held within certain limits or exegetical principles, although it is possible to point out some rather unfortunate exceptions to this rule.

The first of these exegetical principles has already been discussed above: allegorical interpretation must not discard the primary mean-ing of the text, except when this meaning is such that it contradicts what is already known of God's character and dignity. Thus, the historical truth to which scriptural texts refer does not disappear. Although Clement often pays so much attention to the higher level that the historical sense is forced into the background, there are many other instances in which the two levels of interpretation are so blended

---

[23] *Strom.* 2. 16.

together that the resulting exegesis is typological rather than allegorical.[24] Thus, for example, the sacrifice of Isaac, while being an undeniable historical event, is also a sign or type that points to the sacrifice of Jesus Christ; and the relationship between these two is not to be found in some allegorical allusion within the text of Genesis, but rather in the structure and even the details of the historical events themselves.

For he [Isaac] was the son of Abraham, as Christ the Son of God, and a sacrifice as the Lord, but he was not immolated as the Lord. Isaac only bore the wood of the sacrifice, as the Lord the wood of the cross. And he laughed mystically, prophesying that the Lord should fill us with joy, who have been redeemed from corruption by the blood of the Lord. Isaac did everything but suffer, as was right, yielding the precedence in suffering to the Word. Furthermore, there is an intimation of the divinity of the Lord in his not being slain. For Jesus rose again after His burial, having suffered no harm, like Isaac released from sacrifice.[25]

Clement's second exegetical principle is that each text must be interpreted in the light of the rest of Scripture. This means primarily that every text must be understood within its proper and immediate context.[26] But Clement understands this exegetical principle in a much wider sense, so that it leads him to rather involved allegorical interpretations. The manner in which he applies this principle is usually to seek other texts in which the same ideas, the same things, the same names, or even the same numbers appear, to see how they are to be understood allegorically in that second text, and then to transpose that sense to the text that he is currently studying.[27] By appealing to various texts in other parts of Scripture, one can discover unexpected things within a particular passage. Naturally, as Clement's critical and

---

[24] Daniélou, *Origen*, pp. 139-73, stresses the typological character of Clement's exegesis. See also his article "Typologie et allégorie chez Clément d'Alexandrie," *SP*, 4 (1959), 50-57.

[25] *Paid*. 1. 5 (*ANF*, 2: 215).

[26] *Strom*. 3. 11.

[27] Mondésert, *Clément*, p. 139.

historical tools were limited by his times, this method resulted in the most extravagant interpretations. However, one should not forget that there is in this principle an attempt to keep allegorical interpretation within the framework of biblical thought. As an example of the manner in which Clement applies this principle, one can quote the text in which, in order to clarify the meaning of the sixth chapter of the Gospel of John, where Jesus tells his disciples that they must eat his body and drink his blood, Clement appeals to Genesis 4:10, where God says to Cain: "The voice of your brother's blood is crying to me from the ground." On the authority of this latter text, Clement claims that in biblical language "blood" is a symbol for the Word, and that therefore the blood to which the Lord refers is none other than the Word himself.[28]

One of the main characteristics of Clement's theology springs from the distinction between several levels of meaning in the Scriptures, and from his own inclination toward Neoplatonic philosophical research. That characteristic is evident in his distinction between the simple Christians and the "true gnostics." Clement believes that, over and beyond the simple faith that all Christians have, one can also achieve a more profound understanding of eternal truth, a superior "gnosis" that is reserved to those few and privileged spirits who constantly exercise themselves in an intense search after truth. This "true gnosis," which Clement opposes to the "false gnosis" of the heretics, is ethical as well as intellectual. "In contrast with the barely believing, uncultivated beginner, inclined to externalities, stands the Christian who beholds the mysteries of God, and who, with heart and understanding, receives God to abiding fellowship." [29] It is not merely a matter of discovering higher intellectual truth, but also of living a life of a higher order.[30] One achieves this "gnosis" through various means of which Clement speaks frequently, but whose inner relationship he

---

[28] *Paid.* 1. 6.

[29] Reinhold Seeberg, *Textbook of the History of Doctrines* (Grand Rapids: Baker Book House, 1956), 1: 142.

[30] *Strom.* 4. 21, 23; 6. 9, 10; 7. 3, 7-15.

does not clarify: personal inspiration; allegorical exegesis; Platonic dialectics; and a secret tradition to which he appeals repeatedly, but whose character, content, and means of transmission it is impossible to determine.[31] In any case, the important point is that Clement's thought has a markedly aristocratic and esoteric nature, so that in reading his works one must understand that they do not reflect the theology of the church of Alexandria, but rather that of a group of gifted Christians in that city.

Having discussed the basic principles and characteristics of Clement's theology, we now turn to its content. When speaking of God, Clement follows Neoplatonic doctrine in claiming that one must do so mainly in negative terms: God has no attributes; he is beyond the category of substance; nothing can be directly said of him, for he cannot be defined.[32] But to these assertions of a markedly Platonic nature one other must be added which is the result of Clement's Christian faith: God is triune. Next to the Father, and throughout all eternity, stands the Word.[33] As has already been said, the Word is the source of all knowledge, and most especially of the knowledge of God.[34] The Word is also the principle of the whole creation, for "without him nothing has been made." Although Clement places himself within the tradition of the Fourth Gospel in affirming the coeternity of the Word and the Father, his teaching on this point has a certain Platonic flavor, especially when he speaks of the Word as at once one and multiple, that is, as an intermediate being between the ineffable unity of God and the multiplicity of the universe.[35] This

---

[31] *Ibid.*, 6. 7.

[32] Osborn, *Clement*, pp. 25-32.

[33] *Strom.* 5. 1. Clement never says that the word is *homoousios* with the Father. But Harnack thought that he probably knew that term as a way to refer to the community of nature which the Logos possesses, both with God and with men (*HD*, 2: 352, n. 2). On the other hand, Photius affirms that Clement counted the Son among the creatures (*Bibliotheca*, 109; *PG*, 103: 384).

[34] See Erich Fascher, "Der Logos-Christus als göttlicher Lehrer bei Clemens von Alexandrien," in *Studien zum Neuen Testament und zur Patristik* (Berlin: Akademie-Verlag, 1961), pp. 193-207.

[35] Cf. Osborn, *Clement*, pp. 34-44.

Word of God, source of all knowledge and of every creature, has become incarnate in Jesus Christ.[36] The incarnation is the apex to which the Word himself has directed all his previous works, both among the Jews and among the gentiles. Thus, he has inspired philosophy to the Greeks and the Law to the Jews so that one as well as the other might serve as handmaidens to lead men to Christ, the Word incarnate. This leads to an entire doctrine of history, a history that, as Mondésert says,

unfolds, moves forward until it reaches a supreme event; but it only reaches that point in order to begin its march anew, although without saving itself from the influence of that central and high point which it has reached; after that point history is no longer a lineal and horizontal movement, but rather a vast spiral which ascends without ever abandoning the axis which it has discovered.[37]

However, in spite of the importance that Clement grants to the incarnation, one must point out that the manner in which he understands that event would leave much to be desired from the standpoint of Tertullian or that of Irenaeus. According to him, the Word did assume humanity, and there is no doubt that Christ was human in his body as well as in his soul.[38] But this union of the divine and the human is such that some of the fundamental characteristics of humanity are lost. In fact, in the following text, in which Clement is attacking Docetic teaching, he nevertheless is led to a position very close to Docetism, and which springs from the same considerations that led some to embrace that doctrine.

In the case of the Saviour, it were ludicrous [to suppose] that the body, as a body, demanded the necessary aids in order to its duration. For He ate, not for the sake of the body, which was kept together by a holy energy, but in order that it might not enter into the minds of those who were with Him

---

[36] *Exhort.* 11; *Paid.* 1: 74; *Strom.* 5. 16.
[37] Mondésert, *Clément*, p. 188.
[38] *Paid.* 1. 2.

to entertain a different opinion of Him; in like manner as certainly some afterwards supposed that He appeared in a phantasmal shape. But He was entirely impassible, inaccessible to any movement of feeling—either pleasure or pain.[39]

Clement does not develop a clear doctrine of the Holy Spirit. Perhaps the manner in which he makes the Word the illuminator and inspirer of believers makes it difficult for him to assign a parallel function to the Spirit. This does not mean, however, that Clement does not distinguish the person of the Spirit from the other two persons of the Trinity—although without using the term "person," unknown to Clement within this context. For him, the Spirit is above all the principle of cohesion which attracts men towards God. In any case, there is no doubt that Clement clearly affirms the triune nature of God, for one can frequently find trinitarian formulas in his works.[40]

This triune God is the Creator. The world is the result of an action of God. It has not simply emanated from the divinity; nor is it a mere ordering of a preexistent matter.[41] Creation took place outside time—a doctrine for which Clement believes that he can find support in the philosophers as well as in Scripture.[42] Furthermore, creation is not to be confused with the mere preservation of the universe, for Clement believes that God, who made all things in the beginning, no longer creates, but has rather left the preservation and multiplication of things to the natural order that he established at the beginning.[43]

Creation includes not only men and this world in which we live, but also angels and other heavenly beings. Reflecting the seven days that God employed in making the universe, all creation has number seven as its fundamental structure: There are seven members of the first angelic order; the planets are seven; the stars in the Pleiades are

---

[39] *Strom.* 6. 9 (*ANF*, 2: 496). Cf. *Strom.* 3. 7.

[40] *Exhort.* 12; *Paid.* 1. 42; 3. 12; *Strom.* 5. 14.

[41] *Strom.* 5. 14.

[42] *Ibid.*, 6. 16.

[43] In a fragment preserved by Anastasius Sinaita (q. 96). English trans.: *ANF*, 2: 584.

seven, etc.[44] Thus, Clement already exemplifies one of the interests that will be characteristic of a good deal of Christian theology that has suffered Platonic influences: the investigation of the hierarchical and numerical structure of the universe, and above all of the heavenly hosts.

On some points, Clement's doctrine of man approaches that of Irenaeus in a manner that is surprising in two theologians of such different leanings. For Clement, as for Irenaeus, Adam was created with childish innocence, and he was to achieve the purpose of his creation through further growth unto perfection.[45] With the fall, which took place because man made use of his sexual capabilities before God had intended it,[46] man became subject to sin and death. However, Clement differs greatly from Irenaeus in that for him Adam is not the head of mankind, but rather a symbol for that which happens in each of us individually.[47] When a child is born he is not under "the curse of Adam." But in the long run we all sin, and we all become like Adam. Then we are subject to the Devil, and thus become slaves of sin and death. This does not mean that human freedom is utterly destroyed. On the contrary, when God, by means of his Word, offers faith, it is man who must decide whether to accept it or not, thus exercising his freedom.[48] This faith is only the beginning of the new life, which Clement sometimes describes as the resumption of that growth which was interrupted by sin, and sometimes as a process of divinization. Following his own esoteric interest, Clement claims that faith must be followed by fear and hope, which lead to love and finally to a "true gnosis." Whether the totality of this development is to take place in this life, or whether one can continue the process of divinization even beyond his death, is a matter that is not clearly answered in Clement's works.

---

[44] *Strom.* 6. 17.

[45] *Ibid.*, 2. 22.

[46] *Ibid.*, 3. 17.

[47] See John Norman Davidson Kelly, *Early Christian Doctrines* (London: A. & C. Black, 1960), p. 179.

[48] See Osborn, *Clement,* p. 51.

However, one must take care not to interpret Clement's doctrine of salvation in excessively individualistic terms, for the church has an important part in the process of salvation. The church is the Mother of Believers,[49] and it is within her that the process of illumination and divinization takes place which leads the Christian to the life of the "true gnostic." One enters this church through baptism, and is nourished within it by means of the eucharist. Baptism is the washing of sin, and in that act that illumination takes place which is at the root of the Christian life.[50] However, Clement does not believe that in his baptism a Christian receives the fullness of that life, but only the starting point for a further growth that should take him to perfection. On the other hand, the eucharist is really efficacious as a way to nourish faith and to make its partaker share in immortality, but this does not mean that the bread is literally the body of Christ, or that the wine is his blood.[51]

The importance of Clement's theology is to be found mainly in the way in which it is guided by his doctrine of the Word. This doctrine is the bridge by which he relates pagan philosophy with Scripture. It is also the principle of unity within the totality of history, and especially the principle of unity between both Testaments. The illumination and participation of the Word is the basis of the superior life of the "true gnostic." On the other hand, it is in the doctrine of the Word that one can see most clearly the unresolved conflicts between the Hellenistic and Christian traditions: in that doctrine one finds Platonic elements and others taken from Scripture existing side by side in a tension that is not resolved. It is precisely this tension which makes Clement so important for the history of Christian thought. "Platonic and Biblical, he is an original witness to that extraordinary encounter between Greek genius and that of the Orient, and between human speculation

---

[49] *Paid.* 1. 5.

[50] *Ibid.*, 1. 6.

[51] *Ibid.* It spite of Quasten's arguments to the contrary, Clement does not seem to treat the eucharist as a sacrifice. Cf. Johannes Quasten, *Patrology* (Paramus, N. J.: The Paulist/Newman Press, 1953), 2: 28-30.

and divine revelation." [52] One should not be surprised that his attempts at conciliation within that encounter did not always succeed. It could not be otherwise, given the fact that he was a pioneer opening new and untraveled pathways.

Besides, one must remember that the particular purpose of the *Exhortation*, as well as that of the *Instructor*, have been accomplished to such a degree that it is doubly painful that, instead of the promised *Teacher*, we only possess the strange collection of miscellaneous materials called *Stromata*.

Finally, Clement is also important for the history of Christian thought because he was able to communicate some of his fundamental ideas, and especially the basic spirit of this theology, to his disciple Origen, who later systematized them and turned them into an imposing theological edifice.

Origen

Unlike Clement, Origen was born of Christian parents.[53] His father, Leonidas, gave up his life as a martyr in the year 202, during the persecution of Septimius Severus. At that time, Origen exhorted his father to be faithful unto death, and his zeal was such that his mother hid his clothing so that he could not go out and get himself arrested.

Shortly after the death of his father, Origen, who was still in his early youth, began to teach literature and philosophy as a means to earn his living. Soon the Christian community of Alexandria had to face the problem that, on account of the absence of many of its leaders because of the persecution, there was no one to teach the fundamentals of Christianity to those who were requesting training for baptism. By then some converted pagans—a certain Plutarch and his brother Heraclas, who later became bishop to Alexandria—had ap-

---

[52] Mondésert, *Clément*, p. 267.

[53] The main sources for Origen's life are Eusebius (*HE* 6.), Pamphilus of Caesarea (what remains of his *Apologia*), Gregory the Wonderworker (*Oratio*), and Jerome (*De viris illus.* 54. 62).

proached Origen and asked him to instruct them in the Christian faith. Thus, faced by the need to continue the teaching ministry of the church, Bishop Demetrius gave that responsibility to Origen, who was then eighteen years of age and who had studied under Clement. His own temperament led Origen to take that responsibility with great zeal, and he devoted himself not only to intensive studies, but also to the practice of an austere life, which he always took to be an important aspect of the life of the philosopher.

Then, with becoming consideration, that he might not need aid from others, he disposed of whatever valuable books of ancient literature he possessed, being satisfied with receiving from the purchaser four oboli a day. For many years he lived philosophically in this manner, putting away all the incentives of youthful desires. Through the entire day he endured no small amount of discipline; and for the greater part of the night he gave himself to the study of the Divine Scriptures. He restrained himself as much as possible by a most philosophic life; sometimes by the discipline of fasting, again by limited time for sleep. And in his zeal he never lay upon a bed, but upon the ground.[54]

This ascetic tendency of Origen's temperament was brutally shown when he took literally the reference of the Gospel to "those who make themselves eunuchs because of the kingdom of heaven." His resulting action, by which he deprived himself of his sexual organs, later was for him a source of difficulties with ecclesiastical authorities, especially with Bishop Demetrius, who thought that the fact that he had emasculated himself excluded Origen from the possibility of receiving priestly orders.[55]

Meanwhile, Origen's renown was spreading, and soon his disciples were so many that he was unable to teach all of them. It was then that he entrusted the teaching of candidates for baptism to his disciple Heraclas, and concentrated on the instruction of those who came after more profound knowledge. Thus, Origen founded a new school of

---

[54] Eusebius, *HE* 6. 3 (*NPNF*, 2nd series, 1: 252).
[55] Cf. Richard Patrick Crosland Hanson, "Note on Origen's self-mutilation," *VigCh*, 20 (1966), 81-82.

higher studies similar to those of the ancient philosophers, and to those of Justin and Pantaenus. It was through his teaching in that school that he became so well known that even pagans were interested in hearing the great philosopher—among them the Governor of Arabia and the mother of the Emperor.

As he did not have to be ordained in order to teach, Origen remained a layman for several years. When he was finally ordained, this was done in such circumstances that it created new difficulties for him. While he was visiting Palestine, around the year 216, a group of bishops of that region asked him to expound the Scriptures in their churches. Origen agreed, thinking it his duty to accept this occasion to explain the message of the Scriptures. When Bishop Demetrius of Alexandria received word of this, he ordered Origen to return immediately to Alexandria, for a layman was not to be allowed to preach before bishops. Origen agreed to this, and the matter was forgotten until years later, when he returned to Palestine on his way to Antioch. Once again the local bishops asked him to preach, and this time they ordained Origen. Although it seems that the sincere purpose of this step was not to antagonize Demetrius, it was indeed an unwise measure. As soon as Demetrius knew that Origen had been ordained by the bishops of Palestine, he interpreted this as an attempt to evade his authority. Besides, Demetrius believed that Origen's act of emasculating himself should keep him out of the ranks of the clergy, and it is also possible that there may have been a measure of envy in his attitude. There followed a prolonged controversy in which two synods convoked in Alexandria by Demetrius excommunicated Origen and deprived him of his orders. Meanwhile, Origen himself took up residence in the city of Caesarea in Palestine. After the death of Demetrius, Heraclas, who had been a disciple of Origen, became bishop of Alexandria. But he sustained the actions of his predecessor, and Origen gave up every hope of returning to his native city, and spent the rest of his life in Caesarea. There he founded a theological school similar to that which he had organized in Alexandria, and spent almost twenty years devoted to writing and teaching theology, although his renown often made it necessary for him to interrupt his research and teaching in order to visit some part of the Empire where his presence was required.

Very little was known of Origen's activities in these trips until the recent (1941) discovery in Egypt of several papyri that contain, among other things, notes taken during a public disputation that Origen held in Arabia with bishop Heraclides,[56] who was suspected of being a Modalist. In that document, written with such freshness that there is no doubt that it is based on shorthand notes, modern historians have a remarkable witness to the great ability with which Origen could not only refute heretics, but even convince them.

Finally, after long years of teaching and prolific writing, Origen had the opportunity to show in his own life what he had expected and admired in his father, and what he had taught in his *Exhortation to Martyrdom*. During the rule of Emperor Decius a great persecution broke out against the Christians. It was no longer one of the local and sporadic persecutions that followed Trajan's instructions to Pliny—that is, to punish Christians if they were accused, but not seek them out if nobody denounced them. This time it was an organized and systematic persecution. Every citizen was to offer sacrifice to the gods and would receive a document certifying that he had done so. Failure to have such a document was punishable by death. It seems, however, that the purpose of the edicts of persecution was not so much to destroy Christians as to pressure them into abandoning their faith. Therefore, the lot of the martyrs of that time, rather than death, turned out to be prolonged periods of incarceration and torture. Origen was subjected to such tortures for several days and, according to the witness of Eusebius, his behavior was admirable.[57]

History does not record how Origen managed to be freed from prison; but it does record that he died in the city of Tyre, possibly as a result of his tortures, when he was almost seventy years old.

---

[56] Jean Schérer, *Entretien d'Origène avec Heraclide et les évêques ses collegues sur le Père, le Fils, et l'âme* (Le Caire: Societé Fouad I de Papyrologie, 1949).
[57] *HE* 6. 39.

His literary work was unbelievably extensive—so much so that it would be impossible within the space available here to give even a list of the titles of his works. Over the passage of centuries, most of his works have been lost, but that fraction of his production which has survived is by itself impressive. Although Epiphanius affirms that Origen's works were six thousand, about eight hundred of their titles have survived.[58] Yet, even most of these eight hundred have been lost. A very small number of them have been preserved in their original Greek text, whereas most of those which have survived exist only in translations which are probably not very faithful to the original.[59] For these reasons it is very difficult to reconstruct Origen's thought, and it would be completely impossible were it not because—although they are a fraction of his total production—those works which have survived are sufficiently numerous to allow the historian to compare their contents and thus attempt to set aside that which seems to come from an inexact translation rather than from Origen's own mind.

In order to give an idea of Origen's literary production, one should begin with his work as a student of the Bible. Origen always thought of himself as an interpreter of the sacred text, and it was to this task that he devoted his greatest efforts. Among the works that show this aspect of Origen's literary production, one should mention the *Hexapla*, the *Scholia*, the *Homilies*, and the *Commentaries*.

The *Hexapla* is the first attempt in the history of Christianity to provide the student with the necessary instruments to establish the original text of Scripture. This work, most of which has been lost, was a parallel presentation, in six columns, of the Hebrew text of the Old Testament, a transliteration of that text in Greek characters, and the four Greek versions that circulated at that time: the version of Aquila, that of Symmachus, the Septuagint, and the translation of

---

[58] *Pan.* 64. 63. Quoted by Adolph von Harnack, *Geschichte der altchristlichen Literatur,* I/1 (reprint, Leipzig: J. C. Hinrichs Verlag, 1958), 333.

[59] Cf. Vinzenz Buchheit, "Rufinus von Aquileja als Fälscher des Adamantiosdialogs," *ByzZschr,* 51 (1958), 314-28.

Theodotus. If he was able to lay his hand on any other version, Origen included it in an extra column, and the result was that in certain sections—those corresponding to the Psalms—the Hexapla was expanded to nine columns. Yet Origen was not satisfied with this mere compilation, but rather devoted himself to a careful comparison of the Hebrew text with that of the Septuagint, and used a system of signs in order to indicate alterations, omissions and additions.

The *Scholia* are short explanations of individual texts whose interpretation seemed particularly difficult or interesting. Except for a few fragments, they have been lost.

Naturally, Origen wrote his *Homilies* or sermons after he broke with Demetrius. Although most of them have perished, those which have survived show the nature of Origen's preaching. It is mostly a moral exhortation, and the speculations that are so common in the biblical commentaries do not constitute his main theme.

Finally, Origen had ample opportunity to make use of his exegetical method and capabilities in the commentaries. Although none of them has survived in its entirety, there are rather extensive portions of the *Commentary on the Gospel of St. Matthew*, the *Commentary on the Gospel of St. John*, the *Commentary on the Epistle to the Romans*, and the *Commentary on the Song of Songs*. These works are the main source by which it is possible to know Origen's exegetical method, which in turn is an important clue to the rest of his theology.

Besides these exegetical writings, the centuries have spared an apology, a systematic treatise, and some minor works whose practical nature makes them less interesting for a history of Christian thought.

The title of Origen's apology is *Contra Celsum*. Celsus was a pagan philosopher, who several years earlier had written a work against Christianity whose title was *The True Word*.[60] It was a biting and

---

[60] Henry Chadwick, trans., *Origen: Contra Celsum* (Cambridge: Cambridge University Press, 1965); W. den Boer, *Celsus, de eerste bestrijder van het Christendom* (Groningen: P. Noordhoff, 1950); Carl Andresen, *Logos und Nomos: Die Polemik des Kelsos wider das Christentum* (Berlin: W. de Gruyter, 1955). This last author believes that Celsus wrote in

well documented attack, not only on Christian practice, but also and above all on the doctrines and the Scriptures of the new faith. This attack does not seem to have had great consequences, for Origen himself did not know the work of Celsus before his friend and protector Ambrose asked him to refute it. Although at first Origen thought that it was best to ignore Celsus' attacks, he finally decided to acquiesce to Ambrose's plea and wrote the *Contra Celsum*. As Origen refuted Celsus' arguments one by one, this work does not have a principle of internal unity. In spite of that, it is of great importance for the history of the encounter of Christianity with paganism in the first centuries of our era.[61]

Finally, Origen's great systematic work is that which is known as *On First Principles—De principiis*. As this work will serve as an outline for our exposition of Origen's theology, let it suffice to say now that it is an early work (*ca.* 220) of Origen, written in four books. Most of it has survived only in a Latin translation of Rufinus, who took upon himself the task of correcting those opinions of Origen which he took to be too audacious[62]—and thereby complicated the historian's task. Therefore, when one reads this work one must always suspect Rufinus' hand in it, and seek in the rest of Origen's works the clues that will help to discover the meaning of the original text.

The best starting point for an exposition of Origen's theology is the way in which he interprets Scripture,[63] for exegesis was always his main theological interest. Most of his writings are exegetical, and the interpretation of scriptural texts is a central concern even in the systematic work *De principiis*. Besides, a man who spent practically

---

response to Justin. But cf. Quintino Cataudella, "Celso e gli apologeti cristiani," *NDid*, 1 (1947), 28-34.

[61] See Pierre de Labriolle, *La réaction païenne* (Paris: L'Artisan du Livre, 1950), pp. 111-69.

[62] Rufinus claims that in so doing he is not correcting the text of Origen, but rather eliminating corruptions that have been introduced in the text by "heretics and malevolent persons." *Prol. ad De princ.* (*ANF*, 3: 237-38).

[63] Jean Daniélou, "Origène comme exégète de la Bible," *SP*, 1 (1955), 280-90; José María Caballero Cuesta, *Orígenes intérprete de la Sagrada Escritura* (Burgos: Seminario Metropolitano, 1956); Rolf-Geogler, *Zur Theologie des biblischen Wortes bei Origenes* (Düsseldorf: Patmos Verlag, 1963).

his whole life on a work of such ambition as the *Hexapla* must have felt great interest and respect for the biblical text.

Although Origen is very far from being literalistic in his interpretation of the sacred text, he does firmly believe in the literal inspiration of every word in Scripture.[64] In them there is not a single word, or even a letter, that does not contain a mystery.[65] This is the reason why Origen took the task of restoring the original biblical text to be so important.

However, the true sense of the Bible is not always that which follows from a literal interpretation. On the contrary, the fact that God has inspired even the texts that seem most absurd is a proof of the need to interpret the Bible "spiritually." From this follows the doctrine that a biblical text has—or may have—three different but complementary meanings: a literal or physical sense, a moral or psychical sense, and an intellectual or spiritual sense.[66] This is the well-known doctrine of the various biblical senses, which Origen obviously derives from Clement and even from earlier non-Christian exegetes, such as Philo.[67] However, one must not take this doctrine too literally, for it is not an exegetical principle that Origen follows every time he faces a text. On the contrary, very seldom does one find a clear distinction between the three different meanings of a particular text. Origen holds firmly to the doctrine of the various meanings of a text, and especially to the need of seeking, behind the literal sense, that which is hidden and spiritual. But very rarely does he develop his exegesis in a systematic manner upon the basis of the trichotomy between the literal, moral, and spiritual meanings of the text. Moreover, there are

---

[64] Richard Patrick Crosland Hanson, *Allegory and Event: A Study of the Sources and Significance of Origen's Interpretation of Scripture* (London: SCM Press, 1959), p. 187.

[65] *Hom. in Ex.* 1. 4.

[66] *De princ.* 4. 11-13.

[67] In thus classifying the various senses of Scripture, Origen follows the example of Philo and draws a parallelism between the various constituents of man and the senses of Scripture. But Philo argued only for two senses: the physical corresponding to the body, and the spiritual corresponding to the soul. Origen introduces an anthropological trichotomy within this context, and thus allows Hanson to say that he "out-Philos Philo." *Allegory*, p. 237. Cf. H. de Lubac, *Histoire et Esprit: L'intelligence de l'Ecriture d'après Origène* (Paris: Aubier, 1950), pp. 150-66.

cases in which he finds in a single text several spiritual meanings, thereby creating an entire scale of allegorical interpretations.

The foregoing does not mean that Origen usually neglects or pushes aside the literal meaning of Scripture.[68] On the contrary, it was precisely a literal and legalistic interpretation of a Gospel text that led him to deprive himself of his manly organs. Often, when dealing with the miracles of the New Testament or with some of the historical material of the Old, he pauses to underline the historical reality of the events described before he goes on to an allegorical interpretation of their significance.

On the other hand, he does affirm that in certain cases one must discard the literal meaning of a text. Every biblical text has a spiritual sense, but not every one can be interpreted literally. Thus, for example, while commenting on certain Levitical laws, Origen says that he would blush if he had to interpret them as the Jews do, and to claim that they were given by God. According to a literal interpretation, one could not deny that human laws, such as those of the Romans, Athenians, and Lacedemonians, are higher than these laws. But if one interprets them spiritually, "as the church teaches," it should be clear that the Levitical laws are truly of divine origin. Interpreting everything literally is the error of the Jews as well as of the Marcionites.[69]

Origen seems to have taken from Philo the idea of a "moral" exegesis. This type of interpretation is to be found above all in his homilies, although it is not always possible to distinguish it from spiritual exegesis.[70] It is usually an allegorical interpretation of the text, although not with the purpose of reaching great speculative heights, but rather to lead the believer in his moral and devotional life. Origen

---

[68] Cf. *ibid.*, p. 238.

[69] *In Lev. hom.* 7. 5.

[70] Hanson, *Allegory*, p. 243: "On the whole the 'moral' sense plays no significant part in Origen's exegesis, not because he had no occasion to draw edifying or devotional lessons from the text of the Bible but because in the practical work of expounding Scripture he found it impossible to maintain the distinction between the 'moral' and the 'spiritual' sense, and the former became absorbed in the latter." Bardy, "Origène," *DTC*, 11: 1008, also says that the psychic or moral sense "is rather difficult to define."

claims that an example of moral exegesis may be found in the manner in which the apostle Paul interprets the ancient commandment: "Thou shalt not muzzle the ox when he treads out the corn." In referring this commandment to the practical life of the churches, and claiming that this text proves that the apostle has a right to be supported by the church, Paul is showing the moral sense of the text.[71]

But it is in the spiritual meaning of Scriptures that Origen can rise in those speculative flights of which he is so fond, and which are so characteristic of Alexandrine theology—Christian as well as Jewish and even pagan. On the other hand, this spiritual exegesis allows him to discover alleged points of contact between Platonic philosophy and the biblical message, without feeling the need to abandon any of these two poles of his thought—although he never consciously defended the classical tradition over against what he took to be biblical doctrine.

However, one must point out that this spiritual exegesis is not always allegorical in the strict sense. On the contrary, Origen is so submerged in the life and faith of the church that he is inclined to follow the long tradition of typological interpretation that had been established by such men as Paul and Justin. Thus typology is fundamental in Origen's spiritual exegesis, and one finds in his works traditional themes such as that of the sacrifice of Isaac as a "type" or "figure" of the passion of Christ,[72] or that of circumcision as a type of baptism.[73] Besides, as Daniélou points out, Origen's typology goes beyond that which the church had developed up to that point, for he includes the New Testament and even the actual church within the sphere of typological figures. Thus, Origen proposes an interpretation "of the Old Testament as a figure of the New, the New as a figure of the church, and the church as the figure of eschatology, that is to say, the analogy of the same purposes in the various stages of the history of salvation." [74]

---

[71] *De princ.* 6. 12.

[72] *In Gen. hom.* 8. 8-9.

[73] *Comm. in Rom.* 2. 13.

[74] Jean Daniélou, *Message évangélique et culture hellénistique* (Paris: Desclée & Co., 1961), p. 254.

On the other hand, this typological tradition does not prevent Origen from often abandoning the historical meaning of a text and making use of allegorical interpretations in order to find biblical support for doctrines that are extraneous to Scripture. He does this to such an extent that some historians have found it possible to interpret his thought as a philosophical system that is only peripherally related to Christianity.[75] Although such an interpretation is obviously exaggerated, it may serve as a reminder of the dangers of unwarranted allegorization of the biblical text, as found in Origen.

It is difficult, and perhaps even impossible, to list the exegetical principles that Origen follows in his allegorical interpretation. The most that can be said is, first, that every text is pregnant with profound mysteries that are to be discovered through allegory; second, that nothing is to be said of God which is unworthy of him; third, that each text is to be interpreted in the light of the rest of Scripture; finally, that nothing contrary to the rule of faith is to be affirmed.

Origen exaggerates the principle that each text is to be interpreted in the light of the rest of Scripture. Clement had already sought to discover the hidden meaning of a word or number in a text by investigating its use in another passage. But Origen makes this type of research a habitual practice, discovering hidden meanings even in the most clear and simple words. Hanson has compiled a list of some of these mystical meanings which Origen claims that he has found in biblical language:

"Horse" in the Bible usually means "voice"; "today" means "the present age"; "leaven" means "teaching"; "silver" and "trumpet" mean "word"; "clouds" . . . mean "holy ones"; "feet" mean "the counsel by which we tread the journey of life"; "well" means "the teaching of the Bible"; "linen" means "chastity"; "thighs" mean "beginning"; "unmixed wine" means "misfortune"; "bottle" means "body"; "secret" and "treasury" mean "the reason." [76]

---

[75] Thus, Eugène de Faye, *Origène: sa vie, son oeuvre, sa pensée*, 3 vols. (Paris: E. Leroux, 1923-1928).

[76] Hanson, *Allegory*, pp. 247-48.

Although in some cases the normal biblical use of a particular term serves as a clue for the reason that led Origen to give it a particular meaning, the truth is that in most cases the reader receives the impression that the way in which a particular word is to be understood depends on an arbitrary decision of the interpreter. It is on this basis that Hanson pronounces his somewhat hyperbolic but nevertheless justifiable judgment of Origen, saying that he "transforms the Bible into a divine cross-word puzzle the solution to whose clues is locked in Origen's bosom." [77]

On the other hand, this phrase is hyperbolic because there is another element in Origen's theology which restrains and directs him in the interpretation of Scripture: the rule of faith of the church. As has been said in a previous chapter,[78] the "rule of faith" was not a fixed or written formula, but was rather the traditional preaching and teaching of the church, and its content thus showed some slight variations from place to place. Thus, for instance, Origen seems to have understood that the rule of faith included the doctrine of the several meanings of Scripture,[79] whereas such a thing is not to be found in the rule of faith of Irenaeus or Tertullian. But in any case there were certain fundamental doctrines that the rule of faith affirmed and that Origen did not feel free to deny.[80] Therefore, the rule of faith served to keep his theology—at least in part—within the sphere of the traditional doctrine of the church.

The first article of that rule of faith refers to God. According to Origen, God is such that his nature cannot be comprehended by any human intelligence. God is invisible, not only in the physical sense that eyes cannot see him, but also in the intellectual sense, for there is no mind that is capable of contemplating his essence. No matter how perfect our knowledge of God may be, we must constantly be re-

---

[77] *Ibid.*, p. 248.

[78] Chap. VII.

[79] *De princ.*, *praef.*, 8. Cf. Bigg, *The Christian Platonists of Alexandria* (Oxford: The Clarendon Press, 1886), pp. 85-87.

[80] Although in *Comm. in Joh.* 13. 16 he seems to follow a different course, he normally refers to the rule of faith as the church's authoritative interpretation of Scripture.

minded that he is much higher than anything that our intelligence can conceive.[81] God is the simple and intellectual nature, beyond every definition of essence.[82] The anthropomorphic language that Scripture applies to God is to be understood allegorically, as trying to show us some facet of the manner in which God relates to creation and to men. On the other hand, if there is anything that one can say of God in an almost literal sense, that is that he is One.[83] Absolute unity, that unity which is diametrically opposed to the multiplicity of the transient world—and which was one of the characteristic themes of contemporary Platonism—is the main attribute of God's being.

However, this ineffable One is also the triune God of the rule of faith of the church. Origen not only knew and frequently used the term "trinity," but he also contributed to the development of trinitarian doctrine, for his theology is one of the main sources of the trinitarian debates that would shake the church almost a century later.[84]

Following the rule of faith as it was established at that time, Origen affirms that God is Father, Son, and Holy Spirit. But the rule of faith allowed a certain freedom of movement in that which had to do with the exact relationship between these three. It is here that Origen makes use of his originality and speculative ability.

In that which refers to the relationship between the Father and the Son, one can find in Origen two currents or tendencies that he, through his genius, was able to keep in balance, but that would later divide his followers in two violently opposed groups.

The first of these tendencies is that of underlining the divinity and the eternity of the Son, and of making him equal to the Father. For "who . . . can suppose or believe that God the Father ever existed,

---

[81] De princ. 1. 1. 5.

[82] Contra Cels. 7. 38.

[83] De princ. 1. 1. 6.

[84] Cf. Georg Krestschmar, Studien zur frühchristlichen Trinitätstheologie (Tübingen: J. C. B. Mohr, 1956), who probably exaggerates the importance of Origen for the development of trinitarian doctrine.

even for a moment of time, without having generated this Wisdom?" [85] To suppose that there was a time when the Son did not exist would lead one to suppose also that there was a time when the Father did not exist as Father, which would be a great error. On the contrary, the Son

was born indeed of Him, and derives from Him what He is, but without any beginning, not only such as may be measured by any divisions of time, but even that which the mind alone can contemplate within itself, or behold, so to speak, with the naked powers of the understanding.[86]

Furthermore, this Son of God is not only coeternal with the Father, but it can even be said of him that he is divine "according to the essence," and not "through participation." [87]

This tendency to underline the unity between the Father and the Son can be seen in the manner in which Origen, in discussing the generation of the Son, rejects the idea that this can be understood as a mere emanation. Such a doctrine—for which Origen could have found some support in Clement—would tend to turn the individuality of the Son into a limitation of the divine substance.[88] Origen

---

[85] *De princ.* 1. 2. 2 (ANF, 4: 246).

[86] *Ibid.* Although this text could be seen as an attempt by Rufinus to adjust Origen to post-Nicene orthodoxy, there are several undeniably genuine texts that support this one. Such are, for instance, *Comm. in Joh.* 1. 32 and *Comm. in Rom.* 1. 4—*"non erat quando non erat."*

[87] *In Psal.* 135. 2 (PG, 12:1656): "ὁ δὲ Σωτὴρ οὐ κατὰ μετουσίαν, ἀλλὰ κατ' οὐσίαν ἐστὶ θεός." It is possible that Origen knew and used the term ὁμοούσιος in order to refer to the relationship between the Father and the Son. It appears four times in fragments of his *Comm. in Matt.*, and once in the *Apology* of Pamphilus of Caesarea. But the fragments may be due to a later attempt to strengthen Origen's prestige by making him agree with Nicea. On the other hand, Pamphilus, who died in A.D. 310 and who therefore could not have known the Arian controversy, says that according to Origen "the Son of God is born of the same substance of God, that is, ὁμοούσιος, which is to say, of the same substance as the Father; and is not a creature, nor is he a true Son by adoption, but by nature, begotten of the Father himself." (*Apol. pro Origine* 5; PG, 17: 581.)

[88] Cf. Maurice F. Wiles, "Eternal Generation," *JBL*, 79 (1960), 111-18; R. Arnou, "Le thème neoplatonicien de la contemplation créatrice chez Origène et chez S. Augustin," *Greg*, 13 (1932), 124-36.

rejects this theory because it implies that the divinity is corporeal in nature. On the contrary,

we must be careful not to fall into the absurdities of those who picture to themselves certain emanations, so as to divide the divine nature into parts, and who divide God the Father as far as they can, since even to entertain the remotest suspicion of such a thing regarding an incorporeal being is not only the height of impiety, but a mark of the greatest folly, it being most remote from any intelligent conception that there should be any physical division of any incorporeal nature. Rather, therefore, as an act of the will proceeds from the understanding, and neither cuts off any part nor is separated or divided from it, so after some such fashion is the Father to be supposed as having begotten the Son.[89]

There is, however, another current within Origen's theology which tends to underline the distinction between the Father and the Son. Whereas it is true that Origen refuses to define the difference between the Father and the Son as a limitation of the latter, as if his substance were a part of the substance of the Father, he is ready to speak in terms of a limitation that does distinguish the Son from the Father. It is the limitation that is required so that the God who is beyond every essence and definition may be known, and placed within the scope of essence.[90] The Son is the image of God; his name; his face.[91] The Father is absolute Unity; in the Son there is multiplicity, and he can therefore relate with the world and with men.[92] Here one has to subscribe to Daniélou's judgment when he affirms that the main difficulty that Origen encounters within this context—as well as the great difficulty of all ante-Nicene trinitarian theology—is to be found in this principle of basing the distinction between the Father and the

---

[89] *De Princ.* 1. 2. 6 (*ANF*, 4: 248).

[90] Origen uses the illustration of a statue of such immense dimensions that it is impossible for man to comprehend it, and another statue, just like the former, but smaller, so that it is comprehensive to the beholder. *De princ.* 1. 3. 7.

[91] Henri Crouzel, *Théologie de l'Image de Dieu chez Origène* (Paris: Aubier, 1956), pp. 75-83.

[92] *Comm. in Job.* 1. 20.

Son in the contrast between an absolutely transcendent God and a personal God of a limited transcendence who can therefore relate with creatures and establish dialogue with man. As a consequence of this, the divinity of the Son is endangered.[93] Within this frame of thought, which is typical of theological systems that have been influenced by Middle or Neoplatonism, the Word becomes an intermediary being between the unspeakable One and the multiplicity of the world.

Throughout all of Origen's trinitarian theology, one can detect this tendency to make the Son somewhat inferior or less divine than the Father. This is easily understood if one remembers that one of the great heresies of the time was Modalistic Monarchianism, which in its final development turned the Father, the Son, and the Holy Spirit into three temporary manifestations of the same God. This is precisely the doctrine that seems to have been held by Bishop Heraclides, with whom Origen had a debate whose records have been discovered recently, as has been said above. In this dialogue, in order to clarify the distinction between the Father and the Son, Origen goes to the extreme of affirming that they are "two Gods," although they are one in "power." [94]

This unresolved tension in Origen's theology was not kept by most of his disciples, who soon were divided in two groups of which one would emphasize the true divinity of the Son and his equality with the Father while the other would attempt to distinguish between the Son and the Father by making the Son a subordinate being.

Origen affirms that the Holy Spirit proceeds from the Father,[95] and is not a creature, for his beginning is not temporal, but he is rather coeternal with the Father and the Son.[96] With reference to the third person of the Trinity, there is in Origen the same tension that has already been pointed out with reference to the Son, although here

---

[93] *Message*, pp. 348-49.
[94] *Dial.* 124.
[95] *De princ.* 3. 5. 8.
[96] *Ibid.*, 1. 3. 4.

again there is no doubt that Origen believes the Holy Spirit to be divine.[97]

Finally, Origen believes that the three persons of the Trinity have different functions and fields of action in their relationship with creatures. Thus, all creatures derive their being from the Father; in those that are rational the Son is at work; and in those rational creatures that are sanctified one must see the intervention of the Holy Spirit.[98]

Origen's doctrine of creation shows the extent of the influence of Platonic idealism upon his theology. The same argument that served to prove the eternal generation of the Son, and that was grounded on a static conception of the Godhead according to which the Father must always be Father, forces Origen to affirm that creation is eternal, for the omnipotent Creator must always be such.[99]

On the other hand, the character of this eternal creation is also determined by Origen's idealism, and he therefore posits an eternal creation, but not an eternal corporeal creation. The world that God first created is not this visible world, but one composed of pure intellects.[100] The intellects are the primary recipients of God's creative action, as they will also be the final beneficiaries of his saving action. They were created in such a way that their purpose was the constant contemplation of the Image of God, which is the Word. But they were also free, which made it possible for them to forsake the con-

---

[97] This may be the best place to note that one of the main difficulties in interpreting Origen's doctrine of the Trinity lies—as is to be expected in a pioneer—in the imprecision of his terminology. Terms that later received a very precise meaning are used by Origen in various senses, and it is not always possible to determine their meaning in a particular and crucial context. This happens, among others, with the terms *ousía* and *hypóstasis*. See, further on this subject. Antonio Orbe, *Hacia la primera teología de la procesión del Verbo* (Rome: Gregorian University Press, 1958), pp. 431-52, and Crouzel, *Théologie*, pp. 75-128. On the specific issue of the Holy Spirit, see M. Garijo, "Vocabulario origeniano sobre el Espíritu Divino," *ScrVict*, 10 (1964), 320-58.

[98] *De princ.* 1. 3. 7.

[99] *Ibid*, 1. 3. 10.

[100] *Ibid.*, 1. 3. 1.

templation of that Image and turn their gaze toward multiplicity.[101] No created being is good or evil because of its essence, but is so because of the use that it makes or has made of its own freedom.[102]

Making use of that freedom, a certain number of the intellects that God had created turned their gaze away from the Image and thereby became "souls."[103] Yet they did not all go astray in the same measure, and this is the reason why rational beings are diverse and are ordered according to a hierarchy. This hierarchy is multiple, for it includes all the celestial beings of which Scriptures speak. But it is basically composed of three levels: heavenly beings, whose bodies are ethereal; we who have fallen unto this world, with our fleshly bodies; and the demons, whose bodies are even coarser than ours.[104]

This speculation regarding the source of rational beings leads Origen to the doctrine of a double creation, which he derives from Philo.[105] According to this doctrine, the two parallel narratives of creation that are to be found in Genesis correspond to two different divine actions. The first is the creation of the pure intellects, and it is of these intellects that the Bible affirms that God made them "male and female"—that is, not each of a different sex, but each with no sexual distinctions. The other narrative refers to the creation of this visible world, which was made in order to serve as a field for the trial of fallen spirits, and in which God first made the body of man and then that of woman, thereby establishing sexual distinctions.[106]

In this world, we are going through a period of trial so that, making use of our freedom, we may return to the unity and harmony of all intellectual beings, which is the purpose of God. Meanwhile, and in the process of achieving that end, it is probable—for Origen only

---

[101] *Ibid.*, 1. 8. 3.

[102] *Ibid.*, 1. 5. 3-5.

[103] *Ibid.*, 2. 8. 3. Origen claims this on the assumption that ψυχή is etymologically related to ψυχέσθαι

[104] *Ibid.*, 1. 6. 2-3.

[105] Crouzel, *Théologie*, pp. 54-55.

[106] *Ibid.*, pp. 148-53. Cf. *Comm. in Rom.* 2. 13; *Comm. in Cant., prol.*

dares to suggest the possibility—that we may have to undergo a series of incarnations that would take us from one level of the hierarchy of being to the next.[107]

The divine purpose of restoring the original unity includes all rational beings. The demons—and even the Devil, who is the principle of evil and whose fall was the cause of the fall of the rest of the intellects—are also a part of this purpose, and will eventually return to their original state as intellects fully devoted to the contemplation of the Word.[108] Naturally, this implies that hell and condemnation are not eternal. Origen interprets them as a purification that some beings have to undergo—a sort of fever whose purpose is to destroy illness.[109]

Yet, we must still continue our struggle against the Devil and his demons. Although he will be saved in the end, he is now the Adversary, and he has made up his mind to pull down to himself as many rational beings—and especially human souls—as he can. Furthermore, as we have all sinned—if we had not we would not be in this world—we have all been made subject to him, and he rules us with an evil power.[110]

Besides, we are handicapped because our fall has been such that we are unable to make use of our freedom in order to liberate ourselves from our present condition and to return to our previous purely intellectual state. In order to overcome these difficulties, the Word was made flesh. The purpose of the incarnation is, on the one hand, to destroy the power of the Devil; and, on the other hand, to grant men the illumination that they require in order to be saved. Christ is the conqueror of the Devil and the illuminator of men.[111]

In his incarnation, the Word of God was united to an unfallen in-

---

[107] *De princ.* 1. 6. 3; 2. 11. 6.
[108] *Ibid.*, 1. 6. 1.
[109] *Ibid.* 2. 10. 6.
[110] *Ibid.*, 1. 6. 3.
[111] Daniélou, *Origen*, p. 269; Marguerite Harl, *Origène et la fonction révélatrice du Verbe incarné* (Paris: Le Seuil, 1958).

tellect, and through it to a body that was in no way different from the
rest of human bodies, although it was of a different origin.[112] In thus
affirming that the Word was united not only to a human body, but
also to a created intellect—which, although unfallen, is in its essence
similar to human souls—Origen showed an insight into the need to
posit in Christ, not only a human body, but also a human intellect. As
we shall see further on, this insight was later put aside by some Alexandrine theologians.

In Christ divinity and humanity are united in such a way that one
can attribute to the first, actions and conditions that properly correspond to the latter, and vice versa. This is the doctrine of the
communicatio idiomatum, or "communication of properties," which
would later become one of the main tenents of Alexandrine Christology. Origen insists that one cannot understand Christ merely in
terms of his humanity or of his divinity. "If it [the human intellect]
thinks of a God, it sees a mortal; if it thinks of a man, it beholds Him
returning from the grave, after overthrowing the empire of
death." [113] The divine and human natures exist in a single being,
although how that can be is the greatest mystery of faith.

But of all the marvellous and mighty acts related of Him, this altogether
surpasses human admiration, and is beyond the power of mortal frailness to
understand or feel, how that mighty power of divine majesty, that very
Word of the Father, and that very Wisdom of God, in which were created all
things, visible and invisible, can be believed to have existed within the limits
of that man who appeared in Judea; nay, that the wisdom of God can have
entered the womb of a woman, and have been born an infant, and have
uttered wailings like the cries of little children.[114]

As has already been said, the purpose of this incarnation of the Son
of God is to free man from the power of the Devil and to show him
the way of salvation. Christ achieves his victory over the Devil

---

[112] *De princ.* 2. 6. 3-4.
[113] *Ibid.,* 2. 6. 3 (ANF 4: 281-82).
[114] *Ibid.,* 2. 6. 2.

throughout the totality of his life, but most especially in his incarnation and his death. In his incarnation, Christ invaded the dominions of the Devil, and thereby began his victorious work. But it was in this death that Satan himself, being fooled by the seeming weakness of the Savior, introduced him into the deepest shadows of his empire, where Christ defeated him in returning victorious from among the dead. Since then, all the dead who wish to do so may follow him, thereby escaping the claws of death and of its master Satan.[115]

The other basic aspect of the work of Christ is to show man the way of salvation. The Word became incarnate because man was unable, by his own efforts, to achieve that contemplation of divine realities which was necessary so that he could return to his original state as an intellect in communion with God. Therefore Christ is, besides a victorious Savior, an example and illuminator. In him man sees God, and he sees also how he is to direct his life in order to be saved.[116]

Origen's eschatology, being the counterpart of his doctrine of creation,[117] shows the same Platonic influences that have already been pointed out with reference to creation. It is a purely spiritualistic eschatology, in which all intellects will return to their original state of harmony and communion with God. But even that universal restoration or apokatastasis—ἀποκατάστασις—[118] is not strictly final, for after this world there may be many others that will follow in a never-ending sequence. As the intellects are free, and they will continue to be so even after the consummation of this world, it is to be expected that what has happened in this age or aeon will again take place, and once again there will be a material world and a process of restoration.[119] Here Origen lets himself be carried away by his speculative

---

[115] *Comm. in Matt.* 16. 8.

[116] *Comm. in Rom.* 4.

[117] H. Cornélis, "Les fondements cosmologiques de l'eschatologie d'Origène," *RScPhTh*, 43 (1959), 32-80, 201-47.

[118] A. Méhat, "Apocatastase," *VigCh*, 10 (1956), 196-214; G. Müller, "Origenes und die Apokatastasis," *ThZschr*, 14 (1958), 174-90.

[119] *De princ.* 2. 3. 1.

curiosity and discusses the nature of those coming worlds—although he clearly states that he is not to be necessarily followed in this, as if he were expounding the rule of faith.[120] Those worlds will not be mere repetitions of the one that we now know, as the Stoics held.[121] On the contrary, they will be different, and it is impossible to know whether they will be better or worse.[122] In any case, there is at least one thing that Origen can say categorically, and that is that Christ suffered once and for all in this world, and that he is not to suffer again in the future ones.[123]

In spite of the impression that the foregoing exposition of his theology may have given, Origen was not an individualist who set himself over against the life and faith of the church in order to be free for his own speculations. On the contrary, when he is about to depart in one of his most personal and characteristic speculative flights he makes it clear that this is a matter of personal opinion, and that the rule of faith says nothing with reference to the point at issue. Besides, Origen acknowledges the role of the church and of the sacraments in the plan of salvation. Apart from the church, no one can be saved [124]—although it is true that Origen interprets this church not so much in terms of a hierarchical unity as in terms of a community of faith. The sacraments work for the sanctification of those who receive them, and in the eucharist Christ is really and physically present,[125] although, on the other hand, the believer who has certain intellectual gifts must rise above this common interpretation and see the symbolic meaning of the sacrament.[126]

There is no doubt that Origen was the greatest theologian of the early School of Alexandria. His extremely audacious thought gained him a good number of grateful disciples, but also an even greater

---

[120] *Ibid.*, 2. 3. 7.
[121] *Ibid.*, 2. 3. 4.
[122] *Ibid.*
[123] *Ibid.*, 2. 3. 5 (on the authority of Hebrews 9: 26).
[124] *In Lib. Jesu Hom.* 3. 5.
[125] *In Ex. Hom.* 13. 3.
[126] *Comm. in Matt.* 11. 14.

number of enemies. As a consequence, various synods have at different times condemned propositions held or supposed to be held by him. Among his admirers were Gregory the Wonderworker, the evangelizer of Pontus; Eusebius of Caesarea, the first church historian; and Dionysius the Great, who succeeded Heraclas as Bishop of Alexandria. But his influence also reached some of the greatest theologians of the Eastern church—Athanasius, Basil the Great, Gregory of Nazianzus, and Gregory of Nyssa, among others—as well as some Western theologians—Hilary of Poitiers and Ambrose of Milan. However, none of these great churchmen accepted the totality of Origen's theology, and none of them felt inclined to defend his most audacious speculations when they were condemned, first by individual theologians such as Methodius of Olympus, and later by councils such as the one that Justinian called in Constantinople in A.D. 553.

Perhaps the most fundamental difference between Origen's theology and that of Clement is that, whereas Origen is theocentric, Clement places the doctrine of the Word in the center of his theology. For Clement, the Word was the point of contact between pagan philosophy and Christian revelation, and this was the determining factor in his theology. In the case of Origen, on the other hand, everything seems to revolve around the Triune God, and especially the Father. The consequence of this is that Clement lays special stress on the doctrine of the Word as illuminator and thus arrives at his most dangerous doctrine, that of a "gnostic" or aristocratic Christianity that is attainable only by those who receive a special illumination from the Word. This is an immediate consequence of Clement's point of departure, which tends to reduce Christianity to a superior truth that is to be received through the illumination of the Word. Origen starts, not from the doctrine of the Word, but from a God whose main characteristics are determined more by Platonism than by Scripture. The result of this point of departure is a series of doctrines that many Christians have found unacceptable, such as the eternity of the world, the pre-existence and reincarnation of souls, the existence of future worlds, and the final salvation of the Devil.

Origen goes beyond Clement at least in two points: in the wide scope and total coherence of his theological system, and in the audacity of his doctrine. The first made him one of the principal sources of Eastern theology. The second was the reason why that very theology found it necessary to condemn him repeatedly.

IX

Western Theology in the Third Century

During the third century, there was a marked difference between Alexandrine and Western theology. In general, their difference is the same that we have already seen as early as the Apostolic Fathers: the practical character of Western Christianity over against the speculative interest of the Alexandrines; the Stoic influence in the Latin West over against the Platonic influence in the Greek world; the interest in allegory in Alexandria over against the legalistic trend in Rome. These contrasts—which appear clearly when one compares the *Epistle of Barnabas* with the *Epistle of Clement* or Clement of Alexandria with Tertullian—are still marked in the third century, and this is one of the reasons why we would seek in vain in the West for a system of speculative theology that may compare with that of Origen.

This does not mean that Western theology is lacking in interest or importance. On the contrary, during the third century various subjects were discussed and steps taken that would be of great importance for the future development of Western theology. Most of these had to do with practical rather than speculative matters, but even these practical questions were dealt with from a theological perspective. Thus, for instance, during this period the Western church devoted a great deal of attention to the forgiveness of sins and the nature of the church, and both of these subjects are practically, as well as theologically, important.

234

During this time, the centers of theological and literary activity were Rome and North Africa. It was now that the Roman church presented its first two great theologians, Hippolytus and Novatian—both schismatic and both considered by the Roman church as antipopes. In North Africa, on the other hand, the tradition begun by Tertullian continued, and this region produced such writers as Minucius Felix, Arnobius, Cyprian, and—although already in the fourth century, but by reason of his basic situation belonging to the third—Lactantius, perhaps the best Latin stylist of the ancient church. Of these many writers, we shall study here only those whose work is most significant for the history of Christian thought: Hippolytus, Novatian, and Cyprian.

Hippolytus of Rome

Very little is known of the life of Hippolytus,[1] and this is most unfortunate since an understanding of the course of his life would greatly clarify the exact nature of the controversies in which he was involved, and therefore of his theology itself. In any case, Hippolytus was greatly respected among Roman Christians early in the third century. Even Origen went to listen to him when he visited the imperial capital in A.D. 212. Soon friction developed between Hippolytus on the one hand and bishops Zephyrinus and Callistus on the other. It seems that this had to do with personal matters as well as with disagreements regarding the doctrine of the Trinity and the forgiveness of sins. In any case, when Callistus succeeded Zephyrinus in A.D. 217 Hippolytus refused to acknowledge him as bishop and thus produced a schism in the Roman church, which now had two rival bishops: Callistus and Hippolytus. The latter continued opposing Callistus and his successors until the persecution of Maximinus in A.D. 235, when he and his rival Pontianus were deported to Sardinia. There they both died, and tradition affirms that they were reconciled

---

[1] The best biographical study is probably that of R. Reutterer, *Der heilige Hippolytus* (Klagenfurt: S. Jörgal, 1947).

before their deaths. Sometime afterward, their remains were brought back to Rome, where the Christian community itself had been reconciled, and since then both have been honored as saints and martyrs.

Most of the works of Hippolytus have been lost. Sufficient material has survived, however, to draw a picture of his theology.[2] The theology of Hippolytus was greatly influenced by that of Irenaeus. Hippolytus draws from the bishop of Lyon, not only the most and best part of his information regarding the doctrines of heretics, but also the idea that heresies derive from philosophy. Like Irenaeus, Hippolytus usually interprets the Old Testament typologically. The doctrine of recapitulation plays a role in the thought of Hippolytus which is at least as important as that which it plays in Irenaeus. Finally, the eschatology of Hippolytus has the same chiliastic features that we have already noted in the bishop of Lyon. Therefore, one may well place Hippolytus within the tradition that stems from the Apostolic Fathers of Asia Minor and from Irenaeus.

There are two aspects of Hippolytus' theology which are of special interest to us here: his moral rigorism, and his doctrine of the Trinity.

The moral rigorism of Hippolytus is important since it led him to a polemic with Callistus which is one of the focal points in every attempt to reconstruct the development of the penitential system of the church. During the early years of the foundation of the church, as

---

[2] Among these works, the most important for our purposes are: *Philosophumena, Against All Heresies, On the Antichrist, Against Noetus,* and, for the study of church order, the *Apostolic Tradition.* Some scholars have claimed that the differences between the *Philosophumena* and *Against Noetus* are such that they cannot have been written by the same author. The authenticity of the *Philosophumena* but not of *Against Noetus* is held by Marcel Richard, "Comput et chronographie chez saint Hippolyte," *MScRel,* 7 (1950), 237-68; 8 (1951), 19-50; Pierre Nautin, "La controverse sur l'auteur de l'*Elenchos,*" *RHE,* 47 (1952), 5-43. The opposite position, that is, that *Against Noetus* is genuine and the *Philosophumena* is not, is held by Pierre Nautin, *Hippolyte: Contre les héresies, Fragment. Étude et édition critique* (Paris: Éditions du Cerf, 1949). Finally, the authenticity of both is held by a great number of scholars, among them Gustave Bardy, "L'énigme d'Hippolyte," *MScRel,* 5 (1948), 63-68. We shall not discuss here the contents of the *Apostolic Tradition.* There is a good summary in J. Quasten, *Patrology,* 2: 180-94. To the excellent bibliography to be found there, one should add Bernard Botte, *La Tradition apostolique de saint Hippolyte: Essai de reconstitution* (Münster: Aschendorff, 1963).

may already be seen in the *Shepherd* of Hermas, there seems to have been a general consensus that, after that repentance which took place in baptism, it was somehow possible to repent again and thus be forgiven for post-baptismal sin. This took place through the public confession of the sin committed, followed by a period of penance and excommunication, in order to be admitted again within the Christian community through a formal act of restoration. This was not applied, however, in the case of the minor sins that Christians found themselves committing daily, and for whose remission there does not seem to have existed a penitential system except for private prayer and repentance. On the other hand, toward the end of the second century and early in the third there was a general opinion that the church could not or should not forgive those who were guilty of homicide, fornication, or apostasy. This was the opinion not only of Hippolytus, but also of Tertullian and Origen.

Naturally, this denial of the forgiveness of certain sins, while it tended to keep the moral strength of the church, was also a denial of the spirit of love and forgiveness which is characteristic of the gospel. Therefore, it was necessary that sooner or later there would develop a conflict between those who wished to preserve the moral purity of the church at all costs and those who believed that evangelical love should be followed even at the expense of moral rigor. This was one of the bases of the conflict between Callistus and Hippolytus.

It seems that Callistus dared to offer the grace of repentence and restoration to those who were guilty of fornication. It is not possible to know the personal motives of Callistus himself, for what Hippolytus says about his personality is rather difficult to believe.[3] In any case, Callistus appealed to the parable of the wheat and the tares and to the example of Noah's ark, where there were clean as well as unclean animals.[4] Hippolytus, who had other theological and even personal reasons to mistrust Callistus, saw this as an attempt to introduce an unacceptable laxity into the life of the church.

---

[3] *Philos.* 9. 7.
[4] *Ibid.*

Hippolytus' rigorism did not lead him to oppose the penitential system that had slowly developed in the Christian church. On the contrary, he claims that he is not rebelling against the traditional system, but against the innovations of Callistus. The penitential system itself is a fundamental part of Hippolytus' Christianity—including in that system the power of the bishops to forgive sin.[5] Therefore, the controversy had nothing to do with whether or not the church has the authority to forgive sins, but rather with the scope and application of that faculty.

The doctrine of the Trinity was the other focus of the controversy between Callistus and Hippolytus. We have already seen that Tertullian developed his doctrine of the Trinity in opposition to a certain Praxeas, who had established his residence in Rome and whose doctrine consisted in a Modalistic Monarchianism. Hippolytus himself develops his trinitarian doctrine in opposition to Modalism, represented in his case by Noetus of Smyrna, who, according to Hippolytus, "alleged that Christ was the Father Himself, and that the Father Himself was born, and suffered, and died," [6] and by Sabellius, whose defense of Modalism was such that this doctrine was later known as "Sabellianism." [7]

The position of Callistus before this doctrine was not entirely clear. If what Hippolytus says regarding the doctrine of the Roman bishop is not a mere fiction, Callistus does not seem to have been very distant from Monarchianism. According to Hippolytus, Callistus

alleges that the Logos Himself is Son, and that Himself is Father; and that though denominated by *a different* title, yet that in reality He is one indivisible spirit. *And he maintains* that the Father is not one person and the Son another, but that they are one and the same; and that all things are full

---

[5] E. Amann, "Pénitence," *DTC,* 12:766.

[6] *Ag. Noetus* 1 (*ANF,* 5: 223).

[7] The exact doctrine of Sabellius is not known. It is quite possible that his only important contribution to Modalism was to include the Holy Spirit in a system that had previously dealt only with the Father and the Son. Other texts would seem to indicate that he also added a more sophisticated understanding of the Godhead; but all such texts are rather late and it is impossible to know how much credence they deserve.

of the Divine Spirit, both those above and *those* below. *And he affirms* that the Spirit, which became incarnate in the virgin, is not different from the Father, but one and the same. And *he adds,* that this is what has been declared *by the Saviour:* Believest thou not that I am in the Father, and Father in me?" For that which is seen, which is man, *he considers* to be the Son; whereas the Spirit, which was contained in the Son, to be the Father.[8]

If such was the doctrine of Callistus, Hippolytus was not completely mistaken in comparing it with that of Noetus and Sabellius, although Callistus is careful enough to speak, not of the Father suffering *in* the Son, but of the Father suffering *jointly with* the Son. Thus he attempted to avoid falling into Patripassianism. But he still emphasizes the divine unity to such an extent that there is no distinction within the Godhead, and that the term "Son" is used only to refer to the humanity of Christ.

It is in opposition to the clear Modalism of Noetus and Sabellius, and to the less clear doctrine of Callistus, that Hippolytus develops his own trinitarian theology. In so doing, he makes use of the precedent that he finds in Tertullian's *Against Praxeas.* Like his predecessor, in opposing Modalism, Hippolytus emphasizes the distinction between the divine persons to such an extent that it is difficult for him to express the divine unity. Thus he, like Tertullian before him, seems to turn the Word into a secondary God and thus gives Callistus the opportunity of accusing him of "ditheism."

The subordinationism of Hippolytus is seen most clearly in the manner in which the generation of the Word depends on the will of the Father, and even on his purpose of creating the world.[9] Hippolytus accepts the understanding of the Word which the Apologists had, with its subordinationistic tendencies, and he repeats the distinction between the inner and the expressed Words.[10] However, this

---

[8] *Philos. 9. 7 (ANF, 5:130).* In the quotation from Callistus which follows, the term πρόσωπον (face, mask, person) appears for the first time in trinitarian discussion, although it still does not have the technical sense that will later develop.

[9] *Ag. Noetus 10.*

[10] *Philos.* 10. 29. Cf. Bernard Capelle, "Le Logos, Fils de Dieu, dans la théologie d'Hippolyte," *RThAM,* 9 (1937), 109-24.

subordinationism is limited, for Hippolytus himself categorically denies that there are "two Gods," as Justin or even Origen would have said.[11] His doctrine does not in any way deny the divinity of the Word, but rather affirms it explicitly, although it denies the eternal existence of the Word as distinct from the Father.

All this is to be understood, as in the case of Tertullian, in terms of the special divine "economy" according to which "we cannot otherwise think of one God, but by believing in truth in Father and Son and Holy Spirit."[12] This once again clearly shows the influence of Tertullian, who also understood the relationships within the Godhead in terms of an organic oneness that by its own "economy" is threefold.

Also in his Christology, Hippolytus follows the path that was opened by Tertullian. For him, as well as for the African theologian, the union of divinity and humanity in Jesus Christ is the union of "two natures," and in it each of them retains its properties.

And through the flesh He [Jesus Christ] wrought divinely those things which are proper to divinity, showing Himself to have both those natures in both of which He wrought, I mean the divine and the human, according to that veritable and real and natural subsistence, (showing Himself thus) as both being in reality and as being understood to be at one and the same time infinite God and finite man, having the nature of each in perfection, with the same activity, that is to say, the same natural properties; whence we know that their distinction abides always according to the nature of each.[13]

In Rome Hippolytus stands geographically between Irenaeus of Lyon and Tertullian of Carthage. He still writes in Greek, and the basic framework of his theology is the same as that of Irenaeus. But he often reads Irenaeus through Tertullian, and when it comes to specifically important issues, such as the restoration of sinners, the

---

[11] *Ag. Noetus* 8, 14.
[12] *Ibid.,* 14 (*ANF, 5:* 228).
[13] *Ag. Ber. and Hel.* 1 (*ANF, 5:* 231).

doctrine of the Godhead, and Christology, he is closer to the African doctor than to the bishop of Lyon. He is therefore a link in a long chain that will serve to preserve the influence of Tertullian at the same time that his name becomes less and less common.

Novatian

The very little that is known of the life of Novatian serves as a reminder of the importance that the issue of the restoration of the lapsed had in the Western church of the third century. We have already pointed out that this question was one of the factors involved in the dispute between Callistus and Hippolytus. Now, in the case of Novatian, it will be the same issue that will lead him to a rupture with the established episcopacy and thus provoke a new schism in the Roman church. In this case, as well as in that of Hippolytus, it is impossible to determine the relative importance of personal and theological factors. In any case, the fact is that—although it is possible that Novatian's attitude before the schism was different [14]—once the separation took place the discussion had to do with the problem of the restoration of the lapsed.

At this time, the issue did not have to do with those who had fallen into fornication—the battle that Callistus and his followers had already won—but with those that had committed apostasy during persecution. Once again, now in the person of Bishop Cornelius, the authorities of the Roman Church were inclined to forgive sinners. Novatian was opposed to this, and his attitude was parallel to that of Hippolytus three decades earlier.[15] As in the previous case, it was not so much a doctrinal debate regarding the nature of repentance, penance, and absolution as a discussion regarding its scope. In fact, the influence of the schism itself on Novatian's theology is scant and may be seen mostly in his emphasis on the sanctity of the church.[16]

---

[14] On the basis of Cyprian, *Ep.* 30 and 5.4.

[15] As well as to that of Tertullian. Cf. C. B. Daly, "Novatian and Tertullian. A Chapter in the History of Puritanism," *IrThQ*, 19 (1952), 33-43.

[16] Cf. *De trin.* 29.

From the doctrinal point of view, Novatian is important by reason of his work *On the Trinity*. Here he attempts to prove the divinity of the Son of God as well as his distinction from the Father. Jesus Christ is human as well as divine. As human, he is called Son of Man, and as God he is called Son of God.[17] The divinity of Christ is necessary for soteriological reasons: as immortality is "the fruit of divinity," and the purpose of Christ is to give immortality, it is necessary that Christ be divine. "Therefore He is God who proffers eternal salvation, which man, being unable to keep himself for ever, cannot be able to give to another." [18] This Savior God is the Son, who existed from the beginning in God, and whom the Father begat according to his will before the beginning of time, in such a fashion that between the Father and the Son there is a "communion of substance." [19] In Christ, the Son of God is united to the Son of man, and this union of two "natures" is such that the Son of God becomes Son of Man in assuming flesh, and the Son of Man becomes Son of God in receiving the Word.[20]

However, the main interest of Novatian's treatise is not to prove that the Son is God and that this divinity is in Christ, but to prove, against Sabellianism, that the Son is distinct from the Father. This purpose leads him to emphasize the subordination of the Son to such a point that some have seen in him a forerunner of Arianism. This subordinationistic tendency of Novatian takes as its starting point the distinction between the Father as the immutable and impassible God, and the Son as capable of establishing contact and relationship with men, the world, and its events.[21] Thus, when Genesis affirms that God came down to look upon the tower of Babel, and to confuse the languages of man, this does not refer to the Father, who is not in any place, but to the Son.[22] When Abraham saw God, he saw

---

[17] *De trin.* 11.
[18] *Ibid.*, 15 (ANF, 5: 625).
[19] *Ibid.*, 31.
[20] *Ibid.*, 23.
[21] *Ibid.*, 17.
[22] *Ibid.*, 17.

not the Father, who is invisible, but the Son.[23] When God appeared to Jacob in the form of an angel, it was not the Father, but the Son who spoke through him.[24]

This Son proceeds from the Father by generation. Although this generation is qualitatively different from the manner in which creatures come from God, there is a "certain sense"—is it a purely logical sense?—in which the Father is before the Son.[25] The beginning of the Son is in the Father—and Novatian thus attempts to avoid the ditheism into which he would fall if he were to affirm that the Son has his own beginning independently of the Father. If there were two "unbegotten" beings there would be two Gods.[26] But Novatian does not seem to affirm the eternal generation of the Son, nor his eternal existence as a second person in God. On the contrary, the Son or Word was eternally in the Father until an act *of the will* of the latter made the Son to be *with* the Father. It seems that once again we have here the distinction between the inner and the expressed Word.[27]

In his attempt to refute Sabellianism,[28] like Tertullian in attempting previously to refute Praxeas, Novatian so emphasizes the distinction between the Father and the Son that the latter turns out to be "inferior to the Father," or "less than the Father." [29] This, however, does not mean that he doubts the divinity of the Son. As far as the Holy Spirit is concerned, the position of Novatian is the same: the Holy Spirit is God, but the only manner in which Novatian can ex-

---

[23] *Ibid.*, 18.

[24] *Ibid.*, 19. It is these passages—and Chap. 20—which have led to an interpretation of Novatian according to which Novatian believes that the Son is an angelic being, but not divine: Felix Scheidweiler, "Novatian und die Engelchristologie," *ZschrKgesch*, 66 (1954-55), 126-39. But see: J. Barbel, "Zur 'Engelchristologie' bei Novatian," *TrthZschr*, 67 (1958), 96-105.

[25] *De trin.* 31.

[26] *Ibid.*

[27] *Ibid.*

[28] See G. Keilbach, "Divinitas filii ejusque patri subordinatio in Novatiani libro de Trinitate," *Bogoslovska Smotra*, 21 (1933), 193-224. Another interpretation, which claims that Novatian wavered between two positions: M. Simonetti, "Alcune osservazioni sul 'De Trinitate' di Novaziano," *Studi in onore di Angelo Monteverdi* (Modena: Societa Tipografica Editrice, 1959), 2: 771-83.

[29] *De trin.* 27.

press his existence as a distinct person is by making him inferior, not only to the Father, but also to the Son. If the Holy Spirit receives from Christ those things which he is to declare, it follows that "Christ is greater than the Paraclete, because the Paraclete would not receive from Christ unless He were less than Christ." [30]

In short, Novatian is significant for the history of Christian thought as an exponent of two aspects of Western doctrinal and ecclesiastical development during the third century. On the one hand, he was involved in the controversies that necessarily developed with the growth of the penitential system, and that occupied the attention of the Western church during most of the century. On the other hand, he shows how the influence of Tertullian was felt in Western trinitarian theology.

The schism that sprang from Novatian continued even after his death, and his church spread toward the East, where it later merged with some groups of Montanist inclinations.

Cyprian of Carthage

The most remarkable personality of the African church between Tertullian and Augustine is Cyprian of Carthage.[31] He was born early in the third century to a wealthy pagan family, and was not converted until he was approximately forty years old. After his baptism, he followed an austere life, abandoning that rhetoric in which he had made great progress, selling his properties in order to distribute his riches among the poor, and following the road of chastity. In A.D. 248—or perhaps 249—he was elected bishop of Carthage by popular acclaim. Although at first he was inclined to flee in order not to accept such responsibilities, he finally accepted the election as the will of God, and thus began a new stage in his life.

His episcopacy lasted only nine years, but during that brief period

---

[30] *Ibid.* 16 (*ANF,* 5: 625).

[31] The best general study is that of J. Ludwig, *Der heilige Märtyrerbischof Cyprian von Karthago: Ein kulturgeschichtliches und theologisches Zeitbild aus der afrikanischen Kirche des 3. Jarhunderts* (Munich: K. Zink, 1951).

he performed a great pastoral task. His writings are mostly practical, for they are motivated by concrete issues that required his action as bishop. His theology is clearly influenced by Tertullian, whom he called "the master." Like Tertullian, but even more because of his pastoral responsibilities, Cyprian pays most attention to moral, practical, and disciplinary matters. Furthermore, some of his works are mere revisions and annotations of those of Tertullian—*On the Dress of Virgins, On the Lord's Prayer, On the Vanity of Idols*, and *On the Advantage of Patience*.

Early in the year 250, when the persecution of Decius ended a period of relative peace for the churches which had lasted almost half a century,[32] Cyprian fled Carthage and hid. As the policy of the persecution consisted, not only in forcing all to secure a certificate stating that they had offered sacrifice to the gods, but also in attacking mainly the leaders of the church, Cyprian thought that his duty was to hide in order to avoid creating greater difficulties for the church. From his exile, he continued directing the life of the church, mostly through an abundant correspondence. He was greatly criticized for this decision, among others by the Roman clergy, who had lost their own bishop in the persecution and wrote to Cyprian asking for an explanation of his attitude. He replied that his presence in Carthage would only have brought more suffering upon the church and that, in any case, he had not abandoned his pastoral functions.[33]

Finally, the storm blew over, and early in the year 251 Cyprian was back among his flock. He then had to face the problem of the restoration of the lapsed, which had arisen even before the end of the persecution. The recent persecution, besides being the most systematic and severe that the church had known until that time, had sprung unexpectedly after a period of relative peace. When the edict appeared that required all the inhabitants of the Empire to offer sacrifice to the

---

[32] Charles Saumage, "La persécution de Dèce en Afrique d'après la correspondance de S. Cyprien," *Byz*, 32 (1962), 1-29.
[33] *Ep.* 14.

gods, and to obtain a certificate stating that they had done so, many were led by panic to flock to the pagan temples. Others succumbed later to the pressure of friends and relatives, and still others avoided martyrdom by obtaining false certificates. Very soon, and even before the persecution had passed, many of these people expressed their wish to return to the communion of the church. Cyprian believed that they should be given that opportunity, but that this should be done with due discipline and order, and that the decision should be left to the bishops.[34] A group of confessors whose courage during persecution gave them great moral influence was opposed to this policy, and required that those who had fallen and who now claimed to repent were to be restored immediately to the communion of the church. A group of elders who had always been opposed to Cyprian's election joined the confessors. Thus, the problem of the restoration of the fallen led to schism—as it did also in Rome, under the leadership of Novatian.

Faced by these circumstances, Cyprian called a synod which was attended by some sixty bishops. In order to make his position known to the synod as well as to the rest of the church, he wrote two treatises: *On the Unity of the Church*, and *On the Lapsed*. These two treatises are basic for an understanding of Cyprian's ecclesiology, and we shall refer to them repeatedly further on. Let it suffice to say here that Cyprian's position with reference to the lapsed was the following: those who refuse to do penance should not be forgiven, even on their deathbeds. Those who purchased certificates should be admitted immediately; the fallen should do penance for the rest of their lives, and would be restored to the communion of the church on their deathbeds or when they proved the true nature of their repentance in another persecution; finally, the fallen clergy should be deposed. On the other hand, regarding the schism, Cyprian recommended that its followers be excommunicated. In both of these matters the Council followed the suggestions of the bishop of Carthage and—although the

---

[34] J. J. Thierry, "Het conflict tussen martelaar en priester in de jonge kerk van Afrika," *NAKgesch,* n.s. 42 (1957), 63-77.

schism continued for some time, and was later strengthened by an alliance with the Novatians of Rome—this was the end of the controversy.

Two other problems gave occasion to the best of Cyprian's theological production: the plague that developed in A.D. 250, and the controversy regarding baptism.

When the plague broke out in North Africa, a pagan called Demetrianus blamed the Christians for the epidemic, which he claimed was a punishment sent by the gods. Cyprian responded in a brief but pointed treatise *To Demetrianus*. But he also wrote to the faithful trying to help them to face death properly—*On the Mortality*—and to practice the works of charity which the situation required—*On Works and Alms*.

The controversy regarding baptism had to do with whether or not baptism administered by heretics was valid, and whether therefore one should rebaptize converted heretics. The custom regarding this matter differed according to the various regions of the Empire: in North Africa and in Asia Minor it was customary to rebaptize those who had received the rite from heretical hands, whereas in Rome that previous baptism was considered valid, and converted heretics were not rebaptized. This diversity was a cause of concern for some people who consulted Cyprian. The bishop of Carthage then declared himself in favor of the African custom of rebaptizing converted heretics, and he later gained the support of two successive synods of African bishops.[35] Stephen, the bishop of Rome, who had already collided with Cyprian on other matters,[36] in learning of the decision of the African bishops, decided to intervene, and wrote an epistle, now lost, in which he urged the African bishops to follow the Roman custom and to accept the validity of the baptism of heretics. The controversy that ensued was prolonged, and Stephen even threatened

---

[35] The course of the controversy can be followed through Cyprian's *Epistles*, esp. *Ep. 72*, in which Pope Stephen is told of the decision of an African synod; *Ep. 74*, which shows Cyprian's reaction to Stephen's attitude; and *Ep. 75*, in which Bishop Firmilian of Caesarea supports Cyprian's position.

[36] Cf. *Ep. 67, 68.*

Cyprian with breaking the bonds of communion with the African church. But the bishop of Rome died before he could fulfill his threat, and a year later his Carthaginian counterpart offered his life as a martyr. This was the end of the controversy, but somehow the Roman church continued exerting its influence, and early in the fourth century it was customary in Africa to accept the baptism of heretics, although it is impossible to know when the change took place.

If I have given a great deal of time to summarizing the controversies of Cyprian with schismatics and with Rome, it is because these controversies are the context within which he developed his doctrine of the church, and that doctrine is his main contribution to the history of Christian thought.[37] Although Irenaeus and Tertullian opposed heretics by emphasizing the importance of the church and apostolic succession, and even Clement and Origen thought that the church was of great importance in the plan of salvation, none of them took the time to develop a doctrine of the church. Cyprian himself did not attempt to do so in a systematic manner, but through his controversies and the resulting treatises he gave shape to a doctrine of the church that would be very significant for later developments.

Cyprian sees the church as the indispensable ark of salvation.[38] Just as in the time of Noah no one who was not within the ark could be saved, now also only those who are within the church can be saved. "There is no salvation out of the Church," [39] and "he can no longer have God for his Father, who has not the Church for his mother." [40] This is the reason why Cyprian adopts an uncompromising attitude against that baptism which is received from heretical or schismatic hands. If these are not the church, and do not share in it in any fashion, there is no salvation within their community, or forgiveness

---

[37] Günter Klein, "Die hermeneutische Struktur des Kirchengedankens bei Cyprian," ZschrKgesch, 68 (1957), 48-68.

[38] De unit. eccl. 6.

[39] Ep. 73.21 (ANF, 5:384). Cf. G. Nicotra, "Interpretazione di Cipriano al cap. IV, vers. 12, della Cantica," SCatt, 18 (1940), 380-87.

[40] De unit. eccl. 6 (ANF, 5:423). Cf. J. C. Plumpe, "Ecclesia Mater," Transactions and Proceedings of the Amer. Philol. Assoc., 70 (1939), 535-55.

of sins, or direction of the Holy Spirit, or true eucharist, or true baptism. To claim that their baptism is valid would be to acknowledge that their group is ecclesiastically valid. It is therefore necessary to affirm that all the actions of heretics and schismatics, including their baptism, are the work not of Christ but of the Antichrist.[41] But, what can one say, then, about the good persons to be found among schismatics? There are no such persons, for

let none think that the good can depart from the Church. The wind does not carry away the wheat, nor does the hurricane uproot the tree that is based on a solid root. The light straws are tossed about by the tempest, the feeble trees are overthrown by the onset of the whirlwind.[42]

How can this church outside of which there is no salvation be defined and recognized? According to Cyprian this is the church of truth and unity. Although Cyprian affirms that truth is one of the essential characteristics of the church, his opposition to schismatics leads him to emphasize unity. Furthermore, he sees no truth without unity, for the foundation of all truth is love, and where there is no unity there is no love.

The unity of the church is in the episcopate. The bishops are the successors of the apostles, and their authority, which derives from that succession, is the same that Christ granted to the apostles.[43] The bishop is in the church and the church in the bishop, and where the bishop is not there is no church. The episcopate is one, but this is not due to a hierarchy of such a nature that all the bishops are subject to a single "bishop of bishops," but rather to the fact that in every bishop the totality of the episcopate is represented. "The episcopate is one, each part of which is held by each one for the whole." [44]

---

[41] Ep. 70.

[42] De unit. eccl. 9 (ANF, 5: 424).

[43] Ep. 33.

[44] De unit. eccl. 5 (ANF, 5: 423). The Latin says: "Episcopatus unus est, cujus a singulis in solidum pars tenetur" (PL, 4: 516). This may be understood in the sense that each bishop holds a part of the episcopacy. Thus P. Schepens, "Saint Cyprien, Episcopatus unus est cuius a singulis pars in solidum tenetur (De unitate Ecclesiae, V),"

Hence, each bishop is to govern his diocese independently of a monolithic hierachy—and Cyprian shows a high degree of tolerance and flexibility regarding various practices and customs. No bishop has the right to dictate to other bishops, although the unity of the episcopate is such that bishops should consult with one another in matters of importance. This federated view of the episcopate is important for an understanding of Cyprian's position regarding the Roman see.

On the one hand, Cyprian exalts the primacy of Peter among the apostles and also the importance of the Roman Church for the church universal. The confession of Peter on the road to Caesarea, and the repeated command of the Lord to Peter—"feed my sheep,"—show that Peter is the source of apostolic unity. The other apostles had the same honor and authority as Peter, but he was the first who received this authority, and this was done precisely in order to make him the principle of unity.[45] For this reason, as well as for its present importance, the church of Rome and its bishop have a certain priority among Christian churches. The Roman church is "the chief church whence priestly unity takes its source." [46]

On the other hand, Cyprian refuses to grant the bishop of Rome any jurisdiction whatsoever in the internal matters of his diocese.[47] Just as the authority of Peter, although prior to that of the other apostles, was not superior, thus the priority of Rome does not grant

---

RScRel, 35 (1948) 288-89. But it can also be understood as saying that the episcopal authority is indivisible, and yet each bishop shares in it. Thus Maurice Bévenot, "In solidum and St. Cyprian: a Correction," JTS, new series, 6 (1955), 244-48.

[45] De unit. eccl. 4. There is a textual problem regarding this chapter, of which two texts exist. The shorter text clearly affirms the primacy of Rome, whereas the longer text does not. Scholars still debate whether both texts are Cyprian's and, if so, which is earlier.

There is an impressive case against the shorter text in J. Le Moyne, "Saint Cyprien est-il bien l'auteur de la rédaction brève du 'De unitate' chapitre 4?" RevBénéd, 63 (1953), 70-105. But G. S. M. Walker, The Churchmanship of St. Cyprian (London: Lutterworth Press, 1968) believes that both texts are Cyprian's, and that the shorter text is the original.

[46] Ep. 59. 14 (ANF, 5: 344).

[47] The best study on this subject is Bernhard Poschmann, Ecclesia principalis: Ein kritischer Beitrag zur Frage des Primats bei Cyprian (Breslau: O. Borgmeyer, 1933).

it any authority over the other churches. When Pope Stephen attempted to intervene in the decision of the African church, Cyprian's answer was clear:

For neither did Peter, whom first the Lord chose, and upon whom He built His Church, when Paul disputed with him afterwards about circumcision, claim anything to himself insolently, nor arrogantly assume anything; so as to say that he held the primacy, and that he ought rather to be obeyed by novices and those lately come.[48]

Therefore, Cyprian thinks in terms of a federated episcopacy in which every bishop has a certain autonomy, although he must also listen to the fraternal recommendations of other bishops, and must obey the decisions of a council. His own method of government among the African churches shows this understanding of episcopal autonomy, for whenever it was necessary to make a decision that might affect his colleagues Cyprian called them to a council. It is in the acts of one of these councils that the following words may be found, clearly directed against the bishop of Rome, who attempted to impose Roman customs in Africa:

For neither does any of us set himself up as a bishop of bishops, nor by tyrannical terror does any compel his colleague to the necessity of obedience; since every bishop, according to the allowance of his liberty and power, has his own proper right of judgment, and can no more be judged by another than he himself can judge another. But let us all wait for the judgment of our Lord Jesus Christ, who is the only one that has the power both of preferring us in the government of His Church, and of judging us in our conduct there.[49]

In summary, the unity of the church is in its episcopate, of which all bishops share as if it were a common property. This unity is not something to be added to truth, but is rather an essential part of

---

[48] *Ep.* 71. 3 (*ANF*, 5: 377).
[49] *Conc. Carth. sub Cypriano VII, proemium* (*ANF*, 5: 565).

Christian truth, so that where there is no unity there is also no truth. Apart from this unity there is no salvation. Apart from it there is no baptism, or eucharist, or true martyrdom. But this unity does not consist in being subject to a "bishop of bishops," but in the common faith, love, and communion of all bishops among themselves.

Thus we end our rapid glance at Western theology in the third century. We have not studied all the theologians of the time, nor have we discussed the total thought of those whom we have studied. But what has been said should suffice to show that the theology of the West is inclined to practical interests. The most abstract theme that is discussed in the West is the doctrine of the Trinity—and here very little is said which is not a repetition of what was already found in Tertullian. Next to this subject there are others, such as the restoration of the lapsed and the validity of the baptism of heretics. These mostly practical concerns are the occasion for the rise of a doctrine of the church which would become general in the West until the time of Saint Augustine.

X

Eastern Theology After Origen

Origen's imprint was never erased from Eastern theology. In widely varying degrees, the greatest of the Greek Fathers showed his influence, and the repeated condemnations to which his theology was subjected were unable to keep his works from being read and some aspects of his theology from becoming widespread.

One of the characteristics of Eastern theology during the third century was precisely this dominance of Origen in the theological scene. The most distinguished theologians were his followers. Those who were not, and were yet significant, were so through their opposition to the Master. The main theological schools were really various factions within Origenism. And when a wholly independent theology arose, as was the case with Paul of Samosata, it was the Origenists that opposed it and finally succeed in having it condemned.

After Origen's death the theological tradition to which he belonged and which he moved forward continued, not only in Alexandria, but also in Caesarea and in other regions of the East where his disciples settled. In Alexandria, the tradition of Pantaenus, Clement, and Origen was continued in men such as Heraclas, Dionysius the Great, Theognostus, and Pierius. Although only fragments remain of the works of these Alexandrine theologians, they served to continue a tradition that will once again appear in the foreground early in the fourth century. In Caesarea, Pamphilus, who had studied under Pierius in Alexandria and later became bishop of Caesarea, conserved and enlarged Origen's library, and this was one of the main reasons why Eusebius of Caesarea—another Origenist who was in turn a disciple of Pamphilus—was able to write his famous and very valuable *Church History*. In other regions of the Empire, there were such distinguished Origenists as Gregory of Neocaesarea—the Wonderworker—and Lucian of Antioch. Their work was to have enormous consequences, and before the end of this chapter we shall have occasion to refer to it.

However, before expounding the various tendencies that appear within Origenism during the third century, one must pause in order to discuss first the only significant theologian of this period who seems to be totally independent from Origenism—Paul of Samosata—and then, the opposition to Origenism—represented in Methodius of Olympus.

Paul of Samosata

Paul of Samosata was elected bishop of Antioch in approximately A.D. 260. At that time the kingdom of Palmyra was flourishing and, in practically proclaiming itself independent from the Roman Empire, had awakened once again the ancient visions of a great Eastern empire. Antioch was part of that kingdom. Queen Zenobia, as a shrewd politician, favored the various considerable minorities that existed within her kingdom—among them, the Jews and the Christians. This was perhaps one of the reasons why she appointed Paul of Samosata *ducenarius,* a post of which he was so proud that he preferred to use that title rather than that of bishop.[1] As a bishop and a public officer, Paul's conduct seems not to have been very commendable, and there soon arose a wave of protest against his abuses,

---

[1] It is not possible to know exactly what were the functions and authority of a *ducenarius,* but it seems certain that it was a high administrative post that involved the management of large sums.

against the luxury that he attempted to create around himself, and against the innovations that he introduced in the life of the church.[2]

These accusations were accompanied by that of being a heretic. It seems that Paul combined certain Monarchianist tendencies with other adoptionist trends, thus proposing the theory that has been called—rather inaccurately—Dynamic Monarchianism.

The main interest of Paul's theology was in affirming Christian monotheism. Jews were a strong minority in Antioch, and even the general religious trend of Palmyra showed a marked evolution toward monotheism. Christianity itself, in its polemic against the pagans, had insisted in the existence of only one God. All this led Paul to emphasize the unity of God, even at the expense of the distinction between the Father, the Son, and the Holy Spirit.

However, Paul did not follow the way of Modalism, which affirmed that the Father, the Son, and the Holy Ghost were three modes in which God appeared. On the contrary, he attempted to preserve monotheism by establishing a marked difference between the Father and the Son, in such a manner that only the Father is God. As to the Holy Ghost, it is impossible to reconstruct Paul's thought on the basis of the fragments that remain.[3]

The Son is not God, nor is he the Word or Wisdom of God. Furthermore, the Son exists only after the incarnation, after the moment in which Christ is begotten in the womb of Mary by the Holy Ghost.[4] This distinction between the Word and the Son, however, would not have sufficed to condemn Paul as a heretic. It was often used by other theologians in order to distinguish between the Word as he existed before the incarnation, and the Son, who was the Word incarnate. Where Paul did open himself to attack was in denying that

---

[2] The most significant of these innovations was that of forbidding hymns to be sung to Christ. He also allowed women to sing in church, and had them accompany him wherever he went. Gustave Bardy, *Paul de Samosate: étude historique* (Louvain: Spicilegium Sacrum Lovaniense, 1929), pp. 264-73.

[3] Cf. Bardy, *Paul,* pp. 443-48.

[4] Thus, Mary bore not the Word, but the Son, *fragm.* 26 (Bardy, *Paul,* p. 56).

the Word was anything more than the unspoken and immanent reason of God.

Paul's Christology cannot be called "adoptionist" in the strict sense, for the conception by the Holy Spirit and the virgin birth—which he affirms[5]—imply that Jesus, from the moment of his birth, was the Son of God. But there is an adoptionist tendency in this doctrine inasmuch as the sonship of Jesus Christ is not essential—it is not a matter of the eternal Son or Word being made flesh—but consists rather in a "purpose" or "predestination" of God.

In Jesus the Wisdom or Word of God dwelt. But, as that Word is no more than the reason or purpose of God, and as it dwelt also in Moses and the prophets, God's presence in Jesus is only quantitatively different from what it has been or can be in other men. Jesus is in no way divine, but is rather "from below." [6] The union between Jesus and the Word is simply a moral union,[7] in such a way that the Word dwelt in Jesus "as in a temple." [8]

As this Word or Wisdom in no way subsists next to the Father, but is rather his power or δύναμις, this doctrine is usually called "Dynamic Monarchianism" to distinguish it from Modalistic Monarchianism. In the latter, the Word is identified with the Father, so that the divinity that existed in Jesus Christ is the Father himself, and for this reason this doctrine is also called "Patripassianism." Paul of Samosata, on the contrary, affirms that God was in Christ only in the sense that in him the power or Wisdom of God dwelt. For the Modalists, Jesus Christ is God; for Paul, he is a "pure man." [9]

On the other hand, the doctrine of Paul of Samosata should be distinguished from the subordinationist tendency that we have already found in Tertullian, Hippolytus, and even in Origen. In its extreme expressions, subordinationism safeguards the unity of God by turning

---

[5] *Fragm.* 37 (Bardy, *Paul,* p. 63).

[6] Eusebius, *HE* 7. 30. 11.

[7] Such is Bardy's conclusion (*Paul,* p. 466): "In short, Paul conceived only a moral union between Wisdom and Jesus.

[8] *Fragm.* 25 and 27 (Bardy, *Paul,* pp. 54, 57).

[9] Pamphilus, *Apol.* 5; Eusebius, HE 5. 28. 1-2.

the Son—and the Holy Ghost, when explicitly discussed—into a being that is lesser than the Father, but that is distinct from him and with a relatively independent subsistence. Paul safeguarded that unity by rejecting the idea that any sort of higher being, no matter how different from the Father, was incarnate in Jesus. This is probably the context in which he used the term ὁμοούσιος—consubstantial—which his opponents saw fit to condemn.

Thus, Paul's theology had to clash with that of the Origenists, and even with that of other Eastern theologians, at least on two points: in his doctrine of the Godhead, and in his Christology. His denial of the existence of the Word as a hypostasis or person next to the Father, and especially his denial of the real union of that Word with humanity in Jesus Christ, could only scandalize the majority of church leaders and even many of the laity in Antioch.

Soon the neighboring bishops began receiving complaints, regarding not only the conduct but also the orthodoxy of the bishop of Antioch. The Christians of that city were concerned about the attitude and the teachings of their bishop, and the result was a schism. Faced by such circumstances, Bishop Hellenus of Tarsus convoked a council that met in Antioch in A.D. 264 and that was attended by a group of distinguished Origenists. As was to be expected, these men clashed with Paul of Samosata. The latter's defense was such that the council could not clearly determine the nature of his error; but he still promised to modify his position and to teach what had become by then the traditional doctrine of the church. With this promise, and after discussing other matters, the bishops went home.

This however did not solve the problem, for it became necessary to call another council when word was received that Paul was still teaching the same doctrines that he had promised to abandon. This council deposed him after long debate in which the Origenist Malchion showed the weak points in the theology of the Antiochene bishop. But even then, with the support of Zenobia, Paul refused to accept the deposition, and held his episcopal and civil functions until the year 272, when Emperor Aurelian, after defeating Zenobia and consulting the bishops of Italy, applied the decision of the council.

This second council of Antioch has a certain importance for the history of Christian thought, because it was here that the doctrine that the Word is "consubstantial" (ὁμοούσιος) with the Father was condemned. It seems that Paul of Samosata used this term in order to deny that the Word had a subsistence of its own. When, in A.D. 325, the Council of Nicea used this same term—although in a different sense—there were many who suspected that the great council was returning to the ancient doctrine of Paul of Samosata.

Methodius of Olympus

Although the condemnation and deposition of Paul of Samosata had undeniable political overtones, it marked the end in Eastern theology of the last theological system of importance which was independent of Origenistic influence. From this point on—and during the third and fourth centuries—although there were repeated voices of protest against Origen and his followers, these voices themselves still betrayed the influence of the great Alexandrine teacher. In Methodius of Olympus we have an excellent example of this last statement.

Very little is known of the life of Methodius, and the only reason to call him "of Olympus" is that a tradition that is less doubtful than others claims that he was bishop of that city. It is said that he died as a martyr in A.D. 311, although that statement may also be questioned. What is unquestionable is that he was greatly inclined to asceticism, and that he held celibacy in high esteem, as may be seen in his dialogue *Symposium,* the only one of his works whose Greek text has been wholly preserved.

Although Methodius admired and followed Origen for some time, most of his writings present him as an opponent of the great Alexandrine. Probably this opposition itself is one of the reasons why so little is known of his life, for the historian Eusebius, being a fervent admirer of Origen, saw fit not to include Methodius in his *Church History*. In any case, even in opposing Origen, Methodius shows that he is not totally free of his influence. Thus, he coincides with Origen in making use of the philosophy of Plato—whose dialogues he attempts to imitate—as well as in speaking of God as a Platonist, and of the Trinity in terms of subordinationism, although without denying the eternity of the Son.

Methodius is opposed to Origen on four counts: the eternity of the world, the pre-existence of souls, spiritualistic eschatology, and allegorical exegesis. He attacks all these doctrines from the standpoint that is characteristic of that theological tradition which we have already encountered in Melito, in Papias, and in Irenaeus. As they had done before him, Methodius favors a typological interpretation of the Old Testament, a chiliastic eschatology, and an interpretation of the history of salvation in terms of "recapitulation," or of the parallelism between the work of Adam and that of Christ. But Origen's influence may still be clearly seen in the manner in which, while attacking the exaggerated allegorical exegesis of the great Alexandrine, Methodius himself is carried away by other interpretations that are no less allegorical; and it may also be seen in the manner in which he makes use of reason in refuting Origen's rationalism.

In order to show the manner in which Methodius refutes Origen's doctrine, it will suffice to summarize his argument against the doctrine of the eternity of the world, as that argument may be found in a fragment that has been preserved by Photius. As has been said above, Origen affirms that, God being eternally creator, creation itself must be eternal. Methodius points out that dependence constitutes an imperfection, so that the perfect being must be totally independent. Therefore, God's nature as creator cannot depend on creation, but on God himself, for to affirm the contrary would be to deny the divine independence and, therefore, the divine perfection. In conclusion, "we cannot accept the pestilent sin of those who affirm that God is almighty and Creator by reason of the things which he governs and creates." [10] and, as this is the foundation of Origen's doctrine, neither can he accept his opinions regarding the eternity of the world.

However, in that which refers to the issue that will occupy the center of the stage during the fourth century, that is, trinitarian doctrine, the teaching of Methodius is similar to that of Origen, although less precise. For him, as for Origen, there is a real distinction between the Father, the Son, and the Holy Ghost, and this distinction is expressed in subordinationist terms, although without denying the eternity of the three persons. "And thus, after this Beginning without beginning which is the Father, he [the Word] is the Beginning of other things, by which all things were made." [11]

Origenistic Theology

Very little is known about the development of Origenism immediately after the death of its founder. Although Eusebius of Caesarea, who belonged to that school, recorded abundant data regarding some of the main Origenists of the third century and the beginning of the fourth, these data are mostly biographical, and they add very little to our knowledge of the main theological currents of the time. On the other hand, there are references and even quotations of third-century Origenists in later writings. These are very valuable for the history of Christian thought, for through them one can attempt to reconstruct the theological development that leads from Origen to the Arian crisis. But one must not forget that, precisely because these references were made after the Arian issue was posed—that is to say, when the doctrine of the Trinity occupied the center of theological discussion—the witness of these writers of the fourth century is not to be taken as a balanced expression of the position of their predecessors—not only in the sense that the fragments and other data that have been preserved may have been twisted, but also in the sense

---

[10] *Fragm.* from Photius, *Bib. con.* 235 (*PG*, 103: 1144).
[11] *Ibid.* (*PG*, 103: 1148).

that the controversies of the fourth century have served to select those materials of the third which were quoted, thus giving later historians a partial vision of theological concerns during the period that goes from Origen to the first decade of the fourth century. Therefore, in studying Origenistic theology during the third century, one finds himself forced to focus his attention on trinitarian questions, and especially on those which refer to the relationship between the Father and the Son. But one must not forget that, behind the scant remains that we possess, there must have been a great deal of theological activity, not only in that which refers to the Trinity, but also in biblical exegesis, the doctrine of man, the theory of the sacraments, and so forth.

In order to illustrate the course of theology after Origen's death, we shall briefly discuss the thought of three of the most outstanding Origenists of the time: Gregory of Neocaesarea, Dionysius of Alexandria, and Lucian of Antioch.

Gregory was born to a distinguished pagan family of Neocaesarea, in Pontus. His real name was Theodore, but after his conversion and baptism he was called Gregory. That conversion took place in Caesarea in Palestine, through the teachings of Origen. After spending some time in that city learning from the great theologian the mysteries of the faith, he returned to his native city, of which he eventually became bishop. Many miracles were attributed to him, to such a point that he is known as Gregory the Wonderworker. We are also told that when he became bishop of Neocaesarea there were in that city seventeen Christians, and that his evangelistic labors were such that when he died there were only seventeen pagans. As bishop of Neocaesarea, he attended the first council held against Paul of Samosata in Antioch.

The most extensive work of Gregory that has survived is his *Panegyric to Origen*, which is very valuable for studying Origen's teaching methods. But much more interesting to us here is a creed that has been preserved in the biography of Gregory that was written by Gregory of Nyssa.

There is one God, the Father of the living Word, *who is His* subsistent Wisdom and Power and Eternal Image; perfect Begetter of the perfect *Begotten,* Father of the only-begotten Son. There is one Lord, Only of the Only, God of God, Image and Likeness of Deity, Efficient Word, Wisdom comprehensive of the constitution of all things, and Power formative of the whole creation, true Son of true Father, Invisible of Invisible, and Incorruptible of Incorruptible, and Immortal of Immortal, and Eternal of Eternal. And there is One Holy Spirit, having His subsistence from God, and being made manifest by the Son, to wit to men: Image of the Son, Perfect *Image* of the Perfect; Life, the Cause of the living; Holy Fount; Sanctity, the Supplier, *or Leader,* of Sanctification; in whom is manifested God the Father, who is above all and in all, and God the Son, who is through all. There is a perfect Trinity, in glory and eternity and sovereignty, neither divided nor estranged. Wherefore there is nothing either created or in servitude in the Trinity; nor anything superinduced, as if at some former period it was non-existent, and at some later period it was introduced. And thus neither was the Son ever wanting to the Father nor the Spirit to the Son; but without variation and without change, the same Trinity *abideth* ever.[12]

This creed emphasizes the eternal divinity of the Son, and says very little about that which distinguishes him from the Father, except that it certainly is *not* that one is invisible and the other visible, or one incorruptible and the other corruptible, or any such explanation that would make one less divine than the other. It is impossible to know the motives that led to the formulation of this creed, but there is no doubt that it reflects a continuation of one of the two aspects of Origen's doctrine. Whereas the Alexandrine teacher affirmed the eternity of the Son and at the same his subordination to the Father, Gregory takes up the first aspect of this doctrine, and leaves the second aside. This tendency of some followers of Origen has been called, rather inexactly, but still quite usefully, "right-wing Origenism."

On the other pole, some Origenists emphasized the subordinationist aspects of the master's doctrine. These are called, just as inexactly as

---

[12] *ANF,* 6: 7. The words "to wit to men" are probably a later addition.

the others, "left-wing Origenists." They were mostly persons who feared the threat of Sabellianism, which erased the distinction between the three divine persons. These theologians saw subordinationism as an easy means of distinguishing clearly between the Father and the Son, and of thus destroying every kind of Modalism. As examples of these concerns, we shall discuss Dionysius of Alexandria and Lucian of Antioch.

Dionysius of Alexandria—known as "the Great"—was one of Origen's most outstanding followers. He succeeded Heraclas as bishop of Alexandria and director of the catechetical school of that city. During the persecutions of Decius and Valerian he was forced to go into exile, but in both cases was restored to his episcopal charge, which he occupied until his death in A.D. 264. His works, which must have been many, were lost, and only a few fragments were preserved which later writers fortunately felt inclined to quote. Of these fragments, the most significant are those which refer to his correspondence with Dionysius of Rome, for they show how an Origenist, faced by the threat of Sabellianism, leaned towards "left-wing Origenism," and thus emphasized the distinction between the Father and the Son to such a point that he scandalized some of his flock.

According to the record of some later writers,[18] Dionysius of Alexandria, fearing the extremes of Sabellianism, used in his preaching certain phrases and illustrations with which he sought to emphasize the distinction between the Father and the Son. Some of these phrases and illustrations seemed to imply that the Son was a creature. Thus, Dionysius affirmed that there was a time when the Son did not exist, and that he was of a different substance than the Father. He also quoted the words of the Lord—"I am the true vine, and my Father is the husbandman"—in order to establish the difference between the Father and the Son, saying that their relationship is similar to that which exists between the husbandman and the vine, or between a boat and him who makes it.

---

[18] The most important are Eusebius, *HE,* 7; *Praep. evang.* 7. 9; 14. 23-27; Athanasius, *De sententia Dionysii.*

Some Christians from Alexandria, concerned over these doctrines of their bishop, decided to write to the bishop of Rome whose name was also Dionysius, and ask him for his opinion. Dionysius of Rome called a synod that condemned the opinions that seemed to be held by Dionysius of Alexandria, and he also wrote a letter to the latter asking him to clarify his position.

The bishop of Alexandria answered with a *Refutation and Apology*, in four books. This work has been lost; but some fragments have been preserved, and through them it is possible to outline his answer. He set out by complaining that his accusers had taken his words out of context, for he had also used other phrases and illustrations that should have served to show that he did not pretend to turn the Son into a mere creature. Thus, for example, one of these illustrations was that of a light that is lit from another, so that the resulting lights are distinct, but still share in a common nature. As to the term "consubstantial"—*homoousios*—he was willing to accept it as his Roman colleague explained its meaning, but he still pointed out that it was a word not to be found in the Scriptures. In any case, this term must not be understood in such a way that it denies the existence of three who are distinct, for it is always necessary to affirm the threefold nature of God. In short, Dionysius concluded that "we extend the Monad indivisibly into the Triad, and conversely gather together the Triad with diminution into the Monad." [14]

This correspondence between two bishops shows, not only the "left-wing Origenism" that the threat of Sabellianism could produce in a churchman, but also the difficulties posed by the fact that the East and the West used different languages. In the West, since the time of Tertullian, it was common to use the term "substance" in order to refer to the common divinity of the Father, the Son, and the Holy Spirit, and "person" to refer to each of these three. In attempting to cross the language barrier, it was natural to translate "persona" by

---

[14] Quoted by James Franklin Bethune-Baker, *An Introduction to the Early History of Christian Thought* (reprint, London: Methuen & Co., 1958), p. 115. This work contains a good summary of the correspondence between the two Dionysiuses: pp. 113-18.

"prósopon," which means, not only "person," but also "face" or "mask." Therefore, Eastern Christians would tend to see in Western theology an unacceptable Modalistic inclination. On the other hand, terminology in the East was still much more fluctuating than in the West, and the terms "ousia" and "hypostasis" were still ambiguous. The first could mean the particular subsistence of a thing as well as the common substance of which several individual beings share. The same ambiguity existed in the term "hypostasis." Therefore, when an Eastern theologian such as Dionysius of Alexandria spoke of three "hypostases," he was not necessarily establishing between the three persons of the Trinity as marked a distinction as his terminology could suggest to a Latin Christian. This confusion became serious because both *ousia* and *hypostasis* could be translated into Latin as *substantia*. Therefore, when a Western theologian such as Dionysius of Rome learned that an Oriental colleague was speaking of three "hypostases" he was bound to interpret such an affirmation in tritheistic terms, or at least in terms of an intolerable subordionationism. These difficulties, which could already be seen in the correspondence between the bishops of Alexandria and Rome, would be an obstacle in the communication between East and West until late in the fourth century, when, after long and bitter controversies, the ambiguities of the basic terms were clarified.

Finally, it is necessary to say a word about an Origenist whose work had enormous consequences: Lucian of Antioch. It is impossible to reconstruct the course of his life, for the data that seem to apply to him are contradictory. There was a certain Lucian in Antioch who was a follower of Paul of Samosata, and who for this reason was kept outside the communion of the church during the rule of three successive bishops.[15] There was also a certain Lucian who headed a school in Antioch where he had as disciples those who later were the main leaders of Arianism—and who called themselves "Collucianists."[16] It is impossible to coordinate these data, for Arianism is not to be understood

---

[15] Alexander of Alexandria, quoted by Theodoret, *HE* 1. 4. 36.
[16] Epiphanius, *Pan.* 69. 6.

as a further development of Paul's Monarchianism, but rather as an extreme type of Origenism. Were there then two different Lucians in Antioch at the same time? This would seem to be the best solution to the problem, and, in any case, one should not claim that Lucian, the teacher of Arius, who later died as martyr, is a link between Paul of Samosata and Arianism.[17]

Lucian of Antioch, the teacher of the Arians, founded in that city a school that would soon rival that of Alexandria. Although he was an Origenist in every other sense, Lucian was opposed to the allegorical interpretation of the Alexandrians, and he implanted in Antioch the study of Scriptures according to a historical and grammatical method. This method made the sacred text much more difficult to manipulate to one's advantage. But, although this made the theological task more difficult, it was also a great advantage, and even the great Alexandrine teachers of the fourth century, faced by the heresies of their time, were forced to abandon allegorical exegesis in favor of another method of interpretation that was more strict and scientific in character. This historical and grammatical exegetical method, which later became characteristic of the school of Antioch, seems to have been already at the root of the Greek text of the Bible which Lucian edited, and in which the main concern seems to be for clarity of expression.[18]

However, the importance of Lucian for the history of Christian thought is not so much in his contribution to exegetical method as in an aspect of his theology of which we have no trustworthy records: his doctrine of the Trinity.[19] When, some years after his death, the

---

[17] That there were two Lucians, one a disciple of Paul and another the teacher of Arius, is held by Friedrich Loofs, *Paulus von Samosata: Eine Untersuchung zur altkirchlichen Literatur- und Dogmengeschichte* (Leipzig: J. C. Hinrichs, 1924), pp. 180-86. On the other hand, Bardy, *Paul*, pp. 375-85, does not accept Loofs' thesis, but does agree that Lucian cannot be made a link between the widely different doctrines of Paul of Samosata and Arius. See, however, Johannes Quasten, *Patrology*, 2:143: "The Adoptionism of Paul of Samosata survived, with modifications, in the teaching of Arius."

[18] Bardy, *Paul*, pp. 381-82.

[19] The creed attributed to him, which appears in Socrates, *HE* 2. 10, and Athanasius, *Ep. de synodis* 23, is not surely his, and in any case has probably been interpolated (Philostorgius, *HE* 2. 14). But even if it is an authentic witness to Lucian's theology, it does

Arian controversy broke out, all the leaders of Arianism were former disciples of Lucian, and they called themselves "Collucianists." Arius, Eusebius of Nicomedia, Theognis of Nicea, Maris of Chalcedon, Leontius of Antioch, and Asterius the Sophist were his disciples; which leads us to ask: was Lucian actually the first Arian? It is difficult to know whether or not his doctrines were as extreme and clear-cut as those of Arius and his followers; but there is no doubt that he was one of those left-wing Origenists who, in emphasizing the distinction between the Father and the Son, came to such a point that it was difficult for them to say in what sense the Son was divine. Although the dangers of such a doctrine were not recognized during Lucian's lifetime, and his death as a martyr made it even more difficult to attack his doctrines, when his disciples developed his teaching to its logical consequences they could not but reach the conclusions—which Lucian perhaps had already reached—which became identified with the name of Arius, and which shook the Eastern church.

---

not change our general understanding of that theology. Cf. Gustave Bardy, *Recherches sur saint Lucien d'Antioche et son école* (Paris: G. Beauchesne et ses fils, 1936), pp. 119 ff.

XI

The Arian Controversy and the Council of Nicea

The fourth century saw the beginning of a new epoch in the history of the church, and, therefore, in the history of Christian thought. Constantine turned the persecuted church into the tolerated church[1] and later—especially after the foundation of Constantinople[2] —into the favored church. One of the immediate results of these new circumstances was that the fourth century was the era of the great Fathers of the church, for the energy that was previously devoted to training for martyrdom and to the refutation of pagan accusations could now be canalized toward other activities. This is one of the reasons why the fourth century produced not only the greatest Fathers of the church—Athanasius, the Cappadocians, Jerome, Ambrose, and Augustine, among others—but also the first historian of Christianity, Eusebius of Caesarea. Other Christians, now that martyrdom at the hands of the State was no longer possible, gave themselves up to the substitute martyrdom of monasticism, and thus

---

[1] There is still disagreement regarding the exact nature of Constantine's conversion. The main positions may be found in Joseph Vogt, "Konstantin," *RAC*, 3: 306-79. See also Hermann Dörries, *Das Selbstzeugnis Kaiser Konstantins* (Göttingen: Vandenhoeck & Ruprecht, 1954).

[2] This statement is well documented, with ample use of numismatic evidence, by Andreas Alföldi, *The Conversion of Constantine and Pagan Rome* (Oxford: The Clarendon Press, 1948), pp. 105-23.

the fourth century saw hundreds of hermits flock to the Egyptian desert.[3]

Christian art, until that time limited to funerary and other minor expressions, now became a triumphal art, progressively centered on Christ as Lord of heaven and earth.[4] Liturgy, which had remained relatively simple, now began to take up the uses of the Imperial court, for a parallelism was established between Christ and the Emperor.[5] And architecture now undertook the construction of churches capable and worthy of the new liturgical developments.[6]

These new conditions also had their negative consequences. In the first place, there soon began a mass conversion that inevitably detracted from the depth of conviction and the moral life of the church. Secondly, the imperial protection, which gave Christians the possibility of developing their theology to an extent that was previously impossible, also implied the possibility of imperial condemnation or favor to one theological position or another, and this in turn gave theological controversies a political dimension that they had not previously had. This is what happened in the Arian controversy.

Arius was a presbyter in the church of Alexandria who had been a disciple of Lucian in Antioch and who, like his teacher, represented the left wing of Origenism. The bishop of Alexandria, Alexander, was also an Origenist, but not of the same school. Soon they clashed, especially since Arius, who had great gifts as a leader, insisted in teaching an extreme subordinationism, and in attacking the position held by his bishop.

The doctrine of Arius was not a continuation or repetition of the

---

[3] J. M. Besse, *Les moines d'orient antérieurs au concile de Chaldédoine* (Paris: Oudin, 1900); Ph. Gobillot, "Les origines du monachisme chrétien et l'ancienne religion de l'Egypte," *RScRel,* 10 (1920), 303-54; 11 (1921), 29-86, 168-213, 328-61; 12 (1922), 41-68; Karl Heussi, *Ursprung des Monchtums* (Tübingen: J. C. B. Mohr, 1936).

[4] Cf. Louis Bréhier, *L'art chrétien* (Paris: H. Laurens, 1928), pp. 53-59.

[5] Cf. Gregory Dix, *The Shape of the Liturgy* (Glasgow: Dacre Press, 1945), pp. 303-96.

[6] This does not mean, however, that earlier Christians had no churches, or that the basilica was a creation of the Constantinian era. Cf. J. G. Davies, *The Origin and Development of Early Christian Church Architecture* (London: SCM Press, 1952), pp. 12-50.

teachings of Paul of Samosata, in spite of all that has been said to favor such an interpretation, even during the fourth century itself.[7] On the contrary, Arius is to be placed in the line of succession of those Origenists who were instrumental in achieving Paul's condemnation. Whereas the latter denied the independent subsistency of the Word, turning him into a mere "power" of the Father, Arius affirmed that the Word was radically different from the Father. Therefore, in order to understand Arianism, it is to be interpreted as the result of that "left-wing Origenism" which we have already found in Dionysius of Alexandria and Lucian of Antioch.

Arius begins from an absolute monotheism,[8] according to which the Son cannot be an emanation of the Father, or a part of his substance, or another being similar to the Father, for any of these three possibilities would deny either the immaterial nature of God or his unity. The Son cannot be without a beginning, for he would then be a brother of the Father, and not a Son.[9] Therefore, the Son has a beginning, and he was created or made by the Father out of nothing.[10] Before that creation, the Son did not exist, and it is therefore incorrect to affirm that God is eternally Father.[11] This does not mean, however, that there was not always a Word in God, an immanent reason; but this Word or reason of God is different from the Son, which was created later.[12] Therefore, when one says that the

---

[7] It seems that the first to claim that there was a relationship between Arius and Paul of Samosata was Alexander of Alexandria, in an epistle to his namesake of Constantinople, preserved by Theodoret, *HE* 1. 3.

[8] Aloys Grillmeier, *Christ in Christian Tradition* (New York: Sheed & Ward, 1965), pp. 189-92, argues that the doctrine of the incarnation, understood within the Logos-sarx framework, is the starting point for the Arian system. But his argument is not convincing, for he fails to show how, then, Apollinaris could be such a convinced anti-Arian. That Arianism springs from an attempt to make the Logos capable of incarnation, there is no doubt. But even a Logos-anthropos Christology would still pose difficulties as long as divinity is understood in terms of transcendence and immutability.

[9] Reinhold Seeberg, *Text-Book of the History of Doctrines* (Grand Rapids: Baker Book House, 1952), 1:202-3.

[10] Epiphanius, *Pan. 69. 6.*

[11] Athanasius, *Contra Arr. orat.* 1. 2. 5.

[12] *Ibid.*

Son is the Wisdom or the Word of God, this is correct only on the basis of the distinction between the Word that exists always, as the reason of God, and that other Word which is "the first born of every creature." Although all things were made by him, he himself was made by the Father, and is therefore a creature, and not God in the strict sense of the word.[13] This is the core of Arianism and the point that, when expounded in all its extreme clarity, created a violent reaction among many Christians: The Savior is not God, but a creature.[14] All this may be seen in a nutshell in the following quotation, preserved by Athanasius:

God himself then, in His own nature, is ineffable by all men. Equal or like Himself He alone has none, or one in glory. And Ingenerate we call Him, because of Him who is generate by nature. We praise Him as without beginning because of Him who has a beginning. And adore Him as everlasting, because of Him who in time has come to be. The Unbegun made the Son a beginning of things originated; and advanced Him as a Son to Himself by adoption. He has nothing proper to God in proper subsistence. For He is not equal, no, nor one in essence with Him. Wise is God, for He is the teacher of Wisdom. There is full proof that God is invisible to all beings; both to things which are through the Son, and to the Son He is invisible. I will say it expressly, how by the Son is seen the Invisible; by that power by which God sees, and in His own measure, the Son endures to see the Father, as is lawful. Thus there is a Triad, not in equal glories. Not intermingling with each other are their subsistences. One more glorious than the other in their glories unto immensity. Foreign from the Son in essence is the Father, for He is without beginning. Understand that the Monad was; but the Dyad was not, before it was in existence. . . . To speak in brief, God is ineffable to His Son. For He is to Himself what He is, that is, unspeakable. So that nothing which is called comprehensible does the Son know to speak about; for it is impossible for Him to investigate the Father, who is by Himself. For the Son does not know His own essence. For, being Son, He really existed, at the will of the Father. What argument then allows, that He who is from the Father

---

[13] *Ibid.*

[14] Gustave Bardy, *Recherches sur saint Lucien d'Antioche et son école* (Paris: G. Beauchesne et ses fils, 1936), pp. 226 ff; has collected the extant fragments of Arius.

should know His own parent by comprehension? For it is plain that for that which hath a beginning to conceive how the Unbegun is, or to grasp the idea, is not possible.[15]

This extreme subordinationism was not totally lacking in antecedents, for it appears in the history of Christian thought whenever the Word is interpreted in a Platonic sense, as a demiurge that exists between an immutable divinity and a world in which all is change and multiplicity. Justin, because of a similar understanding of the Word, had already affirmed that he was "another God"—which, in view of Christian monotheism, would imply that he was God only in a relative sense. Clement of Alexandria, for similar reasons, had established the distinction between the Father and the Son on the basis of the difference between the invisible and the visible. The innovation of Arius was then simply to take this subordinationism to its logical consequences, and to declare quite clearly that the Word was a creature.

As was to be expected, Alexander, who belonged to the opposite wing of Origenism, attacked the doctrine of Arius with all the means at hand and, after a series of events that it is not necessary to retell here, convoked a synod in which almost a hundred Egyptian bishops were present, and which condemned and deposed Arius. The latter, however, did not consider himself defeated, but wrote to his "fellow Lucianists" and gained their support, especially that of Eusebius of Nicomedia, who was the most influential among them. Eusebius received Arius in his diocese and granted him his protection in spite of the protests of the bishop of Alexandria. Thus, the dispute became a schism that could affect the whole church.

The news regarding these events reached Constantine, who had hoped that Christianity would be "the cement of the Empire," and who had already found himself in the necessity of intervening in the Donatist schism in North Africa. This new threat of schism, in which theological issues were involved which he could not understand, was

---

[15] Athanasius, *De syn.* 15 (*NPNF*, 2nd series, 4: 457-58).

very discouraging. He therefore decided to send to the East his counselor in religious matters, Bishop Hosius of Cordova, who went armed with a letter in which the Emperor asked the belligerent parties to resolve their dispute pacifically. When Hosius informed him that the reasons for the dissension were profound and that it was not possible to solve them by mere efforts of reconciliation, Constantine decided to call a great council of bishops which would deal, not only with the Arian question, but with several problems that needed a common solution.[16]

The council met in the city of Nicea, in Bythinia, in A.D. 325, and was attended by more than three hundred bishops. For these bishops, for many of whom persecution was still a living memory, this great assembly, gathered under the imperial cloak and to which all had come making use of the Imperial post, was a true miracle.[17]

Only a few of the bishops who attended the council had firm opinions regarding the main issue to be discussed. On the one hand, the small group of "fellow Lucianists," headed by Eusebius of Nicomedia—as Arius was not a bishop, he was not a member of the council—seems to have thought at first that it would easily be able to gain the support of the majority. On the other hand, another minority, headed by Alexander of Alexandria and in which there were certainly some bishops of Monarchianist tendencies, was bent on achieving the condemnation of Arianism. But the vast majority does not seem to have understood the importance of the matter at hand, and their fear of Sabellianism made them reluctant to condemn subordinationism in very strong terms. Besides, the Emperor, whose interest was in the unity of the Empire rather than in the unity of God, was inclined to find a formula that would be acceptable to the greatest number of bishops possible.

---

[16] This very brief sketch of events is intended only as an introduction to the Council of Nicea. More detailed narratives may be found in various Church histories. A point of some significance which, however, does not appear in many Church histories may be seen in Henry Chadwick, "Ossius of Cordova and the Presidency of the Council of Antioch, 325," *JTS*, n.s. 9 (1958), 292-304.

[17] Eusebius, *Vita Const.* 3. 7.

The Arians, however, misinterpreted the feelings of the majority, and this was the occasion of their fall. Eusebius of Nicomedia, believing that to be the best policy, read before the assembly an exposition of Arianism in its most clear and extreme form. Faced by the clear consequences of Arianism, the bishops were scandalized, and from that moment the Arian cause was lost.[18] During some time an attempt was made to produce a document that, making use of scriptural terms, would clearly declare that the Son is not a creature. But the Arian party had its own interpretations of all the texts that could be opposed to them.[19] It was then that the Emperor intervened and suggested that the word "consubstantial" (*homoousios*) be included in a creed, in order to make clear the divinity of the Son.[20] With this indication, which possibly was suggested to the Emperor by Hosius of Cordova,[21] a group who were convinced opponents of Arianism was asked to write a statement of faith. The result was the following creed, which the council adopted:

We believe in one God, the Father almighty, maker of all things visible and invisible;

And in one Lord Jesus Christ, the Son of God, begotten from the Father, only-begotten, that is, from the substance of the Father, God from God, light from light, true God from true God, begotten not made, of one substance with the Father, through Whom all things came into being, things in heaven and things on earth, Who because of us men and because of our salvation came down and became incarnate, becoming man, suffered and rose again on the third day, ascended to the heavens, and will come to judge the living and the dead;

And in the Holy Spirit.

But as for those who say, There was when He was not, and, Before being born He was not, and that He came into existence out of nothing, or who assert that the Son of God is of a different hypostasis or substance, or is

---

[18] Theodoret, *HE* 1. 8. 1, 5.
[19] Athanasius, *De decret.* 5. 19-20.
[20] Eusebius, *Ep. ad Caesar.* 4.
[21] But see Heinz Kraft, " Ὁμοούσιος," *ZschrKgesch*, 66 (1954-55), 1-24.

created, or is subject to alteration or change—these the Catholic Church anathematizes.[22]

The traditional interpretation of the origin of this creed was that it was a revision of another formula that Eusebius of Caesarea had read earlier before the assembly. There are, however, several serious objections to this understanding of events, and it seems more probable that what actually happened was that a previously existing creed from the region of Syria and Palestine was interpolated in order to include the typically anti-Arian phrases.[23]

In any case, the significance of the creed adopted at Nicea is to be found in the clauses "that is, from the substance of the father," and "true God from true God, begotten not made, of one substance (homoousios) with the Father," as well as in the anathemas added at the end. From these texts, it is clear that the intention of the creed was to leave no room for Arianism, which henceforth was to be considered heretical.

But how did the bishops gathered at Nicea interpret this creed which they had just adopted and which would be the creed of the universal church? It is difficult to know, and one can well imagine that those who assented to this formula interpreted it in different ways, according to their own theological traditions.

In the first place, to the few theologians who represented the West in the council, but whose influence was great through the presence of Hosius of Cordova, the term "homoousios" must have appeared as an approximate translation of the unity of substance which had become a traditional doctrine in the West since the time of Tertullian. This is precisely the traditional way in which the West has interpreted the Nicene formula. But this interpretation—no matter how orthodox—

---

[22] John Norman Davidson Kelly, *Early Christian Creeds* (London: Longmans, Green & Co., 1950), pp. 215-16. On the sources and variant texts of the creed of Nicea, see: Ignacio Ortiz de Urbina, *El símbolo niceno* (Madrid: Consejo superior de investigaciones científicas, 1947), pp. 8-22.

[23] Kelly, *Creeds*, pp. 211-30.

does not correspond to the historical reality of the problem that was debated, which was not so much the unity between the Father and the Son as the divinity of the latter.

Then, there were also some Eastern bishops who interpreted the term "homoousios" in a similar fashion, and who saw in it an affirmation, not only of the divinity of the Son, but also of the absolute unity between the Father and the Son—a unity without fundamental distinctions. Among these one may mention Eustathius of Antioch and Marcellus of Ancyra, both of whom played an important role in the condemnation of Arianism in Nicea. Eustathius as well as Marcellus were among the opponents of Origenistic speculation. Eustathius was rather in the tradition of Paul of Samosata, although he was careful not to oversimplify his Christology so that he could be accused of the ancient heresy of Paul, or of denying the essential divinity of the Savior. But he did follow Paul of Samosata in approaching a type of Monarchianism, not like that of Sabellius and his followers, but rather one that was archaic in nature, and perhaps influenced by Jewish criticism of Christian doctrine. Although very little is known regarding the trinitarian doctrine of Eustathius, it seems clear that for him the term "homoousios" implied such a unity that the three persons of the Trinity cannot subsist as such.[24]

The doctrine of Marcellus is better known. According to the bishop of Ancyra, God is one, and makes himself known as Father, Son and Holy Ghost, not in three successive stages of revelation, but as three modes of his action. But Marcellus will not go beyond a Trinity for the purpose of revelation, and will not speak of the personal or individual subsistence of each of the three persons.[25] As was to be expected, this insistence upon the unity of God, lacking a corresponding emphasis on the divine Trinity, made Eustathius as well as Marcellus suspect of Sabellianism.[26]

---

[24] Robert V. Sellers, *Eustathius of Antioch and His Place in the Early History of Christian Doctrine* (Cambridge: Cambridge University Press, 1928), pp. 88-93.

[25] Marie-Dominique Chenu, "Marcel d'Ancyre," *DTC*, 9: 1993-1998, discusses the manner in which Marcellus understood the "homoousios."

[26] Cf. Sellers, *Eustathius*, p. 98.

Thirdly, the small minority of followers of Alexander, who had come to the council with the firm purpose of achieving the condemnation of Arius, tended to interpret the formula "homoousios" as an affirmation of the eternity and divinity of the Son, which was precisely the point of conflict between Arius and the "right-wing Origenists." For them, this formula was not as explicit as they would have wished, but in any case it was a clear rejection of any attempt to claim that the Son was a creature.

In the fourth place, the vast majority of bishops had been under the influence of Origen, and were more afraid of Sabellianism than of Arianism. If this group, which was the main body of the council, accepted the creed of Nicea and signed it, this was due, first, to the impact that the extreme exposition of Eusebius of Nicomedia had produced; second, to the overwhelming imperial presence; third, to the possibility of interpreting the phrase "homoousios," not as an affirmation of the absolute and substantial unity of God, but rather only as an affirmation of the divinity of the Son.

Finally, the Arian party interpreted the creed in various manners and adopted different attitudes before it. Most of them, threatened with banishment, signed the creed as well as the anathemas, trying at the same time to find an interpretation of this document which would allow them to submit to the imperial will without violating their conscience. Some others accepted the creed, but refused to sign the anathemas, while two absolutely refused to sign. By imperial decree those who did not sign the entire document were banished, and the books of Arius were burned.

As to the Emperor himself, it is impossible to guess his purpose in suggesting that the term "homoousios" be included. It seems that he thought that that term would stop further speculations regarding the substance of the Father and the Son, and that thus these bitter discussions which he did not understand, but which threatened to divide his Empire, would be ended.

In summary, one may affirm that there was a great ambiguity in the Nicene formula. The creed, whose main purpose was to affirm the divinity of the Son, could also be interpreted as an affirmation of the divine unity. This, coupled with the fact that the formula of Nicea remained silent regarding the distinction between the Father, the Son, and the Holy Spirit, soon made it suspect as a concession to Sabellianism. This is why, in spite of the condemnation of Arianism at Nicea, that condemnation did not prove sufficient to expel it from the church, and for more than fifty years the controversy raged before the church finally and definitively condemned Arianism.

XII

The Arian Controversy After Nicea

Although the Council of Nicea condemned Arianism, that condemnation did not end the controversy, which lasted for more than fifty years beyond that. This was due, on the one hand, to the sincere doubts that some bishops had regarding the Nicene formula and, on the other, to the variations of imperial policy, which since the conversion of Constantine became an important factor in every theological controversy. The dissatisfaction of the bishops with the Nicene decision was to be expected. While the Council was in session, and the main issue was Arianism as it had been expounded by Eusebius of Nicomedia, the bishops there gathered felt inclined to accept a formula that condemned Arianism without saying a word regarding Sabellianism. But upon returning to their own churches, where Arianism was not yet a real threat and where they constantly had to face Sabellian doctrine, the bishops began to doubt the wisdom of their decision in the Council.

Besides, the opposition to Arianism at Nicea had brought together very different interests: the right-wing Origenism of Alexandria, the anti-Origenism of some circles in Antioch and Asia Minor, and the practical and anti-speculative interests of the West. Such an alliance, which is understandable in the presence of Arian speculation, could not present a united front when the Arian leaders began attacking its components separately.

On the other hand, the order of banishment against Arius and his followers, with which Constantine attempted to show his support to the decisions of the Council, established a bad precedent: thereafter, when theological argument failed, and even before making use of it, one could always make use of the resources of politics and have one's enemy banished. Because of Constantine's wavering policies, sometimes supporting the Nicene party and at other times acting against it, and especially because of the uncertainty of politics after Constantine's death, the fourth century—especially in the East—produced extremely complex and fluid positions and alliances. Although the defenders of Nicea as well as its opponents made use of politics and adulation on occasion, there is no doubt that it was the Arians—and especially Eusebius of Nicomedia—who were most distinguished in such arts.

Constantine's ecclesiastical policy consisted in turning the church into "the cement of the Empire." Therefore, and also because he could not see the importance of the subtleties the theologians debated, he easily lost his temper and reacted against those who showed a firm attitude regarding their own theological positions. This was the reason why, after the Council of Nicea, he exiled Arius and all those who refused to sign the Nicene creed. For the same reason Eusebius of Nicomedia was sent into exile a few months later. By ridding himself of these extreme elements, Constantine hoped to solidify the peace that he believed that the Council of Nicea had established.

During some time—approximately five years—the defenders of Nicea were uppermost. The three main sees—Rome, Alexandria, and Antioch—were occupied by bishops who strongly supported the formula and the decisions of Nicea, and at the same time Hosius of Cordova was one of the main counselors of the Emperor. But this situation could not last, for the Arian party soon adopted a position that seemed to be conciliatory and persuaded the Emperor that it was the anti-Arians that were stubborn and rebellious. Likewise, they succeeded in convincing some of the more conservative bishops that the Nicene formula was an unwarranted concession to Sabellianism.

The exile of Eusebius of Nicomedia did not last long, for he soon realized that his strategy of proclaiming the most extreme conclusions of Arianism was wrong. After becoming reconciled with Constantine, he returned to his see in Nicomedia, where the Emperor had his summer residence, and there proceeded to gain the favor of the court and even of Constantine himself. Arius also wrote to the Emperor claiming that he was ready to accept a compromise with the rest of the church, and on those grounds Constantine allowed him to return from exile. Some time later the Emperor ordered Alexander of Constantinople to admit Arius to communion. Alexander believed this to be a sacrilege, and he was still perplexed as to what his action should be when the death of Arius came to solve his problem.

During the first years after the Council of Nicea, the Arians did not themselves attack the decisions of the great Council, which was still Constantine's pride, but rather organized attacks upon those individuals who were the main supporters of the Nicene formula.

Alexander of Alexandria died in A.D. 328 and was succeeded by Athanasius, who had been his righthand man, and who was present at Nicea. Athanasius followed the theological line of Alexander, and soon became known as the greatest defender of the Nicene faith. Therefore, the main opponents that the Arians had in the East were Eustathius of Antioch, Marcellus of Ancyra, and Athanasius of Alexandria. It was against these men that Eusebius of Nicomedia directed a long series of personal attacks whose real target seems to have been the decision of Nicea, although they were often covered under moral or disciplinary accusations.

The first to fall was Eustathius of Antioch. In A.D. 330—that is, five years after the Council of Nicea—Eusebius of Nicomedia managed to have him condemned as an adulterer, a tyrant, and a heretic. At a synod that had been gathered in Antioch in order to judge Eustathius, a woman with a child in her arms claimed that Eustathius was the father. Although there were no further witnesses to strengthen the testimony of the woman, the synod—which in any case had already decided to condemn the bishop—accepted her declarations without any further questioning. The charge of tyranny

281

was not difficult to prove against a bishop of an important see such as that of Antioch, where there were often dissensions that it was necessary to stop. Finally, the main charge—that of heresy—was based on Eustathius' emphasis on the essential unity of God, which made him suspect of Sabellianism. As he affirmed that the Father and the Son were of the same substance, but had no clear means of expressing the distinction between them, the synod decided that he was an exponent of Sabellianism. This accusation was much more easily proved since Eustathius had entered into theological controversies not only with the Arians, but even with moderate left-wing Origenists such as Eusebius of Caesarea. In these controversies Eustathius had attacked the subordinationism of his opponents. In consequence, he was easily condemned and deposed. It was no use for him to appeal to the Emperor, for Eusebius of Nicomedia and his followers also accused him of having spoken disrespectfully of Constantine's mother. As a result, Eustathius was banished to Thrace, where he died sometime later after having composed some works against the Arians. But his history did not end there, for his Antiochene followers did not accept his condemnation, much less the appointment of his successor. Thereby a schism was created that lasted for many years, and that further contributed to the restlessness of the Eastern church. As to the supposed mother of Eustathius' son, on her deathbed she confessed that her testimony had been purchased by the bishop's enemies.[1]

Much more to be feared than Eustathius was Athanasius, now bishop of Alexandria. The importance of that see, its traditional prestige as a center of theological activity, and its close connections with the West, would have been enough to make its bishop a formidable enemy. But now a personal factor was added in that the man who occupied that bishropric was one of the greatest churchmen of all times. As an opponent of Arianism, Athanasius was indefatigable and knew how to take the offensive. Besides, as will be seen in the follow-

---

[1] The story of Eustathius' downfall, with ample reference to sources, may be found in Sellers, *Eustathius*, pp. 39-59.

ing chapter, he was a man with a clear grasp of the central Christian truths, and with an extraordinary ability to distinguish between the central and the peripheral. For these reasons, he was for many years the great defender of the Nicene faith, as well as the main target of Eusebius of Nicomedia and the Arian party.[2]

Already in A.D. 331 Athanasius had to defend himself before the Emperor on charges brought against him by his enemies. At that time, he was able to convince Constantine that the accusations were false. But the Emperor, following always his policy of keeping peace in the church, was not inclined to feel kindly toward a man as firm as Athanasius. Therefore, when some years later a synod gathered in Tyre under the direction of Eusebius of Nicomedia condemned and deposed Athanasius on the same charges, the Emperor did not feel inclined to contradict the synod, but rather sought a pretext to banish Athanasius without thereby seeming to affirm that what he had previously declared to be false accusations now turned out to be true. That pretext was provided by a fresh accusation that Athanasius projected to interrupt the shipment of grain from Alexandria to Rome. As a result, Athanasius left his see in what turned out to be the first of a long series of exiles. But, firm in his conviction that he must defend the Nicene faith, he made use of his exile in order to visit the West and there to establish ties that would later prove very useful.

As to Marcellus of Ancyra—the other Eastern bishop who had taken a firm and aggressive stand against Arianism—his condemnation was not difficult, for he was clearly prone to Monarchianism. In A.D. 336—the year of Arius's death—a synod in Constantinople condemned Marcellus and deposed him "for teaching the doctrine of Paul of Samosata," and the Emperor banished him. Marcellus also went to the West, where he would later come in contact with Julius of Rome and with Athanasius—during the second exile of the bishop of Alexandria. However, Athanasius himself did not feel comfortable with the support of one who was so near to Monarchianism, and in one of

---

[2] On the life of Athanasius, and the events of his times, see Hans Lietzmann, *A History of the Early Church*, Vols. III-IV (London: Lutterworth Press, 1950-1951).

his works attacked the doctrines of the former bishop of Ancyra, although without mentioning his name.[3]

In summary, one can say that during the period that goes from A.D. 330 to the death of Constantine seven years later the defenders of the "Great Council" were repeatedly defeated. The Emperor's main interest was political rather than theological, and this combined very well with the political abilities of Eusebius of Nicomedia in order to give Arianism the upper hand. This situation was made much more difficult on account of the inability of some of the main defenders of Nicea to show how their doctrine differed from Sabellianism. At the same time the Arians abstained from openly attacking the Council that Constantine had convened. The final defeat for the Nicene party during that time, although more symbolic than real, was the fact that Constantine himself was baptized on his deathbed by Eusebius of Nicomedia.

Constantine was succeeded by his three sons, Constantine II, Constans, and Constantius. The East fell under the rule of Constantius, whereas his two brothers shared the West, so that Constans had the region of Italy and Illyria, and Constantine II had Gaul and North Africa.

At first the new political situation seemed to favor the Nicene party, for one of the first acts of Constantine II, upon receiving news of the death of his father, was to order that Athanasius be restored to his see in Alexandria. Other exiles were also allowed to return, among them Marcellus of Ancyra.

But it soon became clear that Constantius, whose inheritance was the government of the East, was a decided defender of Arianism and of its leader Eusebius of Nicomedia, who was now bishop of Constantinople. The motives that Constantius had for this policy are not clear, but it seems that, apart from any theological convictions that may have played a role in his decision, he was interested in pushing forward the importance of the bishop of his capital over those of other sees,

---

[3] *Or. contra Arianos* 4.

especially Antioch and Alexandria. As, from the time when Eustathius had been deposed, Antioch had been ruled by the party of Eusebius, it only remained to subject the see of Alexandria to the same control. Besides, Constantius could not count on permanent good relations with his two brothers who ruled in the West, and in such circumstances he needed an Eastern church united under one doctrine, and somehow indebted to him. Thus a sort of alliance developed between Eusebius and Constantius, and the Arians once again gained the upper hand in the East.

In the West, Arianism had never been able to grow roots, for there was not such a great fear of Sabellianism, and the formula "one substance and three persons" had become commonplace—a formula that, at least in its first part, was in agreement with that of Nicea. But the relationship between the two Western emperors was not wholly friendly, and resulted in a war that continued until the death of Constantine II in A.D. 340. These rivalries in the government of the West diminished its influence upon the East, so that Constantius felt free to follow a policy of supporting the Arians and trammeling the Nicene party. In A.D. 339, Athanasius left Alexandria in a second exile, and he now went to Rome.

After Constantine II died, the West now being united under Constans, Constantius felt compelled to moderate his policy according to the wishes of his brother, and the defenders of Nicea had a brief respite that allowed Athanasius to return to Alexandria in A.D. 346. Contantius, however, did not abandon his policy of supporting the Arians, but only made it more moderate because of the influence of Constans and the West.

During this period of political uncertainty, the Arian party attempted to weaken the Nicene position, not only by attacking its defenders, but also by producing a series of other creeds that hopefully would be used as alternatives to that of Nicea. Thus, a single synod in Antioch in A.D. 345—the so-called "Council of the Dedication"—produced four different creeds.

The strength of the Arian party seemed to grow every day. The three bishops Ursacius, Valens, and Germinius, who opposed the Council of Nicea not simply as conservative anti-Sabellians, but rather as convinced Arians, became personal and close counselors of Constantius, who in A.D. 350, upon the death of his brother Constans, became absolute master of the Empire. Five years later, the Arian counselors of the Emperor suggested to him a formula according to which the Son was clearly inferior to the Father, and which later became known as "the blasphemy of Sirmium." Part of that formula read as follows:

But since some or many persons were disturbed by questions concerning substance, called in Greek οὐσία, that is, to make it understood more exactly, as to ὁμοούσιον [of the same substance], or what is called ὁμοιούσιον [of like substance], there ought to be no mention made of these at all. Nor ought any exposition to be made of them for the reason and consideration that they are not contained in the divine Scriptures, and that they are above man's understanding, nor can any man declare the birth of the Son, of whom it is written, *Who shall declare His generation?* For it is plain that only the Father knows how He begat the Son, and the Son how He was begotten of the Father. There is no question that the Father is greater. No one can doubt that the Father is greater than the Son in honour, dignity, splendour, majesty, and in the very name of Father, the Son Himself testifying, *He that sent Me is greater than I.* And no one is ignorant that it is Catholic doctrine that there are two Persons of Father and Son; and that the Father is greater, and that the Son is subordinated to the Father, together with all things which the Father has subordinated to Him, and that the Father has no beginning and is invisible, immortal and impassible, but that the Son has been begotten of the Father, God of God, Light of Light, and that the generation of this Son, as is aforesaid, no one knows but His Father.[4]

Naturally, the prohibition of all discussion regarding the "ousia" or "substantia" was tantamount to a condemnation of the Council of Nicea, which shows that the Arians now considered themselves suffi-

---

[4] Hilary, *De syn.* 11 (*NPNF,* 2nd series, 9: 6-7). Cf. Athanasius, *De syn.* 28 (*NPNF,* 2nd series, 4: 466).

ciently strong to carry out a frontal attack. The Emperor supported this formula, and even attempted to impose it, not only in the East, where the "homoousios" formula had never been very popular, but even in the West, where the unity of substance was a traditional doctrine of the church. His methods in attempting to impose this decree were violent, and even the elderly Hosius of Cordova[5] and Pope Liberius[6] submitted to the Emperor's demands and signed the "blasphemy."

At that moment, the Arians thought that they had won the battle, and that was their fatal mistake. Although the Nicene creed had never been very popular, the same was true of Arianism, and the ease with which Eusebius of Nicomedia earlier and Ursacius and Valens later were able to produce a reaction against Nicea was due to the fear of Sabellianism which was shared by most Eastern bishops, and not to a true Arian feeling. Among those whom Athanasius called "Arians," most were not really such, and would react against Arianism as soon as it would prove to be a real threat to the traditional doctrine of the church by affirming that Christ was a creature. Therefore, with the political advance of Arianism after the death of Constans there developed also more clarity in the various positions among the opponents of Nicea. Toward the middle of the fourth century, one can discern among the opponents of the "homoousios" formula at least three trends, which may be called the *anomoean*, the *homoean*, and

---

[5] There have been various attempts to clear Hosius of this charge: H. Yaven, *Osio, obispo de Córdoba* (Barcelona: Editorial Labor, 1945); Ramón Serratosa, "Algo más sobre Osio de Córdoba," *Est*, 13 (1957), 65-84; Ursicino Domínguez Del Val, "Osio de Córdoba," *RET*, 18 (1958) 141-65, 261-81; Bernardino Llorca, "El problema de la caída de Osio de Córdoba," *EstEcl*, 33 (1959), 39-56. But it seems clear that he did accept the formula of Sirmium, although probably under extreme duress. The best English work on the subject is V. C. De Clerq, *Ossius of Cordova: A Contribution to the History of the Constantinian Period* (Washington: Catholic University of America Press, 1954). For further references, see Ursicino Domínguez Del Val, "La bibliografía de los últimos tiempos sobre Osio de Córdova," *CD*, 171 (1958), 485-89.

[6] Also in the case of Liberius, there have been attempts to deny that he signed the formula of Sirmium. Such is F. S. Blanes, *La cuestión de Osio, obispo de Córdoba, y de Liberio, obispo de Roma* (Madrid: Espasa Calpe, 1928). But see Monald Goemans, "L'exil du pape Libère," *Mélanges offerts à Mademoiselle Christine Mohrmann* (Utrecht: Spectrum, 1963), pp. 184-89.

the *homoiousian* (note the difference between *homoousian* and *homoiousian*).

The *Anomoeans*—from the Greek, ἀνόμοιος, unlike—were the extreme Arians, who affirmed that the Son was "unlike the Father in every respect." The Son is not of the same substance—*homoousios*—of the Father, nor is he of a similar substance—*homoiousios*—but is rather of a different substance. The Son may be called God, not because of his substance, but because he shares in the power or the activity of the Father.[7] In the strict sense, only the Father is God, for God is by nature unbegotten (*agennetos*) and without origin (*agenetos*), and the Son has his origin in the Father. The Son is a "generation of the ungenerate," a "creature of the uncreated," and a "work of the not made."[8] The main exponents of this position, which was extremely rationalistic,[9] were Aetius[10] and Eunomius.[11]

The *Homoeans*—from the Greek ὅμοιος, similar—are also known as "political Arians." For them, the relationship between the Father and the Son is one of similarity, but they never defined what that meant. As two things that are similar are also different, this position is capable of various interpretations according to different situations. However, the leaders of this party—men such as Ursacius and Valens—were convinced Arians, and did not hesitate in supporting the Anomoeans whenever circumstances permitted.[12] As to the question of the *homoousios*, the Homoeans attempted to evade it, for that would force them to define the character of the similarity between the Father and the Son. This is probably the reason why, as has been said above, Ursacius and Valens advised Constantius

---

[7] A point in which the anomoeans had developed original Arian doctrine. Cf. X. Le Bachelet, "Anoméens," *DTC*, 1: 1324-25; John Norman Davidson Kelly, *Early Christian Doctrine* (London: A. & C. Black, 1960), p. 249.

[8] Eunomius, *Apol.* 28 (*PG*, 30: 868).

[9] Gregory of Nyssa accused them of conceiving of God according to the categories of Aristotle. *Contr. Eunom.* 1. 12.

[10] See the forty-seven arguments of Aetius quoted by Epiphanius, *Pan. 76.*

[11] His *Apologia* may be found in *PG*, 30: 835-68. Because of his influence, the Anomoeans are sometimes called "Eunomians."

[12] Although, on occasion, they were willing to condemn the more extreme form of Arianism. Cf. Athanasius, *Apol. contra Arian. 58.*

to forbid all discussion regarding the consubstantiality or the similarity of substance between the Father and the Son, and why this party studiously avoided such discussion.[13]

The *Homoiousians*—from the Greek ὁμοιούσιος, of similar substance—who are sometimes mistakenly called semi-Arians,[14] are the heirs of the ancient misgivings regarding the formula of Nicea, which had to do, not with the fact that it condemned Arianism, but with its apparent openness to Sabellianism. This party appeared as such when, after the "blasphemy of Sirmium," the more moderate theologians felt the need to oppose not only Sabellianism, but also Arianism. The "blasphemy of Sirmium" affirmed that the Son was substantially different from the Father, and that their relationship could not be expressed by the term *"homoousios,"* or even *"homoiousios."* This is the first time that the term *homoiousios* appears in the texts that have been preserved, but the fact that it is attacked seems to imply that some theologians were already beginning to use it as a means of avoiding both Sabellianism and Arianism. In any case, after the "blasphemy of Sirmium" there appears a group that is usually called the Homoiousians, under the leadership of Basil of Ancyra. At first, the Homoiousians—besides Basil, one should mention Cyril of Jerusalem and Meletius of Antioch—were opposed to Arianism as well as to the Nicene party, but slowly they became aware that, at least in its intention, their position coincided with that of the defenders of the *homoousios.*

The birth of the homoiousian party as a clearly defined group took place in A.D. 358, when a synod gathered in Ancyra under the leadership of Basil produced the first homoiousian formula.[15] In this formula one can see the reaction of the conservative majority to the "blasphemy of Sirmium." Here the substantial similarity between the

---

[13] As may be seen in the "Macrostich confession"—or "long-lined confession"—quoted by Athanasius, *De syn.* 26, and in the creeds of 359 and 360. See Theodoret, *HE* 2. 21, and Athanasius, *De syn.* 30.

[14] So Epiphanius, *Pan.* 73.

[15] Quoted by Epiphanius, *Pan.* 73. 3, 11. See J. Gummerus, *Die homöusianische Partei bis zum Tode des Konstantius* (Leipzig: A. Deichert, 1900).

Father and the Son is categorically affirmed. This similarity is such that, in that which refers to the distinction between the Creator and his creatures, the Son is quite clearly next to the Father and not among the creatures. This does not mean, however, that there is a total identity between the Father and the Son, for their substances—*ousiai*—are not one, but two. This party scored a great victory when Constantius, probably seeking a middle way that would restore some measure of unity to his divided Empire, endorsed it.[16]

The lack of precision in the terms employed in this discussion was one of the difficulties that the church of the fourth century found in attempting to clarify the relationship between the Father and the Son. In the West, a rather fixed terminology had already been achieved, and the term "substance" was used to refer to the one and common divinity, whereas the individuality of the Father, the Son, and the Holy Spirit was expressed by means of the term "persons." In the East, on the other hand, there was not the same precision and fixity in terminology. For Eastern theologians, *ousia* and *hypostasis* were synonymous—and as such are used in the anathemas appended to the Nicene creed—and there was no term that could adequately translate the Latin "*persona*," for the Greek *prosopon* was capable of a Sabellian interpretation. Therefore, when the Nicene defenders spoke of a single *ousia*, most Eastern bishops saw this as an attempt to reintroduce Sabellianism. And when the more conservative bishops—in this case the Homoiousians—spoke of a duality of *ousiai*, the Nicenes thought that this was merely a new form of Arianism.

Such was the state of affairs when the death of Constantius and his succession by Julian the Apostate—who, being a pagan, was not too interested in theological debates—removed the influence of politics upon theological debate and made it necessary for each party to seek victory primarily through theological means.

It was at this juncture that Athanasius took a decisive step[17] that

---

[16] Sozomen, *HE* 4. 13.

[17] A step, however, for which he had been paving the way since 359. Cf. *De syn.* 41. 67, 76.

would ultimately lead to the victory of the Nicene faith: in a synod gathered in Alexandria in A.D. 362, it was declared that verbal differences were not important, as long as the meaning was the same. Thus, both the phrase "three hypostases" and its counterpart "one hypostasis" are acceptable as long as the first is not interpreted in such a way that it supports tritheism or the latter in a Sabellian fashion.[18] With this decision, the Nicene party opened the way to an alliance with the conservative majority. There now remained a long process of clarification of the meaning of various terms in order to reach a generally accepted formula, and the consequent definitive condemnation of Arianism.

The importance of the Alexandrine synod of A.D. 362 is not limited to its conciliating spirit, but is due also to its position regarding the Holy Spirit. Arianism, in denying the absolute divinity of the Word, was led to the same conclusion regarding the Holy Spirit. But the bishops gathered in Nicea, in centering their attention on the divinity of the Word, which was the crucial point of the controversy, did not lay great stress on the question of the Spirit, but simply retained the phrase: "and in the Holy Ghost." Therefore, the Council of Nicea did not discuss the trinitarian question as a whole. But during the years between that Council and the Alexandrine synod of A.D. 362, in attempting to clarify and define the matters at issue, several theologians had paid more attention to the question of the Holy Spirit and his divinity. Futhermore, the long controversy regarding the divinity of the Son had led the majority of theologians to conclude that it was necessary to affirm that divinity in one way or another; but the case was different when it came to the Holy Spirit, for on this point there had not yet been sufficient discussion. Thus, some theologians—such as Eustathius of Sebaste and Marathon of Nicomedia[19]—showed themselves willing to affirm the consubstantiality

---

[18] *Tom. ad Ant.* 5, 6.

[19] Although this group was later called "Macedonian," after Macedonius of Constantinople, there is no evidence that he actually held such a doctrine.

of the Son and the Father, but not that of the Holy Spirit.[20] Over against this position, the synod of A.D. 362, which was rather flexible in matters that were mostly verbal, saw an unacceptable error in the position of these theologians, who were called *Macedonians* and *Pneumatomachians*—that is, enemies of the Spirit. In consequence, the synod condemned Arianism as well as the parallel opinion that the Holy Spirit is a creature.[21] In so doing, it opened the way for the final affirmation of trinitarian doctrine, for it both prepared an alliance between the strict Nicene party and the conservative Homoiousians and widened the discussion so as to include the Holy Spirit.

From that moment the Arian cause was lost. Although a short time later Julian sent Athanasius into a new exile, and the same was done once again by Valens, these two brief periods of banishment could not stop the progress of the Nicene cause. A synod gathered in Antioch in A.D. 363 declared itself in favor of the Nicene creed, explaining that the term *homoousios* means simply that the Son is like the Father according to his essence, and that its only purpose is to condemn the Arian heresy, which turns the Son into a creature. In a letter addressed to Emperor Jovian, the bishops gathered at the synod say:

Wherefore lest we should be included in the number of those who adulterate the doctrine of the truth, we hereby declare to your piety that we embrace and steadfastly hold the faith of the holy Synod formerly convened at Nicaea. Especially since the term *homoousios*, which to some seems novel and inappropriate, has been judiciously explained by the fathers to denote that the Son was begotten of the Father's substance, and that he is like the Father as to substance. Not indeed that any passion is to be understood in relation to that ineffable generation. Nor is the term *ousia*, "substance," taken by the

---

[20] In Egypt, the group that Athanasius called Tropicists explicitly held that the Spirit was "of a different substance" from the Father. Athanasius, *Ep. ad Serap.* 1. 2.

[21] *Tom. ad Ant.* 3 (*NPNF*, 2nd series, 4: 484): "To anathematise the Arian heresy and confess the faith confessed by the holy fathers at Nicaea, and to anathematise also those who say that the Holy Spirit is a Creature and separate from the Essence of Christ. For this is in truth a complete renunciation of the abominable heresy of the Arians, to refuse to divide the Holy Trinity, or to say that any part of it is a creature."

fathers in any usual signification of it among the Greeks; but it has been employed for the subversion of what Arius impiously dared to assert concerning Christ, viz.—that he was made of things "not existing." [22]

Therefore, also in Antioch we now find the spirit of conciliation between Homoousians and Homoiousians which a year earlier was already manifested in Alexandria. The same may be said of a series of synods and episcopal decisions that took place between A.D. 362 and 381.

Furthermore, Julian's brief reign (361-363) was the turning point in imperial policy regarding this matter. Before Julian, the emperors who supported Arianism—in a sense, Constantine the Great, and most certainly his son Constantius—turned out to be the most powerful, while those who supported the Nicene cause ruled only in the West, far from the center of the controversy, and were certainly less powerful than their counterparts. After the brief pagan reaction of Julian there is a long succession of emperors who were either pro-Nicene or at least did not support Arianism. The main exception to this rule is Valentinian II, who—following the advice of his mother Justina—clung to Arianism even after it was a lost cause. But at the other extreme there is Theodosius, without any doubt the most powerful emperor of the second half of the fourth century, who supported the Nicene cause and held the Council of Constantinople (A.D. 381), which marks the final condemnation of Arianism.

In the field of theology, the alliance between Homoousians and Homoiousians—that is, between the strictly Nicene party and the conservative majority—became tighter and stronger. The decision of the synod of A.D. 362 was only the starting point for a series of steps toward the formation and strengthening of that alliance. The most important of those steps was the correspondence between Athanasius and Basil of Ancyra, the leader of the Homoiousians. Thus, the last years of the life of Athanasius saw the beginning of the final solution of the controversy.

---

[22] Socrates, *HE* 3. 25 (*NPNF*, 2nd series, 2: 95). Cf. Sozomen, *HE* 6. 4.

It was, however, another generation that would develop the formulas that would make it possible to reach an understanding among the majority of bishops and theologians. The main personalities of that new Nicene generation are the "Three Great Cappadocians"—Basil of Caesarea, Gregory of Nyssa, and Gregory of Nazianzus. The importance of these three theologians compels us to devote to them a separate chapter—Chapter XIV—but it is necessary to outline at this point their contribution to the final victory of the Nicene cause.

The Alexandrine synod of A.D. 362 had pointed out the confusion that existed in the terminology employed for referring to the relationships between the Father, the Son, and the Holy Ghost; but it had not offered a positive solution to this question of terminology. That synod saw clearly that the word "hypostasis" was ambiguous, and that it was therefore correct to say either "one hypostasis" or "three hypostases," for the same term was used in a different sense in each of the two phrases. But this synod saw no other solution than that of affirming that in a sense there is only one hypostasis in God, and that in another sense there are three.

The Cappadocians took upon themselves the task of defining more clearly the unity and the diversity within the Godhead, and of seeking a terminology capable of expressing both poles of this issue. Their solution was based on the distinction between the terms *ousia* and *hypostasis*. In philosophical literature, and even in the decisions of the Council of Nicea, these terms were used as synonymous, and both were usually translated into Latin by *substantia*. But they were both ambiguous, for they referred to the individual subsistence of a thing as well as to the common essence of which all the members of the same species participate. The Cappadocians distinguished between these two terms, reserving the use of *hypostasis* to refer to the individual subsistence of a thing, and that of *ousia* to refer to the essence that is common to the various members of a species.[23] Then they affirmed that there are in God three *hypostases* and only one *ousia* or, in other

---

[23] See, for instance, Basil, *Ep.* 236. 6.

words, three individual subsistences that participate in one divine essence.[24]

This formula was rather confusing for the West, which was prone to interpret it in terms of Tertullian's formula: one substance and three persons. For Western theologians, the affirmation of three divine *hypostases* seemed to mean that there were three divine substances and, therefore, three Gods. But the work of the Cappadocians, including in their formula the unity of *ousia,* eventually satisfied the West.

Harnack and other historians of Christian doctrine have accused the Cappadocians of having twisted the doctrine of Nicea.[25] According to them, the Cappadocians did not affirm the doctrine of Nicea, which consisted in the unity of God, but rather affirmed the existence of three divine substances with a common nature. This criticism must be corrected at least on two points. In the first place, it presupposes that the bishops gathered in Nicea were concerned above all with affirming the unity of God. But this interpretation of the Great Council is incorrect. Although it is true that some of the bishops at Nicea saw in the *homoousios* an affirmation of divine unity, most of those present saw it as an affirmation of the divine nature of the Son with sufficient strength to reject the doctrines of Arius and his "fellow Lucianists." In the second place, those who criticize the trinitarian doctrine of the Cappadocians err in that they forget that, given their Platonic presuppositions, the Cappadocians would assert that the common essence of which several individuals share is more real than the particular subsistence of each. Thus, it is not correct to interpret the formula "three *hypostases* and one *ousia*" as a veiled tritheism, and therefore as a betrayal of the Nicene faith.

When Emperor Theodosius called a council that met in Constantinople in 381—and that was later called the Second Ecumenical

---

[24] Some concrete examples of their explanation of this formula will be found in Chap. XIV, which deals specifically with the Cappadocians.

[25] Harnack, *HD,* 4: 84-88.

Council—it was the Cappadocian formula that won the day. Although there were no Western bishops present at this council, there was a wide representation of all the East, and shortly thereafter the Western church accepted its doctrinal decisions. The bishops gathered at Constantinople did not draw up a new creed, but rather reaffirmed that of Nicea,[26] and condemned Arianism, not only in its primitive form, but also in its new modalities—*anomoean, homoean,* and *pneumatomachian*—and Apollinarianism.[27]

With the actions of the Council of Constantinople, Arianism ceased to be an important factor in theological discussion. However, this was not the end of that doctrine, for it had already spread extensively among the barbarians,[28] and in later centuries, when those barbarian peoples invaded the West, they took with them their Arian faith. Thus, the Vandals in North Africa, the Visigoths in Spain, and the Lombards in Italy established Arian kingdoms. The Franks were the only ones among the main invading peoples that were converted to orthodox Christianity rather than to Arianism. The result was that the West, which had not really been challenged by that doctrine until then,[29] now had to face a bitter struggle. But in this confrontation theology did not play a major role. It was mostly a matter of the stronger implanting their faith among the weaker, and of a higher civilization conquering its conquerors. At first, the Arian barbarians persecuted the orthodox in the lands that they invaded. But soon they began attempting to assimilate the culture of the vanquished, and with it they assimilated also their Nicene faith, so that one after

---

[26] There has been a great deal of discussion regarding the so-called Constantinopolitan Creed and its relation with the Nicene Creed and with the Council of A.D. 381. If the Council did indeed promulgate the Constantinopolitan Creed, it probably did not create it, nor did it offer it as a substitute for the Nicene formula. Cf. Kelly, *Early Christian Creeds,* pp. 296-331.

[27] A christological doctrine to be discussed in Chap. XVI.

[28] See H. E. Griesecke, *Die Ostgermanen und der Arianismus* (Leipzig: B. G. Teubner, 1939).

[29] Gustave Bardy, "L'Occident et les documents de la controverse arienne," *RevScRel,* 20 (1940), 28-63 traces the introduction into the West of documents pertaining to the Arian controversy.

another the great Arian kingdoms became orthodox. Another contributing factor in this development was the growth of Frankish power, for its Arian neighbors were thus compelled to follow the beliefs of that growing empire.

The defeat of Arianism was due in part to the intellectual superiority of its adversaries; in part to the fact that, during the prolonged controversy, the West was always in favor of the Nicene party, and in part to the divisions among the Arians having to do with subtle distinctions, while their opponents tended to unite and form ever wider alliances. But one could also see in the inner nature of Arianism one of the main causes of its defeat. Arianism can be interpreted as an attempt to introduce within Christianity the custom of worshiping beings which, while not being the absolute God himself, were divine in a relative sense. The general Christian conscience reacted strongly against this limited understanding of the Savior's divinity, as was clearly seen every time the Arians expressed their doctrine in its extreme fashion. The Nicene faith, although less strictly rational than Arianism, and although it required more than half a century to clarify its actual meaning, was able to affirm in a more clear and radical way the fundamental Christian doctrine that "God was in Christ reconciling the world unto himself." Besides, the Arian intent of producing such a paganized Christianity by allowing the worship of a being that was not quite God himself had strong competition in popular piety that was already beginning to follow the custom—no less pagan, but certainly less detrimental to the divinity of Christ than Arianism—of rendering to the saints a type of worship similar to that which antiquity offered to demigods.

There is no doubt that the Arian controversy was to some extent the result of the penetration of the Hellenistic spirit within Christian theology. But one must ask whether the extreme form of that penetration is to be found in the Nicene party or in the Arians. It has been traditional to interpret the doctrine of Arius as derived from Paul of Samosata through Lucian of Antioch, and therefore as a defense of the ancient Jewish monotheism against the invasion of Hellenism. But it

297

has already been pointed out that Arius is not to be interpreted as a successor of Paul of Samosata, but on the contrary, as an exponent of the same type of Origenism that condemned Paul. The Hellenizing tendency of Arianism was constantly manifested in the course of the controversy, when its leaders repeatedly appealed to arguments drawn from philosophical speculation, while the Nicene theologians—and especially Athanasius, as will be seen in the following chapter—usually took Christian soteriology as their point of departure. There is no doubt that the Nicene formula, and even more so the theology that was developed in order to support it, shows a marked Hellenistic influence. The obvious case is the term *homoousios* itself, which, as was already pointed out in the fourth century, is nowhere to be found in Scripture. But the influence of the Hellenistic spirit was greater in Arianism than in the Council that condemned it. Therefore, the result of the controversy is not, as has sometimes been claimed, the victory of a Hellenized Christianity over another more primitive and Judaic understanding of the faith, but the setting of a limit, by a moderately Hellenized Christianity, to the exaggerated influence of philosophical speculation on Christian theology.[80]

---

[80] Pierre-Thomas Camelot, "Le dogme de la Trinité: Origine et formation des formulas dogmatiques," *LumVie*, 30 (1956), 9-48.

XIII

The Theology of Athanasius

One of the best patristic scholars of our time has said about Athanasius that "the history of dogma in the fourth century is identical with the history of his life."[1] In fact, the life and work of Athanasius are so interwoven with the development of theological discussion in the fourth century that it is impossible to tell the history of that development apart from the biography of Athanasius. He became the symbol of the Nicene faith, and his repeated exiles and returns serve as a weather vane to show which way the doctrinal and political winds were blowing. This is why the preceding chapter, while recording the course of the Arian controversy after the Council of Nicea, has also outlined the biography of Athanasius. It is not necessary to repeat that story here. Let it suffice to say that Athanasius was without any doubt the most remarkable bishop that ever occupied the ancient see of Alexandria, and that he was as well the greatest theologian of his time. The purpose of this chapter is, therefore, not to repeat what has already been said about the life of that great churchman, but rather to attempt to show what were the major theological concerns that led him in his bitter struggle against Arianism, as well as to outline some of the main aspects of his theology.

---

[1] Johannes Quasten, *Patrology* (Utrecht: Spectrum Publishers, 1960), 3: 66.

Athanasius was a churchman and a pastor rather than a systematic or speculative thinker. This does not mean that his thought is not orderly, or that it lacks system, but that his work and his theology developed in response to the needs of each moment rather than on the basis of the requirements of a system. Therefore, one would seek in vain among his works for one that attempts to present the totality of his theology. His works are pastoral, polemical, exegetical, and there is even a biography among them; but in none of them does he attempt to theologize for the mere pleasure or curiosity of it. The oldest of his writings is a single work usually published as two treatises: *Against the Heathen* and *On the Incarnation*. These were probably written before the beginning of the Arian controversy;[2] but in them—especially in the second treatise—one can already find the theological principles that would later serve Athanasius as points of departure in his controversy with the Arians. Among his other works of theological interest, one should mention his *Discourses against the Arians*, *On the Incarnation against the Arians*, *Apology against the Arians*, *History of the Arians*, and the *Four Epistles to Serapion*. On the other hand, the *Life of Saint Anthony* which he wrote, although not concerned primarily with doctrinal issues, did greatly influence the further development and popularity of the monastic movement, for it was through this work that the great ascetic deeds of Anthony became widely known.

Athanasius' theology is more concerned with religious matters than with those which are purely speculative in nature. It was precisely this difference of interest which led him away from the Origenistic school, to which most of his predecessors in the see of Alexandria had belonged. Yet, in his trinitarian doctrine, and perhaps even without being conscious of it, Athanasius had been influenced by that form of right-wing Origenism which prevailed in Alexandrine circles.

---

[2] E. Schwartz, "Der sogenannte *Sermo maior de fide* des Athanasius," *SBAW*, 41 (1925), 44-46, places this work at a later date (A.D. 335-337), but his arguments have not been generally accepted. Of the two extant recensions, the longer one seems to be the original. The shorter recension may well be also by Athanasius, but is probably a revision of the other.

The content of his theology is often very near that of Origen, but his method is radically different from that which the ancient Alexandrine theologian followed, for his interest is practical and religious rather than speculative or academic. This does not mean that he discusses only practical themes and leaves doctrinal questions aside, but rather that he is constantly seeking the religious significance of every doctrinal issue.

This religious significance is to be found in the implications that each doctrine has for certain basic principles that are at the heart of Christianity. The truth or falsehood of a doctrine is to be judged on the basis of the degree and manner in which it expresses the principles of the Christian religion. For Athanasius, these principles are basically two: monotheism and the Christian doctrine of salvation.

Even before the Arian controversy developed, Athanasius had given some thought to the nature of God and the means by which man can know him. This may be seen in his early treatises, *Against the Heathen* and *On the Incarnation*.

In *Against the Heathen*, after attacking pagan polytheism in a manner similar to that of the ancient apologists, Athanasius discusses the means by which God can be known. These are principally two: the soul and nature.

God may be known through the human soul, for "although God Himself is above all, the road which leads to Him is not far, nor even outside ourselves, but is within us, and it is possible to find it by ourselves." [3] Every man has been on this road which is the soul, although some have refused to follow it. By studying the soul we may infer something about the nature of God. The soul is invisible and immortal, which makes it superior to all things visible and perishable.[4] Therefore, the idols that pagans worship, being visible and destructible, are not gods, but are even inferior to the men who make them.[5] The true God, like the soul, must be invisible and immortal. By its

---

[3] *Contra gentes* 30. 1.
[4] *Ibid.*, 33. 4.
[5] *Ibid.*, 34. 2.

own nature, the soul is capable of seeing God, although sin prevents it from attaining that vision. The soul was made according to the divine image and likeness, and it was intended to be like a mirror in which that image, which is the Word of God, would shine. Sin, however, dulls that mirror, so that without a previous cleansing it is impossible to see the Word in it.[6] This is a Platonistic theme that had become part of Alexandrine theological tradition since the time of Origen.

On the other hand, it is possible to know God through his creation, which "as though in written characters, declares in a loud voice, by its order and harmony, its own Lord and Creator."[7] God created the world in order to make himself known to men. As he is by nature invisible and incomprehensible, he has placed around us this universe so that we may know him, if not in himself, at least through his works.[8] From the observation of this universe one can infer the existence of God.[9]

The order of the universe shows, not only that there is a God, but also that he is one. If there were more than one God, the unity of purpose that can be seen throughout the universe would be impossible. "The rule of more than one is the rule of none."[10] The order of the universe, in which opposites are balanced and distributed in an admirable fashion, must have only one source.[11] This source is the Christian God. Over against it, pagan gods seem weak, for several of them are needed in order to create and rule a single world.[12]

Finally, the order and reason within nature show that God has created it and rules it through his Reason, Wisdom, or Word.[13] This Word is not to be understood as the Stoic Logos, that is, as an impersonal principle that is the order itself of nature. The Word of God

---

[6] Ibid., 34. 3.
[7] Ibid., 34. 4 (NPNF, 2nd. series, 4: 22).
[8] Ibid., 35. 1.
[9] Ibid., 35. 4–36. 1.
[10] Ibid., 38. 3 (NPNF, 2nd series 4:24).
[11] Ibid., 38. 4.
[12] Ibid., 39. 2.
[13] Ibid., 40. 2-3.

who rules the world is the living Logos of God. That is, the Word who is God himself. This Logos or Word is not a mere sound, as human words are, but is rather the unchangeable image of the Father. He is the one and only-begotten God. This Word has taken a hand in all created things because they are made out of nothing, and they would therefore perish if the Word did not constantly keep them in existence. Therefore, the Word is the great sustainer and the source of order in the universe. He administers and rules the opposing principles of which the world is made—cold and heat, air and water, and so forth—so that they all coexist in harmony, and do not destroy each other.

But by Word I mean, not that which is involved and inherent in all things created, which some are wont to call the seminal principle, which is without soul and has no power of reason or thought, but only works by external art, according to the skill of him that applies it,—nor such a word as belongs to rational beings and which consists of syllables, and has the air as its vehicle of expression,—but I mean the living and powerful Word of the good God, the God of the Universe, the very Word which is God, Who while different from things that are made, and from all Creation, is the One own Word of the good Father, Who by His own providence ordered and illumines this Universe. For being the good Word of the Good Father He produced the order of all things, combining one with another things contrary, and reducing them to one harmonious order. He being the Power of God and Wisdom of God causes the heaven to revolve, and has suspended the earth, and made it fast, though resting upon nothing, by His own nod. Illumined by Him, the sun gives light to the world, and the moon has her measured period of shining. By reason of Him the water is suspended in the clouds, the rains shower upon the earth, and the sea is kept within bounds, while the earth bears grasses and is clothed with all manner of plants.[14]

This shows that, probably even before being involved in the Arian controversy, Athanasius had developed a doctrine of the Word that was different, not only from that of the Arians, but also from that

---

[14] *Ibid.*, 40. 4-5 (*NPNF*, 2nd series, 4: 25-26).

which had been held by many earlier theologians. Before Athanasius, there was a tendency among many theologians to establish the distinction between the Father and the Word on the basis of the contrast between the absolute God and a subordinate deity. Thus, Clement, for instance, affirmed that the Father was immutable and inaccessible, and the reflected light of the Son was adequate for human eyes. As Athanasius would show during the course of the Arian controversy, this view turned the Word into a subordinate deity, which was incompatible with Christian monotheism. On the other hand, as will be shown later on, Athanasius was convinced that the Savior must be God. There was, therefore, no alternative left but to affirm that the Word was God in the strictest sense. This view, which would become explicit during the Arian controversy, is to be found already in the earliest work of Athanasius that has been preserved.

Whereas *Against the Heathen* shows how Christian monotheism is one of the pillars on which Athanasius builds his theology, the second part of that work, usually called *On the Incarnation,* shows the other pillar upon which that theology is grounded: the doctrine of salvation.

According to Athanasius, the salvation of which men stand in need is continuous with creation, for it is in fact a re-creation of fallen man.[15] The most merciful God, when he created man, did not wish that this creature of his, made out of nothing, would have to return to nothingness. In order to avoid this necessity, he created him according to his image, that is, according to his Word, so that man, through being a participant in the Word, would also partake of being and reason. Therefore, although man was by nature mortal, in his very creation he received the gift of immortality, which he would retain as long as he duly reflected the Image according to which he had been made.[16]

But man sinned and abandoned that Image, and ever since he has

---

[15] *De incar.* 7. 5.

[16] *Ibid.*, 3. 3-4. Cf. Régis Bernard, *L'image de Dieu d'après St. Athanase* (Paris: Aubier, 1952), pp. 21-56.

been a prisoner in the claws of death.[17] Sin is not, therefore, a mere mistake that man has made and that now must be corrected; nor is it a debt that it is now necessary to pay; nor is it even that man has forgotten the way that leads to God and must be reminded of it. Sin is rather the introduction within creation of an element of disintegration that leads man toward destruction, and that can only be expelled through a new work of creation.

From this follows the core of Athanasius' doctrine of salvation: only God himself can save mankind.[18] If the salvation that we need is really a new creation, only the Creator can bring it to us. Besides, as the immortality that we have lost consisted in existence according to the Image of God, and was therefore an existence similar to that of God, the salvation that we now need is a sort of divinization (θεοποίησις).[19] This also requires that the Savior be God, for only God can grant an existence similar to his.

Although the foregoing has been taken from a work of Athanasius which was probably written before the Arian controversy broke out, his later works clearly show that the principles that are expounded above led him in the formulation of his arguments against the Arians. In fact, the difference between his arguments and those of the Arians is surprisingly great: whereas his opponents usually appeal to logical analysis and subtle distinction, Athanasius constantly refers to the two great pillars of his faith: Christian monotheism and the Christian doctrine of salvation.

Let us now see some of those arguments which Athanasius develops.

The Arian doctrine according to which the Word is of a different substance from that of the Father and is not God in the absolute sense, destroys Christian monotheism and leads us back to pagan poly-

---

[17] *De incar.* 6. 1-2.
[18] *Ibid.,* 7.
[19] *Ibid.,* 54. 3 (*NPNF,* 2nd series, 4: 65): "For He was made man that we might be made God."

theism.[20] If the Son does not share in the nature of the Father in such a way that it is possible to speak of both as of a single God, and if at the same time we worship the Son, as the Church has always done, there is no reason left why Christians should condemn polytheism, for they are in fact practicing it.

Besides, the doctrine that sees the Word as an intermediate being between the world and the wholly transcendent God does not solve the problem posed, for it would then be necessary to place other intermediate beings between God and the Word and between the Word and creation, so that the difficulties would only be multiplied unto infinity.[21] In fact, the doctrine that takes as its starting point the absolute transcendence of God and leaves his immanence aside, turns the question of the relationship between God and the world into an insoluble problem. The introduction of the Word within that framework does not solve the difficulty, but merely postpones it.

Likewise, if the Son is mutable, and is the result of an act of the Father's will and not of the divine nature itself, it is impossible to see the immutable Father through him. If the Son reveals the Father to us, this can be not because he is less than the Father, but because he is like him.[22]

Furthermore, the Arian doctrine regarding the Word destroys the possibility of salvation, for a being who is not God cannot attempt to restore creation.[23] If God is the Creator, God must also be the Savior.

Finally, as divinization is part of the work of the Savior, and only God can achieve this, the Savior must be God.[24]

In short, there are two fundamental reasons why Athanasius abhors Arian doctrine: first, that Arianism approaches polytheism and, second, that it implies that salvation comes from a creature. In conse-

---

[20] *Ad. episc. Aegypti* 14; *Or. contra Ar.* 1. 8; 2. 23; 3. 8; 3. 15-16; *De syn.* 50; *Ep. lx ad. Adel.* 3.
[21] *Or. contra Ar.* 2. 26.
[22] *Ibid.*, 1. 35.
[23] *Ibid.*, 2. 14.
[24] *Ibid.*, 2. 70.

quence, it is clear that Athanasius is opposed to Arianism, not because it attacks or denies some point of his theology, but because it is incompatible with the two pillars on which his faith stood, even before the controversy.[25]

Leaving aside the Arian controversy, we must now turn to other important aspects of Athanasius' theology.

In his doctrine of the Godhead, Athanasius shows once again that balance and fine perception which make him one of the greatest theologians of all times. He sees God as a transcendent being, but this is not to be interpreted in such a way that God cannot enter into direct contact with his creatures.[26] Although God exists apart from and above the world, he has established a direct relationship with it in the work of creation itself, and even now is in constant contact with it in order to keep it in existence. This concept of God's relationship with the world is important, for now it is no longer necessary to posit the Word as an intermediate being between God and the world. Those who affirm the absolute transcendence of God turn the Word into a subordinate deity that serves as an intermediary between the absolute God and this transient world. Athanasius, because of the way in which he understands the relationship between God and the world, can affirm that the Word or Son is truly and eternally God, and yet can assert that this does not hinder his relationship with creatures.

This God is triune, for he exists as Father, Son, and Holy Spirit. Athanasius contributed in a positive way to the development of trinitarian doctrine, for his insistence in the divinity of the Son was one of the main factors that led to the defeat of one of the greatest

---

[25] There are certainly some arguments adduced by Athanasius in which he simply makes use of the same type of logic that the Arians employed. Such is his use (*Or. contra Ar.* 1. 28, 29) of Origen's argument that, if the Son is not eternal, the Father is not eternally such. But this argument, which would ultimately lead to the eternity of creation, is not central in Athanasius, who uses it and other similar ones as so many additional supports for a doctrine that in any case is established on firmer grounds. On Athanasius' arguments in general, see: Samuel Laeuchli, "The Case of Athanasius against Arius," *CTM*, 30 (1959), 403-20.

[26] *Or. contra Ar.* 2. 25; *De decretis* 7.

enemies of that doctrine as it finally evolved, Arianism. But the struggle itself against Arianism led Athanasius to devote his attention to the relationship between the Father and the Son to such an extent that the discussion regarding the Holy Spirit was pushed into the background. Later on, with the rise of the Pneumatomachians, who accepted the divinity of the Son but denied that of the Holy Spirit, Athanasius developed his doctrine on this point and affirmed that the Spirit is also of the same substance as the Father.[27]

The main weak point in Athanasius' trinitarian theology is his lack of a fixed terminology that could serve to express the multiplicity as well as the unity within the Trinity. Athanasius did become aware of the need for such a terminology, as can be seen by the action taken by the synod that met in Alexandria in 362. Yet, he himself never developed that terminology, which was a task left for the Cappadocians. Here, as well as in the rest of his theological work, Athanasius showed that he was a man of sharp religious perception, but without great interest or gift for the formal systematization of thought. Without him, the work of the Cappadocians would have been impossible. Without the Cappadocians his work would not have come to its final fruition.

As far as the relationship between the Word and the human nature of Jesus is concerned, the Christology of Athanasius is similar to that of Arius—actually, both theologians can serve as examples of the type of Christology that was current among Alexandrine theologians of the fourth century.[28] Athanasius and Arius are opponents on the question of the divinity of the Word, but they both interpret the union of that Word with humanity in a similar way. According to Athanasius, the Word was united to flesh, but one never finds a clear affirmation in his works that the term "flesh," within this context, has to do with both the body and the soul. It seems that Athanasius takes for granted that there was in Jesus no human rational soul, and the

---

[27] This may be seen in his *Four Letters to Serapion*, to which I have referred earlier.
[28] There is some question as to whether or not Arius did consciously hold that there was no human soul in Jesus. This will be discussed in another chapter (see Chap. XVI, n. 1).

Word took the place of that soul.[29] This doctrine, which was later called "Apollinarianism" and which will be discussed in another chapter, was condemned by the Council of Constantinople in 381. Although Athanasius does not seem to have become aware of this,[30] this interpretation of the person of Jesus Christ does not agree with his own soteriological principles, for—as the Cappadocians would later point out—the Word took human nature in order to free it from sin, and as the soul is also involved in sin, the Word must also have taken it in order to save it.

Likewise, Athanasius emphasizes the unity between the divine and the human in Christ in a fashion that is characteristic of Alexandrine Christology. In this union, the divinity becomes the subject of all the actions of Jesus Christ. It is an unbreakable unity, which is different from all the cases that one finds in the Old Testament of men in whom the Word of God dwelt.[31] In Christ, the flesh becomes an instrument of the Word, and the union between these two is such that that which is properly said of one of the terms of that union can also be transferred to the other term.[32] This is the typical Alexandrine doctrine that is usually called "communication of properties"— *communicatio idiomatum.* Thus, for instance, Athanasius affirms that it is proper to worship the man Jesus, although worship belongs only to God.

---

[29] Marcel Richard, "Saint Athanase et la psychologie du Christ selon les Ariens," *MScRel,* 4 (1947), 5-54. Against this view, Aloys Grillmeier, *Christ in Christian Tradition: From the Apostolic Age to Chalcedon* (New York: Sheed & Ward, 1965), pp. 193-219, attempts to prove that, although the soul of Christ is not a "theological factor" for Athanasius, it is indeed a "physical factor," in the sense that it does exist. This argument, however, does not seem convincing.

[30] There is a possible indication that at a late date he became aware of this in the following very ambiguous words, in which it is still not clear whether Jesus had a human soul or whether it was the Word that performed in him the functions of the soul: "that the Saviour had not a body without a soul, nor without sense or intelligence; for it was not possible, when the Lord had become man for us, that His body should be without intelligence: nor was the salvation effected in the Word Himself a salvation of body only, but of soul also." (*Tom. ad. Ant.* 7; *NPNF,* 2nd series, 4: 485.) Cf. *Ep. ad Epict.* 7.

[31] *Or. contra Ar.* 3. 31.

[32] *Ibid.,* 31-32.

We do not worship a creature. Far be the thought. For such an error belongs to heathens and Arians. But we worship the Lord of Creation, Incarnate, the Word of God. For if the flesh also is in itself a part of the created world, yet it has become God's body. And we neither divide the body, being such, from the Word, and worship it by itself, nor when we wish to worship the Word do we set Him apart from the Flesh, but knowing, as we said above, that "the Word was made flesh," we recognize Him as God also, after having come in the flesh.[33]

In consequence, Athanasius affirms that Mary is Mother or Bearer of God (θεοτόκος).[34] This doctrine is also typically Alexandrine, and in the fifth century would be the catchword of bitter controversies. Athanasius believes that this title is to be given to Mary as a clear consequence of the indivisible union between divinity and humanity in Jesus Christ, and of the resulting *communicatio idiomatum*. To deny that Mary is the Mother of God would be tantamount to denying that God was born of Mary, and this in turn would be a denial of the incarnation of the Word.

In conclusion, Athanasius is a typically Alexandrine theologian, although he is free of the excessive speculation that is perhaps the greatest weakness of that theological tradition. Instead of the Alexandrine speculative method, Athanasius takes certain basic principles of the Christian faith, and from their standpoint judges every other doctrine. These principles are monotheism and the doctrine of salvation, and they are the ground on which Athanasius opposes Arianism.

However, the particular nature of Athanasius' interest and of his intellectual gifts, although allowing him to show with greater clarity than others why Arianism was inacceptable, kept him from developing a formula that would serve as a rallying point for those who found Arianism unpalatable. This would be the task of the Three Great Cappadocians, to whose work we must now turn.

---

[33] *Ep. lx ad Adelph.* 3 (*NPNF,* 2nd series, 4: 575).
[34] *Or. contra Ar.* 3. 14.

XIV

The Three Great Cappadocians

This is the common name given to three bishops and theologians who are foremost in the theological scene during the second half of the fourth century. They are Basil, bishop of Caesarea in Cappadocia, and known as "the Great"; his younger brother Gregory, who eventually became bishop of the small town of Nyssa; and their common friend Gregory of Nazianzus, who for a brief period occupied the patriarchal see of Constantinople. These three friends worked in close collaboration in order to achieve the victory of the Nicene faith, and therefore their trinitarian doctrine is practically common to all three of them. This does not mean, however, that they were in total agreement on every other matter, and it is therefore necessary to study them separately, although showing their unity by including them in one chapter.

Basil (300?-379) was the oldest and most distinguished of the three. Born into a relatively wealthy family, from a very early age he experienced the intense religious life of a home whose center was the Christian faith. His older sister, Macrina, led an ascetic life that left its imprint in the spirit of young Basil. Two of his brothers, Gregory and Peter, eventually became bishops, the former of Nyssa and the latter of Sebaste. Basil himself received a careful education, first at nearby Caesarea, and later in Constantinople and Athens.

It was in Caesarea that Basil met young Gregory, later to become bishop of Nazianzus, who was to be his friend and collaborator throughout all his life. Later, in Athens, they met again, and it was there that their warm friendship developed.

Gregory of Nazianzus (329?-389?) had a very different personality from his friend Basil. The latter was a man of great courage and stability, sometimes to the point of being inflexible. Gregory, on the contrary, was extremely sensitive, sometimes to the point of weakness. For these reasons, Gregory's life is a succession of monastic retreats separated by brief incursions into active ecclesiastical life. Basil loved the quiet life as much as his friend Gregory—and perhaps even more—but once he had taken upon himself the tasks of a bishop he never abandoned them, as his friend was prone to do. Gregory's talents were also different from those of Basil: whereas the latter was the administrator and statesman, Gregory was the great and eloquent orator.

The third of the Great Cappadocians, Gregory of Nyssa (335?-394?), was Basil's younger brother. Although he studied rhetoric and was also a bishop, his main talents were not as a preacher or as an organizer, but he was rather the foremost exponent of mysticism among the three Great Cappadocians. As we shall see further on, his gifts as a theologian, and especially his systematic work, go beyond those of his two colleagues and friends.

Basil of Caesarea

Basil did not devote any time to theological research for the mere pleasure of that work. Therefore, he wrote no work in which he attempted to expound the totality of Christian doctrine in a systematic manner. On the contrary, all his dogmatic works have the clear purpose of refuting errors of the time, especially those of the Arians and the Pneumatomachians. It was with this purpose in mind that he wrote his two most important works: *Against Eunomius* and *On the Holy Spirit*. The former is a refutation of the arguments put forth by the Anomoean Arian Eunomius, while the latter is a defense of the doxology, "Glory be to the Father, with the Son, jointly with the Holy Spirit."

As was characteristic among the Arians, Eunomius' argument[1] was based on the contrast between the absolute God and the relativity of the Son. He bases his argument on the divine nature as being unbegotten (ἀγέννετος),[2] and unable to beget one who shares in his unbegottenness.[3] Therefore, the Son is begotten (he is a γέννημα),[4] and is not God in the strict sense of the word, for God has not communicated his essence to him.[5]

Basil answers that the essence of God cannot be defined simply as not being begotten. Unbegottenness (ἀγεννησία) is a mere negation like invisibility or immortality. But essence (οὐσία) is not a negation, but is rather God's being itself, and one would have to be completely mad in order to count it among the negative attributes.[6] This, however, is precisely what Eunomius does in affirming that God's essence consists in being unbegotten.[7]

On the other hand, according to Basil, Eunomius bases his argument on an erroneous passage from the corporeal to the divine, thus affirming that, as generation is a property that applies only to material beings and has no relationship with the divine, the Son, being begotten, is not God. Basil responds that the generation of living and mortal beings takes place through the action of the senses, but that in the case of God this is not so. When dealing with the divine nature, one must think in terms of a generation worthy of God and therefore "impassible, without parts, nor division, nor time." [8]

From the distinction between the unbegotten Father and the begot-

---

[1] His treatise may be seen in *PG*, 30: 837-68.
[2] *Apol.* 7-8.
[3] *Ibid.*, 9.
[4] *Ibid.*, 12.
[5] *Ibid.*, 28.
[6] *Adv. Eun.* 1. 10.
[7] *Ibid.*, 11.
[8] *Ibid.*, 2. 16 (*PG*, 29: 604).

ten Son, Eunomius draws another argument whose purpose is to prove the Arian point that there was a time when the Son did not exist. The argument itself is very simple: the Son cannot have existed when the Father begat him, for that which already exists does not need to be begotten.[9]

Against this argument, Basil points out that Eunomius confuses eternity with being unbegotten. The latter is said of that which is its own cause, whereas eternity corresponds to that which exists beyond the limits of time. Therefore, there is no contradiction in affirming that the Son is begotten and eternal, or that he is eternally begotten.[10] And if someone requires more precision and logical clarity, Basil responds that the doctrine of the eternal generation cannot be understood by human reason. But this should not surprise us.

> Do not ask me: What is this generation, and of what kind, and how can it take place? The manner of this generation is ineffable and incomprehensible, but we must still build our faith on the foundation of the Father and the Son. For, if we were to judge everything according to our intellect, and to decide that that which our mind cannot comprehend is impossible, gone is faith, gone the reward of hope.[11]

In all this Basil has not gone beyond the position of Athanasius and the earlier defenders of Nicea. Perhaps there is a certain loss, for the soteriological interest that was at the basis of the theology of Athanasius has been abandoned, and the faith of Nicea is defended on the basis of purely logical arguments and of a certain fideistic tendency.

But, on the other hand, Basil's logical interest, which is not, however, as intense as that of his brother Gregory of Nyssa, led him to affirm and defend for the first time the formula that would eventually lead to the definitive solution of the trinitarian controversy: one *ousia*

---

[9] *Ibid.*, 2. 14.
[10] Cf. *NPNF*, 2nd series, 8: xxxvi-xxxvii.
[11] *Adv. Eun.* 2. 24 (*PG*, 29: 625-28).

and three *hypostases* (μία οὐσία, τρεῖς ὑποστάσεις). Basil claims that these two terms are not synonymous, and that they therefore are not to be used indistinctly in referring to the Godhead.[12] What he means by this distinction may be seen in the following paragraph:

The distinction between οὐσία and ὑπόστασις is the same as that between the general and the particular; as, for instance, between the animal and the particular man. Wherefore, in the case of the Godhead, we confess one essence or substance so as not to give a variant definition of existence, but we confess a particular hypostasis, in order that our conception of Father, Son and Holy Spirit may be without confusion and clear. If we have no distinct perception of the separate characteristics, namely, fatherhood, sonship, and sanctification, but form our conception of God from the general idea of existence, we cannot possibly give a sound account of our faith. We must, therefore, confess the faith by adding the particular to the common. The Godhead is common; the fatherhood particular. We must therefore combine the two and say, "I believe in God the Father." The like course must be pursued in the confession of the Son; we must combine the particular with the common and say "I believe in God the Son," so in the case of the Holy Ghost we must make our utterance conform to the appellation and say "in God the Holy Ghost." Hence it results that there is a satisfactory preservation of the unity by the confession of the one Godhead, while in the distinction of the individual properties regarded in each there is the confession of the peculiar properties of the Persons. On the other hand those who identify essence or substance and hypostasis are compelled to confess only three Persons, and, in their hesitation to speak of three hypostases, are convicted of failure to avoid the error of Sabellius.[13]

This contribution of Basil of Caesarea to the development of trinitarian doctrine was later taken up by Gregory of Nazianzus and Gregory of Nyssa, whose work led to its final victory.

---

[12] The most detailed exposition of the distinction between *ousia* and *hypostasis* is to be found in *Ep.* 38. However, as there is some doubt as to the authenticity of that epistle, we shall here use other texts.

[13] *Ep.* 236. 6 (*NPNF*, 2nd series, 8: 278). Cf. *Ep*, 214. 4. Also, on Basil's objections to Sabellianism, *Ep.* 210. 5.

Basil also contributed to the development of trinitarian doctrine in devoting more attention to the Holy Spirit than had been done by earlier theologians. We have already pointed out that the Council of Nicea was content with a brief phrase referring to the Holy Spirit. Athanasius himself did not give too much thought to this issue until the Pneumatomachians brought it to the foreground. In Basil's time, when the Pneumatomachians were a strong force, and when some seemed to be ready to abandon Arianism in that which referred to the Son, but not in that which had to do with the Holy Spirit, it was impossible to attack Arianism without somehow attempting to clarify the nature of the Holy Spirit. This is why, in the last of his three books *Against Eunomius*[14] and in his treatise *On the Holy Spirit*, Basil attempted to show the consubstantiality of the Holy Spirit with the Father and the Son.[15] That this issue was in the air is clearly shown by the fact that, besides the three Cappadocians, other distinguished church leaders of that time felt compelled to write treatises on the Holy Spirit. Among them, one should mention those of Amphilochius of Iconium—to whom Basil's treatise is addressed—Didymus the Blind, and Ambrose of Milan.

Given these circumstances, one is surprised to find that in his treatises composed for publication, Basil abstains from stressing the divinity of the Holy Spirit, and his clearest affirmations of that divinity were made in his epistles.[16] The reason for this is probably that, being interested in convincing rather than in crushing his enemies, Basil attempted to lead them to the recognition of the divinity of the Holy Spirit, rather than to antagonize them.[17] This does not mean, however, that he himself hesitated regarding the divinity of the Holy Spirit, nor that he refrained from affirming that divinity before those

---

[14] Books 4 and 5 are not his.

[15] Hermann Dörries, *Der Beitrag des Basilius zum Abschluss des trinitarischen Dogmas* (Göttingen: Abhandlungen der Akad. d. Wiss., 1956); S. de Boer, "Basilius de Grote en de 'homoousie' vom Hl. Geest," *NedTheolTschr*, 18 (1964), 372-80.

[16] Quasten, *Patrology* (Utrecht: Spectrum Publishers, 1960), 13: 231-33.

[17] Such was at least the understanding of Athanasius (*Ep.* 62-63) and Gregory of Nazianzus (*Pan. Basil.* 68-69), quoted in Quasten, *Patrology*, 3: 231-32.

that denied it. On the contrary, in his third book *Against Eunomius* as well as in the treatise *On the Holy Spirit* Basil affirms and attempts to prove the divinity of the Holy Spirit. But his affirmations and arguments are always restrained, as if he were afraid to scandalize those who, in spite of their goodwill, have not yet been convinced of the divinity of the Holy Spirit. This pastoral interest may also be seen in the manner in which Basil altered the doxology that was used in the Caesarean liturgy, thus attempting to lead his congregation through worship to the conviction of the divinity of the Spirit. The ancient doxology said: "Glory be to the Father, through the Son, in the Holy Ghost"; Basil's doxology said "Glory be to the Father, with the Son, jointly with the Holy Ghost." When he was criticized for this change, Basil wrote his treatise *On the Holy Spirit*, in which, in showing that his version of the doxology is acceptable, he also shows the divinity of the Holy Spirit, although without calling him "God." This reticence can perhaps be understood if one takes into account the presence of certain Arians who were only waiting for the moment when the bishop of Caesarea would make a vulnerable assertion in order then to accuse him of heresy and attempt to claim possession of his important see.

This is the reason why Basil, instead of affirming categorically the divinity of the Holy Spirit in his treatise on that subject, prefers to refute the doctrine that claims that the Spirit is a creature. In spite of this, a careful reader of his treatise has to conclude that Basil believed in the divinity of the Holy Ghost. This conclusion is amply supported by his epistles, in which he categorically affirms the divinity of the Holy Spirit. In any case, the Pneumatomachian position is excluded when Basil affirms that the Spirit is in no way a creature, and that he is worthy of being worshiped.

One, moreover, is the Holy Spirit, and we speak of Him singly, conjoined as He is to the one Father through the one Son, and through Himself completing the adorable and blessed Trinity. Of Him the intimate relationship to the Father and the Son is sufficiently declared by the fact of His not being ranked in the plurality of the creation, but being spoken of singly; for he is not one of many, but One. For as there is one Father and one Son, so is there one Holy Ghost. He is consequently as far removed from created Nature as reason requires the singular to be removed from compound and plural bodies; and He is in such wise united to the Father and to the Son as unit has affinity with unit.[18]

Thus, with his insistence on the person of the Holy Spirit—which is really a reaction of all the main theologians of his time against the Pneumatomachians—Basil contributed to turn the Arian question into a fully trinitarian one. Until that time, what was at issue was mostly the relationship between the Father and the Son. Now the place of the Holy Spirit in the divine Trinity had begun to be given due attention. This was in no way an innovation. The Council of Nicea itself had affirmed its faith in the Holy Ghost, and Athanasius in learning of Pneumatomachian doctrine did not hesitate in condemning it. But Basil's treatise was a landmark for the definitive introduction of the Holy Spirit in the Arian controversy.

Finally, a word must be said about Basil's importance as a liturgist and as an organizer of monasticism. As a witness to his liturgical activities, there is a "Liturgy of Saint Basil," which the Greek orthodox church still uses during Lent, and whose basic traits seem to be the result of the work of Basil himself. On the other hand, there are several works that have been attributed to Basil and that deal with the ordering of monastic life. Some of these works are genuine, others are amply interpolated and perhaps altered, and others should not be in any way connected with his name.

Gregory of Nazianzus

Whereas Basil was the organizer and diplomat among the three Great Cappadocians, Gregory of Nazianzus was the orator and poet. He was a man of quiet and peaceful nature, with a high aesthetic

---

[18] *De Sp. Sancto* 45 (*NPNF*, 2nd series, 8: 28).

sensibility, who always felt inclined to follow the life of monastic retreat and actually attempted it more than once. But his sense of responsibility at a time when the church was involved in great struggles led to him to sacrifice his own tranquillity and to take upon himself the responsibilities of a bishop.[19] As such, he never gave signs of the vigor of his friend Basil, but he did know how to place his great literary talents at the service of the orthodox cause. This is why the best of his theological production is to be found not in systematic treatises, but in his sermons, poems, and epistles. Gregory's sermons show his rhetorical ability, although they go far beyond the beauty of sound and deal with the most difficult theological and moral problems. His poems, although not exceptional jewels of Greek literature, do show a refined artistic taste, and a good number of them are theological in character. Finally, his epistles are exemplary to such a point that Gregory himself decided to publish them on the insistent advice of a relative who admired their style and content. In some of them he discusses theological issues, especially those having to do with Christology, with such clarity and foresight that his exposition of this subject was later adopted by the Councils of Ephesus and Chalcedon.[20]

As that which is most interesting to us here is Gregory's contribution to the final victory of the Nicene faith, we shall begin by expounding his trinitarian doctrine. As in the case of Basil, the great theological opponents of Gregory are the Arians—especially Eunomius and his Anomoean party—and the Pneumatomachians. They are the target at which he aims many of his sermons, epistles, and poems, and especially his five sermons usually called "Theological Orations." [21]

---

[19] The first of these episodes in which Gregory abandoned his personal peace in order to serve the Church was when his own father asked him to collaborate in the leadership of the Church in Nazianzus. Gregory fled, and later composed his "Defence of His Flight," in which he confessed: "I have been defeated, and own my defeat" (*NPNF*, 2nd series, 7: 204). Few documents in patristic literature give a clearer insight into the personality of their authors.

[20] See Chap. XVI for Gregory's Christology.

[21] *NPNF*, 2nd series, 7: 284-328.

The first of the *Theological Orations* deals with the principles of theological research and discussion. Here Gregory attacks the custom of the Arians, who hold theological discussions at all times, and before all types of audiences.[22] Theological discussion must deal only with subjects that are within the grasp of our mind, and must be pursued only to that point at which the mind shows itself incapable of going further.[23] Furthermore, these subjects cannot be discussed by all persons, not only because some lack the necessary intelligence to understand what is discussed, but also and above all because few persons have the virtue necessary to receive properly what is said. Mere intelligence is not enough in order to become a true theologian. It is also necessary to "polish our theological self to beauty like a statue." [24] Those who are unable to develop the necessary virtue should not attempt to discuss the nature of God, but should rather limit their interest to lower subjects, such as the world, matter, and the soul.[25]

The third [26] and fourth *Theological Orations* deal with the Son, and here Gregory directly refutes the arguments of Eunomius which we have already expounded in discussing Basil of Caesarea. Many of the arguments of Eunomius consist in dilemmas whose purpose is to show the logical impossibility of the Nicene doctrine. Gregory takes these dilemmas in order, and shows the fallacies involved in each of them. Thus, for instance, the Anomoeans propose the following dilem-

---

[22] *Or.* 27. 3 (*NPNF*, 2nd series, 7: 285): "Not to every one, my friends, does it belong to philosophize about God; not to every one; the Subject is not so cheap and low; and I will add, not before every audience, nor at all times, nor on all points; but on certain occasions, and before certain persons, and within certain limits."

[23] *Ibid.*, 4.

[24] *Ibid.*, 7 (*NPNF*, 2nd series, 7: 287).

[25] *Ibid.*, 9.

[26] The second *Theological Oration* is a further attempt to force humility upon theological discourse by showing the distance between the theologian and the object of his thought, and the consequent impossibility of conceiving God properly. No matter how exalted a thing may be, the distance between us and it is a great deal shorter than that which exists between it and God (*Or.* 28.3). Plato is wrong when he claims that to conceive God is difficult and that it is impossible to express him in words, for the truth is that it is impossible to express him, and even more impossible to conceive him (*ibid.*, 4). A comprehensible God would be a limited God (*ibid.*, 10).

ma: if the Father begat the Son, he did so either voluntarily or involuntarily. If he begat him involuntarily, some other force compelled him to do so, and it would then be necessary to affirm that there is a higher power than that of God. If, on the contrary, he begat the Son voluntarily, the Son is the Son of Will, and not of the Father.[27] Gregory answers that his enemies attempt to bind him, but that the cords that they use are very weak. The Anomoeans themselves, who dare speak with such boldness regarding the divine generation, should ask the same question regarding their own generation. Was it voluntarily or involuntarily that their fathers begat them? Quite clearly it was not involuntarily, for they were not forced to beget them. But if it was voluntarily that their fathers begat them, the Anomoeans are sons of the Will, and not of their own fathers! Thus, Gregory shows that the supposed dilemma that Eunomius poses is no more than "a few syllables," that is, words lacking content. In any case, the generation of the Son of God would be "no great thing" if we who are unable to understand our own begetting were able to understand it. Therefore, it is "stupid to discuss the question whether that which was begotten from the beginning existed before its generation or not."[28]

However, the core of Gregory's argument is in his insistence that the terms "Father," "Son," and "Holy Spirit" are terms of relation. His opponents pose the following dilemma: the term "Father" must refer either to an essence or to an action; if it refers to an essence, the Son cannot be "of the same essence" as the Father—*homoousios*; if, on the other hand, it refers to an action, that action can be no other than that of the Father as creator, and therefore the Son is a creature. Gregory refutes this argument by saying that "Father" refers neither to essence nor to action, but to relation: that relationship of communion of essence which exists between the Father and the Son.[29] This led Gregory to pay more attention to the question of the relationship

---

[27] Or. 29. 6.
[28] Ibid., 9 (NPNF, 2nd series, 7: 304).
[29] Ibid., 16.

between the three divine persons, which was his great contribution to the development of trinitarian doctrine.

In his fifth *Theological Oration*, Gregory discusses the Holy Spirit. Here he does affirm categorically that the Spirit is God, and that all the predicates of divinity are to be attributed to him.

If ever there was a time when the Father was not, then there was a time when the Son was not. If ever there was a time when the Son was not, then there was a time when the Spirit was not. If the One was from the beginning, then the Three were so too.[30]

However, the point in which Gregory's doctrine goes beyond that of Basil is not the divinity of the Holy Spirit—which Basil accepted, although perhaps not as outspokenly as his friend—but the relations between the three persons of the Trinity. The attempt to distinguish the Father, the Son, and the Holy Spirit on the basis of their attributes, distinguishing between the absolutely transcendent Father and the Son or Word, which is capable of relating to the world, necessarily led to subordinationism and eventually to Arianism. Athanasius had been aware of this and therefore had categorically and repeatedly denied every attempt to understand the transcendence of the Father in such a way that he would appear to be further away from creation than the Son. This emphasis on the equal transcendence of the Father and the Son, while destroying one of the foundations of Arianism, was unable to show how the Nicene doctrine differed from Sabellianism. This was the great task of the Cappadocians. Gregory's approach led him to deal with this problem on the basis of the inner relations of the three divine persons within the Trinity.

According to Gregory, the only distinctions that can be established between the three persons of the Trinity are those which refer to the origin of each of them. These distinctions have nothing to do with the substance or nature, but only with the source of each of the persons.

---

[30] *Or.* 31. 4 (*NPNF*, 2nd series, 7: 318).

And when I speak of God you must be illumined at once by one flash of light and by three. Three in Individualities or Hypostases, if any prefer so to call them, or persons, (πρόσωπα), for we will not quarrel about names so long as the syllables amount to the same meaning; but One in respect of the Substance—that is, the Godhead. For they are divided without division, if I may so say; and they are united in division. For the Godhead is one in three, and the three are one, in whom the Godhead is, or to speak more accurately, Who are the Godhead. Excesses and defects we will omit, neither making the Unity a confusion, nor the division a separation. We would keep equally far from the confusion of Sabellius and from the division of Arius, which are evils diametrically opposed, yet equal in their wickedness. For what need is there heretically to fuse God together, or to cut Him up into inequality?

For to us there is but One God, the Father, of Whom are all things; and one Lord Jesus Christ, by Whom are all things; and One Holy Ghost, in Whom are all things; yet these words, of, by, in, whom, do not denote a difference of nature . . . , but they characterize the personalities of a nature which is one and unconfused. . . . The Father is Father, and is Unoriginate, for He is of no one; the Son is Son, and is not unoriginate, for He is of the Father. But if you take the word Origin in a temporal sense, He too is Unoriginate, for He is the Maker of Time, and is not subject to Time. The Holy Ghost is truly Spirit, coming forth from the Father indeed, but not after the manner of the Son, for it is not by Generation but by Procession . . . ; for neither did the Father cease to be Unbegotten because of His begetting something, nor the Son to be begotten because He is of the Unbegotten (how could that be?), nor is the Spirit changed into Father or Son because He proceeds, or because He is God.[31]

The three characteristics of origin which Gregory establishes in this text were soon accepted, not only by the East, but also by the West, as a means of expressing the distinction that exists within the Trinity: the characteristic of the Father is that of not being begotten (ἀγεννησία); that of the Son is being begotten (γέννησις); and that of the Spirit is his procession (ἐκπόρευσις).[32] With these terms,

---

[31] Or. 39. 11. 12 (NPNF, 2nd series, 7: 355-56).
[32] Or. 29. 2.

Gregory gave further meaning to the characteristic formula of the three Cappadocians: one *ousia* and three *hypostases*.

Gregory contributed to the development of doctrine, not only in his trinitarian teachings, but also in his christological clarifications. Opposing especially the doctrine of Apollinaris—who has already been mentioned in the previous chapter and whose Christology will be discussed further on—Gregory offers formulas that would later be used as means of solving the christological controversies. However, as the main subject of this chapter is trinitarian doctrine, and as we have not yet expounded the issues involved in the christological controversies, the discussion of Gregory's Christology will be postponed for a later time—Chapter XVI.

Gregory of Nyssa

As an administrator, Gregory of Nyssa was not a man of great abilities, to the sorrow and almost despair of his brother and metropolitan bishop Basil of Caesarea. As a speaker and writer, Gregory does not reach the heights of his namesake of Nazianzus. But as a theologian and as an exponent of mystical experience he goes far beyond most of his Eastern contemporaries. Yet, one should not forget that the work of the three Cappadocians was carried on in close cooperation and mutual inspiration, and that Gregory was able to achieve what he did with the collaboration of his two friends.

Gregory of Nyssa makes more and better use of pagan philosophy than the other two Cappadocian theologians.[33] A constant reader of Origen, Gregory agrees with the Alexandrine master in the usefulness of philosophy for theological research. But he is also much more aware than Origen of the dangers that philosophy involves for theology.

Like Origen, Gregory often interprets the Bible allegorically.[34]

---

[33] Cf. Quasten, *Patrology*, 3: 283-85; Hermann Dörries, "Griechentum und Christentum bei Gregor von Nyssa," *ThLit*, 88 (1963), 569-82.

[34] In all of Gregory's works, allegorical exegesis is paramount, except in his *Commentary on the Six Days of Creation* and *On the Creation of Man*. In these two works, Gregory is attempting to complete the work of his late brother Basil on creation. As

This trait is more marked in his mystical works, where persons and historical events become symbols of the various stages of mystical ascent.[35] However, even in such works, Gregory never forgets the historical character of biblical revelation.[36]

But Origen's influence upon Gregory goes far beyond exegetical principles. Gregory's temperament and interest are similar to those of Origen, and he therefore uses the writings of the Alexandrine as a constant source of theological principles. Like Origen, he builds his own theological system on the doctrine of the freedom of the intellects, and he emphasizes that freedom to such a point that the doctrine of grace seems endangered.[37] The origin of evil is to be found in the freedom of created intellects, and not in an autonomous negative principle.[38] Evil exists only as an absence, a certain negativity, and not as a subsisting essence. Therefore, evil is not eternal, and when the day comes in which God will be "all in all" evil will no longer exist, and those who have been evil will be saved.

On the other hand, Gregory did not follow Origen with servility. On the contrary, he took the principles of Origen and applied them within the context of his time, when theological development had reached a point where it was necessary to correct some of Origen's conclusions.

An example of this dual relationship between Origen and Gregory may be seen in the doctrine of the pre-existence of souls. Origen affirmed that souls, although creatures, had existed from the beginning, so that there was not a time where there were no souls. In making such statements, Origen showed that he had not clearly thought out the difference between the Christian doctrine of creation and the

---

Basil had clearly stated (*PG,* 29 : 188) that he would not follow an allegorical method, Gregory continued in the same direction.

[35] The best exposition and defense by Gregory of the allegorical method is to be found in his introduction to his *Homilies on the Song of Songs* (ed. Jaeger, 6: 3-13).

[36] Thus, for instance, in his treatise *On the Life of Moses,* Gregory first tells the story of that life and then moves on to its mystical interpretation.

[37] *De virgin.* 46; *De hom. op.* 44; *In Cant. Hom.* 2. 44 (where the words are to be found: αὐτεξούσιος χάρις).

[38] *Or. Cat.* 6; *De beat.* 5. 44.

Neoplatonic doctrine of emanations. Later, especially during the Arian controversy, theologians had given more thought to the meaning of the word "creature," and had concluded that a creature cannot be eternal. Therefore, Gregory affirms that souls are pre-existent only in the mind of God.[39]

On the other hand, at some points Gregory shows himself to be more of an idealist than Origen himself, as for instance when he affirms that only intellectual creatures and God are substantial in the strict sense; body is only a concomitance of qualities and ideas: weight, color, form, extension, etc.

The corporeal creation, on the other hand, must certainly be classed amongst specialties that have nothing in common with the Deity; and it does offer this supreme difficulty to the Reason; namely, that the Reason cannot see *how* the visible comes out of the invisible, *how* the hard solid comes out of the intangible, *how* the finite comes out of the infinite, *how* that which is circumscribed by certain proportions, where the idea of quantity comes in, can come from that which has no size, no proportions, and so on through each single substance of body. But even about this we can say so much: *i.e.* that not one of those things which we attribute to body is itself body; neither figure, nor colour, nor weight, nor extension, nor quantity, nor any other qualifying notion whatever; but every one of them is a category; it is the combination of them all into a single whole that constitutes body. Seeing, then, that these several qualifications which complete the particular body are grasped by thought alone, and not by sense, and that the Deity is a thinking being, what trouble can it be to such a thinking agent to produce the thinkables whose mutual combination generates *for us* the substance of that body?[40]

For these reasons Gregory of Nyssa, like Origen, is a difficult theologian to evaluate, for one is tempted to understand him as being excessively tied to Neoplatonic categories and thereby not do justice to

---

[39] *De hom. op.* 28; *De an. et res.*
[40] *De an. et res.* (NPNF, 2nd series, 5: 458).

his genuine theological concerns and his contribution to the clarification of trinitarian doctrine.

Although it is difficult to determine how much of Gregory's trinitarian doctrine is original with him, and how much he derives from his brother and teacher Basil—a difficulty that is augmented by the impossibility of determining with absolute certainty which of the two was the author of certain very important treatises—one can at least expound Gregory's trinitarian doctrine and show how his Neoplatonic convictions and interest help him to solve some of the difficulties that his contemporaries found, and to achieve a greater clarity than they.

In order to expound Gregory's trinitarian doctrine, one may follow his two treatises *On the Holy Trinity*[41] and *On Not Three Gods*,[42] although always making use of his book *Against Eunomius*,[43] with which he attempted to continue the work of his late brother Basil.

In the treatise *On Not Three Gods*, Gregory responds to Ablabius, who posed the question of why, if we refer to Peter, James, and John, whose nature is the same, as three men, we are not to do the same with the three persons of the Trinity, and refer to them as three gods. Gregory responds that when we speak of Peter, James, and John as "three men" we are speaking rather inexactly, and letting ourselves be led by a habit of speech. In truth, human nature is only one, and the man who is in Peter is the same man who is in John. Naturally, such an explanation derives directly from Gregory's Platonic traditions, no matter how surprising it may sound to men who are not used to think in such terms.

From this point, Gregory goes on to say that, whereas an inexact use of language is acceptable in speaking of the humanity of Peter, James, and John, that very inexactitude may be tragic if applied to the divine nature. To deny the essential unity of Peter and James is a philosophical error, whereas denying the unity of God is an impiety.

---

[41] Ed. Jaeger, III/I, 3-16; *NPNF*, 2nd series, 5: 326-30.
[42] Ed. Jaeger, III/I, 37-57; *NPNF*, 2nd series, 5: 331-36.
[43] Ed. Jaeger, I/II; *NPNF*, 2nd series, 5: 33-314.

In another treatise[44] Gregory adds that this is precisely the impiety of those who deny that Jesus Christ is God, for if they adore him their own premises show that they are impious, worshiping one who is not true God; if they do not worship him they are mere Jews who refuse to worship Christ.

Furthermore, there is another reason why one may choose to speak of several men and not of several gods: the operations of various men are multiple and individual, whereas the operations of the three divine persons are always common to the three.

Thus, since among men the action of each in the same pursuits is discriminated, they are properly called many, since each of them is separated from the others within his own environment, according to the special character of his operation. But in the case of the Divine nature we do not similarly learn that the Father does anything by Himself in which the Son does not work conjointly, or again that the Son has any special operation apart from the Holy Spirit; but every operation which extends from God to the Creation, and is named according to our variable conceptions of it, has its origin from the Father, and proceeds through the Son, and is perfected in the Holy Spirit. For this reason the name derived from the operation is not divided with regard to the number of those who fulfil it, because the action of each concerning anything is not separate and peculiar, but whatever comes to pass, in reference either to the acts of His providence for us, or to the government and constitution of the universe, comes to pass by the action of the Three, yet what does come to pass is not three things.[45]

Someone might object to this that "divinity" is not an operation but an essence. Gregory rejects that objection, claiming that "divinity" is only a name, and that, as the essence of God is beyond every name, the term "divinity" cannot describe him.[46]

From the paragraph quoted above it is clear that the distinction be-

---

[44] *Ad Simplicium de fide* (Ed. Jaeger, III/I, 61-67; *NPNF*, 2nd series, 5: 337-39).

[45] *Quod non sint tres dei* (*NPNF*, 2nd series, 5: 334). Cf. Jaeger, III/I, 47-48.

[46] *Ibid.*

tween the three divine persons cannot be established on the basis of their external relations. Gregory adds that that distinction can neither be established on the basis of a subordinationism that posits a difference of power or glory between the three persons. Therefore, the only distinction that can be made must be grounded on the inner relations of the Trinity.

If, however, any one cavils at our argument, on the ground that by not admitting the difference of nature it leads to a mixture and confusion of the Persons, we shall make to such a charge this answer;—that while we confess the invariable character of the nature, we do not deny the difference in respect of cause, and that which is caused, by which alone we apprehend that one Person is distinguished from another;—by our belief, that is, that one is the Cause, and another is of the Cause; and again in that which is of the Cause we recognize another distinction. For one is directly from the first Cause, and another by that which is directly from the first Cause; so that the attribute of being Only-begotten abides without doubt in the Son, and the interposition of the Son, while it guards His attribute of being Only-begotten, does not shut out the Spirit from His relation by way of nature to the Father.[47]

Gregory's Christology is not as profound as that of his namesake of Nazianzus. But he too, in opposing Apollinaris, defends the integrity of the human nature of Christ.[48] On the other hand, although the distinction between the human and divine natures does not disappear in the incarnation, the union is such that there is a *communicatio idiomatum*, that is, the communication of the properties of one nature to the other. This is why Gregory affirms, as was already customary in his time, that Mary is "mother of God," and not simply "mother of the man Jesus." [49] There is, however, a certain idealistic and Docetic tendency in the affirmation—which will later become general—that

---

[47] *Ibid.* (*NPNF*, 2nd series, 5: 336). Cf. Jaeger, III/I, 55-56.
[48] See Chap. XVI.
[49] *Ep.* 3. 24 (*Ep.* 17 in *NPNF*).

Mary continued being a virgin even after the birth of Jesus, "for that birth did not destroy the virginity." [50]

Finally, and although this is not our main interest in this chapter, a word must be said regarding Gregory's mystical theology.[51] His mysticism is typically Neoplatonic, and is developed within the framework of a series of successive steps of purification and ascent, in a constant and perpetual progress. This aspect of Gregory's theology greatly influenced the thought of the unknown author of certain works that later circulated under the name of Dionysius the Areopagite. Through him, Gregory made his influence felt in Medieval mysticism—a subject that will be discussed in the second volume of this *History*.

Conclusion

Apart from their great achievements in other fields of ecclesiastical life—liturgy and administration in the case of Basil, rhetoric and poetry in Gregory of Nazianzus, and mysticism in Gregory of Nyssa—the work of the three great Cappadocians consisted in clarifying, defining, and defending trinitarian doctrine. They were instrumental in the defeat of Arianism as well as of the Pneumatomachians. Basil set the foundation for the work of the other two, and he also divulged trinitarian doctrine through his liturgical innovations. Gregory of Nazianzus placed the best resources of language at the service of the Nicene faith, and composed hymns that contributed to the popularizing of that doctrine, as had been done earlier by the Arians. Gregory of Nyssa, building upon the foundations of Basil and Gregory of Nazianzus, gave greater precision and logical coherence to their doctrine.

One may ask whether in these developments the Cappadocians were in truth faithful to the Nicene faith, or, on the contrary, their exposi-

---

[50] *De virg.* 19 (Ed. Jaeger, VIII/I, 323-24; *NPNF*, 2nd series, 5: 365).

[51] See Jean Daniélou, *Platonisme et théologie mystique: Doctrine spirituelle de saint Grégoire de Nysse* (Paris: Aubier, 1944).

tion of trinitarian doctrine, while claiming to defend and expound the doctrine of Nicea, in reality abandoned the intention of the bishops gathered in the Great Council.

This last alternative has been expounded and defended by several historians of Christian thought, who see a marked difference between the "ancient Nicenes" and the "new Nicenes." One of these historians is Harnack, who believes that the Cappadocian formula is a seemingly Nicene manner of expressing the ancient doctrine of the *homoiousios*—that is, that the Father and the Son are not of the same substance, but of similar substances. Thus, Harnack categorically affirms that "it was not the 'homousios' which finally triumphed, but on the contrary the homoiusian doctrine, which fixed the terms of agreement with the 'homousios.' " [52]

There is no doubt that there are ample reasons that justify the distinction between the "ancient" and "new" Nicenes. Among those present at Nicea there were many who did not understand the points at issue, and some of those who there condemned Arius and his followers were really Monarchians whose own doctrine was later condemned. On the other hand, if one gives the name of "ancient Nicenes" to the group that later gathered around Athanasius, there is no doubt that there are great differences between them and the Cappadocians. But these differences must not be exaggerated to the point that they become an opposition that in reality did not exist.

Some of the differences between Athanasius and the Cappadocians are due to their different historical context, and others to their diverse theological methods. Athanasius and the Cappadocians had to face opponents who, although all Arians, were, however, different. Athanasius faced Arianism when its final consequences had not yet been manifested, and it was therefore necessary to refute and condemn it by showing its negative consequences for the Christian faith. The Cappadocians, on the other hand, were opposed to a mature Arianism whose fruits are already known. Therefore, their task was not so much attempting to discover the consequences of Arianism, but

---

[52] *HD*, 4: 82.

refuting such consequences and developing an alternative. Thus, in a good measure the distance that separated the "ancient" from the "new" Nicenes can and must be explained on the basis of the distance that separated the "ancient Arians" from the "new."

Furthermore, the Cappadocians differed from Athanasius on theological methodology. The great Alexandrine bishop referred every question having to do with the divinity of the Son to its soteriological consequences. The Cappadocians tended to make use of logical and scriptural arguments, without a constant and conscious effort to relate trinitarian doctrine with soteriology.[53] For them, what is at issue is a fundamental doctrine of Christianity, rather than a necessary point of departure for Christian soteriology. The battle is almost at its end, and the task of the Cappadocians consists in systematizing the faith of the Church and expounding it with as much logical clarity as is possible. This is probably one of the reasons why, with Gregory of Nyssa, we find ourselves once again in the Origenistic atmosphere that Athanasius seemed to have left behind.

But what Harnack wishes to say with his clear-cut contrast between the two Nicene generations is much more than this. According to him, the Cappadocian formula is a betrayal of the Nicene faith. In Nicea, the unity of substance between the Father and the Son was affirmed. The Cappadocians—in affirming that there is in God one *ousia* and three *hypostases,* and that the unity of God is similar to that which exists between Peter, James, and John—interpreted the unity of God as a community of nature, and they thus reintroduced under the cloak of the *homoousios* what was in fact *homoiousian* doctrine.

This evaluation of the work of the Cappadocians seems unacceptable on two scores: it does not correctly interpret the Nicene decision, and it also errs in its understanding of the doctrine of the Cappadocians. Regarding the Council of Nicea, we have already pointed out that its intention was not proclaiming the unity of the di-

---

[53] One should note, however, that when it came to the question of the human soul of Christ the tables were turned, and Athanasius failed to see the soteriological issue at stake, while the Cappadocians placed it at the center of the discussion.

vine substance, but rather affirming the divinity of the Son. Regarding the Cappadocians, their doctrine that the unity of God is analogous to that which exists between three men is not as far from Nicea as it seems at first sight, once we remember that for a man such as Gregory of Nyssa, given his philosophical presuppositions, the man that is common to Peter, James, and John is more real than the three individuals themselves. This Cappadocian doctrine is placed within the framework of a Platonic realism, and it is unfair to interpret it within the context of our modern nominalism.

XV

Trinitarian Doctrine in the West

In the West, Arianism was not as great a threat as it was in the East. This seems to have been due to three main reasons: the trinitarian tradition of Latin Christianity, its occupation with other matters of a more practical nature which seemed more urgent, and the influence of Stoicism. The first of these reasons is obvious when one remembers that with Tertullian the West had already developed the trinitarian formula that would prevail throughout its history: "One substance and three persons." This was coupled with the practical inclination of the Latin West, thereby preventing the Arian controversy from becoming as widespread an issue as it was in the East. Finally, the fact that in the West Stoicism was the most common philosophy may well have contributed to avoiding some of the pitfalls of the Neoplatonist East. In earlier chapters we have seen how Western discussions of the Trinity, in their concern to refute Modalism, usually were inclined to subordinationism. But this never reached the extreme of Arianism, and this may well have been due, at least in part, to the fact that the influence of Alexandrine theology, with its emphasis on the divine transcendence, was very little felt in the West. When God is conceived as an absolutely transcendent being, one is tempted to see the Word as an intermediate being between God and the world, as is the case with Arianism. Stoic influence, with its emphasis on divine immanence, thus contributed to saving the West from the ravages of Arianism.

This does not mean, however, that Arianism and the trinitarian controversy did not penetrate into the West. There were times and places in which Arianism made its influence felt. During the reign of Constantius, all the West felt the imperial pressure in support of Arianism, and even Pope Liberius, as well as the elderly Hosius of Cordova, were forced to sign documents that contradicted the Nicene faith. However, even during this period, Arianism was able to make strong inroads only in the border zones, where military necessity led men to be more acquiescent to imperial policies. Some years later, when Justina attempted to impose Christianity in that part of the Empire which was ruled by her son Valentinian II, popular reaction—under the very able leadership of Ambrose of Milan—clearly showed that Arianism had no inner vitality.

In spite of this, the West did produce a number of works with which it attempted to reflect on the issues involved in the controversy that was raging in the East. At first, such works followed the general outlines of those written in the East, and some of them were little more than revised versions of Greek works. But the West did slowly develop its own forms of discussing and expressing trinitarian doctrine, and this development reached its climax in Saint Augustine's treatise *On the Trinity*.

Early in the second half of the fourth century, Hilary of Poitiers wrote twelve books *On the Trinity,* which clearly reflect the influences that he received during his exile in the East. His discussion of the Trinity has no great originality, and its importance lies rather in having offered to the Latin-speaking world a treatise that summarized the issues at stake in the Arian controversy and the arguments in favor of the Nicene faith.[1]

Nor does Saint Ambrose, the great champion of the Nicene faith in

---

[1] Pierre Smulders, *La doctrine trinitaire de S. Hilaire de Poitiers* (Rome: Gregorian University Press, 1944); Jules Lebreton, "A propos de la doctrine Trinitaire de saint Hilaire de Poitiers," *RScRel,* 33 (1946), 484-89.

Northern Italy, have anything new to contribute to trinitarian doctrine. He defended the Nicene faith mostly as a very able churchman and a preacher. But when Emperor Gratian asked him to compose a treatise on the Holy Spirit, Ambrose simply took Basil's work on the same subject and produced a free version and slight adaptation of it.[2]

Another Western opponent of Arianism is Lucifer of Calaris in Sardinia.[3] In his works, written in the Latin of the people, he openly attacks Emperor Constantius, and even makes some offensive remarks about him. He became involved in the schism that had taken place in Antioch when Eustathius was condemned and deposed, and after his death those who did not accept the ease with which the Church had reinstated former Arians took him as their symbol and were thus called "Luciferians." Lacking in doctrinal content, this sect was not long lived, although it did produce some able teachers and writers—most noteworthy among them Gregory of Elvira, who wrote a treatise *On the Orthodox Faith Against the Arians*.[4]

It was early in the fifth century, with Augustine, that the West showed the depth and originality of which it was capable. In his fifteen books *On the Trinity* (399-419), Augustine determined the way that Western trinitarian theology would follow, so that the later differences between Eastern and Western trinitarian theology stem from this work. It is therefore necessary to discuss here Augustine's trinitarian doctrine, although the global discussion of this theology will be part of the second volume of this history.

---

[2] Cf. Ludwig Herrmann, "Ambrosius von Mailand als Trinitätstheologe," *ZeitschrKgesch*, 69 (1958), 197-218, who claims that Ambrose leans toward a homoiousian understanding of the Trinity.

[3] The most detailed biography that I know is that found in G. Cerretti, *Lucifero vescovo di Cagliari ed il suo "Moriendum esse pro Filio Dei"* (Pisa: Nistri-Lischi, 1940). On his trinitarian doctrine see: C. Zedda, "La dottrina trinitaria di Lucifero di Cagliari," *DivThom*, 52 (1949), 276-329.

[4] The following are general introductions to his work and theology: Angel Custodio Vega, "Una gran figura literaria española del siglo IV," *CD*, 156 (1944), 205-58, J. Collantes Lozano, *San Gregorio de Elvira: Estudio sobre su eclesiología* (Granada: Imp. F. Román Camacho, 1954); F. J. Buckley, *Christ and the Church According to Gregory of Elvira* (Rome: Gregorian University Press, 1964).

Augustine accepted Trinitarian doctrine as a matter of faith that is beyond every doubt. Therefore, his work *On the Trinity* is not devoted, as most of its predecessors, to offer proofs of the divinity of the Son and of the Holy Spirit, nor to prove their essential unity with the Father. Basically, Augustine builds upon the foundation laid by the three Cappadocians, although he did not know their theology directly but only through Hilary.

Like the Cappadocians, Augustine makes it clear that the distinction between the persons[5] of the Trinity is due not to their external actions but to their inner relationship.[6] This does not mean that it is impossible or wholly incorrect to refer to one of the divine persons a particular action of the Trinity, as is done when one affirms that "the Word became flesh." What actually happens is that the limitations of our vocabulary and our mind do not allow us to express or understand how the Trinity as a whole acts in each of the works of God, and we therefore refer those works to one of the divine persons. This is what medieval theologians would call "appropriations," [7] and their justification is to be found in the following words of Saint Augustine:

But I would boldly say, that the Father, Son, and Holy Spirit, of one and the same substance, God the Creator, the Omnipotent Trinity, work indivisibly; but that this cannot be indivisibly manifested by the creature, which is far inferior, and least of all by the bodily creature: just as the Father, Son, and Holy Spirit cannot be named by our words, which certainly are bodily sounds, except in their own proper intervals of time, divided by a distinct separation, which intervals the proper syllables of each word occupy. Since in their proper substance wherein they are, the three are one, the Father, and the Son, and the Holy Spirit, the very same, by no temporal motion, above the whole creature, without any interval of time and place,

---

[5] Although Augustine avoids using the term "person" in referring to the Trinity. Cf. R. Boigelot, "Le mot 'personne' dans les écrits trinitaires de saint Augustin," *NRT*, 57 (1930), 5-16.

[6] José Morán, "Las relaciones divinas según San Agustín," *Aug*, 4 (1959), 353-72.

[7] See A. Chollet, "Appropriations aux personnes de la Sainte Trinité," *DTC*, 1: 1708-17.

and at once one and the same from eternity to eternity, as it were eternity itself, which is not without truth and charity. But, in my words, the Father, Son, and Holy Spirit are separated, and cannot be named at once, and occupy their own proper places separately in visible letters. And as, when I name my memory, and intellect, and will, each name refers to each severally, but yet each is uttered by all three; for there is no one of these three names that is not uttered by both my memory and my intellect and my will together [by the soul as a whole]; so the Trinity together wrought both the voice of the Father, and the flesh of the Son, and the dove of the Holy Spirit, while each of these things is referred severally to each person. And by this similitude it is in some degree discernible, that the Trinity, which is inseparable in itself, is manifested separably by the appearance of the visible creature; and that the operation of the Trinity is also inseparable in each severally of those things which are said to pertain properly to the manifesting of either the Father, or the Son, or the Holy Spirit.[8]

Although Augustine follows Greek theologians in his discussion of Trinitarian doctrine, theologians such as the Cappadocians tend to take as their point of departure the diversity of the persons or hypostases, and from it move to the unity of essence or *ousia*, whereas Augustine, on the other hand, begins from the essential unity of God, and from it moves to the distinction of persons. He never quite understood what the Cappadocians meant by *hypostasis*—which he translated as *substantia*.[9] But what separates him from Greek theologians is more than a purely verbal difference. It is not merely that Augustine rejected the term *hypostasis* and then used *persona* as its equivalent. The difference is rather that Augustine will not grant to the diversity of persons the importance that it had in the Cappadocians. His manner of understanding the divine unity and simplicity leads him to reject every attempt to speak of God as a

---

[8] *De Trin.* 4. 21. 30 (*NPNF*, 1st series 3:85-86).

[9] *Ibid.*, 5. 8. 10 (*NPNF*, 1st series, 3: 92): "They indeed use also the word hypostasis; but they intend to put a difference, I know not what, between οὐσία and hypostasis: so that most of ourselves who treat these things in the Greek language, are accustomed to say, μίαν οὐσίαν, τρεῖς ὑποστάσεις, or, in Latin, one essence, three substances."

"triple" being, as had been done by Marius Victorinus, a famous intellectual who had been converted to Christianity and whom Augustine otherwise admired.[10]

Neither, since He is a Trinity, is He therefore to be thought triple; otherwise the Father alone, or the Son alone, will be less than the Father and Son together. Although, indeed, it is hard to see how we can say, either the Father alone, or the Son alone; since both the Father is with the Son, and the Son with the Father, always and inseparably: not that both are the Father, or both are the Son; but because they are always one in relation to the other and neither the one nor the other alone.[11]

Furthermore, even the term *persona,* which by that time was generally accepted in Western trinitarian discourse with the prestige given to it by a long tradition, is simply a conventional way of expressing what is inexpressible. "What therefore remains, except that we confess that these terms sprang from the necessity of speaking, when copious reasoning was required against the devices or errors of the heretics?" [12] In any case, it would be much more exact to speak of "relations," for this is what is meant when one speaks of the different "persons."

But in God nothing is said to be according to accident, because in Him nothing is changeable; and yet everything that is said, is not said according to substance. For it is said in relation to something, as the Father in relation to the Son and the Son in relation to the Father, which is not accident; because both the one is always Father, and the other is always Son: yet not "always," meaning from the time when the Son was born [*natus*], so that the Father ceases not to be the Father because the Son never *ceases* to be the Son, but because the Son was *always* born, and never began to be the Son. But if He had begun to be at any time, or were at any time to

---

[10] Cf. Paul Henry, "The Adversus Arium of Marius Victorinus, the First Systematic Exposition of the Doctrine of the Trinity," *JTS,* n.s. 1 (1950), 42-55.

[11] *De Trin.,* 6. 7. 9 (*NPNF,* 1st series, 3: 101).

[12] *Ibid.,* 7. 4. 9 (*NPNF,* 1st series, 3: 110).

cease to be, the Son, then He would be called Son according to accident. But if the Father, in that He is called Father, were so called in relation to Himself, not to the Son; and the Son, in that He is called the Son, were so called in relation to Himself, not to the Father; then both the one would be called Father, and the other Son, according to substance. But because the Father is not called Father except in that He has a Son, and the Son is not called Son except in that He has a Father, these things are not said according to substance; because each of them is not so called in relation to Himself, but the terms are used reciprocally and in relation each to the other; nor yet according to accident, because both the being called the Father, and the being called the Son, is eternal and unchangeable to them. Wherefore, although to be the Father and to be the Son is different, yet their substance is not different; because they are so called, not according to substance, but according to relation, which relation, however, is not accident, because it is not changeable.[13]

This theory of the divine relations is Augustine's point of departure for his two great contributions to trinitarian thought: his theory of the procession of the Holy Spirit, and his doctrine of the vestiges of the Trinity in creatures.

Earlier theologians had found it difficult to express the difference that exists between the generation of the Son and the procession of the Holy Spirit. The Arians profited from these difficulties, asking how it is possible that, while both the Son and the Holy Spirit derive their being from the Father, one is called Son and the other is not. Augustine sets out by confessing his ignorance regarding the proper way to distinguish between the generation of the Son and the procession of the Holy Spirit. But he later proposes the theory—which would become common in the West—that the Holy Spirit is the bond of love that exists between the Father and the Son.

Therefore the Holy Spirit, whatever it is, is something common both to the Father and Son. But that communion itself is consubstantial and co-eternal; and if it may fitly be called friendship, let it be so called; but it is more

---

[13] *Ibid.*, 5. 5. 6 (*NPNF*, 1st series, 3: 89).

aptly called love. And this is also a substance, since God is a substance, and "God is love," as it is written.[14]

This understanding of the procession of the Holy Spirit is important for its later consequences, for the medieval debate between Eastern and Western theologians regarding the *filioque* clause had its roots in it.

Augustine's other contribution to the development of trinitarian thought is his theory of the *vestigia Trinitatis*—the vestiges or signs of the Trinity to be found in its creatures. In all created things, and especially in the human soul, one can see the imprint of the Creator and of his triune nature. This does not mean simply that certain things of the natural order can be used as means to explain or illustrate trinitarian doctrine—a rather common procedure in earlier theologians—but rather that *all things,* by the mere fact that they have been created by the triune God, carry the imprint of the Trinity. Later this doctrine would be systematically developed by medieval theologians, who would distinguish between shadows, vestiges, images, and likenesses of the Trinity in its creatures.[15] Augustine himself, however, centered his attention on man, of whom the Scripture says that he was made in the image and after the likeness of the Trinity—this being the reason why, in Gen. 1:26, the plural form is used: "Let us make man." [16]

Although Augustine uses several different trilogies to show the imprint of the Trinity in the human soul, the most common, and that which later had a more distinguished career throughout the history of Christian thought, is that which refers to the memory, the understanding, and the will.

---

[14] *Ibid.,* 6. 5. 7 (*NPNF*, 1st series, 3: 100). Perhaps Augustine has drawn this doctrine from Marius Victorinus, for whom the Holy Spirit is such a bond. Cf. *PL,* 8: 1146.

[15] See, for instance, Saint Bonaventure's *Itinerarium mentis in Deum.*

[16] An interpretation which is not original with Saint Augustine, but is rather commonplace in earlier Patristic literature. Cf. Irenaeus, *Adv. haer.* 4. *proem.*; Tertullian, *De res. car.* 6; Novatian, *De Trin.* 17; 26. Among the earlier Gnostics, it was common to use this text as a proof of the participation of several angels or powers in the work of creation.

Since, then, these three, memory, understanding, will, are not three lives, but one life; nor three minds, but one mind; it follows certainly that neither are they three substances, but one substance. Since memory, which is called life, and mind, and substance, is so called in respect to itself; but it is called memory, relatively to something. And I should say the same also of understanding and of will, since they are called understanding and will relatively to something; but each in respect to itself is life, and mind, and essence. And hence these three are one, in that they are one life, one mind, one essence; and whatever else they are severally called in respect to themselves, they are called also together, not plurally, but in the singular number. But they are three, in that wherein they are mutually referred to each other; and if they were not equal, and this not only each to each, but also each to all, they certainly could not mutually contain each other; for not only is each contained by each, but also all by each. For I remember that I have memory and understanding, and will; and I understand that I understand; and will, and remember; and I will that I will, and remember, and understand; and I remember together my whole memory, and understanding, and will. For that of my memory which I do not remember, is not in my memory; and nothing is so much in the memory as memory itself. Therefore I remember the whole memory.[17]

Thus, Augustine uses the inner relationships of the faculties of the soul—and there is no doubt that the bishop of Hippo is a man of deep psychological sensibility—in order to attempt to understand, insofar as possible, the inner relationships within the Trinity.

In summary, one can say that Augustine pointed the way that Western trinitarian theology would later follow at least in three fundamental points: his insistence upon the divine unity above the diversity of persons; his doctrine of the procession of the Spirit; and his theory of the *vestigia Trinitatis,* especially in the field of human psychology.[18]

The first of these points, while avoiding the danger of tritheism

---

[17] *De Trin.* 10. 11. 18 (*NPNF,* 1st series, 3: 142).

[18] Cf. Michael Schmaus, "Das Fortwirken der augustinischen Trinitätspsychologie bis zur karolingischen Zeit," *Vitae et veritati: Festgabe für Karl Adam* (Düsseldorf: Patmos-Verlag, 1956), 44-56.

which existed in other theologians, came very close to that Sabellianism which earlier conservative Eastern bishops had feared would be the result of the Nicene *homoousios*.

The second point greatly contributed to clarifying and pointing the way for the Western doctrine of the Holy Spirit, and its most important consequence would be the later controversy regarding the *filioque*.

Finally, the third point was paramount in Western medieval theology, and eventually became the basic framework of a mystical theology that attempted to reach God through the contemplation of his imprint in creatures.

While Augustine was working on the trinitarian problem, the East was beginning to stir with a new subject of controversy: the person of the Savior. What had been discussed up to this time was mostly the divinity of the Son. Now the main question will be how that divinity relates to humanity in Jesus Christ. This is the main theme of the christological controversies to which we must now turn.

XVI

The Beginnings of the Christological Controversies

The controversies that we have just studied revolved around the questions of the divinity of the Son and of the way in which his divinity relates him to the Father and to the Holy Spirit. There is another question that theologians would have to ask themselves, once they considered the divinity of the Son settled: How are divinity and humanity related within Jesus Christ?

Even from the earliest periods of Christian thought, we have seen some of the possible answers to this question. On the one hand, it is possible to affirm Christ's divinity and deny his humanity. This solution, called Docetism, was condemned by the great majority of Christians, for it made the cardinal doctrine of the incarnation meaningless. On the other hand, it is possible to affirm Christ's humanity and call God's revelation in him the result of his moral excellence. This position, which was probably that of the Ebionites, was also unsatisfactory to the religious sensibility of the majority of Christians, who affirmed categorically that "God was in Christ."

Most Christians took a stand somewhere between these two positions, though sometimes leaning in one direction or the other. On certain occasions—as in the case of Paul of Samosata—they neared one or another extreme and were generally rejected. But the theologians whose Christology was more orthodox—Ignatius, Irenaeus, Origen, and even Tertullian—had not really tried to arrive at precise definitions concerning the union of the human and the divine in Jesus Christ.

During the fourth century, and especially in the early stages of the Arian controversy, there was too much interest in the trinitarian question for theologians to give careful thought to Christology itself. For instance, although the Christology of Arius was very different from that which the Western Church had considered orthodox from the time of Tertullian, and likewise, from that of some of the Eastern bishops who met at Nicea—Eustathius of Antioch, among others—the Nicene creed has not a word to say against such Christology. Athanasius himself, champion of the struggle against Arianism, seems to have been quite close to Arius in his Christology.[1] While they debated the question of the Savior's divinity, who would feel inclined to reflect on the relationship between that divinity and his humanity?

But the trinitarian controversy had to lead inevitably to the christological debate. Arianism, intent upon making the Logos a being subject to change, developed a Christology to sustain such a position.[2] Thus, as soon as the later Nicene theologians took time to reflect on the person of Jesus Christ, they found it necessary to refute, not only the Arians' doctrine of the Word, but also their Christology.

Moreover, through the years each one of the principal intellectual and doctrinal centers of Christianity had become accustomed, almost unconsciously, to formulate and solve the christological question in a way typical of itself. These centers were the West, Antioch, and Alexandria.

---

[1] This is not to say that either Arius or Athanasius had a fully developed Christology in the sense that they explicitly denied that Christ had a human soul, but only that they took such a denial for granted. Cf. William P. Haugaard, "Arius: Twice a Heretic?" *CH*, 29 (1960), 251-63.

[2] Aloys Grillmeier, *Christ in Christian Tradition*, pp. 190-92, argues that the relationship between trinitarian and christological thought within Arianism was the reverse of what is stated here. This interpretation does not seem to the present author to do justice to the extant texts, especially since Athanasius, Apollinaris, and others who held a similar Christology were anti-Arians.

In the West, the basic tenets of the christological dogma had been established from the time of Tertullian. More than a century before the Council of Nicea, Tertullian had faced the problem of the duality of natures in Christ, and the way in which these two "substances"—as he would call them—are united in a single person. His solution, though it lacks the clarity and precision that could be attained only through long controversy, is definitely superior to many of the fourth- and fifth-century proposals, for Tertullian is aware of the need to insist on the divinity of the Word and at the same time to affirm the integral humanity of Jesus Christ, including a rational soul.[3]

Tertullian's formula, that in Christ two substances were joined in a single person, was not immediately accepted by Western theologians, most of whom followed his doctrine of the "two natures" but did not draw on his reference to the unity of the "one person."[4] Their Christology, however, was basically that of Tertullian, with its insistence on the reality of the two natures, and on their union in such a way that there is between them a real *communicatio idiomatum*. Later on, Augustine, who very soon gained preeminence as the great teacher of the West, recovered the term "persona" in its christological context and thereby led the West once again to Tertullian's forgotten formula of the two natures in one person.[5] The West thus developed an intermediate position between the confusion of the human and the divine in Christ, and their extreme distinction. Therefore, while the christological controversies raged in the East, the West looked upon them with interest, but without deep involvement, for the dispute was never a crucial issue in the West. Moreover, the position of the Westerners, with Tertullian's christological formula, constituted an intermediate position between the two principal tendencies that the East was discussing. For this reason, when an accord

---

[3] *De carne Christi* 13.
[4] Tarsicius J. van Bavel, *Recherches sur la christologie de saint Augustin* (Fribourg, Switzerland: Editions Universitaires, 1954), p. 13.
[5] *Ibid.*, pp. 25-26.

was reached and the controversy died down, it was Tertullian's old formula that served as the link to join the divergent theories.

In the East, the situation was different from that in the West, for the ranks were divided into two divergent christological tendencies that could not but collide: the Antiochene and the Alexandrine. It should not be thought, however, that these two tendencies are to be wholly identified with the cities for which they are named; rather, it is more a matter of the conflict between a theology of Hellenistic bent, centered in Alexandria, but which had its representatives even in Antioch itself; and a theology centered in Antioch and with a strong Syrian element, which emphasized the narratives of the Gospel and the true humanity of Jesus. While theologians in Alexandria were practically a homogeneous group, those in and around Antioch were divided into two branches: one patterned on Alexandria, and the other typically Antiochene. For this reason the city of Antioch often became the battleground between the two groups, whereas Alexandria was never invaded by Antiochene teachings.

By the middle of the third century these divergent trends already existed in Antioch. In fact, the controversy between Paul of Samosata and his opponents was one of the first episodes in the great battle that was to divide Eastern Christendom a century and a half later.

Although Paul of Samosata did small service to the Syrian party by exaggerating his position and thus giving occasion to Malchion and the rest of the Hellenists to condemn him, this did not end the Syrian tradition in Antioch. Thus, it is not surprising that at the beginning of the fourth century, with Eustathius of Antioch, the Syrian party had again obtained control of the bishopric. In Eustathius the history of Paul was repeated, and once again, though now with less reason, the Syrian followers of Origen—who in this case were Lucianists and therefore defenders of the Arian position—with the help of Eusebius of Nicomedia, condemned and deposed a bishop of Syrian and anti-Origenist tendencies.[6]

---

[6] On the condemnation of Eustathius, see Chap. XII.

Let us pause for a moment to examine Eustathius' Christology.[7] In it one finds the fundamental characteristics that were later to separate the Antiochene school from that of Alexandria. Like Paul of Samosata, Eustathius believed that the divinity to be found in Jesus Christ was not personal—a doctrine soon abandoned by his successors in the Antiochene school. He was interested in safeguarding the reality of Christ's humanity, and he sought to attain this end by distinguishing clearly between the divine and the human in him, at the expense of the true union of the two natures. Thus, the union of the divine and the human in Christ was due to the conjunction of the human will with the divine, in such a way that the former always wills the same as the latter. In addition, Jesus was a true man, with human body and soul, who really grew and developed, just as other men. In Christ, the impersonal "Wisdom" of God dwelt as in a temple, but the personality was human.

This tendency to emphasize the distinction between the two natures of Christ, and likewise the genuineness of his humanity, persists in Eustathius' followers. Among these, it is enough to mention briefly Diodore of Tarsus and Theodore of Mopsuestia.

Diodore of Tarsus was one of the most distinguished theologians of this time, and among his disciples may be found such celebrated men as Theodore of Mopsuestia and John Chrysostom. His treatises, however, have disappeared, destroyed by those who saw in them the beginnings of Nestorianism, and their only remains are fragments quoted in more fortunate works.[8] At any rate, we know that the great majority of his literary work consisted of Bible commentaries, and that in these Diodore followed the historical and grammatical exegesis that Lucian of Antioch had implanted in that city—quite in contrast to Alexandrine allegorization. Naturally, his emphasis on the literal sense of the Scriptures led Diodore—like the rest of the An-

---

[7] Robert V. Sellers, *Eustathius of Antioch and His Place in the Early History of Christian Doctrine* (Cambridge: Cambridge University Press, 1928), pp. 100-120.

[8] The best edition is that of Abramowski, "Der theologische Nachlass des Diodor von Tarsus," *ZntW*, 42 (1949), 19-69.

tiochene theologians—to give more attention to the historic Jesus as the Gospels present him. However, at the time of Diodore—who died in A.D. 394—the personal character of the divinity of Jesus Christ was an established thing, and in this Diodore diverged from Paul of Samosata and from Eustathius of Antioch. This in turn posed the problem of the relationship between the humanity and the divinity of Jesus Christ, which Diodore attempted to solve—in a typically Antiochene fashion—by establishing and emphasizing the distinction between the two.[9] The Word dwelt in Jesus "as in a temple," or "as it dwelt in the Old Testament prophets," though in the case of Jesus the union was permanent. Moreover, it is not only a case of the difference between the dwelling—or temple—and he who dwells in it; it is also a case of the distinction between the Son of God and the Son of David—and it was precisely this doctrine of the "two sons" that led to the destruction of his works by posterity.[10]

It seems as though Diodore arrived at this emphasis on the distinction between the humanity and the divinity of Christ through his opposition to Alexandrine Christology, which we have already seen represented by Athanasius, and later in this chapter we shall see reappear in Apollinaris. Alexandrine Christology insisted on the requirement that the union between the divine and the human in Christ be such that there be a true *communicatio idiomatum*—that is, that the attributes of his humanity can also be predicated of the Word. Nevertheless, when they tried to apply this principle, the Alexandrine theologians did it in such a way that the human nature of Jesus Christ was mutilated—that is, Jesus lacked a rational human soul. Diodore,

---

[9] This exposition of the Christology of Diodore depends, of course, on the authenticity of the fragments of his writings which have survived. As these fragments have come to us through quotations in later authors who were interested in proving the heterodoxy of Diodore, there is always the possibility that they have been mutilated or that their meaning has been changed in one way or another. However, Francis A. Sullivan, *The Christology of Theodore of Mopsuestia* (Rome: Gregorian University Press, 1956), pp. 172-81, has given reasons to believe in the authenticity of a good number of these fragments.

[10] This is also the reason why M. Jugie claims that the fundamental principles of Nestorianism are to be found in Diodore: "La doctrine christologique de Diodore de Tarse d'après les fragments de ses oeuvres," *Euntes Docete*, 2 (1949), 171-91.

on his part, saw the error of the Alexandrines but seems not to have been convinced of the need to assert the *communicatio idiomatum*. This led him to propose a Christology in which he affirmed that the Word had been united to a man, not only to human flesh[11]—a position that would eventually be generally accepted; but it also led him to establish an extreme distinction between the Word and the "assumed man," so that there could not be any *communicatio idiomatum* between them.[12]

The doctrine of Theodore of Mopsuestia follows the traditional Antiochene pattern and is therefore very similar to that of Diodore, though adjusted to theological developments of his era—Theodore died thirty years later than Diodore. Furthermore, as Sellers says, "The system of Theodore is but the acceptance of the principles of Eustathius, which are now set out in accordance with the doctrinal thought of the age." [13] This does not mean that Theodore's thought is lacking in value and originality; rather, quite the contrary, it is the culmination of the theological efforts of the Antiochene school.

Because of recent discoveries, in which certain works of Theodore, previously unknown, have come to light, the teachings of the bishop of Mopsuestia have become an object of study and controversy.[14]

---

[11] This can be affirmed, in spite of the different interpretation to be found in Grillmeier, *Christ*, pp. 260-70.

[12] Sullivan, *The Christology of Theodore*, pp. 188-89: "Diodorus has in fact rejected not only the errors of the Apollinarists, but also the unity of person which they were trying, in their own mistaken fashion, to defend. We believe that Diodorus has failed to recognize the difference between the legitimate predication of human attributes to the incarnate Word as their ultimate subject, and their attribution to the Word by virtue of an Apollinarist composition with human flesh. The failure to make such a distinction, coupled with a lofty concept of the divinity of the Word, excludes all predication of human attributes to the Word. But the inevitable consequence of such an exclusion is nothing less than a denial of the reality of the incarnation. For if no human attribute can be predicated of the Word as its subject, then one cannot say that the Word has been born of the Virgin Mary according to the flesh, or that the Word has become man."

[13] Sellers, *Eustathius*, p. 117.

[14] The main subject of these controversies is the relationship between Theodore's Christology and that of Nestorius. Until recently there had been very little doubt as to the judgment of the Fifth Ecumenical Council which met at Constantinople in 553— which turned Theodore into a Nestorian before Nestorius. The recently discovered texts

Nonetheless, we may assert that Theodore, following the old Antiochene tradition, emphasized the distinction between Christ's two natures much more than the unity of his person. However, Theodore did not carry this to the extreme of affirming—as Diodore seems to have done before him—that in Christ there are two Sons or two Lords.[15] There is, to be sure, the indestructible difference between the one who assumes and the assumed; but there is also the union of the two, also indestructible and permanent. This distinction and union between the humanity and the divinity is such that Theodore could speak of the union of "two natures" in "one person," [16] just as Tertullian had already done and as every orthodox Christian would do later. He understood this "person," however, as that which results from the union of the two natures,[17] and not as the Second Person of the Trinity, to which is joined the impersonal nature of the "assumed man." [18]

Like his predecessors Eustathius and Diodore, Theodore interpreted the presence of God in Jesus Christ in terms of the dwelling of the Son in him. This presence is different from the omnipresence of God in the world. God is present in the world "because of his nature and power," but he is present in Jesus Christ "because of his gracious will." It is also in this way that God dwells in the saints and the prophets. In the

---

seem to prove that the Council made use of texts that had been interpolated and twisted by Theodore's enemies. See, in favor of Theodore's orthodoxy: Robert Devreesse, *Essai sur Théodore de Mopsueste* (Vatican City: Bibliteca Apostolica Vaticana, 1948); against his orthodoxy: Francis A. Sullivan, "Some reactions to Devreesse's New Study of Theodore of Mopsuestia," *ThSt*, 12 (1951), 179-207. The issue is further complicated by the question of what it was that Nestorius actually taught.

[15] Although there are texts in which Theodore establishes a polarity between the Lord and the Son of David, there are others in which he explicitly denies that there are "two Sons" or "two Lords." See Quasten, *Patrology*, 3 (Utrecht: Spectrum, 1960), 415-16.

[16] The most relevant texts are to be found in Devreesse, *Essai*, p. 115, n. 1. One should note, however, that Theodore prefers to speak of the union in one "prosopon" rather than in one "hypostasis." Sullivan, *The Christology of Theodore*, pp. 78-82; 259-84.

[17] Sullivan, *The Christology of Theodore*, p. 265; Richard A. Norris, *Manhood and Christ: A Study in the Christology of Theodore of Mopsuestia* (Oxford: Clarendon Press, 1963), pp. 228-33.

[18] As will be seen further on, the latter was the interpretation that eventually became most common, mostly through the influence of Cyril of Alexandria.

case of Jesus Christ in particular, it is necessary to add that God dwells in him "as in a son." This God who dwells in Jesus Christ is not an impersonal force, but rather, he is the Second Person of the Trinity, who has assumed human nature in such a way that an absolute harmony exists between the two natures.[19] This "conjunction," however, does not deprive Jesus Christ's humanity of any human characteristics; thus there can be a true development from the Child of Bethlehem to the Teacher of Galilee—and here we find another typically Antiochene theme.[20]

For Theodore, the "man assumed" by the Word continues to be the proper subject of human attributes, and these are not transferable to the Word except with the safeguard that this is possible only "by relationship" and not directly.[21] The true *communicatio idiomatum* goes only in one direction: the attributes of the Word are extended to the man; but not vice versa.[22]

Thus, Theodore's affirmations about the "unity of person" in Jesus Christ never quite erase the impression that he is saying that in Christ there are really two persons who act with such harmony that they seem to be one—and it is significant to recall here that the term *prosopon*, which Theodore applies to the "person" of Jesus Christ, has precisely, though not necessarily, the connotation of an external appearance. At this point the doctrine of the incarnation seems to be endangered—though no more than when the Alexandrines emphasized the unity of Christ at the expense of his humanity.[23]

---

[19] This "indwelling" of the Word in the assumed man according to Theodore is very clearly expounded and discussed by Norris, *Manhood and Christ*, pp. 216-28.

[20] The theme of Christ's development according to the School of Antioch is emphasized by Robert V. Sellers, *Two Ancient Christologies: A Study in the Christological Thought of the Schools of Alexandria and Antioch in the Early History of Christian Doctrine* (London: S.P.C.K., 1954).

[21] It is thus that Theodore's position with respect to the title "Mother of God" is to be understood. He does not reject it, but he insists that this title can be given to Mary only if one keeps in mind that she is truly "Mother of the Man" and "Mother of God" only by virtue of the relationship between the Word and the man who was born of her. See: Norris, *Manhood and Christ*, pp. 215-16.

[22] Sullivan, *The Christology of Theodore*, p. 287.

[23] Before leaving Theodore, it is necessary to underline his importance as an exegete. If we have devoted our attention to his Christology, it is because that is our particular

Briefly, we may characterize the Antiochene doctrine as a "Logos-man" Christology, in contrast to the "Logos-flesh" Christology of the Alexandrines. In other words, while the Alexandrines, especially those of the fourth century, were satisfied to affirm the union of the Word with human flesh, the Antiochenes found it necessary to postulate the union of the Word with a complete man. On the other hand, while the Antiochenes were willing to cede a point in reference to the unity of the person of Jesus Christ, the Alexandrines insisted on preserving and emphasizing this unity, even at the expense of the Savior's human nature.

Alexandrine Christology was thus very different from that of Antioch. With their Neoplatonist tendencies, Alexandrine theologians—from Clement on—believed they should sustain the immutability of the Word even though the human integrity of Jesus suffered thereby. We have already seen the Docetic tendency of Clement's assertion that Christ was lacking in human passions. Origen himself, although he felt it necessary to condemn Docetism, states that the bodily constitution of Jesus was different from that of other human beings.

This point of view continued to develop in the third and fourth centuries, when the necessity of affirming the personal presence of the Son in Jesus Christ, and of postulating at the same time his union with humanity, gave rise to the "Logos-flesh" Christology. According to this teaching, it was not humanity that was assumed by the Word, but rather, human flesh. Although the first important representative of this position was Apollinaris of Laodicea, we should point out some of the antecedents in whom he may have found justification for his position.

---

concern in this chapter, and because posterity paid more attention to Theodore's Christology than to his hermeneutical work. However, his disciples called him "The Interpreter"—a title that shows his renown as an exegete. See: L. Pirot, *L'oeuvre exégétique de Theódore de Mopsueste* (Rome: Pontificius Institutus Biblicus, 1913); Rowan Greer, *Theodore of Mopsuestia: Exegete and Theologian* (Philadelphia: Westminster Press, 1961), pp. 86-152; Devreesse, *Essai*, pp. 53-93. This aspect of his work, as well as his Christology, shows Theodore as a typical Antiochene.

Thus, for example, the little that we know about Malchion and the other Origenists who condemned Paul of Samosata in 268 would seem to indicate that their Christology was of the "Logos-flesh" type. According to them, "the divine Word is in Him the same as the inner man in us."[24] Jesus Christ is a being composed in the same way as other men: just as in man there are flesh and soul, so also in the Savior there are the human flesh and the divine Word.[25]

At the beginning of the fourth century, when Eusebius and Pamphilus of Caesarea wrote their *Apologia pro Origine,* there were those who criticized the great Alexandrine teacher for having stated that Jesus had a human soul, and on this account Eusebius and Pamphilus felt obliged to point out that the Scriptures mention Jesus' soul.[26] But Eusebius himself, in expounding his own christological doctrines, abandoned Origen's position and affirmed that the Word moved the Savior's body in the same way that the soul moves other men's bodies.[27]

As was to be expected, this type of Christology came into conflict with Antiochene doctrine. The first encounter of which we have record was the debate between Paul of Samosata and Malchion.[28] Some time later, at the beginning of the Arian controversy, the two schools confronted each other again when Eustathius of Antioch was condemned by Eusebius of Nicomedia and his fellows—whose Christology was of the Alexandrine type. Shortly afterward, this time in the city of Corinth, the two groups faced each other once more, but the results of this confrontation have not come down to us.[29]

---

[24] *Frag.* 30. Greek text to be found in Gustave Bardy, *Paul de Samosate* (Louvain: Spicilegium Sacrum Lovaniense, 1929), p. 59. Bardy himself, however, does not interpret this text as a case of Logos-flesh Christology (see pp. 481-88).

[25] *Frag.* 36, in *ibid.,* pp. 61-63.

[26] *Apol. pro Orig.* 5.

[27] *De eccl. theol.* 1. 20. 90. Quoted by Kelly, *Early Christian Doctrines,* p. 160.

[28] See Chap. XI.

[29] The basis for this assertion is Athanasius, *Ep.* 59, *Ad Epictetum.* One must point out that this epistle does not allow us to affirm categorically the nature of the two tendencies that were to be found at Corinth. Charles E. Raven, *Apollinarism: An Essay on the*

At any rate, by the beginning of the fourth century Alexandrine Christology in its characteristic form dominated the theological scene. Both Arius and Athanasius, who seem to have agreed on nothing else, were participants in the Logos-flesh Christology.

This doctrine was used by the Arians as an argument in favor of the mutability of the Word. If the Word can establish such a close union with human flesh, and it is capable of receiving sense impressions transmitted by that flesh, how can it be immutable?

Thus it is clear that the trinitarian question necessarily led into the christological, since it was important to remove the Arian argument that seemed to prove that the Word was inferior to God. And, even if we ignore the Arian argument, the definitive affirmation of the divinity of Jesus Christ had to lead to the question of the way in which this divinity is related to his human nature. However, the earliest defenders of Nicea did not seem to recognize the situation, so that the merit and the misfortune of such recognition fell to Apollinaris of Laodicea: merit, because his works bear testimony to an alert mind and a sharp theological perception that showed him the need to include the christological question in his discussions; misfortune, because his solution was less fortunate than his perception of the problem, and he was soon condemned by his former companions in the defense of the Nicene doctrine, who now saw in his teachings a danger as serious as Arianism.[30]

Apollinaris was born early in the fourth century in the Syrian city of Laodicea. He received a careful education that made him a skilled orator and a true scholar not without a sense of humor. Sometime after the Council of Nicea, Apollinaris became friendly with Athanasius

---

Christology of the Early Church (Cambridge: Cambridge University Press, 1923), pp. 104 ff., takes them to be Docetic and Ebionite teachings. On the other hand, Sellers (*Two Ancient Christologies*, pp. 36-37) claims that we have here an encounter between Alexandrine Christology and its rival from Antioch. Sellers' argument is convincing.

[30] No work has survived under the name of Apollinaris. There are fragments of his writings in works composed against him—such as the *Antirrheticus* of Gregory of Nyssa. Besides, a few of his works have survived under the names of more orthodox theologians, such as Athanasius, Gregory the Wonderworker, and Pope Julius I.

and Basil,[31] and later was made bishop of his native city, where he had distinguished himself for his opposition to the Arian bishop, George.

In his efforts to refute Arianism, Apollinaris became aware that one of the basic arguments of the later Arians was christological: if the Word was joined to a human body, and such a body is by nature mutable, then the Word itself must be mutable. Faced with this argument, he must develop a Christology capable of demonstrating exactly *how* the immutable Word could unite with mutable humanity. To this task Apollinaris dedicated his best speculative talents, but the result was the doctrine known as *Apollinarianism,* which Christians of clearer theological vision felt obliged to reject.

On the other hand, in the city of Laodicea, located near Antioch, Apollinaris was a great defender, not only of the Nicene faith, but also of the Alexandrine theology that opposed the ancient Antiochene tradition. Thus, at the same time that he was attacking Arius, he had to take care that his arguments should not be in line with Antiochene Christology, with its tendency to distinguish between the divine and the human in Jesus Christ in a way that Apollinaris felt was erroneous. Thus it was that Apollinaris' Christology, though opposed to that of Arius in affirming the immutability of the Word, was in agreement with the latter in its fundamental structure, and is therefore of the Logos-flesh type.

Apollinaris shows two principal interests in formulating his Christology: the integrity of the person of Jesus Christ—as against the Antiochenes—and the immutability of the Word of God—as

---

[31] There has been some discussion among scholars regarding the friendship between Apollinaris and Basil. This has to do mostly with the authenticity of four letters that are to be found among Basil's epistles, bearing numbers 361-364 (*PG,* 32: 1100-1108). Such distinguished historians as Loofs and Lietzmann deny their authenticity. But there is strength in the arguments to the contrary proposed by George L. Prestige, *St. Basil the Great and Apollinaris of Laodicea* (London: S.P.C.K., 1956). This correspondence, if genuine, took place while Apollinaris was still regarded, not as a heretic, but as a champion of the Nicene faith.

against the Arians.[32] The first of these interests is manifest when Apollinaris states that

God the Word is not one person, and the man Jesus another person, but the same who subsisted as Son before was made one with flesh by Mary, so constituting Himself a perfect, and holy, and sinless man, and using that economical position for the renewal of mankind and the salvation of all the world.[33]

On the other hand, his interest in safeguarding the immutability of the Word can be seen in the following quotation:

God, having been incarnated in the flesh of man, retains also His proper energy pure, possessing a mind unsubjected by the natural and fleshly affections, and holding the flesh and the fleshly motions divinely and sinlessly, and not only unmastered by the power of death, but even destroying death.[34]

The Christology of Apollinaris, conceived in part to refute Arianism, arises from the trichotomist presupposition that man is composed—according to I Thess. 5:23—of body, soul, and spirit. This tripartite constitution of human nature was then interpreted in the light of the triple division that Plato established among the different constituents of the rational being. Thus human nature is composed of body, soul, and spirit or reason. In this distinction, the soul is merely the vital principle that gives life to the body. Therefore, the soul is impersonal and not conscious, whereas all the rational faculties are attributed to the spirit, which becomes the seat of personality.

Basing his explanation on this trichotomy, Apollinaris believed he could explain the way in which the Word was united with the hu-

---

[32] The ancient historians interpret Apollinaris' Christology from the anti-Arian point of view, whereas most modern historians tend to emphasize the anti-Antiochene nature of his thought. It seems best to interpret him as opposed to both Arians and Antiochenes, although underlining this latter trend. Actually, there is no mention of Eunomius and the other Arian leaders in the christological texts of Apollinaris which have survived, while there are frequent references to the Antiochene theologians.

[33] Pseudo-Gregory the Wonderworker, *Conf. of Faith* 19 (*ANF*, 6: 45).

[34] *Ibid.*, 16 (*ANF*, 6: 44).

manity in Christ without thereby losing its immutability: in Christ, the Word occupied the place of the spirit, so that in him a human body and soul were joined to the divine reason.[35] In this way Apollinaris saved the immutability of the Word, which is always the active agent and never passive, in the life of Christ. At the same time, he solved the problem of how two natures—the divine and the human—can unite without forming a new nature. Christ is human because his body and his soul—or vital principle—are human; but he is divine because his reason is the very Word of God. If in Christ there were united a complete man, with his own personality and his own reason, to the Son of God, two persons would result, and this would destroy the reality of the incarnation, which states that in Christ God was united with man.[36] Apollinaris, then, found no other solution than to mutilate the human nature of Christ, taking away its rational faculties, and putting the Word in the place these should occupy.

In order to show forth the unity of the Savior which he deemed so important for a correct Christology, Apollinaris repeatedly spoke of Christ as "one nature." By this he probably meant that, just as man is only one "nature," so Christ, even after the incarnation, is only one and cannot be divided into "the man" and "the Word." As one of his most typical phrases, "one nature of God the Word incarnate," was found in a work erroneously attributed to Athanasius, and thus preserved for posterity under the cloak of orthodoxy, the "one nature" formula would influence several orthodox theologians, even after Apollinarism was formally condemned. Eventually, it would become one of the points at issue in a new encounter between Alexandrine and Antiochene Christology.

In the teachings of Apollinaris we have the natural conclusion of the Logos-flesh type of Christology, and Apollinaris has not added any more than the logical precision of his powerful mind. This, and the

---

[35] It is hardly necessary to document this aspect of Apollinaris' doctrine. One can point, however, to fragments 74 and 151 in Lietzmann, *Apollinaris von Laodicea und seine Schule* (Tübingen: J. C. B. Mohr, 1904).

[36] *Ibid.*, fr. 92.

prestige he enjoyed as a defender of the Nicene faith, made many loath to attack him. But the time came when his doctrines began to be propagated and gave origin to a schismatic group, and then some of the most distinguished bishops, convinced as they were of the errors of his Christology, found themselves obliged to attack Apollinaris in his old age.

In general, we may say that the strong opposition to Apollinaris and his group, from both East and West, was due to their implied soteriology. In the West he was condemned repeatedly during the reign of Pope Damasus I (366-384), and soteriological reasons were always involved in such condemnations.[37] But it was in the East that the Three Great Cappadocians felt obliged to refute the Apollinarian teachings.[38] As we have seen, Athanasius was led to his strong opposition to Arianism by consideration of the requirements of the doctrine of salvation. But even Athanasius, who saw clearly the soteriological consequences of a denial of the true divinity of the Son, was unable to perceive that a Christology that denied the human integrity of Jesus Christ also endangered the Christian doctrine of salvation.[39] The Cappadocians were the first to recognize the danger hidden within this Christology, which for all practical purposes denied the reality of Christ's human nature, and to show how such a Christology would destroy what they saw as the Christian doctrine of salvation.

For the Cappadocians, as for most of the Greek Fathers, the doctrine of deification constituted a fundamental aspect of Christian soteriology. As Athanasius, echoing Irenaeus, had said: "He became

---

[37] See, for instance, the Roman decree of 382, in Denzinger, *Enchiridion Symbolorum*, p. 65.

[38] The Cappadocians were by no means the only theologians who attempted to refute Apollinaris, and a fuller study of the controversy would require consideration of the various Roman synods that condemned him, as well as of the writings of Epiphanius and others. Our purpose here is simply to show the main reasons that led to the condemnation of Apollinarism, and to this end a brief mention of the objections raised by the Cappadocians against Apollinaris should suffice.

[39] As stated above, (Chap. XIII, n. 30), the synod of 362 in Alexandria is not necessarily to be understood as a departure from a Logos-flesh Christology. The text of *Ad Antioch.* 7 is not decisive. Finally, the two treatises *Against Apollinaris*, attributed to Athanasius, are spurious.

man so that we might be made gods." [40] When God assumed humanity, his purpose was not only to participate in human life, but also and above all, to enable man to participate in the divine life.

According to the Cappadocians, all this is lost by Apollinaris, and so he must be condemned as emphatically as possible.

If anyone has put his trust in Him as a Man without a human mind, he is really bereft of mind, and quite unworthy of salvation. For that which He has not assumed He has not healed; but that which is united to His Godhead is also saved. If only half Adam fell, then that which Christ assumes and saves may be half also; but if the whole of his nature fell, it must be united to the whole nature of Him that was begotten, and so be saved as a whole. [41]

Such is the essence of the Cappadocian argument, which also occurs in the treatises against Apollinaris falsely attributed to Athanasius.

But the above, although it requires the inclusion of the soteriological implications of each doctrine in the christological debate, does not offer guidelines to the solution of the problem presented by Apollinaris. His own solution was unacceptable. Could a solution be found that would satisfy Apollinaris' requirements and at the same time the soteriological conditions that the Cappadocians were now advancing?

As a matter of fact, most of the Greek theologians, although they had not given themselves to a precise formulation of their Christology, were very close to the position of Apollinaris, even the Three Great Cappadocians. For this reason, in his first attacks against Apollinaris, Basil accused him of schism rather than of heresy. [42]

Even Gregory of Nazianzus, whose two epistles to Cledonius constitute a solid refutation of Apollinarian Christology, does not succeed

---

[40] *Oratio de inc.* 54.

[41] Gregory of Nazianzus, *Ep.* 101 (*NPNF*, 2nd series, 7: 440).

[42] *Ep.* 263. There are in this epistle some accusations of heresy, but they refer to the doctrine of the Trinity and to eschatological questions. Regarding Christology itself, Basil accuses Apollinaris only of vague and useless speculation.

in developing a Christology much more satisfactory than his opponent's.[43] Since the "Word-flesh" type of Christology had demonstrated its ultimate consequences in the doctrines of Apollinaris, Gregory abandoned it and made use of the "Word-man" terminology.[44] But this by no means indicates that Gregory leaned toward Antiochene Christology with its concern for the total and real humanity of Jesus Christ. On the contrary, after having denied Apollinaris' Christology, Gregory thought it necessary to affirm that the center of the Savior's personality is in his divinity, so that his humanity is, as it were, absorbed by the divine nature. The divine and human natures are like the sun and the stars: although the stars have their own light, when the sun appears the starlight is absorbed into the sunshine, and all the light becomes one.[45]

The Christology of Gregory of Nyssa also fails to break away from the Alexandrine tendency to take the divinity of Jesus Christ as the starting point and to attribute to him only the highest degree of humanity that may be compatible with this starting point. Just as his namesake of Nazianzus, Gregory rejects the Word-flesh type of Christology and speaks in terms of the union of the Word to a complete humanity. But he also follows his friend in asserting that divinity and humanity intermingle in Christ in such a way that the latter is absorbed into the former. His best known example is that of a drop of vinegar dissolved in the sea: in the same way that the vinegar does not lose its own nature, so also the humanity continues its existence when absorbed by the divinity, although for all practical purposes there seems to be only the latter.[46]

The Cappadocians have been much criticized for their condemnation of Apollinaris, when their Christology appears to differ so slightly from that of the bishop of Laodicea. However, if we place ourselves in the perspective of the Cappadocians, we shall understand why they

---

[43] *Ep.* 101-2. See also *Ep.* 125 and 202.
[44] *Ep.* 102.
[45] *Ep.* 101.
[46] *Adv. Eunomium* 5. 5. One should note, however, that this text refers to the post-resurrection Christ.

saw a chasm between their Christology and that of Apollinaris. For the Cappadocians, as for the greater part of the Greek Fathers, salvation consisted essentially in deification. The Word became flesh, not so much to give an example to humanity or to pay man's debt to God, as to defeat the forces of evil that had imprisoned us, and at the same time to open the way to the deification of man. Since God assumed humanity, the latter is enabled to attain deification. Thus, for the Cappadocians the important thing was that in Christ God truly assumed humanity, and not that his humanity remained identical to ours or as free as ours. Therefore, Apollinaris' doctrine was not acceptable to the Cappadocians. And for this reason, also, they were able to describe the union of the divine and the human in Christ in such terms that the human seemed to lose itself in the divine, without thereby destroying the soteriological significance of the incarnation as they understood that significance.

It was mostly on the basis of these objections raised by the Cappadocians and by other theologians that the christological doctrines of Apollinaris were condemned by the council gathered at Constantinople in A.D. 381—usually known as the Second Ecumenical Council.

XVII

The Nestorian Controversy and the Council of Ephesus

The rejection of the theories of Apollinaris was in no way a solution of the christological problem. The Cappadocians themselves, although they were convinced that it was necessary to condemn the elderly Laodicean theologian, did not have a clear alternative to offer. Although Alexandrine Christology suffered a severe blow in the condemnation of Apollinaris, it was still a very strong current in Eastern theology, and it necessarily had to collide with Antiochene Christology. Furthermore, the fifth century marks a further step in the process by which the Church of the humble and crucified Lord became involved in struggles for prestige and power which were no less bitter than those that took place in the Byzantine court. All the great Christian sees—Rome, Alexandria, Antioch, and Constantinople —were struggling against their rivals in an attempt to gain preponderance, and each of them in turn allowed these political interests to influence its theological decisions.

In an attempt to simplify a very complex development, one may say that the christological controversies of the fifth century began early in A.D. 428, when the Antiochene Nestorius came to occupy the patriarchal see of Constantinople. Even if Nestorius had been a prudent man, the ancient tension between Alexandrine and Antiochene theology, and the determination of Alexandria that it was not to be supplanted by the new capital, would have been enough to create serious difficulties.[1] But Nestorius was not a prudent man, and that which could have been limited to some difficulties ended in tragedy.

The conflict broke out when Nestorius declared himself against the title "Bearer of God" (θεοτόκος), as applied to Mary.[2] By that time, this title was rather common among most Christians; and Alexandrine theologians, who had been used to it since the time of Bishop Alexander, saw it as a necessary consequence of the *communicatio idiomatum*. Even Theodore of Mopsuestia was willing to accept it as long as one took care to interpret it correctly. But Nestorius saw in the title Bearer of God as applied to Mary a confusion of the divine and the human in Jesus Christ. According to him, one may call Mary Bearer of Christ, but not Bearer of God.

The reaction was not slow in coming. Cyril, the bishop of Alexandria, was a zealous defender of the authority of his see, as well as a convinced partisan of Alexandrine Christology. For him, Nestorius' position was a denial of the Alexandrine principle of the unity of the Savior, as well as an occasion to reaffirm the authority of the Alexandrine see over that of Constantinople. Therefore, one must not interpret Cyril as a mere church politician or as a theologian driven by purely theological considerations.

As soon as he learned of the preaching of Nestorius against the title "Bearer of God," Cyril mustered all the forces that could help him to

---

[1] The Council of Constantinople, in its third canon, granted to "the new Rome" an authority in the East similar to that which old Rome had in the West. This was not well received in Rome or in Alexandria, which by that time had come to see itself as the most important see in the East. In consequence, Alexandria became a vigorous opponent of Constantinople, especially when the latter see was occupied by a man of Antiochene leanings. This opposition may be seen, not only in the struggles described in this chapter and the next, but also at an earlier date, in the bitter antagonism of Theophilus of Alexandria toward John Chrysostom, patriarch of Constantinople, who was deposed and sent into exile in A.D. 404.

[2] In so doing, he was not actually taking the initiative, but was rather attempting to settle a controversy that had been going on in Constantinople for some time. When Anastasius, his chaplain, attacked the use of θεοτόκος, Nestorius refused to excommunicate him. Later, Nestorius himself preached his famous sermons against the title of θεοτόκος.

achieve the condemnation of the patriarch of Constantinople. As patriarch of Alexandria, he had at his disposal a strong argument to obtain the support of the court: gold. Through the centuries, the Alexandrine see had collected great wealth, which could now be employed in the struggle against Nestorius. With these resources, Cyril obtained the support of some high authorities who were more interested in gold than in theology. His second source of support was the Roman see. Ever since the Council of Constantinople had claimed for that city a rank similar to that of Rome, Alexandria had been able to count on the ancient capital as an ally against the pretensions of the upstart see. This Roman inclination to support Alexandria against Constantinople became more marked when Nestorius offered asylum to a group of Pelagians who had been condemned in the West.[3] For these reasons, as well as for his authoritarian and bellicose tone, Nestorius was condemned by a synod gathered in Rome in August, A.D. 430, under the leadership of Pope Celestine. Finally, Cyril had the support of the Egyptian monks, who were convinced that the Alexandrine cause was that of orthodoxy and who, since the times of Athanasius, had become staunch defenders of what they took to be the true faith.

Nestorius, on the other hand, had the support of John, the patriarch of Antioch. Although he was not as powerful as his Alexandrine counterpart, John was a power to be reckoned with, as was amply shown during the course of the controversy.

The Roman Synod of A.D. 430 appointed Cyril to represent it in the East in the task of asking Nestorius to recant. Cyril did write to Nestorius asking him to withdraw his statements; but he did so in terms that Nestorius, even had he been of a more tractable character, would never have been able to accept. After writing twice to the patriarch of Constantinople, Cyril sent him a third letter to which were appended twelve anathemas that Nestorius must accept. These anathemas not only condemned Nestorius' position, but they were also an exposition

---

[3] The doctrine of Pelagius and his followers will be discussed in the second volume of this *History*.

of Alexandrine theology, as if only it were orthodox.[4] Thus, Cyril pretended to turn the defeat of Nestorius into the definitive victory of Alexandrine theology over its Antiochene rival. As a response, Nestorius sent back twelve anathemas against Cyril.[5]

These mutual condemnations created such troubles in the Eastern church that the emperors Valentinian III and Theodosius II called a general council that was to meet at Ephesus on June 7, A.D. 431.

On the date set for the great gathering, only a few of the supporters of Nestorius had arrived at Ephesus. Cyril was already there with a multitude of bishops and monks who were convinced that it was necessary to condemn and depose Nestorius. The local bishop, Memnon, who was also a supporter of Cyril, took charge of organizing a campaign to incite the masses against Nestorius. On June 22, John of Antioch and his group had not arrived, and Cyril opened the sessions of the Council, overriding the protests of seventy-eight bishops as well as of the imperial legate. That very day, in a brief session of a few hours in which he was not given a hearing, Nestorious was condemned and deposed.

Patriarch John of Antioch and his party arrived four days later. When they learned of the Council's decision, they gathered separately, and declared that they were the true council. They then condemned and deposed Cyril as well as Memnon.

Meanwhile, the papal legates had also arrived at Ephesus. They joined Cyril's council, and together they ratified the condemnation of Nestorius, and added to it all those who took part in the rival council headed by John. In exchange for this support from Rome, Cyril's council condemned Pelagianism, which was the heresy that most preoccupied the Pope.

Given all this confusion, and fearing that the result would be an ir-

---

[4] Trans. in *NPNF*, 2nd series, 14: 206-18. Original text in *PG*, 77: 119, and in August Hahn, *Bibliothek der Symbole und Glaubensregeln der alten Kirche*, 3rd ed. (Breslau: E. Morgenstern, 1897), pp. 312-16.

[5] Hahn, *Bibliothek*, pp. 316-18.

reparable schism, Theodosius II ordered Cyril as well as Nestorius and John to be imprisoned. But soon Cyril showed that he was an able politician, and managed to have the Emperor convoke a group of delegates from each of the two factions to meet with him in Chalcedon, and there to try to overcome their differences. Once before the Emperor, Cyril and his supporters gained his favor, with the result that Nestorius was deposed and forced to return to Antioch, while a new patriarch was appointed for Constantinople. As for Cyril himself, he soon returned to Alexandria where the Emperor would find it difficult to take any action against him, should he decide to do so.

This, however, did not end the controversy, for many theologians claimed that Cyril's twelve anathemas against Nestorius were themselves heretical.[6] Thus, the controversy that at first had to do only with Nestorius, now involved Cyril himself. Rome, with a christological tradition that was very different from that of Alexandria, found Cyril's document very embarassing. Cyril was being criticized even in Egypt itself, where some of his former defenders found in his actions much that was disagreeable. On the other hand, John of Antioch and the other Syrian bishops had broken communion with the rest of the Church, so that the schism had now materialized.

In view of the seeming incapability of the bishops to come to an agreement by themselves, the Emperor decided to intervene in the dispute. His legate Aristolaus traveled to Antioch and Alexandria and, after long and complicated negotiations, a compromise was achieved. Cyril did not withdraw his anathemas, but he did reinterpret them in such a fashion that many thought that he had in fact retracted. Futhermore, he agreed to sign a formula based on a credal statement that had been proposed at Ephesus by the council led by John of Antioch.[7] On the other hand, the patriarch of Antioch agreed to confirm

---

[6] See Robert V. Sellers, *The Council of Chalcedon* (London: S.P.C.K., 1953), pp. 8-9.

[7] "We thus confess our Lord Jesus Christ, the only-begotten Son of God, perfect God and perfect man, of rational soul and body; begotten of the Father before all time

the condemnation and deposition of Nestorius. As some in his own party refused to accept this decision, John was forced to depose them also. As for Nestorius, he spent four years in a monastery in Antioch, but his presence there was too cumbersome for John and threatened the precarious peace that had been achieved, and he was therefore sent to more remote places, first the city of Petra and later an oasis in the Libyan dessert. There he was forgotten to such an extent that a few years later those in Constantinople no longer knew what had become of him. However, he did live beyond the time of the Council of Chalcedon (A.D. 451), in which he thought that his own doctrine was vindicated. He spent his last years trying to make himself heard from his remote exile and to show the world that he had been right, for his doctrine was in agreement with that of the Fathers gathered at Chalcedon. It was all in vain; Nestorius, although still alive, was a man of the past, and in the imperial court as well as in the great centers of ecclesiastical life no one seemed to have the time to listen to his pleas.

Was Nestorius really a heretic? In other words, was his doctrine such that it denied some of the fundamental principles of the Christian faith? Or was he condemned rather for his lack of tact and Cyril's ambition and political ability? Did those who condemned him understand his doctrine correctly? Or did they condemn rather a caricature of his thought? These are questions on which scholars are not in agreement. And these questions are further complicated by the tendency of some historians to interpret the Nestorian controversy in

---

according to his divinity, and the same in the last days begotten of the virgin Mary according to his humanity, for us and for our salvation; the same consubstantial with the Father according to his divinity, and consubstantial with us according to his humanity; who is a union of two natures; we therefore confess one Christ, one Son, one Lord. According to this doctrine of the union without confusion, we confess that the holy Virgin is Mother of God (θεοτόκος), for God the Word was incarnate and made man, and from its conception united unto himself the temple which he took from her. As to the evangelical and apostolical words regarding the Lord, we know that the theologians interpret some as being common, and referring to the one person (πρόσωπον), and others as referring differently to the two natures; and they understand those that pertain to the divine as referring to the divinity of Christ, and the lower ones as referring to his humanity." Translated from the Greek text in Hahn, *Bibliothek,* pp. 215-16.

the light of later issues. Thus, many Protestants have seen in Nestorius a forerunner of Protestantism, on no other grounds than his rejection of the title "Mother of God." [8]

Nestorius began to be discussed on new grounds early in the twentieth century, mostly because of the work of Loofs, Bethune-Baker, and Bedjan. The first published in 1905 a new edition of the fragments of Nestorius, and he included in it many fragments previously unknown.[9] Bethune-Baker, making use of a copy of the text on which Bedjan was working, published in 1908 a study in which he attempted to establish the orthodoxy of Nestorius.[10] Finally, in 1910, Bedjan published a Syriac version—discovered in 1889—of the *Book of Heraclides*, by Nestorius,[11] which had been lost. Since then, scholars have not ceased discussing the theology of Nestorius, but they have not yet reached a unanimous verdict as to exact nature of his doctrine.[12]

Generally speaking, the heart of the controversy is in the difficulty of establishing an agreement between what Nestorius says in his *Book of Heraclides* and what seems to follow from the fragments of his

---

[8] Thus, already a seventeenth-century Calvinist wrote a treatise with the title *Disputatio de suppositat, in qua plurima hactenus inaudita de Nestorio tanquam orthodoxo et de Cyrillo Alexandrino alliisque episcopis in synodum coactis tanquam haereticis demonstrantur.*

[9] *Nestoriana: die Fragmente des Nestorius gesammelt, untersucht und herausgegeben* (Halle: Max Niemeyer, 1905).

[10] *Nestorius and His Teaching: A Fresh Examination of His Teaching, with Special Reference to the Newly Recovered Apology of Nestorius* (Cambridge: University Press, 1908).

[11] *Nestorius: Le Livre d'Héraclide de Damas* (Paris: 1910). The Syriac translation probably dates from the sixth century. The English version of G. R. Driver and L. Hodgson was published in 1925.

[12] The various studies and conclusions are summarized in Carl E. Braaten, "Modern Interpretations of Nestorius," *CH*, 32 (1963), 251-67, and in Grillmeier, *Christ in Christian Tradition*, pp. 496-505. The best recent studies are those of Luigi I. Scipioni, *Ricerche sulla cristologia del "Libro di Eraclide" di Nestorio: La formulazione teologica e il suo contesto filosofico* (Fribourg: Edizioni universitarie, 1956), which shows the influence of Stoicism on Nestorius' anthropology and Christology, and Luise Abramowski, *Untersuchungen zum Liber Heraclidis des Nestorius* (Louvain: Corpus scriptorum christianorum orientalium, 1963), who deals more with the literary composition of the *Book of Heraclides,* although she also discusses its teaching.

other works that have been preserved in the writings of his adversaries. Those who attempt to defend the unfortunate patriarch affirm that his true thought is to be found in the *Book of Heraclides,* and that the fragments have been twisted and quoted out of context with the intention of justifying his condemnation. But others claim that the divergence between the fragments and the *Book of Heraclides* stems from their different times and situations: the fragments were written when Nestorius believed that he was powerful and therefore took upon himself the task of arguing resolutely against every doctrine that he believed to be heretical, whereas the *Book of Heraclides* is the apology of a defeated man who is trying to show the injustice of his lot. The proponents of this theory point out that twenty years had gone by between the fragments and the *Book of Heraclides,* and that those years had shown Nestorius the folly of his previous attitude and had helped him to moderate his thought. Finally, others claim that even in his final work Nestorius shows that his Christology was not in agreement with that of the Church at large.

There seems to be an element of truth in each of these interpretations. On the one hand, it is true that what Cyril and his followers condemned at Ephesus was not the theology of Nestorius, but a mere caricature of it. On the other hand, it is also true that Nestorius exaggerated his own positions in the heat of controversy, that some of his disciples seemed to be proud of the manner in which they could draw the most extreme consequences from the teachings of the Patriarch, and that Nestorius himself did not attempt to destroy the caricature that was being made of his theology. When, condemned, deposed and exiled, he discovered his error, it was too late to correct it.

In order to understand Nestorius' Christology, one must first attempt to clarify his terminology, for the manner in which his theology is interpreted greatly depends on the meaning of terms such as "nature," "hypostasis," "prosopon," "union," etc.[18]

---

[18] The following section is greatly dependent on Scipioni, *Ricerche,* pp. 45-97.

In the *Book of Heraclides,* the term "nature" often appears together with the adjective "complete." As Nestorius sees it, a nature can be either complete or incomplete. Incomplete natures are those which in coming together form a new nature—which can also be called "natural composition." Thus, for instance, the body and the soul are incomplete natures, for their union produces the complete human nature. On the other hand, human nature is complete, for its union with another complete nature—in the case of Christ, the divine nature—does not produce a new nature. What makes a nature complete is the totality of its "distinctions," "differences," or "characteristics"; that is, what Nestorius calls its "separation," although this term is not to be understood in the sense of a distance, but rather as that distinction, that particular character, which makes a nature definable and knowable.

When Nestorius refers to a complete nature, he often uses the term "hypostasis." This hypostasis is not something different from the nature itself, something that is added to a nature, but is rather that nature itself inasmuch as it is "complete."

The term "prosopon" is used by Nestorius—besides its common uses meaning "function" and "human individual"—in the sense that it has within the context of trinitarian doctrine.[14] The Father, the Son, and the Holy Spirit are three prosopa. However, Nestorius also uses it in an ambiguous fashion, for he sometimes affirms that there are in Christ two prosopa, and at other times says that there is only one. Therefore, it is necessary to clarify the different manners in which Nestorius uses the term prosopon within a christological context.

When Nestorius speaks of two prosopa in Jesus Christ, he is using the term in the sense of "natural prosopon." For him, the natural prosopon is the form of a nature, the totality of the properties and distinctions that make a nature complete, so that it may be called a hypostasis. Each complete nature is known and distinguished by its

---

[14] Quite naturally, he also uses the term hypostasis in its trinitarian context, although he prefers to use the term prosopon.

prosopon. Therefore, in the case of Christ, if humanity and divinity are to subsist as complete natures, without being dissolved into a third, each of them must have its own prosopon. Hence the claim that there are two prosopa in Christ.

But there is another sense in which, according to Nestorius, one must affirm that there is in Christ only one prosopon. This prosopon is that which Nestorius calls "prosopon of union," "prosopon of the dispensation," "common prosopon," or "voluntary prosopon." [15] This prosopon is that of the Son; it is identical to the second person of the Trinity.[16] In Jesus Christ, God has united his divine prosopon to a human nature—but this in no way destroys the two natural prosopa, which correspond to each of the two "complete natures" or hypostases which are united in Christ.

What is one to say, then, regarding the union of divinity and humanity in Christ? In the first place, Nestorius believes that it is necessary to reject every interpretation that claims that the union is "natural" or "hypostatic." As he understands these terms, a natural or hypostatic union is that in which two natures come together to form a third. If such were the case in Christ, one should no longer speak of a union but of the *result* of a union. If the distinctions of the two natures that are united disappear, the natural prosopa will also disappear, and therefore all that may be said of the resultant nature can be said only of it and not of its components. Furthermore, only two incomplete natures can unite in such a fashion, and Nestorius believes that the integrity of the two natures that are united in the Savior is an inviolable principle. Therefore, the union in Christ cannot be such that the two natures become only one. The doctrine of a hypostatic union—which he understands as synonymous with natural union—is anathema for Nestorius.

---

[15] The references may be found in Scipioni, *Ricerche*, pp. 59-60.

[16] Nestorius does deny that this "prosopon" is the Word. But this must be understood in the light of his use of the terms "Son" and "Word." The latter is applied to the Second Person of the Trinity in referring to his divine nature; the former is used for the same Person as a distinct prosopon. This distinction is not real, but merely conceptual, and it does not mean that the "Son" came into existence only after the incarnation.

For Nestorius, a natural union is a union *of* natures which takes place *in* the natures and terminates *at* the nature, whereas the union in the *prosopon* . . . is the union *of* natures and not *of prosopa*, which takes place *in* the *prosopon* and not *in* the nature, and terminates *at* the *prosopon* and not *at* the nature.[17]

The fundamental difference between these two types of union is that in the union "in the prosopon" the natures that are joined are not changed, whereas Nestorius conceives the natural or hypostatic union as a mixture in which the distinctions that are proper to each nature are confused and lost.

This union is "voluntary"—one of the aspects of Nestorius' doctrine which was most severely attacked. This does not mean that it is a purely psychological union. As Nestorius understands it, the term voluntary union does not refer primarily to a union that is the result of a decision, but to one that does no violence to the natures that are united. A natural union—that is, one of two incomplete natures in order to form a third nature—is involuntary, for the united natures lose their properties. The union of divinity and humanity in Christ is voluntary, not because there has been an act of adoption—a doctrine that Nestorius explicitly condemns—but because in it no violence is done to the properties and distinctions of the natures. Furthermore, the union of the two natures in Christ is voluntary in the sense that it results from the free will of God, as well as in the sense that the will of the human nature agrees with the divine will. But this does not mean that Nestorius believes that the union can be properly interpreted as a mere agreement of two wills.

In emphasizing the integrity of each of the two natures in Christ and claiming a prosopon for each of them, Nestorius placed himself in a position in which it was difficult to claim a real sense for the union of the two natures. For him, this union is rather a "conjunction," so that each of the two natures retains its own predicates, which must

---

[17] Scipioni, *Ricerche*, p. 76.

not be confused. Therefore, he could not accept the doctrine of the *communicatio idiomatum,* which by that time was common, not only among Alexandrine theologians, but also among those of the West and to a certain extent even among the more moderate Antiochenes. This is the basis for his opposition to the title Bearer of God as applied to Mary.[18]

Mary is not the Bearer of God because God cannot have a mother. The distinction between the creature and the Creator precludes such a possibility. Mary is the mother of the man who serves as an "instrument" or "temple" for the divinity, and not of the divinity itself. Mary is "Bearer of the man," or more exactly "Bearer of Christ," but not Bearer of God. To affirm the opposite would be to "confuse the natures," and would result in a third nature that would be neither human nor divine, but an intermediate nature.

Where Nestorius made himself vulnerable was in his excessive distinction between the human and the divine natures of Christ, and in his inability to speak of their union in strong enough terms. If the relationship between the two natures is such that at each step one can and must distinguish between them, how is it possible to say that God dwelt among us? Therefore, the Nestorian controversy did not have to do simply with whether or not Mary was the Mother of God, but also and primarily with the person and work of Jesus Christ[19]—although it was unfortunate for Nestorius that his other theological concerns led him to attack a title given to Mary which by that time had developed firm roots in worship and piety.

It was against this divisive Christology of Nestorius that Cyril developed his own Christology. Before the beginning of the controversy, Cyril had held a Christology that was very close to that of

---

[18] Cf. the *Book of Heraclides,* 129, 136, 244. Also, Loofs, *Nestoriana,* p. 252.

[19] After the controversy, Nestorius came to the conclusion that there was a valid place for the *communicatio idiomatum,* at least in that which refers to the central events of salvation. Thus, he affirms in the *Book of Heraclides* (118) that through the incarnation God has willed to attribute death to his prosopon, so that his victory might be attributed to man.

Apollinaris, for, although he agreed that there was a human soul in Christ, that soul had no christological significance.

At the base of his Christology stands the idea that man is an incarnate spirit and that, in consequence, a spirit becomes man, not by uniting itself with a soul, but by uniting itself to a flesh. Within this perspective, the soul is of no account in the process of the incarnation.[20]

Furthermore, Cyril was prone to Apollinarianism because in certain texts that he believed to come from very orthodox hands, but which were really Apollinarian, he found the formula "one incarnate nature of the Word of God." This formula, as used in Apollinarianism, denied the integrity of Christ's humanity, which could not be called a "nature," for it had no soul. Thus, Cyril, in accepting this formula as part of the orthodox tradition, placed himself on rather shaky ground.

But the Nestorian controversy, and later the negotiations with John of Antioch, forced him to elaborate and define his christological doctrine.

According to the Christology that Cyril thus developed, the divine and the human are united in Christ in a "hypostatic union"—a term that may well have been new with Cyril,[21] and that later became a mark of orthodoxy. This union he understood in terms of the Apollinarian formula "one nature of God the Word incarnate." But this does not mean that the terminology of those who spoke of "two natures" was wholly unacceptable to him. On the contrary, he himself does on occasion speak of two natures, although always making it clear that they cannot be separated.[22] Likewise, he speaks of the humanity of Christ as a "hypostasis." [23] But, on the other hand, both "nature" and "hypostasis" as well as "prosopon" may be used to refer

---

[20] Jacques Liébaert, *La doctrine christologique de saint Cyrille d'Alexandrie avant la querelle nestorienne* (Lille: Facultés catholiques, 1951), p. 158.

[21] Cf. Grillmeier, *Christ*, p. 412, n. 1.

[22] Several texts are quoted by Hubert du Manoir de Juaye, *Dogme et spiritualité chez saint Cyrille d'Alexandrie* (Paris: J. Vrin, 1944), pp. 126-28.

[23] *Ibid.*, pp. 129-30.

to that being which has its own individual subsistence.[24] It is in this latter sense that he understands the formula "one nature of God the Word incarnate." In this sense, the humanity of Christ does not have its own hypostasis or nature, for it does not subsist in itself, but only in the hypostasis of the Word.[25]

According to some historians, Cyril affirmed that the Word was united to humanity in general, and not to an individual man.[26] This interpretation claims that Cyril took such a position because of the influence of Platonism upon him. There are certain texts that would seem to support this interpretation.[27] But Cyril does not in fact deny the individuality of the Savior's human nature. When he says that the Lord's humanity does not have its own hypostasis, Cyril only wishes to point out that it does not subsist by itself, but that the principle of its subsistence is in the Word.[28]

This doctrine of the "hypostatic union" of the divine and the human in Christ is the foundation of the *communicatio idiomatum*. As the Word is the "hypostasis" or principle of subsistence of the Savior's humanity, it is to him—i.e., to the Word—that everything which is said of that humanity must be referred. Mary is Mother of God, not because the divinity of Christ began to exist in her—which would be absurd—but because she is the mother of a humanity that subsists only by its union to the Word, and of which one must therefore say

---

[24] *Ibid.*, pp. 131-32.

[25] It is also in this sense that the distinction is to be understood: two natures before the union, one thereafter. In an ideal sense, one could think of the human nature subsisting in itself; but in fact—after the union—this never happened.

[26] Such is the interpretation of Harnack, *HD*, 4: 176: "What is really characteristic in Cyril's position is his express rejection that an individual man was present in Christ, although he attributes to Christ all the elements of man's nature."

[27] Cf. du Manoir de Juaye, *Dogme*, pp. 263-64. Also, Cyril, *Ep.* 45. 2.

[28] The main objection to this interpretation of Cyril's Christology is grounded on the texts in which he says that "we were all in Christ," or that "the Word has come to dwell in all through one." But these texts should be understood in the light of Cyril's view of the unity of mankind, which leads him to make several similar statements regarding Adam—and there is no doubt that he believed that Adam was an individual man. Furthermore, if Cyril had held that in Christ the Word was united to humanity in general, his Antiochene rivals would have hastened to attack him on that score, which they did not.

that all its predicates are to be applied to that Word.[29] Therefore, it is necessary to affirm, not only that God was born of a virgin, but also that God walked in Galilee, and that he suffered, and that he died.[30]

As to Nestorius, Cyril never made a real attempt to understand his thought. On the contrary, he made a caricature of his opponent's theology and then attacked that caricature. According to him, Nestorius does not distinguish between the manner in which the Word dwelt in Christ and the manner in which the Spirit dwelt in the prophets of the Old Testament. According to him, Nestorius affirms that Christ was only a God-bearing man. According to him, Nestorius teaches that the union of the divine and the human in Christ began only after the birth of Jesus. According to him, in short, Nestorius is a mere adoptionist similar to Theodotus or Paul of Samosata.

In point of fact, the teachings of Cyril were almost as vulnerable as those of Nestorius. If the latter found it difficult to show how he understood the divine and the human to be really united in Christ, Cyril—at least in his early years—emphasized the unity of the Savior to such an extent that it was difficult for him to show in what sense he was truly and wholly man, and to avoid having that humanity absorbed by the Word that was united to it. And yet, Cyril is known by posterity as one of the main defenders of christological orthodoxy, whereas Nestorius is listed among the great heresiarchs of the history of Christianity. This good fortune of Cyril is due to a large extent to the moderation that he was forced to show in his negotiations with John of Antioch and the other theologians of that school. This in turn led him to clarify his own doctrine against his former allies who turned against him on account of his moderation in becoming reconciled with the Antiochene party. But in spite of this, Cyril always emphasized the unity of the Savior over every distinction between the

---

[29] Ep. 1, 4, 17; Quod sancta Virgo deipara sit et non Christipara; Quod beata Maria sit deipara.

[30] See Sellers, Two Ancient Christologies, p. 88.

two natures. He believed that the Apollinarian phrase "one nature of God the Word incarnate" was strictly orthodox, and developed his Christology so that it would be in agreement with that formula. This is why, in the next episode of the christological controversies, the monophysite party was able to claim the support of the late Cyril.

XVIII

The Council of Chalcedon

The reunion formula of A.D. 433 could be no more than a brief truce in the long struggle between Alexandrine and Antiochene Christology. Although Cyril achieved an important victory in the condemnation of Nestorius, subsequent events proved that he must be more moderate in his attempts to impose his own understanding of Christology. This is what led him to accept the reunion formula of A.D. 433, to which he was faithful for the rest of his life.

But Cyril himself, in his struggle against Nestorius, had unleashed forces that were difficult to contain. Many of his former allies, convinced as they were that the true faith required the confession of the single nature of the Savior, and that every acceptance of the Antiochene doctrine of the two natures was tantamount to apostasy, refused to consider the peace of A.D. 433 as definitive.[1]

On the other hand, something similar had taken place among the Antiochenes. Although John of Antioch had not abandoned what his more extreme allies considered to be the true faith—for the formula of 433 affirmed the duality of natures in the Savior—he had betrayed his former ally Nestorius, who according to them had committed no

---

[1] A situation very well described by Sellers, *Chalcedon*, pp. 22-29. Cf. P.-Th. Camelot, "De Nestorius à Eutychès: l'opposition de deux christologies," *DKvCh*, 1: 213-42.

other crime than that of attacking the error of those who confused divinity with humanity.[2]

Because of this situation, the delicate balance achieved in 433 could not last long. As soon as circumstances would allow, the conflict would flare up again. This was what happened when in A.D. 444 Dioscorus succeeded Cyril as patriarch of Alexandria.

Dioscorus went far beyond his predecessor both in his zeal for what he believed to be orthodoxy and in his willingness to use all means available in order to achieve the final victory of his own cause. He saw the reunion formula of 433 as a victory of heresy over the true faith, and as a humiliation of the ancient see of Alexandria, which should enjoy the primacy of the East.

When Dioscorus succeeded Cyril circumstances seemed to be ideally set for the project of achieving the final destruction of Antiochene Christology as well as of the humiliation of the see of Antioch. In the ancient Syrian city, the Episcopal throne was occupied by Domnus, who had succeeded John in A.D. 441 and was more interested in monastic life than in active participation in ecclesiastical matters. He therefore entrusted the government of his diocese to Theodoret of Cyrus. Theodoret was respected by many on account of his great erudition, but he was also widely suspect because of his close personal ties with Nestorius. Therefore, the bishop of Antioch and his colleague were in a rather vulnerable position. Besides, political conditions also favored Dioscorus, for Theodosius II, being too old and weak to rule, had practically placed the affairs of the state in the hands of the Great Chamberlain Chrysaphius, who was a man to be easily tempted by Alexandrine gold. Finally, Dioscorus had the support of a host of monks scattered throughout the East—and even in Antioch—who were begging for an opportunity to defend the true faith against heretics.

---

[2] While some members of the Antiochene party were willing to declare Cyril orthodox, but not to condemn Nestorius, others went further, claiming that Cyril was a heretic and that in agreeing to a reunion with him John had betrayed the true faith. See Sellers, *Chalcedon*, pp. 20-22.

Theodoret's activities in Antioch were the occasion for Dioscorus' attack. Theodoret had prohibited a certain Pelagius—not to be confused with the other monk of the same name who gave rise to "Pelagianism"—to teach theology, for his doctrines were opposed to that which was generally held by Antiochene theologians. Somewhat later, Theodoret wrote three dialogues that are usually known as *Eranistes,* in which he defended the doctrine of two natures. It is a moderate and respectful work; but it leaves no doubt as to its author's opinion regarding those who "confuse" the two natures of Christ.

Dioscorus saw in the activities of Theodoret the weak link in the Antiochene chain. He had Chrysaphius convince the emperor to publish an "anti-Nestorian" edict that was in fact directed against Antiochene Christology. As was to be expected, this edict caused such consternation in Antioch that from then on it was easy for Dioscorus to claim that Theodoret and his followers were unruly. As a result, the emperor ordered Theodoret to remain in Cyrus and not to continue disturbing the peace with his synods and other activities. Theodoret attempted to continue his work from Cyrus mostly through his writings; but it was evident that Dioscorus had managed to restrict the field of action of the most distinguished Antiochene theologian alive.

The matter could have ended there; but Dioscorus was bent on achieving the final victory of Alexandria over Antioch, and he therefore decided to use the case of Eutyches as a means to that end. Eutyches was a monk in Constantinople, where he was admired by many and respected by most, for he was godfather to Chrysaphius. As to his doctrine, he was a decided opponent of Nestorianism and of every doctrine that seemed to approach it; but he did not formulate his own Christology in precise terms.

In A.D. 448, in a local synod gathered in Constantinople, Eutyches was accused of heresy by Eusebius of Dorilea, who was known for his antiheretical zeal, to the point that some of his fellow theologians felt that his attitude was excessively bellicose. In attacking Eutyches, Eusebius based his case on the fact that the monk refused to accept the reunion formula of A.D. 433, which the bishops gathered at Constantinople considered as a standard of orthodoxy. In point of fact, in denying the validity of the formula of 433 Eutyches was not alone, for many of his Eastern colleagues were not quite willing to accept the doctrine of two natures contained in that formula; but Eutyches, trusting perhaps on the support of Chrysaphius and Dioscorus, openly opposed the agreements of 433.

After a long series of maneuvers by both parties, Eutyches appeared before the Constantinopolitan synod, although—probably to show that the bishops gathered there were dealing with an important personage—he came surrounded by soldiers and court officials. He does not seem to have been aware that he was merely an instrument for the designs of Dioscorus, who seems to have instructed the imperial legate to make sure that Eutyches was condemned. After such condemnation, Dioscorus could become the champion of the cause of Eutyches, and in achieving his reinstatement he would also deal a fatal blow to his opponents. As Dioscorus expected, Eutyches was condemned by the synod of Constantinople.

It is difficult to ascertain exactly what was the doctrine of Eutyches.[3] He refused to accept the formulas "consubstantial to us," and "two natures after the incarnation"—both taken from the reunion formula of A.D. 433—although he was willing to affirm that the Savior was "of two natures before the union." It was later claimed that he had said that the human body of Christ descended from heaven. But this seems to be an exaggeration, and probably what Eutyches taught was that, because of the incarnation, the body of Christ was deified in such a way that it was no longer "consubstantial to us." In any case, there is no doubt that Eutyches was—as Pope Leo would say—"very unwary and exceedingly ignorant," [4] and that his interpretation of Cyril—in whom he claimed to base his theology—

---

[3] See A. van Roey, "Eutychès," DHGE, 16: 87-91; Camelot, "De Nestorius à Eutychès," pp. 235-42.

[4] Ep. 28. 1 (NPNF, 2nd series, 12: 38).

was rather superficial. The same may be said regarding his interpretation of Nestorius, which led him to discover "Nestorianism" in every affirmation of two natures in Christ. It is probably fitting that he who gave the names of Cyril and Nestorius to doctrines that these theologians never held gave his own name to a doctrine that he himself never held—Eutychianism.

After being condemned by the Constantinopolitan synod, Eutyches appealed to the bishops of the main sees, including Leo, the bishop of Rome. On his part, Flavian, the patriarch of Constantinople who presided over the trial of Eutyches, also wrote to Rome. This is probably what Dioscorus had hoped, for now the local conflict became universal, and there was therefore good reason to convoke a general council that would not be difficult for Dioscorus to control. If that council absolved Eutyches and condemned those who had judged him, that would be a great victory for Dioscorus and for the see of Alexandria. Meanwhile, in order to show the need for a general council, Dioscorus rejected the decisions of the synod that had gathered in Constantinople and offered communion to Eutyches.

Finally, the emperor called a council that was to meet at Ephesus in A.D. 449. This council was attended by some 130 bishops, and from the very beginning it was clear that Dioscorus—whom the emperor had appointed to preside at the assembly—was not willing to tolerate any opposition to his own policies. Unexpectedly for Dioscorus, Rome sided against him, for Pope Leo sent Flavian of Constantinople an epistle—usually known as the *Tome*—in which he supported the condemnation of Eutyches. Although the *Tome* is conciliatory in tone, it clearly states that Eutyches was correctly condemned, and it sets forth the christological position of Leo himself. According to the Pope, Eutyches is to be counted among those who "stand out as masters of error because they were never disciples of truth," [5] and his main error consists in denying the consubstantiality of the Savior with humanity, for the glory of the incarnation does not destroy the human nature of

---

[5] *Ibid.*

Christ. "For as God is not changed by the showing of pity, so man is not swallowed up by the dignity." [6] On the contrary, the distinction of the two natures is necessary even after the union.

> Without detriment therefore to the properties of either nature and substance which then came together in one person, majesty took on humility, strength weakness, eternity mortality: and for the paying off of the debt belonging to our condition inviolable nature was united with passible nature. . . . Thus in the whole and perfect nature of true man was true God born, complete in what was his own, complete in what was ours.[7] . . . The Word performing what appertains to the Word, and the flesh carrying out what appertains to the flesh. One of them sparkles with miracles, the other succumbs to injuries. And as the Word does not cease to be on an equality with His Father's glory, so the flesh does not forego the nature of our race.[8]

This does not mean, however, that Leo "divides" the natures as Nestorius was accused of doing, for he categorically affirms that in Christ there is only one person, and that this unity is to be constantly reaffirmed. "For it must again and again be repeated that one and the same is truly Son of God and truly son of man." [9]

In this exposition of christological doctrine, Leo is not making an innovation nor attempting to be original. On the contrary, his formula is the same that was used by Tertullian two and a half centuries earlier, although it is true that Tertullian only referred to the "one person" incidentally, and that it took the work of Ambrose, Jerome, and Augustine, a few years before Leo, to generalize in the West a formula that could already be found in Tertullian.[10]

---

[6] *Ibid.*, 4 (*NPNF*, 2nd series, 12: 40). This is why Leo cannot accept Eutyches' formula "of two natures before the incarnation, and in one nature after the union." This would imply that humanity has been absorbed by the divinity (*ibid.*, 6).

[7] *Ibid.*, 3 (*NPNF*, 2nd series, 12: 40). Note the use of "nature" and "substance" as synonyms, as had been done much earlier by Tertullian.

[8] *Ibid.*, 4 (*NPNF*, 2nd series, 12: 40-41).

[9] *Ibid.* (*NPNF*, 2nd series, 12: 40-41).

[10] See Tarsicius J. van Bavel, *Recherches sur la christologie de saint Augustin: L'humain et le divin dans le Christ d'après saint Augustin* (Fribourg, Switzerland: Éditions universitaires, 1954), pp. 176-80.

Thus, in the controversy that took place around Eutyches the three main christological currents of the ancient church met: the Alexandrine, the Antiochene, and that of the West. All these agree that it is necessary to affirm a union of divinity and humanity in Jesus Christ, but they do not agree as to how this is to be done.

The Alexandrines had a long tradition of teachers who—abandoning Origen at this point—had attempted to find a formula of union by proposing a christological doctrine of the Logos-flesh type. In Apollinaris this doctrine had reached its natural conclusion, and since that time no orthodox theologian supported it consciously. But there were some works that were Apollinarian in origin but that circulated under the name of orthodox theologians—notably Athanasius—and this led the Alexandrines to continue seeking solutions similar to that of Apollinaris. During the fifth century, the most common was the doctrine of Cyril regarding the hypostatic union and the lack of a human hypostasis in Christ. However, some of his own successors saw his doctrine as an extremely dangerous approach to the "division of the natures," and returned to the ancient affirmation of the single nature of the Savior. Naturally, as Cyril was very much respected and had affirmed that Christ was "of two natures," it was necessary to solve this difficulty, and the Alexandrines did so through the formula "of two natures before the incarnation; in one nature after the union." That is, that Christ was truly man and God, but that this distinction could only be made on an intellectual level—"before the incarnation"—for "after the union" humanity had been absorbed by the divinity to such a point that it was no longer possible to speak of a human nature as such.

The Antiochene theologians set out from the human reality of the Savior, although after the cases of Paul of Samosata and Eustathius of Antioch they had become convinced that it was necessary also to affirm his personal divinity. Furthermore, after the condemnation of Nestorius, the Antiochenes became generally aware that the denial of the *communicatio idiomatum* was in fact a denial of the incarnation itself, and therefore of the saving work of Jesus Christ. For this reason they were willing to affirm that the union of humanity and divinity in Christ was such that a true *communicatio idiomatum* could take place. But they were not ready to accept a doctrine that would "confuse" divinity with humanity, so that the latter would lose its proper character.

Finally, Western theologians started from the ancient formula of Tertullian, as generalized by Ambrose, Jerome, and Augustine. As the West was beginning to conceive the saving work of Christ in what would later be its characteristic form, that is, as the payment of a debt that man owed God, it was necessary to affirm that the Savior was such that that work could be performed. This required the union of divinity and humanity in Christ, but it did not demand any particular understanding of that union. Therefore, it was enough to repeat the ancient formula, although showing at the same time that this does not mean that the humanity of the Savior was absorbed by his divinity. This is what Leo did in his *Tome*.

These three christological currents met in the council gathered at Ephesus in A.D. 449. The results of that council could be foretold even before its first session. Dioscorus had the support of Chrysaphius, and through him of the Emperor himself. Furthermore, he had brought with him a host of bishops and fanatical monks who were bent on achieving the victory of the "true faith" at all costs. Theodoret of Cyrus, the most able of the defenders of the Antiochene cause, received orders from the emperor forbidding him to take part in the sessions of the council. Finally, in a decree published two days before the council opened, the emperor appointed Dioscorus to preside over the assembly, and gave him authority to impose silence on any one who attempted to add or subtract something from the faith proclaimed by the bishops gathered in Nicea (325) and in Ephesus (431).[11]

---

[11] The council of Ephesus of A.D. 431 had forbidden anyone to "propose, write, or compose a different faith, besides that which was set forth by the holy fathers gathered at Nicea with the Holy Ghost." This is what is known as "the Ephesian canon," and was the basis for this imperial decree as well as for much of the later opposition to the steps taken at Chalcedon.

Under such conditions, the Ephesian council of A.D. 449 could not be anything but what Leo later called it: "a robbers' synod." [12] In spite of the protests of Flavian and of the Papal legates, the *Tome* of Leo was never read. It is possible that Flavian was treated with such violence that he died a few days later. Eusebius of Dorilea, who had been the first in accusing Eutyches, was condemned and deposed for teaching the doctrine of the "two natures after the union." Eutyches was declared perfectly orthodox, and several of the bishops who earlier had condemned him now changed their position, and anathematized those who condemned Eutyches. Next, the council took up the task of condemning and deposing the main exponents of Antiochene Christology—among them, Domnus of Antioch, Theodoret of Cyrus, and Ibas of Edessa.[13] Finally, the council decreed that from that time on only those men could be ordained who did not hold the doctrines of Nestorius and his followers. Thus, the final victory of Alexandria over Antioch seemed to have taken place, both theologically and politically.

Pope Leo did not feel inclined to accept the decrees and decisions of a council that he took to be a gathering of robbers. He soon received letters from Flavian, Theodoret, and Eusebius of Dorilea. Besides, the deacon Hilarius, who had been part of the Papal delegation to Ephesus, brought direct news regarding the manner in which the council had been conducted. Immediately, Leo began his campaign against what had taken place at Ephesus. He wrote to bishops, monks, politicians, and even members of the imperial family. But all his efforts were in vain. The Emperor and those who ruled with him were not willing to open once again the discussion that had led to the recent council of Ephesus.

---

[12] *Ep. 95. 2: "in illo ephesino non iudicio sed latrocinio."*

[13] Ibas is significant for the later development of Christian theology because, through his close relationship with Barsumas of Nisibis, he is one of the links that explain the so-called Nestorianism of the school of Nisibis and of Persian Christianity. Ibas himself, however, was no Nestorian, in spite of what the council of 449 decided concerning him.

The situation changed radically when, less than a year after the "robbers' synod," the Emperor fell from his horse and died. He was succeeded by his sister Pulcheria and her husband Marcian. Pulcheria had always been one of the main hopes of Pope Leo—in fact, it is probable that one of the reasons why she was expelled from court during the reign of her brother was her opposition to Dioscorus and Chrysaphius.[14] Now she and her husband set out to undo what had been done by the recent council of Ephesus. Soon the bishops who had been deposed by Dioscorus returned to their posts; the remains of Flavian were taken with great pomp to the Basilica of the Apostles; the new bishop of Constantinople, who had previously followed Dioscorus, now declared himself in favor of the *Tome* of Leo; in the provinces, many followed the example of the bishop of the capital; finally, the emperors called the bishops to gather in a new council at Nicea in May, A.D. 451.

For practical reasons, this council—which is generally known as the Fourth Ecumenical Council, although the so-called Nestorian and Monophysite churches do not acknowledge it—took place in Chalcedon.[15] Five hundred and twenty bishops—the greatest number ever gathered in a council up to that time—met at the Basilica of Saint Euphemia,[16] together with an imperial legation of eighteen members.

Accepting a request of the Papal legates, the council began by discussing the case of Dioscorus and of the synod of A.D. 449. The acts of that synod were read and discussed, and by the end of the reading several of the bishops who had taken part in the previous gathering confessed that they had allowed themselves to be influenced by threats and by fear; others claimed that they had been confused.

---

[14] See Paul Goubert, "Le rôle de Saint Pulchérie et de l'eunuque Chrysaphios," *DKvCH*, 1: 303-21.

[15] See Sellers, *Chalcedon*, pp. 254-301; Monald Goemans, "Chalkedon als 'Allgemeines Konzil'," *DKvCh*, 1: 251-89.

[16] See Evagrius, *HE* 2. 3. Also, Alfons M. Schneider, "Sankt Euphemia und das Konzil von Chalkedon," *DKvCh*, 1: 291-302.

Dioscorus remained firm in his position, affirming that Christ was "of two natures" but not "in two natures," and that this was why Flavian, Domnus, Ibas, and the rest had been deposed. The result was that Dioscorus was condemned, deposed, and banished. He died some time later, still in exile, venerated by the monophysites, who saw him as the great champion of the true faith, and almost forgotten by the orthodox, to whom he was no more than a fanatic who made use of the power and influence of his see in order to impose his doctrine on others. His fellow members of the "robbers' synod" were forgiven when they confessed their previous error. Finally, the bishops who had been deposed in 449 by Dioscorus and his followers were returned to their sees—except Domnus of Antioch, who preferred to continue a life of monastic retreat rather than to resume the responsibilities of the episcopacy.

Some difficulties were encountered by the council when it came to draw up a confession of faith. The seventh canon of the Third Ecumenical Council (Ephesus, A.D. 431) said that no one was to compose or propose a different faith than that which had been affirmed at Nicea. Many understood this as a prohibition to set forth new creeds, and were therefore opposed to having the council of Chalcedon compose a doctrinal formula. This opposition had to give way before imperial pressure, as well as before the obvious fact that the symbol of Nicea was not sufficient to end the controversy at hand, for both sides of the current debate were willing to accept that creed and to claim it in their support.

Another difficulty was found in the differences between Cyril and Leo. Cyril had always preferred to speak of "one incarnate nature of the Word of God," and had been suspicious of those who distinguished too clearly between that which corresponded to the divinity of Christ and that which corresponded to his humanity. As to the two natures, Cyril had been willing to speak of them "before the incarnation," and even had said that Christ was of two natures, but he had never said that he was in two natures. Over against this, Leo's

Tome affirmed that in Christ there were two natures after the union, and that it was possible to distinguish between the humanity and the divinity of Christ, so that certain things could be attributed to the one and certain things to the other, although without forgetting the *communicatio idiomatum*, without which the incarnation would be meaningless.[17] Both formulas were perfectly compatible, as long as one did not understand the phrase "of two natures" in such a way that it would imply that the duality of natures existed only in an ideal moment, "before the incarnation," and that in the concrete person of Jesus Christ, "after the union," there was only one nature. Such was the position that Eutyches took in the synod in Constantinople which condemned him, and it was also the declaration of the synod of Ephesus in A.D. 449. For this reason the Western delegates and some Antiochenes, although accepting the authority and orthodoxy of Cyril, thought that his formula "of two natures" was insufficient, and preferred the formula "in two natures." [18]

After long debates that it is not necessary to discuss here,[19] a formula was drawn up, known to posterity as the *Definition of Faith* of Chalcedon.

Following, then, the holy Fathers, we all with one voice teach that it should be confessed that our Lord Jesus Christ is one and the same God, the Same perfect in Godhead, the Same perfect in manhood, truly God and truly man, the Same [consisting] of a rational soul and a body; *homoousios* with the Father as to his Godhead, and the Same *homoousios* with us as to his manhood; in all things like unto us, sin only excepted; begotten of the Father before ages as to his Godhead, and in the last days, the Same, for us and for our salvation, of Mary the Virgin *Theotokos* as to his manhood; One and the same Christ, Son, Lord, Only-begotten, made known in two

---

[17] See Paul Galtier, "Saint Cyrille d'Alexandrie et Saint Léon le Grand à Chalcédoine," *DKvCh*, 1: 345-87.

[18] Some extreme Antiochenes went further, and claimed that the formula "of two natures" was equivalent to the Apollinarian formula "one incarnate nature of the Word of God," and should be condemned.

[19] See Sellers, *Chalcedon*, pp. 103-23.

natures[20] [which exist] without confusion, without change, without division, without separation; the difference of the natures having been in no wise taken away by reason of the union, but rather the properties of each being preserved, and [both] concurring into one Person (*prosopon*) and one *hypostasis*—not parted or divided into two persons (*prosopa*), but one and the same Son and Only-begotten, the divine Logos, the Lord Jesus Christ; even as the prophets from of old [have spoken] concerning him, and as the Lord Jesus Christ himself has taught us, and as the Symbol of the Fathers has delivered to us.[21]

In composing and accepting this formula, and also sanctioning the *Tome* of Leo and the doctrinal epistles of Cyril, the bishops gathered at Chalcedon did not believe that they were violating the Ephesian canon that prohibited the teaching of a different faith from that of Nicea. On the contrary, the *Definition of Faith* of Chalcedon seemed to them a commentary on the faith of Nicea, although relating that faith with the controversies that had developed after the Great Council. The creed of the church would still be that of Nicea, although it was now to be interpreted as was proposed by the *Definition* of Chalcedon, which condemned not only those who, like Eutyches, "confused" the natures of the Savior, but also those who, like Nestorius, "separated" them. The phrase "of two natures," used by Cyril as well as by Eutyches, is not explicitly condemned, although the manner in which Eutyches seems to have understood it is rejected. Likewise, although the phrase "in two natures" is accepted, the manner in which it was thought that Nestorius used it is explicitly rejected.[22]

The purpose of Emperors Marcian and Pulcheria in convoking the

---

[20] Some Greek manuscripts say "of two natures." But there is no doubt that the majority of Greek manuscripts, as well as all the ancient versions, are correct in their reading: "in two natures."

[21] Translation taken from Sellers, *Chalcedon*, pp. 210-11. The Greek text is readily accessible in *DKvCh*, 1: 389-90.

[22] Although Nestorius, then in exile, claimed that he had been proved right by the condemnation of extreme Alexandrine Christology at Chalcedon.

Council of Chalcedon seemed to have been achieved. After condemning the extreme positions, as well as earlier heresies, the Council had produced a *Definition of Faith* on which most bishops agreed. But the unity that had been achieved was more apparent than real. It was soon evident that there were strong minorities that were not willing to accept the *Definition of Faith,* and therefore dissident groups arose which would continue their separate existence at least until the twentieth century. Furthermore, even among those who accepted that which had been done in Chalcedon, there were differences regarding the manner in which the *Definition* was to be interpreted. These differences sometimes led to violent disagreements. Rome herself contributed to the undermining of the authority of the Council by rejecting its twenty-eighth canon, which granted to the see of Constantinople "equal privileges" to those of Rome. As a consequence, the christological controversies continued for several centuries. But the story of such later controversies properly belongs in the next volume of this *History.*

XIX

Apostolic or Apostate?

Everything seems to indicate that as the bishops left the great hall of Saint Euphemia they were convinced that they had been faithful to the faith of the apostles. But were they correct in such an assumption? Is it not possible to see the development of Christian thought from the day of Pentecost to the days of Chalcedon as a vast, although unknowing, apostasy in which the original gospel was abandoned for the sake of vain philosophies and dogmatic minutiae? Was not the originally Jewish message Hellenized to such a point that it practically ceased to be Jewish? Probably so. But there are certain factors that must be taken into consideration, and which will show that the issues involved are more complex than would appear at first glance.

First, if Christianity is the message of the incarnation, that is, the message of the God who has come into this world by becoming man, how can it be blamed for entering into the Hellenistic world by becoming Hellenized? The alternative would have been a rigid, nonincarnational Christianity that would perhaps have preserved its original formulation, but that would never have entered into the world around it.

A second consideration must be made, however, if one is to appreciate the dangers involved in the course that Christian theology followed in its development. Hellenism was not only a general cultural attitude. It also had a content that could endanger the faithfulness of Christianity to its original message. Classical Greek philosophy was a major factor in the formation of the Hellenistic mind, and that philosophy understood being in basically static terms. When Christians began speaking of God as the "prime unmoved mover," how would this affect their understanding of his relationship with history, and of his becoming part of history in Jesus Christ? Once they began defining God in terms of a negation of all human characteristics, how could they affirm that a God so defined had become man? Thus, a great deal of the difficulties encountered by Christian thought in its development were the result of an attempt to reconcile what was said of God in the original Judeo-Christian tradition with what seemed to be known of him through that which the Greek tradition called reason—which is certainly not the only possible understanding of reason.

Finally, one must point out that—in spite of a rather widespread opinion that the development of doctrines was an unwarranted Hellenization of Christianity—it was often the "heretics" that proposed the most radically Hellenized versions of Christianity, and that in condemning them the Church at large, while often using the tools of Hellenistic philosophy, in fact set a limit to the influence of that philosophy upon the understanding of the Christian faith. Such was the case, for instance, when the Council of Nicea condemned the doctrine of Arius, which followed from a Hellenistic way of understanding the Godhead, by proposing and canonizing the unscriptural term *homoousios*. And a similar assertion may be made regarding the Council of Chalcedon and the doctrines that it condemned.

Thus, in summary, a general evaluation of the development of Christian thought up to the time of the Council of Chalcedon should affirm that that development involves without any doubt a profound Hellenization of Christianity. That Hellenization has to do not only with matters of form or vocabulary, but also with the very understanding of the nature of Christianity, and it therefore created problems that ideally could have been avoided by following other avenues of philosophical interpretation. But it is hard to see any viable alternative that Christian thought could in fact have followed, given the intellectual atmosphere of the times. And furthermore, the general development of Christian doctrine, while making use of a Hellenistic understanding of Christianity, instinctively excluded those extreme forms of Hellenization which would have denied the basic tenet of the Christian faith: that God was in Christ reconciling the world unto himself.

Index of Subjects and Authors

Principal references are in bold type; references to footnotes are in italics; all other references are in Roman type.